JOURNAL

OF A

LADY OF QUALITY

Being the *Narrative* of a
Journey from
SCOTLAND
to the *West Indies, North Carolina*,
and *Portugal*, in the years
1774 to 1776

Janet Schaw

Edited by
EVANGELINE WALKER ANDREWS

in collaboration with
CHARLES MCLEAN ANDREWS

Introduction to the Bison Books Edition by
STEPHEN CARL ARCH

UNIVERSITY OF NEBRASKA PRESS
LINCOLN AND LONDON

∞

First Nebraska paperback printing: 2005

Library of Congress Cataloging-in-Publication Data
Schaw, Janet, ca. 1731–ca. 1801.
Journal of a lady of quality: being the narrative of a journey from
Scotland to the West Indies, North Carolina, and Portugal, in the
years 1774–1776 / Janet Schaw; edited by Evangeline Walker An-
drews in collaboration with Charles McLean Andrews; introduction
to the Bison Books edition by Stephen Carl Arch.—Bison Books ed.
p. cm.
Originally published: New Haven: Yale University Press, 1934.
Includes index.
ISBN-13: 978-0-8032-5953-9 (pbk.: alk. paper)
ISBN-10: 0-8032-5953-0 (pbk.: alk. paper)
1. Schaw, Janet, ca. 1731–ca. 1801—Diaries. 2. Schaw, Janet, ca.
1731–ca. 1801—Travel. 3. Scots—Diaries. 4. Women travelers—
Diaries. 5. North Carolina—Description and travel—Early works
to 1800. 6. West Indies—Description and travel—Early works to
1800. 7. Lisbon (Portugal)—Description and travel—Early works
to 1800. I. Andrews, Evangeline Walker. II. Andrews, Charles
McLean, 1863–1943. III. Arch, Stephen Carl. IV. Title.
F257.S37 2005
910.4'082—dc22   2005011384

INTRODUCTION TO THE
BISON BOOKS EDITION

Stephen Carl Arch

In 1904, while researching colonial history in the British Museum, Charles McLean Andrews and Evangeline Walker Andrews chanced upon Janet Schaw's long-forgotten, unpublished manuscript account of her travels. Their subsequent investigations into the manuscript and its history definitively established Schaw as the author of the unsigned narrative, provided background on some of the people and places she visited, and confirmed the historical significance of her account. Yet today, more than one hundred years later, we know little more about Janet Schaw than the Andrews did when they finally put Schaw's manuscript into print in 1923.

The known facts of Schaw's life can be gleaned for the most part from her narrative: in 1774, as an unmarried, approximately thirty-year-old woman of some education and fairly extensive reading, Janet Schaw accompanied her brother Alexander and the three adolescent children of John Rutherford, a family friend, from Scotland to the West Indies and then to North Carolina. Alexander was to take up a colonial appointment as a customs officer on the island of St. Christopher (St. Kitts); as it turned out, however, he continued on to North Carolina with Janet, and was then re-routed back to London carrying dispatches from the governor of North Carolina to the British government. The children who accompanied Schaw on her trip had completed their education in Scotland and were being delivered to their father, a Loyalist planter and former customs official who lived near Wilmington, North Carolina. Janet Schaw's other brother, Robert, a planter and businessman, also lived in Wilmington, so the second leg of her journey conveniently combined business and pleasure.

Though the book's first editors uncovered some information about Schaw's life, one mystery they did not solve was the identity of her correspondent. Like another more famous, fictional narrative written in the 1770s, Hector St. John de Crèvecoeur's *Letters from an American Farmer* (1782), Schaw's narrative is imagined as a series of letters, written from a first-time traveler to a more experienced friend. The form is that of a journal, its entries written not daily but whenever time and opportunity (and paper and ink) were available, and the accounts sent on at intervals to her correspondent. The advantage of working in these narrative conventions of the letter and the journal—and they *are* conventions—is a sense of immediacy: "[E]very subject will be guided by my own immediate feelings," Schaw wrote (20). For weeks or months at a time she could not dispatch what she had written to her friend in Scotland, but by recording her immediate impressions of people, things, scenes, and events, she could permit that friend to "connect" with her sometime in the future.

The eighteenth century valued what it termed "sensibility," the heightened emotions that connect two or more individuals on the level that, many philosophers and writers theorized, most distinguishes us as humans. Early on in particular, Schaw waxes emotional when viewing certain scenes or views, and she then shares these emotions with her correspondent: "[M]y attention was caught by one of the most affecting scenes that could be presented to a feeling heart, and, I thank God, mine is not composed of very hard materials. . . . [I]f I am able to paint it the least like what I feel it, I am sure you will share my feelings" (33).

Though the internal evidence is inconclusive, Schaw's correspondent and friend was in all probability a man, perhaps someone whom she could not hope to marry because of extenuating circumstances. Something awkward or troubling occurred between them before she sailed for the New World: "Do not suppose however that I repent," she implores him or her, "or in the least regret what I have done—that is far from the case" (130). For us today it is important to keep in mind that intended audience of one specific friend, whose imagined sympathy permits Schaw to reveal an inner, private self: one that is ironic (even sarcastic at times), playful, intelligent, insightful. "As you know," she writes at one point, "my tongue is not always under my command" (156). This is self-deprecating, to be sure, and was possibly true in real life, but on the page her conventionalized immediacy is skillfully conveyed and quite revealing. She writes with careful craft.

Although Schaw does reveal something of an inner, private self, I think it is misguided to refer to this as her "true" self. We know from other eighteenth-century memoirs, journals, and personal narratives (the word "autobiography" was not coined until the last decade of the eighteenth century) that both private and public personae were constructed in accordance with given social roles and expectations. Individualism was largely a nineteenth-century invention. For the eighteenth century, sociability was both the norm and the goal. How one "fit" in one's social milieu was more important than any desire to stand apart or stand alone. Robinson Crusoe's complete solitude on a deserted island was the eighteenth-century European's nightmare, however much Henry David Thoreau might have yearned for something like it in the nineteenth.

Thus readers might note, superficially, how little time Janet Schaw actually spent *alone.* On a small ship in the mid-Atlantic, her "private" space is shared and social, and even the thoughts and impressions in her journal are intended to be read by another. "[I]t is the Social Circle . . . that constituted my happiness" (21), she laments upon leaving Scotland, and she manages (or at least tries) to reconstitute such a circle of friends in all the places she disembarks. So it is that when her ship meets another ship in the mid-Atlantic, Schaw and the other passengers feel a pleasure that is "impossible to describe" (45), an emotion generated not by the simple surprise of meeting another ship in that immensity but because man is "by nature a kindly Social animal" (46).

Modern-day readers will likely take interest in what Janet Schaw observed during her travels. Book-learned but naive, unmarried but constrained by her gender, Schaw serves as one kind of lens through which to view the eighteenth-century colonial world. Although at first she is repulsed by the poor, dirty Scots emigrants hidden on board her ship, she comes to understand that the Highland emigration of the 1760s and 1770s had its root in economic upheaval in Scotland, and she then revises her impression of the emigrants. Schaw portrays the rich settlers in the West Indies and in North Carolina as in-

dolent creatures who lounge in the shade while servants and
slaves attend to their every whim. She witnesses strange rituals, such as the farce that is played out on her ship while
passing "under the Tropick" (69–71) and the "holiday" for slaves
between Christmas and New Year's Day (107–9); and like a
modern-day anthropologist, she notes in some detail the ceremonies that gave those rituals their significance. She describes
the terrific abundance of food available to the wealthy planters
in the West Indies (see, for example, 95–100) as well as the
slimmer pickings on board the ship after a great storm. Indeed,
food and its consumption is something she takes note of everywhere. She watches in fascination and, eventually, sympathy
as an alligator is tortured and killed in North Carolina. She
sees the high drama and pageantry of the Catholic churches
during the Christmas season in Portugal. She sees herself, hi-
lariously, covered in molasses and candles after her ship has
nearly foundered in the mid-Atlantic. In short, Janet Schaw has
her eyes open, and like many other travelers to the New World,
from Columbus's time to the present day, she observes many
interesting things both in the unusual and in the commonplace.

Yet it is what Janet Schaw sees but cannot fully comprehend
that is most revealing about her personally and about her position as a middle-class, white, female traveler within the first
British empire. In *Imperial Eyes: Travel Writing and Transculturation*, Mary Louise Pratt looks at colonial travel narratives
of the eighteenth and nineteenth centuries. She shows how
many privileged travelers and adventurers depended in their
written accounts upon "strategies of representation whereby
European bourgeois subjects [sought] to secure their innocence
in the same moment as they [asserted] European hegemony"
(7). Like the travelers whom Pratt studies, Schaw, an educated
member of the British empire, carries her cultural baggage
wherever she goes: her Protestantism to Catholic Portugal, the
virtue of hard work to the luxurious West Indies, deep loyalty to
the Crown to North Carolina, and the genteel qualities of true
ladies to all places and at all times. To Schaw, these were "self-
evident" truths; unfortunately, her strong adherence to these
values often prevented her from fully understanding the world
in which she found herself.

The slaves in the West Indies are, in Schaw's mind, healthy

and well fed and cheerful; and their masters are "kind and beneficent" (104). These were self-evident truths espoused by the planter class, by most colonists, and by many Westerners, at least until the first abolitionist movement began to undermine the myth in the 1770s and 1780s. Yet Schaw also sees evidence of darker, hidden truths. For instance, she describes a little mulatto girl who stands, "as a pet," in attendance on Schaw's childless friend Mrs. Hamilton (123–24). Just a few pages earlier, Schaw notes the "licentious and even unnatural amours" (112) that produced such offspring in the West Indies (and in the American South). Where else would Mrs. Hamilton's "pet" have come from, if not her husband's "amours"? These sorts of relationships prove uncomfortable for both the wives of the planters (who keep their thoughts to themselves) and Schaw herself. Though Schaw could be receptive to new ideas—as when she changed her attitude toward the Scots emigrants—she struggles here to maintain the myth of the well-treated slave in order to, as Pratt puts it, "secure [her] innocence." To this end she casts white women as "modest, genteel, reserved, and temperate" (113); and never being subjected to the sun, "the tincture of [their] skin is as pure as the lily, and as pale" (114), she reports. Black women, meanwhile, are simply whores who "lay themselves out for white lovers" (112) who, though blameworthy, can hardly be expected to resist such seductions. And black men are merely brutes who do not possess mind or soul. There is no need to waste any sympathy when one sees them being whipped and in chains, she reports; sensibility is only for equals.

Race, class, gender, nationalism: in all her confrontations with manifestations of these phenomena, Schaw struggles to assert and re-assert what is "natural" and normal, even though she often sees, quite literally, evidence of the fictions upon which those conceptions were and must be built. The drinking water in Antigua, she notes, is presented to the wealthy planters in a coconut shell fixed on the end of a stick—"lest the breath of the Servant who presents it should contaminate its purity" (111). The rich and the poor have an invisible line between them across which the "disease" of the poor cannot be allowed to reach. Yet look carefully at Schaw's account and note who prepares the food, who makes the beds, who cleans the houses:

How can the rich hope to be separated entirely from those who make their leisure possible? Look carefully at Janet Schaw's own position: Is she rich or poor? Aristocrat or a servant? Pure or contaminated? White or suntanned brown? She tells us that the American revolutionaries—"ragamuffins" all, she snorts— "are infected by [the] unfortunate disease" of rebellion, but men of property and credit are free of the disease (194). Yet at the same time she criticizes the Carolina planters for their indolence, degenerate manners, and ignorance. The smartest man she meets in Carolina is not "prized and courted" by the other men of property and credit but is ignored by them (165). Loyalists and revolutionaries have a line drawn between them, she says, but in fact it is hard to see their differences.

The original discovery and publication of Janet Schaw's manuscript narrative was a gift to those of us who study the colonial past, and its republication now comes at a timely moment when the United States, for good or for ill, is itself involved in the enterprises of empire. Schaw's is one of the few accounts we have of an eighteenth-century Scotswoman abroad in the empire, and she joins other early women writers, such as Mary Wollstonecraft, Anna Maria Falconbridge, and Maria Graham, in her attempt to comprehend the world that Great Britain was making in the late eighteenth century. We should celebrate Schaw's ability to bring that world to life, her incisiveness in noting the rituals and drama and details of the societies she encountered, and her reporting of even those things that she could not "see" so clearly from her vantage point. For, like her, we are also stuck in our own moment and place, and as we travel about a world that has become much smaller than hers, we too are blinded by the myths we carry with us. But by traveling to unknown lands, by planes as well as by books, we all pass through customs, as it were, and have the opportunity to see more clearly how our world was made and how others have made theirs.

FURTHER READING

Additional information about Janet Schaw and her writings has been published in Elizabeth A. Bohls, "The Aesthetics of Colonialism: Janet Schaw in the West Indies, 1774–1775," *Eigh-*

teenth-Century Studies 27 (1994): 363–90; and, more recently, in Deirdre Coleman, "Janet Schaw and the Complexions of Empire," *Eighteenth-Century Studies* 36 (2003): 169–94.

Travel writings—especially letters and published journals—from this time period and earlier abound. Fictionalized accounts also exist. Caryl Phillips is a writer born in the West Indies and raised in England, and his novel *Cambridge* (New York: Knopf, 1992) draws extensively on Schaw's journal and other period writings.

Recommended scholarly works related to gender, travel writing, and colonial history that help contextualize Schaw's work include Thomas W. Krise, ed. *Caribbeana: An Anthology of English Literature of the West Indies, 1657–1777* (Chicago: University of Chicago Press, 1999), which comprises selections from some of the most important early literary and historical accounts of the West Indies. Mary Louise Pratt's *Imperial Eyes: Travel Writing and Transculturation* (London: Routledge, 1992) is now a classic scholarly analysis of the strategies of representation used by colonizers and the colonized in the eighteenth and nineteenth centuries. Also recommended are Sara Mills, *Discourses of Difference: An Analysis of Women's Travel Writing and Colonialism* (London: Routledge, 1991); Felicity Nussbaum, *The Autobiographical Subject: Gender and Ideology in Eighteenth-Century England* (Baltimore: Johns Hopkins University Press, 1989); and Orlando Patterson, *The Sociology of Slavery: An Analysis of the Origins, Development, and Structure of Negro Slave Society in Jamaica* (London: MacGibbon and Kee, 1967).

CONTENTS

ILLUSTRATIONS

Note. The map of the Parishes of Basseterre, the map of the Lower Cape Fear, the plan of the Town of Wilmington, and the Entries of the *Jamaica Packet* and the *Rebecca* are heliotypes from photographs of the original documents. The remaining maps and plans are from drawings by W. A. Dwiggins.

INTRODUCTION

THE finding of an interesting manuscript is much like the
sighting of an unexpected island by a mariner sailing in
strange seas, for the exploration of either, whatever may be
the ultimate value of the discovery, affords all the excite-
ment that accompanies an adventure into the unknown. Nor
has this "Journal of a Lady of Quality," stumbled upon
accidentally in a search for other material, failed in any particular to fulfill the expectations of its discoverers or the
promise of its charming title and opening pages; and one
can only marvel that such a treasure should have lain so long
unproclaimed.

That an incredulous reader may not have to speculate
regarding the genuineness of the Journal, the editors hasten
to say that it is no twentieth century fabrication, but that the
manuscript from which the present text is printed is known
as Egerton, 2423, and is even now in the British Museum.
It is a quarto volume labelled "Travels in the West Indies
and South Carolina, 1774, '75"; and in the Museum Cata-
logue it is entered as a "Journal by a Lady, of a Voyage from
Scotland to the West Indies and South Carolina, with an
account of personal experiences during the War of Independence, and a visit to Lisbon on her return 25 October
1774—December 1775." Quite a long description that, but
withal an inaccurate one; and surely he was a careless re-
tainer of the British Museum who did the labelling, for even
a cursory reading of the beautiful manuscript shows that

"North Carolina" should be substituted for "South Carolina," and that the narrative itself deals, at most, with only the preliminary events of the American War for Independence and continues nearly to the beginning of February, 1776.

As a narrative, the Journal falls naturally into four parts, dealing respectively with the voyage from Scotland to the West Indies; with life and experiences in the West Indies at Antigua and St. Kitts, and the voyage from St. Kitts to the Cape Fear River; with life on the Cape Fear just before the American War of Independence; and, finally, with the various adventures and experiences of Miss Schaw and her companions in Portugal on her way back to Scotland. Nowhere in our manuscript does the name of the author occur, and, for the most part, the names of persons referred to are in blank; so that only after much following of clues and searching in the records of England, Scotland, Ireland, the West Indies, and America have the editors been able to trace the careers of those who play the leading parts in the story. With the blanks filled out as far as possible, with but few corrections in spelling and capitalization, and with here and there a change in the diverting, but somewhat erratic, punctuation, the Journal, in the form now presented, is the same as that of the British Museum manuscript.

But of more importance than these slight changes in form is the fact that two other copies of the Journal are known to exist, one of which, the Vetch manuscript, owned by a descendant of the Schaws and recently bequeathed to a descendant of the Rutherfurds,—the two families that play the chief rôles in the Journal,—we have not been allowed to examine, even for purposes of textual comparison. The other, now in the possession of Mr. Vere Langford Oliver, the distinguished author of a history of Antigua, was purchased by him a few years ago in the belief that it was unique; and although this is not the case, it is of particular value in that it gives the name of the author and is dedicated to Alexander Schaw, Esqr, "the Brother, Freind, and fellow traveler of the Author, his truly affect. Jen. Schaw, St. Andrews Square, March 10, 1778." Mr. Oliver, who has compared his copy with that in the British Museum, says that although there are differences in binding and pagination, the two manuscripts are in the same handwriting and differ but slightly in phraseology. Our belief is that both are copies of the same manuscript, which, in turn, may have been the original; for these letters, written to a dear friend, probably a woman back in Scotland, by this same "Jen. Schaw" while on her eventful journey to the West Indies and North Carolina, were probably copied many times for circulation among relatives and friends. Thus, from 1904, when the editors of the present volume came upon the British Museum manuscript, these other manuscripts have been appearing, first Colonel Vetch's and later Mr. Oliver's, to claim the title for the only and original; and almost comically, have been masquerading, like three Dromios, somewhat to the confusion and dismay, but also to the amusement, of some of the discoverers of the prize.

If further proof were needed, both of the authenticity of the Journal and also of the accuracy and truthfulness of the author in describing places, events, and individuals, that is supplied by the notes and appendices of this volume, in which Professor Andrews has checked up or amplified each point of personal and historical interest. Scholarly research has been applied to the work of this delightful "Lady of Quality," but she holds her ground firmly and ably, as with ease and fluency she discusses manners and customs, climate and scenery, sugar-culture and farming, friends,—their houses, amusements, recreations, and sorrows,—and, fortunately for posterity, happenings and human beings as she saw both in the West Indies and North Carolina just before the American War for Independence. Rarely is she caught napping, and with her enthusiasm and humour, her ability to make us see and feel with her, she carries us to a triumphant end. Reluctantly we close the volume, for we would know all her story; but she leaves us abruptly in Portugal, with never a hint as to how she got back to Scotland or how and where she spent the later years of her life: and we ask ourselves, Who was this "affect. Jen. Schaw," where did she come from and whither did she go, this vivacious, adventurous, aristocratic lady, this devoted sister, who willingly faced great discomfort and hardships in order to accompany one dear brother to his new home in the West Indies and to visit another in the far distant British colony of North Carolina? What manner of woman is this who suddenly appears on our field of vision, leaves an unforgettable account of herself and her relatives and friends, and vanishes as suddenly as she came? What is her achievement, and what is the significance for us of this Journal of hers? It is in the search for answers to these questions that one begins a real voyage of adventure.

The Journal relates that there sailed from the Firth of Forth on October 25, 1774, a small craft, the *Jamaica Packet*, bound for the West Indies and North Carolina, the chief passengers of which were a young Scotsman and his sister, the author of the Journal, who from other sources we discover were Alexander and Janet Schaw of Edinburgh. Travelling with them were Fanny, an attractive girl of eighteen or nineteen, John, Jr., or Jack, a lad of eleven, and William Gordon, the nine-year-old "Billie" of the Journal, connections of the Schaws, and children of John Rutherfurd, a prominent resident of the colony of North Carolina. Besides these five, there were also Mrs. Mary Miller, Miss Schaw's maid, whom she called her Abigail, and who is a comic figure in the story; and the faithful, efficient Robert, Mr. Schaw's grave East Indian servant, who almost magically made up for deficiencies in the menu when live stock and food had been swept overboard and the passengers were facing possible starvation. And that the Journal might lack no element of romance, there were the fine English sailors, the honest mate, the subservient supercargo, hand in glove with the unscrupulous captain; the pitiful emigrants smuggled aboard and treated like slaves; frightful storms and rumours of pirates; and hovering in the background, always the sinister figure of Parker, the rascally owner of the vessel, whose evil deeds constantly came to light during the perilous voyage on which the Schaws were embarked. Nowhere, we think, does our author display so well her own sterling qualities of character and charming personality, as in this, the opening chapter of the Journal. From the start she captures our interest for herself and for her companions of what she picturesquely calls her "little wooden kingdom," and with a real sense of climax, sustains it at high pitch, until she and they, after a stormy passage of seven weeks, from which they but barely escape with their lives, sail safely into the beautiful harbour of St. John's at Antigua. For months, off and on, regardless of storms, severe cold, intense heat, or the distractions of travel, Miss Schaw wrote her journal-letters, describing, as the case might be, the tropical and almost Oriental luxury of the West Indies, the exciting and interesting events of our pre-revolutionary history, or the details of her amusing experiences in Setubal and Lisbon, never forgetting her promise to the fortunate and adored friend in Scotland who was her inspiration. Dating her first letter "9 o'clock evening, October 25, 1774," Miss Schaw says: "I propose writing you every day, but you must not expect a regular journal. I will not fail to write whatever can amuse myself; and whether you find it entertaining or not, I know you will not refuse it a reading. As every subject will be guided by my own immediate feelings, my opinions and descriptions will depend on the health and humour of the moment in which I write; from which cause my sentiments will often appear to differ on the same subject." It is not surprising that the journal of such a delightfully whimsical and candid author as this letter shows Miss Schaw to be, should be both accurate and refreshing, and that its author should win for herself at the outset the affectionate interest of her readers. Fortunately for us she was blessedly unaware, as she jotted down her opinions and descriptions according to the "humour of the moment" that she was writing for posterity a document of rare interest and importance, one which, as far as we know, and especially as it bears on the Scottish phase of American colonial history, is unique. Little did she suspect that she was to be caught in the net of the future historian and labelled as a valuable specimen of those Scots who figured in the colonizing movements of the seventeenth and eighteenth centuries.

In the lowlands of Scotland, amid the hills and valleys and along the rivers and firths from the Grampians to the Tweed and the Clyde, were scores of Scottish families of old-time stock whose attention was attracted early to the islands and mainland of the New World. Even before the end of the seventeenth century, young Scotsmen had begun to wander across the seas, either to fill civil offices in the colonies, to find cheap land upon which to set up farms and plantations, or to serve in regiments, stationed for longer or shorter periods in Boston, New York, or some one of the island colonies. As lands in the West Indies became more difficult to obtain, because of the growth of the sugar industry, many of the settlers turned to the mainland of America, to North Carolina in particular, and after the opening of the Cape Fear section, colonized there in great numbers— Hamiltons, Martins, Mackinnens, Hallidays, Murrays, Duncans, Rutherfurds, Pringles, and Schaws—all of whom figure in this Journal. Before the end of the colonial period both Lowland and Highland Scots were to be found in North Carolina, Georgia, New York, and Nova Scotia, with a few in Maryland and Virginia as well; and some of them, men of the old covenanting blood and spirit, alive to the opportunities offered by commerce or the development of large plantations, became important officials or planters and tradesmen of prominence and influence. Wherever these Scotsmen found themselves, whether in the West Indies or on the American Continent, in Oporto or in Lisbon—Portuguese cities where treaty relations with Great Britain made it possible for English and Scottish merchants to monopolize commerce—there they established homes and places of business, and retaining their devotion to their mother-country, their king, and their traditions, created centres of Scottish life that became in reality little Scotlands. Mutual affection and devotion characterized these Scottish families, wherever their members settled. Eager for news from home, those in the colonies extended generous hospitality to the wandering members of their own family, or the families of their friends; those that remained in Scotland never lost interest in their kin across the sea, aided them with money, and welcomed them back whenever they could come. Thus had the stage been set for Alexander and Janet Schaw, who, all unconscious of so much preparation for their advent into history, wandered happily from one to another of the West Indian islands, to various plantations and centres of the colony of North Carolina, and finally, Miss Schaw herself, to Lisbon, meeting old friends and acquaintances, and enjoying the lavish hospitality that clannish Scotsmen naturally offered to such charming and distinguished guests.

It is a matter for congratulation that Miss Schaw made her visit to the West Indies and the Cape Fear just when she did, for had she come a few years later, she would have found Antigua and St. Kitts, not at the height of their prosperity as they were in 1774, with the Hamiltons, Martins, and Paynes dispensing almost royal hospitality, but suffering from the somewhat devastating effects of the American

Revolution: and had she come earlier, we should have lacked a chronicler of a period of our own revolutionary history for which there exists no finer contemporary document than her Journal. Not only does she describe graphically and interestingly the natural scenery and social life of the places she visited—for she is a gifted letter writer, as other extant letters of hers prove—but she gives us pictures of political life in North Carolina during the stormy pre-revolutionary days which are typical, not only of the Cape Fear, but also of many other colonial centres, and which help us to understand, even if they do not induce us to accept, the conservative point of view held by those who in such troublous times remained loyal to their mother-country. From the moment of her arrival at Brunswick until she sailed for Portugal in the autumn of 1775, Miss Schaw gives a running account of affairs in the Cape Fear, both social and political, as seen by one of the group of loyalists and conservatives, of whom many undoubtedly were forced into active opposition to the colonial government by the violence of the extreme radicals. In this connection it is interesting to learn that of the men of Brunswick and Wilmington whom the Schaws knew well, those who moved to the Cape Fear from Charleston, such as Richard Quince, William Dry, Joseph Eagles, James Moore, and others, became the nucleus, as it were, of the united provincial group, which often, and especially after the actual outbreak of hostilities, opposed those "newcomers and foreigners" of English or Scottish birth, such as Dr. Cobham, Robert Hogg, the Rutherfurds, and the Schaws. Such cleavages of friendship were unhappily frequent, for political feeling ran high in all the colonies; and it is not difficult to understand Miss Schaw's indignation when she saw the radical group of North Carolina politicians, self-styled "patriots," forcing into rebellion a colony which she believed had itself no real grievance against the mother-country. Her accounts of the persecutions of such refined, intellectual men as Dr. Cobham and Archibald Neilson, and of such honorable business men as Robert Hogg, Samuel Campbell, and Thomas Macknight—persecutions that drove them either out of the colony entirely or most unwillingly into the ranks of the king's party; her story of the tarring and feathering of Neilson's valet; of the enforced drilling of unwilling "volunteers"; of the threats against the lives of peaceful citizens who refused to "sign the Association"—all these details, vividly and feelingly described, together with her own impressions of individuals and events, constitute a story that challenges the attention of all those genuinely interested in our movement for independence. Such contemporary evidence makes us realize that our forefathers, however worthy their object, were engaged in real rebellion and revolution, characterized by the extremes of thought and action that always accompany such movements, and not in the kind of parlour warfare, described in many of our text books, in which highly cultivated and periwigged American gentlemen of unquestioned taste and morality, together with farmers of heroic mould, engaged life and limb for principles of democratic government, which developed, in fact, only during later periods of our national life. A definitive account of the loyalists in our revolution has yet to be written, but such a contribution should help to clarify our minds about the facts of our colonial history, and counteract the false judgments and prejudices which perpetuate what a recent writer so aptly describes as "the ancient grudge."

But this Journal, valuable as it undoubtedly is as history, claims recognition for itself also as a literary and human document, and places its author among the littérateurs of her country and century. Researches, amply rewarded in other respects, unfortunately have failed to secure much information about the personal life of Janet Schaw herself; but we know that she was born in Lauriston, a suburb of Edinburgh, in a house which is still standing, and conjecture that at the time of her voyage to the West Indies and America she was possibly thirty-five or forty years of age. She came of an old Scottish family that counted as blood relations or connections by marriage Murrays, Rutherfurds, and Scotts, and was herself a third cousin once removed of Sir Walter Scott. The common ancestor of all was a certain John Schaw, minister of Selkirk, who had married Anne, daughter of an early Sir John Murray of Philiphaugh. On January 23, 1723, Janet's father, Gideon Schaw, was married to an Anne Rutherfurd, also a cousin of Sir Walter's and great-aunt of the three Rutherfurd children who accompanied Alexander and Janet Schaw to America. By this marriage there were six children, of whom three only, Robert, Janet, and Alexander, figure in this Journal. As early as 1726 Gideon Schaw and his wife were living at Lauriston Yards, a fourteen acre farm just outside Edinburgh, now included in the city proper; and we know that there the eldest daughter, Anne, was born; but inasmuch as from 1730 to 1751 Gideon Schaw held positions in other parts of Scotland, and as we can find no records of birth or baptism for Janet or Alexander, we can only guess as to where they were born and when. Janet probably spent many years at Lauriston, and we believe that she was residing there at the time of her father's death in 1772, two and a half years before her narrative opens; but of her later life, after her return from Lisbon in the winter of 1776, we know almost nothing. That she was living in Edinburgh, at least for a time, is indicated by the dedication in 1778 of one copy of the Journal from "St. Andrews Square" in that city, and also from an entry in the Edinburgh directory of 1778-1779, which gives her residence as "New Town," a northern section of Edinburgh which included St. Andrew's Square. Such are the meagre facts of the life of our charming "Lady of Quality." Had she, like her brother Alexander or her relative John Rutherfurd, held positions of public trust, or, like her brother Robert and the Rutherfurd children, owned land

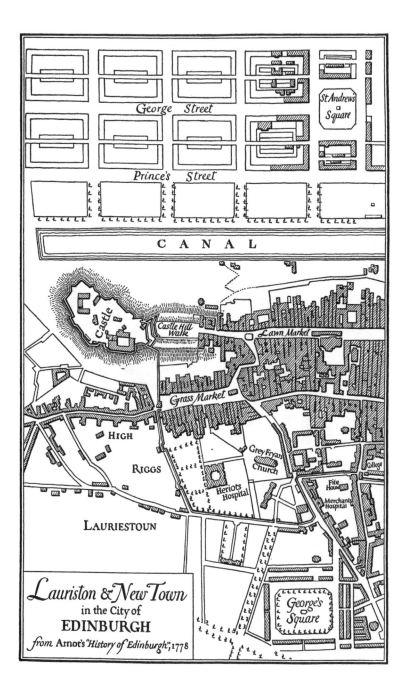

George Street

St Andrews
Square

Prince's Street

C A N A L

Castle

Castle Hill
Walk

Lawn Market

Grass Market

HIGH

RIGGS

Grey Fryars
Church

Heriots
Hospital

Fife
House

Merchants
Hospital

College

LAURIESTOUN

George's
Square

Lauriston & New Town
in the City of
EDINBURGH
from Arnot's "History of Edinburgh", 1778

on the Cape Fear, public records would have been available for her history as they have been for the history of these others; but she, the most important person connected with the Journal, remains for the most part unrecorded. Nor is the elusive lady to be caught anywhere it seems, for as far as we know she did not marry; and having made her contribution to history and letters, she passes on—what woman but will envy her!—without date, ageless, just Janet Schaw, the author of "The Journal of a Lady of Quality."

But if records fail to furnish the life history of our author, her Journal is rich in revelations of her character and ability and shows her to be a well-born Scotswoman, loyal to her country and her king, in her tastes and preferences an aristocrat, and in religious, social, and political views a typical member of the educated class in Scotland in the latter half of the eighteenth century. Her prejudices and antipathies, though largely temperamental, are to a certain extent also those of her class; and although they do not invalidate her sense of fact, at times they warp her judgment and blind her to the real significance of the events in which she plays an important part. But, on the whole, Miss Schaw exhibits a tolerance and breadth of view, especially in matters pertaining to religion and faith, that seem unusual, unless one recalls the fact that she was living and writing at a time when Scotland was not only passing through a period of great material prosperity, marked by extension of trade and rapid development in agriculture; but was also making her greatest contribution to science, philosophy, and literature, and through such men as David Hume, Adam Smith, Black, Leslie, Hutton, and above all Macpherson, was exercising a profound influence on the contemporary thought of the intellectual world. It is not surprising, therefore, to find Miss Schaw discussing scientific methods of tilling the soil and harvesting the crops, and drawing comparisons between the thrifty intensive farming she had seen in East Lothian and the shockingly wasteful methods employed by whites and blacks alike on the plantations of the Cape Fear. Also, it is natural that, inheriting as she did the literary traditions of Allan Ramsay and James Thomson, and living in the midst of a metaphysical and philosophical renaissance, she should take great pride in the philosophers and poets of her country, should quote them frequently with admiration and approval, and adopt them as guides in the conduct of life. We almost catch the contemporary thrill when she exclaims over the magic beauty of Ossian; and share her amusement when she finds that the book from which Fanny Rutherfurd was reading aloud when the boat seemed to be sinking, was not the Bible but, as Miss Schaw laughingly confesses, Lord Kames's *Elements of Criticism*! However, she is deeply religious and revels in hymns and the Scriptures, as her frequent quoting of both attests; and although she disclaims being a bigot and really is a very tolerant person, she acknowledges that the force of habit is too strong to allow her to be anything more than a spectator at the ceremonies of other churches than her own. She prefers, so she says on one occasion with her characteristic frankness, "the snivelling of a sincere-hearted country precentor" to the impressive service and grand music of the beautiful church at Antigua, and doubts whether there is much real religion in the ceremonious procedure of the Anglican church.

Her antipathies, however, are not only religious, they are political and social as well; but inasmuch as she is never ill-humoured in her criticism, her strong feelings on various subjects only tend to make her more vivid, and produce in any portrait of her an effect of earnestness and force that contrast delightfully with the varied and lighter sides of her character. As might be expected, from a Lowland Scot, a staunch Presbyterian, and a Hanoverian, she is thoroughly distrustful of her neighbors the French, who, she says with much contempt are, like "chattering, grimacing monkeys,

. . . subtle enemies and false friends, and as little ashamed
of defeat as a French admiral or general." We can only hope
that she lived to know that the "little Billie" of her journal
became the Captain William Gordon Rutherfurd of the
Swiftsure, who, serving with distinction under the great
Lord Nelson, took part in the defeat of the hated French at
the battle of Trafalgar.

It is in character, too, that she should condemn the radical
American colonists as rebels and savages, and be shocked and
enraged by some of the events she witnessed in the Cape
Fear; for by temperament and education Miss Schaw de-
tested violence and cruelty, advocated the authority both of
the family and the state, and cherished always the good form
and courtly manners characteristic of the refined society to
which she was accustomed. That in social matters she was
conservative and valued the conventions of life for society
at large, there is ample evidence; though it is also true that,
aristocratically, she sometimes claimed exemption for herself, as when she humorously defied custom and drank wine
at a ladies' luncheon in Antigua, or, for purposes of safety
and convenience, travelled with Archibald Neilson in Portugal as his wife. Also, she took for granted a certain laxity
of morals in her own class, when, for instance, she describes
the terror of one of the emigrants, "a lovelorn youth," who
but for herself and her brother would have fared badly at
the hands of an outraged husband, "a rough fellow," she
calls him, "who had not the patience of your husbands of
fashion." But her prejudices and points of view, such as
they are, only relate her more closely to the very fine type
to which she belonged; while her intelligence, kindly human
sympathies, and freshness of heart and mind save her from
provinciality, and leave on our minds the impression of a
truly admirable and delightful woman. A real love of fun
and humour and an instinctive passion for fair play—such
are the qualities which she shared largely with her brother

Alexander, and of which they both gave evidence again and again during the eventful sixteen months of which the Journal treats. They make a charming picture, this highly bred, high-spirited brother and sister, who faced life wherever it found them with courage and equanimity, good nature and kindliness—he, the educated, intelligent man of affairs, prompt in action, impatient of brutality and injustice, resourceful in emergencies both on land and at sea; she, the candid, warm-hearted, quick-witted woman of the world, a person of very real distinction and charm. Whether or not she was beautiful, we do not know, for although she loves the flower-like beauty of Fanny Rutherfurd and has much to say of the good looks of the men and women of Antigua, she refers to her own appearance but twice: once when she writes jocosely that a passion is begun between Mr. Baird, the collector, and herself, "which, as it is not raised on beauty, it is to be hoped will be lasting"; and again, when speaking of the masks worn by the ladies of Antigua, she says, "As to your humble servant, I have always set my face to the weather, wherever I have been. I hope you have no quarrel with brown beauty." But that she was genial and sociable, liking both men and women and liked by them in return, there is ample proof; and it is not surprising that two such visitors as she and her brother Alexander received a warm welcome wherever they went, and that their journey resembled more a royal progress than a tour of ordinary travellers.

But it is not only as a faithful chronicler of what she saw and experienced, or as an interesting and charming woman, that Janet Schaw claims attention, but above all as an artist, as a lover of beauty and form, who uses her masses of material with reserve and discrimination, securing her backgrounds and atmosphere with delicacy and precision, and drawing her figures with swift, sure strokes of her pen. Her imagination plays about the subjects that interest her, and feeling and emotion lift her work above the commonplace into the realm of artistic achievement. She revels in the smell of the air, as it comes to her "warm off the African coast"; in the colour and perfume of Mrs. Dunbar's garden; in the richness and elegance of architecture of churches and houses and public buildings. Picture after picture she paints for us —landscapes of rugged mountains and bleak, barren lands with an almost arctic atmosphere; frightful storms with boats battling for their existence; sea-scapes of tropical islands in an almost motionless ocean, langourous under the rays of a burning sun; vivid little genre pictures of a lady going to a ball dressed out in all her "British airs with a high head and a hoop"; of emigrants at play in the sunshine on the deck of a sailing vessel; of marvellous banquets where the varieties of food and drink seem infinite in number, and where one is presented with a refreshing liquid "in a crystal cup with cover of silver"; of slaves going to market in joyful troops, carrying animals and fruits and flowers "like a set of devotees going to sacrifice to their Indian gods." Her portrait of the exquisite Lady Belle Hamilton seated in her magnificent hall at "Olivees," her handsome young husband near her, and beside her a little mulatto girl "dressed out like an infant Sultana" possesses in its effects of contrast the quality achieved by Rossetti in his lovely picture of "The Bride"; whereas in such a description as that of the great storm at sea, when the ship with her sails fluttering in rags was all but lost, our author seems almost inspired.

Miss Schaw knows, also, the uses, for artistic purposes, of fun and humour,—broad at times as was characteristic of the period,—of balance and rhythm, of imagery, of pathos and emotion, and even of sentimentality, and sketches picture after picture instinct with warmth and colour and motion and the joy of living. Very often, especially in the descriptive parts of her work, and in her characterizations, she suggests her compatriot Stevenson, who might have said of her subjects what he says of Raeburn's, that "the people who sat for these pictures are not yet ancestors, they are still relations. They are not yet altogether a part of the dusty past, but occupy a middle distance within cry of our affections." Her contribution both to history and to literature is a real one, and so vivid and human are the events and the people she depicts as to make us feel that we have suddenly, and with real understanding, touched hands, as it were, with our forebears of the colonial period.

Before the visitor has been long in the beautiful state of North Carolina, he will have realized, as have the editors of this volume, that from Miss Schaw's day to our own North Carolina has been one of the great southern triumvirate of states noted for the charm of their climate and scenery and the hospitality of their people. In pursuit of material connected with this Journal the editors have journeyed from Great Britain to North and South Carolina, finding everywhere such generous interest and such a delightful welcome as to make them feel that those who have coöperated in the volume are a veritable band of brother adventurers. Especially are they indebted to Dr. J. Maitland Thomson of Edinburgh, who has contributed genealogical information of great value and photographic copies of letters written by Janet Schaw; and to the present members of the Hewlett family, owners of the fine colonial house of "Rockhall," at Lawrence, Long Island, at times the home of the last royal governor of North Carolina, Josiah Martin, who with his father, Colonel Samuel of Antigua, are prominent in the Journal. In North Carolina, they have wandered from Raleigh to the Cape Fear and Albemarle regions, familiarizing themselves with the historical background of the Journal, and enjoying the innumerable courtesies that the North Carolinian lavishes upon the stranger within his gates. Everywhere have they met with coöperation, but especially have they to thank The North Carolina Society of the Colonial Dames of America, who are contributing financially to the publication of this volume; Mr. John D. Bellamy, Jr., who has furnished many facts of real value; the late Mr. John G. Wood of Edenton, from whose important collection of papers at "Hayes" they have obtained much information concerning the Rutherfurd family; and even more particularly Mr. R. D. W. Connor, secretary of the North Carolina Historical Commission, who not only put at their disposal the manuscript material under his charge, but at every turn helped on the work with real interest and generous assistance. Finally, and with peculiar gratitude, the editors recall the hospitality and coöperation of Mr. James Sprunt of Wilmington, himself a Scot, under whose kindly guidance they were able to study Wilmington and the Cape Fear, and to whom most affectionately they dedicate this volume.

Today one perceives very little of the isolation that Janet Schaw felt in Wilmington, now a beautiful city echoing to the hammers of new shipbuilding enterprises that sprang up during the war; but a sail down the Cape Fear River to the plantation of "Orton," sole survivor of the many interesting plantations that dotted the Cape Fear in colonial times, recalls her descriptions, and carries one into the heart of what was once old Brunswick, the first settlement that she saw on her arrival in the province. Today all that is left of the original town are the impressive brick ruins of St. Philip's Church, its roof open to the sky, its fine deep windows framing sunny bits of out of doors, and its nave and aisles picturesquely overgrown with grass and trees. In the old churchyard can be found graves and tombstones that testify to the burial there of some of Janet Schaw's friends; and starting from the centre of what was once Brunswick Town are here and there magnificent live oaks, still tenacious of life though heavy with years, and clothed in the fantastic, parasitic moss that is treacherously destroying them. To the north the fine colonial mansion of "Orton" brightly offers hospitality to the delighted stranger, giving

him a sense of stability and security; but neither the delicious warm sunshine of early spring, nor the odours of sweet-
scented flowers and shrubs drifting in from well-kept gardens, nor the drowsy washing of the river along the sandy
shore can entirely dispel his fear lest in time the luxuriant
jealous forest, which even now threatens to overwhelm both
church and churchyard, shall reduce to jungle and obliterate
forever the old Brunswick that once knew Janet Schaw.

EVANGELINE WALKER ANDREWS.

Orton Plantation,
    March 30, 1920.

CHAPTER I.

The Voyage to the West Indies.

Burnt Island Road* on board the Jamaica Packet
9 o'Clock Evening 25ᵗʰ Octʳ 1774.

WE are now got on Board, heartily fatigued, yet not
likely to sleep very sound in our new apartments, which I
am afraid will not prove either very agreeable or commodious; nor, from what I can see, will our Ship be an
exception to the reflections thrown on Scotch Vessels in
general, as indeed, nothing can be less cleanly than our
Cabin, unless it be its Commander, and his friend and bed-
fellow the Supercargo. I hinted to the Captain that I thought
our Cabin rather dirty. He assured me every Vessel was so
'till they got out to Sea, but that as soon as we were under
way, he wou'd stow away the things that were lumbering
about, and then all wou'd be neat during the Voyage. I
appear to believe him; it were in vain to dispute; here we
are, and here we must be for sometime. My brother has laid

---

* Burntisland is a seaport of county Fife, on the north side of the Firth
of Forth, five miles across from Leith and Edinburgh. As there was a ferry
from Leith, it is quite probable that Miss Schaw and her party drove to
Leith in carriages and there boarded the ferryboat for Burntisland. The
seaport has an excellent harbour and was a favorite anchorage for vessels
entering or leaving the firth, but the fact that the owner of the vessel lived
at Burntisland may furnish an additional reason for the place of departure.
Some of the Scottish regiments serving in the Revolutionary War sailed
from this port, and as early as 1627 we meet with a vessel called the
Blessing of Burntisland.

in store of whatever may render our Situation agreeable, and I have laid in a store of resolution to be easy, not to be sick if I can help it, and to keep good humour, whatever I lose; and this I propose to do by considering it, what it is, merely a Voyage.

As we have no passengers but those of our own family, we will have all the accommodation the Vessel is capable of affording, and we can expect no more.

My Brother has not yet got on Board, I dare say he will be sadly fatigued with the business he has had to go thro'. I will send this on shore with the boat that brings him off.

I propose writing you every day, but you must not expect a regular Journal. I will not fail to write whatever can amuse myself; and whether you find it entertaining or not, I know you will not refuse it a reading, as every subject will be guided by my own immediate feelings. My opinions and descriptions will depend on the health and the humour of the Moment, in which I write; from which cause my Sentiments will often appear to differ on the same subject. Let this therefore serve as a general Apology for whatever you observe to do so thro' my future Letters.

I am just now contemplating the various Sensations our intended Voyage and its destination produce in the little Group around me.* The two young Rutherfurds have not the most distant remembrance of their Father, yet such is the power of natural affection on their little hearts, that they are transported with the Idea of seeing him, and were they to draw his Portrait I dare say it wou'd be the most charming picture in the world; as the three people they love best are with them, they have nothing to damp their pleasure. The case however is different with their Sister, she perfectly

---

*Miss Schaw was accompanied by her brother, Alexander, and by the three children of John Rutherfurd, of North Carolina—Fanny, aged eighteen or nineteen, John Jr., aged eleven, and William Gordon, aged nine, all of whom, though born in North Carolina, had been sent to Scotland in 1767 for their education.

remembers her Father, and tho' she is equally rejoiced at the hopes of being once more clasped to the bosom of a fond Parent, yet her satisfaction is check'd by various considerations. In the first place, her Modesty makes her afraid he has drawn a picture of her person in his own Imagination, to which she will by no means come up, and her diffidence of her own attainments makes her fear he will not find her so accomplished as he has reason to expect. I believe she may make herself easy as to these, for few Fathers ever had better reason to be satisfied.

But there is another Source of distress, to a sensible mind, still more severe. In this Country* all her early friendships and connexions have commenced, which can only be form'd in the delightful Season of Youth; to break these all at once, and bid them an eternal farewell, requires the utmost exertion of fortitude, and I have reason to believe it has been no easy task. As to myself, the approbation of my own conduct is my support against a thousand invading Passions. I had long taken root in my native Soil, yet it is not the spot of Earth that gave me being I call my Country. No! it is the Social Circle of such friends, as few can boast their brightest hours of prosperity were enriched with, it was these that constituted my happiness; the western world may shew me higher Scenes of riches, and Luxury may bid me view the difference, and how far they exceed us, but never can they afford my soul such evening Conversations as I have feasted on in the friendly Circle of our Chearfull Hearth.

> Give me again that glowing sense to warm,
> The song to warble, and the wit to charm.

My going will chear the Travils of the best of Brothers, and once more give me the other, lost from childhood.† Time will

---

* Scotland.

† The "best of brothers" was, of course, Alexander; "the other, lost from childhood," was Miss Schaw's brother Robert, probably older than herself. Later in the narrative, she says that he "had not seen a bleaching-washing

restore me to you, perhaps to my dear Native land, on which
may Heaven shower its choicest blessings. But farewell, my
spirits are quite worn out, and my fatigues require rest, tho'
I fear my narrow bed will be no great inducement to the
drowsy powers. Adieu, sound and peaceful be the slumbers
of my friend, whatever Mine prove.

Sleep was more obliging than I expected; it was not long
before all my cares were lost, which wou'd sooner have happened, but from the music of Mrs Mary's nose who had got
the start of me.*

Our Bed chamber, which is dignified with the title of
State Room, is about five foot wide and six long; on one side
is a bed fitted up for Miss Rutherfurd and on the opposite
side one for me. Poor Fanny's is so very narrow, that she is
forced to be tied in, or as the Sea term is lashed in, to prevent
her falling over. On the floor below us lies our Abigail, M^rs
Mary, now Mrs Miller. As she has the breadth of both our
Beds and excellent Bedding, I think she has got a most
envyable berth, but this is far from her opinion, and she has
done nothing but grumble about her accommodation, and
I fear will prove a most complete Abigail indeed.

We had not slept above an hour, when my Brother
arrived, he let down the half door to enquire after our
healths. We both waked with pleasure at his well-known and
friendly Voice, and made him happy by assuring him we
found ourselves much better than we expected. After delivering the affectionate Compliments of merry friends, he
warned us not to be alarmed if We heard a noise and screaming on Deck, for that the boat had gone off to bring Ovid,
our owners poor Devil of a Negro man on Board, who was to

since he was a boy," which would mean that he must have left Scotland at
a very early age. For a further account of him, see Appendix XII.

* "Mrs Mary" was Mrs. Mary Miller, Miss Schaw's waiting woman, who
accompanied her mistress on her travels. Whether she attended Miss Schaw
during her Lisbon sojourn is doubtful (see below, page 210, note).

be laid in Irons, 'till we were fairly out at Sea. We desired to know what crime the poor wretch had committed to deserve so hard a sentence. He replied, he knew of none, for he believed he was a much worthier man than his Master, whom he had reason to think a very great scoundrel without heart or feeling. Just then we heard the Boat along side: my brother left us, and went on Deck to mitigate, if possible, the rigours intended against this unfortunate creature, and we lay trembling in fearful expectation of the event, but happily for our feelings, poor Ovid finding himself overpowered by numbers, submitted without resistance.

Just then Mrs Miller awoke, was much surprised how we could sleep in so odious an hole, for her part, she never expected to close an eye in this Vile ship, was deadly sick with the motion (tho' by the bye it had not yet begun to move), and fell fast asleep with the words half pronounced on her Tongue. I am sure she is to be a great plague, but as she has left her Country with us, nothing shall prevent her being kindly treated, however little she may deserve it from her behaviour. My brother, who was sadly fatigued, had got into his Cott, which swings from the roof of the Cabin; our two little men were fast asleep in a bed just below him, when we were informed from the Deck that they were going to weigh anchor. Every body that was able, got up to see this first grand operation. My Brother descended from his Cot, the boys sprung out of bed, all hands were on Deck, hurry, bustle, noise, and confusion raged thro' our wooden kingdom, yet it was surprizing how soon every thing was reduced to order. In little more than a quarter of an hour, all was over, the watch was set, and nothing to be heard, but the sound of the man's feet moving regularly backwards and forwards at the helm, and the crowing of a Cock that the noise had waked in the Hen Coop. My Brother, as he again retired to his airy couch, informed us in passing our state room, that we were now underway, and that we wou'd be in the Channel* in a few hours, where we wou'd have the finest view of the finest Country in the World. He then gave poor Fanny some Saline drops to settle her stomach, which had felt the very first motion of the ship; a circumstance that gives me much concern, as I fear she will find it too much thro' our Voyage. As yet I am very well, and hope I will not be much hurt, tho' I must expect a little touch as well as others. My Brother now mounted into his Cot, the boys got to bed, we shut up our half door, and in a few moments, we were all again in the arms of Sleep.

But short must be the slumber in so unquiet and uncertain a situation, we were soon roused again by the Voice of our Cap^n,† who was talking to my Brother, and it was with no small vexation that we were informed by him that the wind had chopt about, and being now full in our Teeth, it was impossible for him to proceed up the channel, and that it was necessary to change his course, and go round by the North of Scotland. It is hardly possible to imagine a more disagreeable passage at this Season of the Year than this must be. The many Islands, Shelves and Rocks, render it very dangerous, which, with the addition of a rough sea, sudden squalls, and the coldest climate in Britain, gives as uncomfortable a prospect as one wou'd wish. However my brother agreed, all hands were called, hurry again filled the Vessel, "About Ship" was now the word, in the performing of which operation, every thing was tumbled topsyturvy. A few moments however settled us once more, and quietness wou'd again have restored us to rest, had not the Cock, as harbinger of day, repeatedly told us it was now morning. Nor were we the only passengers on Board whom this information con-

---

* The "Channel" is the Firth of Forth.

† The captain was Thomas Smith, and the vessel a brig or frigate of eighty tons, built in Massachusetts in 1772 and registered at Kirkcaldy, a seaport of Fife, northeast of Burntisland and the nearest port with a naval office. Captain Smith had registered the vessel on October 22, three days before sailing (see below, page 144, note).

cerned, his wives and children who now heard him, made such an outcry for Breakfast, as shewed their Stomachs suffered nothing from the Sea Air.

Their demands complied with, the outcry ceased, but they kept such a Peck Pecking directly over head, that it was impossible to rest, and banished all desire to sleep. This was a Misfortune much less felt by me than my poor young friend, who was now sick to death. I prevailed on Mrs Miller to get up and give us a dish of Tea, this she actually tried, but was not able to stand on her feet, as she was now really sick, and the motion of the Ship very violent. It was in vain for either of us to think of moving, and we were almost in despair, when fortunately I bethought me of Robert, my brother's Indian servant, a handy good fellow. "Oh!" cried I, to the first that I saw, "oh! for Heaven's sake send us Robt, Black Robt." Robt approached our state room, with all the dignity of a slow-stalking Indian Chief. "Dear Robt," exclaimed I, "cou'd you be so good as to get us a dish of Tea?" "To be certain, my Lady," replied he, "but Miss is very badly, and Tea is not good for her; I will get her a little good Chicken broth." "Do, dear Robt," cried poor Fanny, in a voice of the utmost thankfulness. Robt stalked off, and it was not long before he made his appearance with a Mess of the most charming chicken broth that ever comforted a sick stomach; and if ever you are again at Sea, pray, remember Robert's receipt, and if you do not find it the best thing you ever tasted, surely I have no judgment in Broths. Robt dealt out his benefits in Tea cup-fulls, every one had a little, and every one had a desire for more, so that his broth went thro' many Editions.

My Brother was now up, and tho' he wou'd not own he was sick, yet confessed he was a degree at least beyond squeemish. This he attributed to the smell of the Cabin, and to say the truth, this alone was enough. This sense of his has often been troublesome to him, and I am much mistaken, if he will find pleasure from it during his abode in the Jamaica Packet. Even the boys complain of being, they do not know how-ish, so he and they have gone on deck to try the Air. But tho' I make no doubt this is a good receipt, it is not in Miss Rutherfurd's power or mine to follow their Example, for, besides that we cannot keep our feet one moment, the Climate, we are in, is one of the coldest and worst in the World. The air is bitter beyond expression, with the addition of a constant dragling rain which renders it unsufferable, even to the poor Sailors, who are hardly able to stand out the watch; and as they never fail to be wet thro' and thro', my Brother is become very anxious about their healths, as he observes we have not half the compliment the Owner bargained with him for; his being obliged to stay so long at London made him trust to this fellow Parker the owner of the Ship,* and I am afraid we will find he has not paid much regard to the confidence that was reposed in him.

He came and pressed this Vessel on us, declaring that as he had the highest obligation to Mr Rutherfurd and my brother in Carolina, he had brought this ship from Newcastle, where he was destined for a different Voyage, on purpose to accommodate us, as she was an excellent Vessel, and he could let us have her entirely to ourselves. He affected a perfect indifference as to terms, which, however, in the end,

---

* The owner of the ship, the *Jamaica Packet*, was George Parker, who had lived in Wilmington from 1762 to 1771 as a householder and merchant, and was well known to Rutherfurd and the Schaws. He had been a town commissioner in 1764, and in 1766, as owner of the ship *Nancy*, had taken part in the protest against the stamps during the Stamp Act troubles. In 1771 he decided to leave Wilmington and go to Burntisland, where he had a brother. Consequently, he sold his house on Market Street, his lands, negroes, pettiauger, furniture, chaise, etc., for £910 (Wilmington, Register's Office, Conveyances, F, 157-160) and returned to Scotland. He seems to have been under some obligation to Rutherfurd, but in his dealings with Miss Schaw and her party showed very little honesty or friendship. There are references to him in the Brunswick County Records, Conveyances, A, 129-130, the *North Carolina Colonial Records*, VI, 177-178, and the Wilmington Town Records.

turned out very high. We had the precaution however to have her Hull viewed, which was declared vastly good, and I hope is so. He told us his plan was to send her with a light lading to the West Indies, where she would dispose of her Cargo, and, after taking in some Rum, Sugar, etc., wou'd sail with my Brother (as soon as he had settled his affairs at St Kitts*) to whatever American Port he desired.

There is no such thing as being warm, do what we will, and tho' we have but little wind hitherto, yet we are jaulted to death by the motion of the ship in these rough seas. Yet the Capt is every moment congratulating us on the smoothness of our Vessel, which he declares is so soft in her Motion, that one may play at Bowls on the deck. However as I am like to beat out my teeth every time I try to drink, and often after all am not able to bring the cup to such a direction as to obtain my desire, I cannot help thinking he rather overrates the gentleness of her Motions, tho' the mate in confirmation of what his Captain says, asserts, that last time he crossed the Atlantick even in a calm, they were forced to ly flat on their faces, which the hogs stubbornly refusing, had their brains knocked out against the sides of the ship. How happy are we, who are only in danger of losing teeth and breaking limbs.

As I was amusing myself with my pen, and Fanny with her book, a little while ago, my brother came into the Cabin, and informing us the weather was tolerable fair. He had provided watch-coats to secure us from the cold, and begged we would go with him upon deck, as he was sure a little fresh air would do us much good. We immediately accepted his invitation, and while we were preparing for this excursion, I asked my brother, if he had seen all our crew, and what sort of hands they were; for that as I lay awake last night in bed, I heard a heavy groan, (from that part of the steerage†

* Alexander was going out as searcher of customs at St. Christopher.
† "Steerage" in the sailing vessels of the day was the space below decks

which is only divided by a few boards from our State room,)
when presently a Voice called out, "What's the matter,
man," on which the groaner (as I supposed) replied, "Alas!
alas! this is a hard pillow for three score years to rest on."
My brother smiling took me by the hand, and reaching out
the other to Fanny, bade us come along, and we wou'd probably discover our groaning Neighbour. We now ascended the
Companion or Cabin stair, when, judge of my surprize, I saw
the deck covered with people of all ages, from three weeks
old to three score, men, women, children and suckling infants. For some time I was unable to credit my senses, it
appeared a scene raised by the power of Magic to bring such
a crowd together in the middle of the Sea, when I believed
there was not a soul aboard but the ship's crew and our own
family. Never did my eyes behold so wretched, so disgusting
a sight. They looked like a Cargo of Dean Swift's Yahoos*
newly caught.

It was impossible to account for this strange apparition,
till the Captain informed me, that they were a company of
Emigrants,† whom the owner had made him smuggle aboard
privately, and had ordered to be kept close under the hatches
till we were out at sea. He vindicated himself, by declaring,
he was under the most absolute necessity of obeying the
owner, whom he sincerely believed to be one of the greatest
Villains upon earth; that he and every one was much surprized how we came to trust him, for that his character as a
scoundrel was notorious wherever he had lived, that he himself had been ruined by him, and was now forced to serve
him, as he had got his all into his possession, and put it out
of his power to make bread in any other way. To this he

---

aft, that is, in the stern of the vessel. The accommodations, as the narrative
shows, were straitened and uncomfortable. "Steerage passengers" are mentioned quite early in the eighteenth century.

* The Yahoos of *Gulliver's Travels* are described as brutes with human
forms and vicious and uncleanly habits.

† For the highland emigration of these years, see Appendix I.

added many other particulars, and summed up all by the comfortable intimation, that C——r, the supercargo,* was just such another, and put on board for the express purpose of cheating and deceiving us; he, the Captain, being thought too honest to perform this piece of duty. This tale he has also told my brother, which the goodness of his own heart induces him to believe: but for my own part, I take it to be a forged story altogether, and that they are all alike. The mate, however, notwithstanding the story of the hogs, seems an honest plain fellow, and I am inclined to think much better of him than of the others. Indeed he does not entertain a very high opinion of his messmates himself, nor appears much satisfied with his present berth, but says it is like Padie's Candles, it will not mend. He so often mentioned

---

* Though it is hardly possible to recover the name of the supercargo, his character as "a republican and a violent American" is a sufficient indentification. He will be met with again (pp. 64, 65). It is evident that Miss Schaw did not like him, deeming him a silly fellow and a fool.

A "supercargo" was an officer of a merchant ship who was entrusted with the sale of the cargo and other commercial transactions. Such an officer required not only a knowledge of business, but also a certain amount of diplomatic skill to deal with extraordinary situations. The following explanation of the origin of this functionary is given by an old American naval commander. "Captains of ships were not often educated men; they began to go to sea very young, they learned just enough to navigate their ships in the simple way and with the crude instruments of that day. They could handle their ships under all circumstances and they were proficients with lead and line, etc., but they were not merchants, and generally knew nothing about buying and selling cargoes; consequently it was necessary that a merchant should go with the ship to do the cargo-selling and buying, and that man was the Supercargo. They were always men of mercantile education, often of extensive education, collegiate, etc., etc. At sea, after preparing their account-books, etc., they had little to do and they often learned to handle the ship, to navigate, etc., and became expert seamen. Bowditch, whose work on Navigation [1802] is the basis of most navigation books and whose own work is used by three-fourths of the navigators of the world, was the supercargo of a ship. He learned seamanship for want of something else to do. He was a college graduate and stood high as a mathematician, and when he took up navigation on board the ship he found the methods in use were crude and erroneous and he proposed to make new rules and processes and actually did make new rules from day to day, which the captain used and pronounced much better than the old methods." Letter from Commander Edward Hooker, November 9, 1894 (Connecticut Historical Society).

Padie's candles, that I became curious to know what sort of
things they were, and found it was a favourite foremast joke
of a teague,* who hung some candles before a fire to dry, and
as they melted, swore, arrah, on my soul, now the more they
dry the more they wet. This may be no joke to you, but has
been such a one to us, that I am afraid the youngsters will
make the poor man ashamed of his only piece of wit.

As I am resolved no more to encounter these wretched
human beings, I will have the more time to write. Indeed you
never beheld any thing like them. They were fully as sensible of the motion of the Vessel as we were, and sickness
works more ways than one, so that the smell which came
from the hole, where they had been confined, was sufficient
to raise a plague aboard. I am besides not a little afraid, they
may bestow upon me some of their live-stock, for I make no
doubt they have brought thousands alongst with them.
Faugh! let me not think of it; it affects my stomach more
than this smooth sailing Vessel, or this shocking rough Sea,
in which we are tumbling about so, that I can hardly hold
the pen.

I am warm nowhere but in bed, and it is really surprizing
how sound we sleep; we wake indeed regularly at the calling
of every watch; but I begin to think it chearful. Poor Fanny
is still vastly sick; when out of bed, she sits like a statue of
monumental Alabaster, so white, so cold and so patient. This
is by no means the case with my brother, who is deadly sick
and even as impatient as it is possible. I am quite distressed
to see him in such a plight, and can discover nothing to give
him relief. I have exhausted all my physic and cookery to no
purpose, poor soul, nothing sits on his stomach, nor can he
rest a moment thro' the Night, but bounces in and out of his

---

* "Teague" was a word for a simple, unsophisticated Irishman, used
generally in a half contemptuous sense. In origin the name was that of a
faithful Irish servant, blundering and inefficient, one of the characters in Sir
Robert Howard's comedy, "The Committee" (1665).

cot, every quarter of an hour, the ropes of which not being originally strong, down it comes, then all hands to tie him up. He gives them many a hearty curse, and truly I am often tempted to join him. His sufferings however never get the better of his good humour, he laughs at himself, and would freely allow me the same liberty, had I the heart to use it; he comforts poor Fanny; tho', thank God, she is not near so ill as he is.

I must now go and prepare for bed, which, I assure you, is no easy task, the toilet engages much more of my time at Sea than ever it did at land; we sit in bed till we dress, and get into it, when ever we begin to undress.

Mrs Miller is in such bad humour that we dare hardly speak to her. This, you may believe, would be matter of little moment, were she not mistress of the provisions, and will let us have nothing but what she chuses; we have, particularly, a large quantity of eggs prepared to keep thro' the Voyage. Miss Rutherfurd, this morning, humbly begged one, but had not interest sufficient to obtain it, tho' she saw Mary eat a couple very comfortably to her own breakfast. If you have a mind to learn, they say, go to Sea. I remember an Anecdote of the Ship's Crew aboard which the Duke of Glocester first went abroad. The Sailors were all drawn up to pay they Comp^ts as he came on board, but his highness hurried into the Cabin, without taking the least notice of them. "I think," cries Jack to Tom, "this same prince or Duke, has d—d little manners." "Why, where the devil should he have got them," returned Tom, "when he never was at Sea before." And so, dearest friend, good night, dream of me, as I shall try to do of you.

My poor brother has passed another night, with as little comfort as the former. He finds himself worst in the Cabin, and for that reason, stays continually on deck, notwithstanding the constant Rains, the oze and even the waves that wet him thro' and thro'. The Vessel is so deeply loaded, that she is within a few inches of the water, by which means the waves come all over the Deck. This indeed looks frightful, but as yet we have only a rough Sea to combat, for we have no more wind than is necessary to swell our sails and bear us along, and this, they assure us, is the reason we feel it so rough, as the ship lies tumbling about amongst the waves, and has not her sails sufficiently filled to buoy her above them; and this reasoning I begin to comprehend, yet cannot find in my heart to wish an increase of wind.

We have just finished breakfast, a meal which costs no little trouble. Miss Rutherfurd can get nothing she is able to taste. Tea without milk she cannot drink, and Coffee is reprobated by us all for the same want. We tried chocolate, but found it much too heavy. I have carried one point and got eggs, but we unfortunately trusted the provideing the bread to our owner, and there is not a bisket on board fit for any thing but the hogs. However, my brother had swallowed an egg, and was just going to drink a cup of burnt Claret with spiceries, which Robert was cooking over the Cabin stove, with much care and attention, when the Nasty Captain coming down to take a dram from his gin case, set all our stomachs topsy turvy by the smell. My brother flew to the deck, Miss Rutherfurd to her state room, I applied to my smelling bottle, while Mrs Miller more wisely than any of us joined the Captain, and finds herself much the better for it.

Notwithstanding my resolutions of going no more on deck, I must attend my brother there just now, as he has sent to let us know that we are passing the fine islands of Orkney and Shetland. I little expected even to have had an opportunity of seeing them, so will give them a look in spite of the cold that flows off their frozen mountains.

I left you yesterday to view the Scotch Islands, which I accordingly did. We were almost opposite to Shetland, when we came on deck, but it afforded nothing to please my eye, or atone for the cold, that I suffered in looking at its barren heaths, frozen mountains and wild tracts of frightful rocks; and I was turning in disgust from so chearless a scene, when my attention was caught by one of the most affecting scenes that could be presented to a feeling heart, and, I thank God, mine is not composed of very hard materials. It is so warm on my mind that I fear I will not be able to reduce it into order, but if I am able to paint it the least like what I feel it, I am sure you will share my feelings.

You remember I told you some days ago how much I had been surprized, as well as disgusted, at the appearance of a company of Emigrants, who had been privately put aboard our Ship. I was too much chagrined at their being with us to give myself the trouble of inquiring who they were, but now find they are a company of hapless exiles, from the Islands we have just passed, forced by the hand of oppression from their native land.

The Islands were now full in sight,* and they had all crowded to that side of the ship next to them, and stood in silent sorrow, gazing fondly on the dear spot they were never more to behold. How differently did the same sight affect them and me? What chilled my blood and disgusted my eye, filled their bosoms and warmed their hearts with the fondest, the most tender sensations, while sweet remembrance rushed on their minds and melted the roughest into tears of tenderness. The rude scene before us, with its wild rocks and snow-

---

* At this point the route of the vessel is obscured by Miss Schaw's confusion of the Orkney and Shetland Islands. The islands they had "just passed" were not the Shetlands but the Orkneys, from one of which the Lawsons and others must have come. Miss Schaw could not have seen the Shetlands at all, for the next land, which the vessel must have passed on the south side, was the Fair Isle, a small island three miles long and two broad, lying midway between the two larger groups. The "safe basin" referred to was the only harbor that the island possessed, a shallow indentation on the eastern side, rarely, if ever, frequented by ships. All habitations were on the south, so that in watching what was going on Miss Schaw stood at the rail facing north. An excellent map and description of this Fair Isle may be found in Tudor, *The Orkneys and Shetland*, ch. xxxiii.

cover'd mountains, was dear to them, far more dear than the most fertile plains will ever appear. It was their native land, and how much is contained in that short Sentence, none but those who have parted with their own can be judge of. Many, whom I now beheld, had passed year after year in peace and sweet contentment; they wished, they imagined nothing beyond what it afforded, and their gray hairs seemed a security that they should mingle their dust with that of their fathers, when the cruel hand of oppression seized on their helpless age, and forced them (at that late season) to seek a foreign grave across the stormy main.

Hard-hearted, little Tyrant of yonder rough domains, could you have remained unmoved, had you beheld the victims of your avarice, as I have done, with souls free from guilt, yet suffering all the pangs of banished villians; oh! had you seen them, their hands clasped in silent and unutterable anguish, their streaming eyes raised to heaven in mute ejaculations, calling down blessings, and pouring the last benedictions of a broken heart on the dear soil that gave them being; perhaps even a prayer for the cruel Author of all their woes* mixed in this pious moment. Lord require not our blood at his hands, he is the descendent of our honoured, our loved Master, the son of him I followed to the field of Fame in my happy youthful days, of that loved Lord, who diffused peace, plenty and content around him. The eager eye now went forth in search of particular spots marked by more tender remembrance; there a loved wife reared with fond maternal pride a blooming offspring. "Yonder is my paternal cottage, where my chearful youthful hours were passed in sweet contentment. Ah! little then did I think of braving the wide Atlantick, or of seeking precarious bitter bread in a foreign land."

---

* We have been unable to identify the "cruel Author of all their woes," though the reference seems very specific and the charge is directed against a very definite and seemingly prominent person.

In this general group of Sorrow, there was one figure that more particularly engaged my attention. It was that of a female, who supported with one arm, an Infant about a month old, which she suckled at her breast; her head rested on the other, and her hand shaded her face, while the tears that streamed from under it bedewed her breast and the face of the Infant, who was endeavouring to draw a scanty nourishment from it. At her knee hung a little Cherub about two years old, who looked smiling up into her face, as if courting her notice, and endeavouring to draw her from her melancholy Reflexions; while a most beautiful little girl about eight years old stood by, and wept at the sight of her Mother's tears. I wished for Miss Forbes, with her pencil of Sensibility, to have done justice to this group of heart-affecting figures. I longed to address the Mother, but there is a dignity in Sorrow and I durst not intrude, but respectfully waited, till she gave me an opportunity. In a few minutes she raised her head from her hand and shewed me a face that had once been beautiful, was still lovely, but had a broken heart impressed on every feature. When she observed me looking at her, she stood up and courtesied. I returned her civility and moved towards her. "You are from one of these Islands," said I, "Yes, madam," returned she, "from that one we have just past." She looked abashed, and added with a heart-breaking smile, "You, no doubt, wondered to see me so much affected, but I was just then within view of my fathers house, he is the best of men as well as fathers, and I could not help thinking that perhaps, at that moment, he was pouring out his aged soul in prayers, for a lost and darling daughter"; but her words were choaked; something too seemed to choak myself; so I relieved both by speaking to her of her children, who are indeed extremely lovely. She told me, two were left with her father, and that she had one more on board. Just then a neat pretty girl about eighteen came up to take the child. "Is that your daughter?" said I, "No, madam," returned she, "that is an orphan niece of my husband, whom, in better days, he bred with a father's fondness. The poor child had no occasion to leave her own country. Many of her friends would gladly have taken her, but she would not leave us in our misery." I looked at Marion, for so she is called. I thought I never beheld any thing so beautiful. I wish to learn the history of this woman, which I will easily do, as they all know each other. I hope it will prove worth your reading and will give it a letter by itself. Tho' it be a hundred to one you never see these letters, yet as they give an idea of conversing with you, they afford myself infinite satisfaction.

Pity, thou darling daughter of the skies, what a change do you produce in the hearts where you vouchsafe to enter; from thee the fairest social virtues derive their being; it is you who melt, soften and humanize the soul, raising the man into a God. Before the brightness of thy heavenly countenance every dirty passion disappears—pride, avarice, self-love, caution, doubt, disdain, with all which claim Dame Prudence for their mother; and how different a set appears in thy train, those gently-smiling Goddess-charity, meekness, gentle tenderness with unaffected kindness. What a change has she wrought on me since my last visit to the deck. Where are now the Cargo of Yahoos? they are transformed into a Company of most respectable sufferers, whom it is both my duty and inclination to comfort, and do all in my power to alleviate their misfortunes, which have not sprung from their guilt or folly, but from the guilt and folly of others.

I have made many friendships since these last two days, and was not a little vain, on my coming on deck this morning, to hear the children with infantine joy, call to each other: "O there come the Ladies." We rewarded their affection with some apples, which we gave the young Rutherfurds to bestow, a task which, they declared, afforded them more pleasure than the best apple-pye would have given them. I find the woman I formerly mentioned is considered as superior to the rest of the company, and what is not always an effect of superiority, she is greatly esteemed by them. I was at no loss to obtain her history, as every one seemed willing to do justice to her miseries and misfortunes.

Mr and Mrs Lawson, (for so they are called while the rest are only called John or Margt), were, till lately, in very affluent circumstances. He rented a considerable farm, which had descended in a succession from father to son, for many generations, and under many masters. He had also become proprietor of a piece of ground, on which he had built a neat house, and was thought a good match for Margt Young, the daughter of a neighbouring Farmer, more remarkable for his learning and respectable for his many virtues, than for his herds or flocks. The term of Lawson's Lease being out sometime ago, advantage was taken of the strong attachment he had for what he considered his natural inheritance; and his rent raised far beyond what it could ever produce. He struggled hard for some time, but all his industry proving vain, he was forced to give up his all to the unrelenting hand of oppression; and [to see] the lovely family, I have been so much admiring, turned out to the mercy of the winter winds. While I listened to this melancholy story, many of the Emigrants joined the person who was relating it, and added circumstances with which their own sad fate was connected; all, however, composed a tale of wo, flowing from the same source, Vizt the avarice and folly of their thoughtless masters.

I shall finish this account by a few circumstances regarding poor Mrs Lawson particularly, who is, it seems, the only surviving child of her fond parent, her two brothers having been killed [in the] last war in America.* It is needless to

* By the "last war in America" probably the French and Indian War is meant.

make any comment on the conduct of our highland and
Island proprietors. It is self-evident, what consequences must
be produced in time from such Numbers of Subjects being
driven from the country. Should levys be again necessary,
the recruiting drum may long be at a loss to procure such
soldiers as are now aboard this Vessel, lost to their country
for ever, brave fellows, who tho' now flying from their
friends, would never have fled from their foes. I have just
seen Lawson, he is a well looking fellow, between forty and
fifty, has a bold, manly, weather-beaten countenance, with
an eye that fears to look no man in the face, yet I saw it
glisten, when I complimented him on the beauty of his
family. "Yes, Madam," said he, "they deserved a more fortunate father," turning abruptly away to hide a tear, which
did him no discredit, in my opinion.

I am just now summoned to the deck to take a view of the
Fair Isle. For what reason it bears so pretty a name I cannot
guess, for I expect little beauty in these Seas.

The Fair Isle, which we passed yesterday, is the last land
which belongs to Scotland, and has indeed as little beauty
as I expected. The side that lay next us, is one continued
chain of perpendicular rugged Rocks, and in many places the
upper parts hang over, so that a ship that was to be driven
against them, would have very little chance of Salvation.
I observed almost in the centre of the Island however, a very
safe Bason, which would admit tolerable large Vessels, and
very convenient for boats to land from, and I should think
it a snug place to carry on a contraband trade. Yet I dont
find any such use made of it, the inhabitants living entirely
on what the Island affords, together with a little trade for
provisions, which, ships who are passing purchase of them.
It was peopled many years ago from Denmark, and has kept
so clear of foreign connection, that they still retain their
looks, their manners and their dress, and tho', in their intercourse with strangers, a bad sort of English is spoken by the

men, yet, on the Island, nothing is spoken but their original language. Within our view was one very well-looking house, which, we were told, belongs to the proprietor of the Island; and at a little distance, a town composed of hutts with a church. I observed several stack-yards, but neither a tree nor a shrub.

I have been the more particular as to this Island, as I do not recollect ever to have read any description of it, or indeed even heard of it, till the Captain advised me to trust to it for Sea-Stock, as an inducement to us to go north about, which, however at that time, we refused to do. He assured me, we would get poultry of all kinds extremely cheap, also eggs, fine dried fish and the best Cabbages, in the world. By the time we came on deck, he had hung out his flag and was plying off and on in the offing. The Sea was at that time running high, and it had begun to blow pretty fresh. I felt myself very uneasy for the boats, which, they told us, were extremely small. The signal was not out above a quarter of an hour, when we observed the shore full of people of both sexes, who were scrambling amongst the rocks, when presently they seemed to part, as if by consent, the one half making towards the town, while the other descended to the bason I formerly mentioned; and we soon saw them distinctly launch a number of boats, and put out on this rough Sea, a sight which greatly encreased my Anxiety. But as they came nearer, I was much pleased with the lightness with which they bounded over the waves. They are indeed light, pretty, neat Vessels, all extremely clean, and painted with various colours. They were each manned with four rowers and are long and narrow. I fancy they resemble Indian canoes, but appear extremely proper for these Seas. A number of them arrived safe at our ship, in a few Moments after they put off from the shore, and no sooner got along side the Vessel, than three of them quitted every boat—the fourth remained to take charge of her—and bearing their merchan-

dize in their arms, were aboard in a moment. The novelty
of their appearance greatly amused me. They are entirely
different from the Inhabitants of Scotland in general, and
even from those of the Islands that lay next them; they are
of a middling Stature, strong built and straight, their complexions uncommonly fair, their skins remarkably smooth,
their features high, aquiline noses and small eyes. Their hair
is not red but real yellow, and the older ones wore it long on
the bottom of the chin, which is very peaked. They wore red
caps lined with skin and Jackets of the same with a Paulice
[pelisse] of coarse cloth and boots of undressed skin, with
the rough side outmost, over which were trousers made of
cloth. They are very active and their figures tho' uncouth,
are by no means disagreeable.

This fleet, however, brought us no provisions, but were
loaded with the Island manufactures: such as knit caps, mit-
tens, stockings, and the softest coarse cloth I ever saw made
of wool. They informed us that the people we saw making
to the town were gone for provisions, with which they would
load their boats and be with us presently, that the best hen
and duck was sold at four pence, a goose for sixpence,
Chickens in proportion, eggs eighteen for a penny and plenty
of Cabbage to boot. This was a most agreeable account; and
while those concerned were settling their bargains, which
was not to be done without much haggling, Fanny, my
brother and I leaned over the side of the Vessell, diverting
ourselves with the motions of this second fleet, which made
towards us with surprizing celerity. While we were thus engaged and thinking all was peace and kindness round us, the
cry of "Murder, help, murder," made us turn suddenly round.
Nor can I describe what were our sensations, when we beheld
our Captain, Supercargo and even some of the sailors binding
one of the Islanders to the mast and stripping off his cloths.
The poor creature applied to us for protection, which he
would have instantly got, had not my Brother's attention

been called off to an object that more immediately engaged his humanity. This was one of the boats, which with a single rower on board, had got under the stern of our ship. The sea was so rough, that the motion of the Vessel was very violent, and she must have been dashed to pieces and the poor lad drowned, had not my brother flown to his assistance, part of the crew who had not joined the Captain and all the Emigrants engaging in this humane labour. The young man was saved, tho' the boat was all broke to pieces. As soon as they had got him safely on board, my brother turned sternly to the Captain and demanded the meaning of this outrage. "Oh D——n them," cried the Captain, "they know well enough." "Oh, your honour," cried the poor wretch frighted to death, "we never did him any harm, we did all we could to save his Ship and Cargo." This brought out a secret; and we now found, that, some months before this, our Captain had lost a ship on the frightful coast, I have been just describing. He could not deny they had used their utmost endeavours to serve him on that occasion; but that he had lost a chest which contained sundry articles and which he supposed was stolen, and was determined to have it back. And this noble motive, we have reason to believe, was the reason we have been brought round this dangerous and shocking navigation. This account, however, added stronger reasons still for my brother's interesting himself to obtain them good treatment, that of some future Vessel, perhaps, having a like fate, when it was not to be doubted, but these people would remember the reward they had from our grateful and humane Captain. He therefore assumed such an air of Authority as awed our commander into compliance. He let fall the rope's end, unbound the Victim of his resentment, and released those he had made prisoners below, who were now permitted to return to their boats, but unfortunately for us, had time enough to give a scream of caution to their friends, who were now just at hand, and, who understanding the signal, instantly turned and rowed back to the shore as fast as they were able. And here ended our last Scotch adventure, with every hope of adding to our stock of provisions, which luckily, however, is sufficiently large to last us till we reach Antigua, which will now be the first land we will see. Adieu then, thou dear, loved native land. In vain am I told of finer Climates, or of richer soils, none will ever equal Scotland in my estimation. And in the midst of all the luxuries of the western world, I will envy the Cottager in his snow-surrounded hamlet. The wind encreases very fast, we will not have the prayers of the fair Islanders.

We have had a very blowing night, and my poor brother is ready to die with sickness. He begins to lose his colour, and I fear much this constant straining at his stomach will bring on some serious illness. Fanny, thank God, is now quite well, and bears every thing without repining; that is indeed the sole employment of Abigail and we leave it entirely to her. I was set this morning very gingerly by the fire-side in an elbow chair I had made lash to for me close by the Cabin Stove, with my back to the door. I had taken up a book and was reading as composedly as if sitting in my closet. I did not however enjoy this calm situation long, for presently I heard a rumbling just behind me. This I took for a barrell of spoilt Callavans pease, which made part of the ship's provision, but which no body would eat, and it was an amusement to kick them over, two or three times a day, but what was my surprize, when the Cabin-door burst open and I was over-whelmed with an immense wave, which broke my chair from its moorings, floated every thing in the Cabin, and I found myself swiming amongst joint-stools, chests, Tables and all the various furniture of our parlour. Fanny escaped this and has laughed heartily at me, but I fancy we will all have our share before the Voyage be over. It Blows harder and harder, the shrouds make a terrible rattling, it is a horrid sound. Oh Lord! here comes the Captain, who tells us the dead lights* must be put up. I know the meaning of the word and yet it makes me shudder. He says, he expects a hard gale, I suppose he means this, a soft word for a hard storm. Very well, Winds, blow till ye burst. I know the same protecting providence which rules at land, commands at Sea. Thou great, infinite, omnipotent Creator, who formed by thy word this vast, this awful profound, into thy hands I commit myself and those dearest to me. If death is to be our fate, afford us the necessary fortitude to support thy awful sentence. But be it life or be it death, thy will be done.

Thank God, the storm is at last subsided,† and tho' the sea still looks frowningly, yet it does not wear the same face of horror it lately did. Beautiful and Emphatick is that expression of the Psalmist, "Those who go down to the great waters see thy wonders and on the deep behold thy mighty works, awfully magnificent indeed they appear."

> Where wave on wave and gulph on gulph
> O'ercomes the pilots art.

I wou'd willingly give you a description of the horrors we have sustained for these ten or twelve days past, but tho' they made a sufficient impression on my own mind, never to be forgot, yet I despair of finding words to convey a proper idea of them to you. You remember I gave over writing, just as the Carpenter came in to put up the dead Lights, and a more dreary operation cannot be conceived; my heart, at that moment, seemed to bid farewell to Sun, Moon and Stars. But I now know one God commands at Sea and at Land, whose omnipotence is extended over every element. I praise him for his Mercys past, and humbly hope for more.

The dead lights were no sooner up and a candle made fast to the table, by many a knot and twist of small cord, than my

---

* Dead lights were the heavy double windows or shutters put up outside the cabin windows to keep out the water in case of a storm.

† Twelve days have passed.

young companion took up a book, and very composedly
began to read to herself. I begged her to let me share her
amusement by reading aloud. This she instantly complied
with. She had however taken up the first book that came to
hand, which happened not to be very apropos to the present
occasion, as it proved to be Lord Kaims's Elements of Criticism.* She read on however and I listened with much seeming attention, tho' neither she nor I knew a word it contained. And by this you may guess at our feelings during that
time, which were indeed too confusedly felt by ourselves to
be very accurately described. The storm roared over and
around us, the Candle cast a melancholy gleam across the
Cabin, which we now considered as our tomb. We did not,
however, assist each other's distress, for neither of us mentioned our own. During this time, all was in the utmost hurry
and confusion on deck. The melancholy sound of the Sailors
pulling with united strength at the ropes, the rattling of the
sails and every thing joined to render the fearful scene more
frightful. My brother was still obliged to keep on deck and
brave the fury of the waves that now came continually
aboard, and was every moment in danger of washing off our
people.

* The reference is to Lord Kames's *Elements of Criticism*, three volumes,
Edinburgh, 1762. There was a third edition with additions, published in
1765, in two volumes. An American edition in one volume was issued in 1871.
Henry Home, Lord Kames, was a judge of the court of sessions in Scotland,
who died in 1782. He was a well-known barrister, judge, and writer, who
tried several cases in which some of those who emigrated to North Carolina
—James Hogg, for example—were plaintiffs. There is a good account of
him in the *Dictionary of National Biography* and records of cases tried before him can be found in the *Scots Magazine*. Boswell, in recording Dr.
Johnson's prejudices against Scotland, cites his opinion of Kames. "But Sir,"
said Boswell, "we have Lord Kames." "You have Lord Kames" (replied
Johnson), "keep him, ha, ha, ha! We don't envy you him" (Boswell's *Life*,
II, 54).
The books in the cabin were brought on board by Alexander Schaw for
the use of the party. They were left at St. Christopher on his departure from
that island in January, 1775, but whether afterwards recovered or not we
cannot say. Alexander Schaw's will (1810) mentions books among his possessions.

We did not continue above an hour in this dreary situation, tho' to us it appeared many, when the Captain came down and entering the Cabin with a chearful and assured countenance, congratulated himself and us on the fine breeze which was carrying us ten knotts an hour, and so elated was he with his good fortune, that tho' no singer, he could not help concluding with a favourite ballad of "How happy are we when the winds blow abaft." Tho' this was mere affectation in him, it had an immediate effect on our Spirits; our terror vanished in a moment, and we laughed at our own fears. It was now we discovered we were meeting death, like philosophers not Christians: with a Lord Kaims in our hands in place of a Bible. This imaginary calm did not, however, last long. As the evening advanced, the storm gathered strength, and not only encreased all that night, but all next day. The Sea was now running mountain high, and the waves so outrageous, that they came aboard like a deluge; and rushing from side to side of the Vessel, generally made their way into the Cabin, and from thence into the state-room, which was often so full of water as almost to reach us in our beds. Poor Mary had now real cause to complain, as she was actually very near drowned while asleep, and could no longer ly in the state room but was forced to peg in with the boys who could easily let her share with them, fear and curiosity never suffering them to be in bed above a quarter of an hour at a time. But disagreeable as you will think our present situation, it was no more than a prelude to what followed. As we were constantly assured there was no danger, we made ourselves as easy as we could.

On the second day of this breeze (as it was still termed) the joyful cry, "a sail, a sail," made us run on deck, regardless of the Weather, to see at a distance, a thing which contained within its wooden sides, some fellow-creatures, and tho' these were to us unknown, it is impossible to describe the pleasure every one felt on looking at her. She came within hail of us and proved to be a brig from Liverpool loaded with merchant goods for Philadelphia; her figure shewed the nation she was from, neat, clean and lightly loaded. She seemed to rise above the waves, yet notwithstanding these advantages over our poor heavy hulk, she had her dead lights up also, and dipt them so often under the water, that it shewed us plainly the necessity there was for this precaution. As our course was different, we soon parted, and every heart felt a pang at losing sight of a ship we knew nothing of and being separated from people with whom we had no concern. Man is certainly by nature a kindly Social animal. The law of affection was planted in his breast for the best of purposes. The depravity of Individuals makes us on our guard amidst a populous world, and, indeed, has rendered caution so necessary, that it has cooled the best propensities of the heart and obliged us to set a guard on our feelings, least they betray us into kindness. But no sooner are we divided from our natural associates than humanity regains its superiority; we forget their faults; we love them as brethren and all our philanthropy instantly returns. To this I attribute the benevolence, sincerity and warm hearts we generally meet with in Sailors. They have no use of Prudence on board and scorn to make up an acquaintance with such an old mercenary Jade ashore, and tho' being strangers to her often hurts their purses and still oftener their health they never mind that.

> A light heart and a thin pair of breeches
> Goes round the wide world, brave boys.

It was now about fifty hours the wind had been very high, tho' not dangerous. The sailors, however, began to complain heavily of their hard duty; besides, many things about the Vessel were beginning to give way: the ropes particularly, (which were not originally good,) were rendered so slight by the constant rain, that they every moment snapt in the working, by which means the Ship underwent such sudden and violent evolutions, that we were often thrown off our seats. This forced us to ly abed nor were we even safe there from its effects.

The rains continued, and the winds seemed to gain new strength from a circumstance that, in general, calms them. The sailors's hands were torn to pieces by pulling at the wet ropes. Their stock of Jackets were all wet, nor was there a possibility of getting them dried, as the Steerage was quite full of the Emigrants and hard loading; a piece of inhumanity, that I do not believe even Avarice ever equalled in any other owner. However our honest Johns did their best to keep a good heart, and weather out the gale. And when the wind would permit us to hear them, we were still serenaded with true love-garlands, and histories of faithful sailors and kind-hearted lasses. But on the fourth evening of the gale (as it was now termed) the whole elements seemed at war: horror, ruin and confusion raged thro' our unfortunate wooden kingdom, and made the stoutest heart despair of safety.

Just after the midnight watch was set, it began to blow in such a manner, as made all that had gone before seem only a summer breeze. All hands, (a fearful sound) were now called; not only the Crew, but every man who could assist in this dreadful emergency. Every body was on deck, but my young friend and myself, who sat up in bed, patiently waiting that fate, we sincerely believed unavoidable. The waves poured into the state-room, like a deluge, often wetting our bed-cloths, as they burst over the half door. The Vessel which was one moment mounted to the clouds and whirled on the pointed wave, descended with such violence, as made her tremble for half a minute with the shock, and it appears to me wonderful how her planks stuck together, considering how heavy she was loaded, Nine hogsheads of water which were lashed on the deck gave way, and broke from their

Moorings, and falling backwards and forwards over our heads, at last went over board with a dreadful noise. Our hen-coops with all our poultry soon followed, as did the Cab-house or kitchen, and with it all our cooking-utensils, together with a barrel of fine pickled tongues and above a dozen hams. We heard our sails fluttering into rags. The helm no longer was able to command the Vessel, tho' four men were lash'd to it, to steer her. We were therefore resigned to the mercy of the winds and waves. At last we heard our fore main mast split from top to bottom, a sound that might have appaled more experienced Mariners, but we heard all in Silence, never once opening our lips thro' the whole tremendous scene:

> "At last from all these horrors, Lord,
>   Thy mercy set us free,
>   While in the confidence of prayer,
>   Our Souls laid hold on thee."

About seven in the morning, my Brother, the Capt and our young men came down to us. They too had been on deck all night, fear not suffering them to stay below. Jack had behaved thro' the whole with great fortitude, but poor Billie, who is scarcely ten years old, had been sadly frighted, and could not refrain from crying. "Why, you little fool," said my brother to him, "what the duce do you cry for; you are a good boy, if you are drowned, you will go to heaven, which is a much finer place than Carolina." "Yes, uncle," returned he sobbing, "Yes, Uncle, I know if I had died at land, I would have gone to Heaven, but the thing that vexes me is, if I go to the bottom of this terrible sea, God will never be able to get me up; the fishes will eat me and I am done for ever"; at this thought he cried bitterly, it was annihilation the poor little fellow dreaded, for as soon as he was convinced that God could get him up, he became quite calm and resigned.

Tho' the immediate danger was now over, the storm had not subsided. The sea was in most frightful commotion, and the waves so tumultuous, that the deck was never a moment dry. Judge then what must have been the sufferings of the poor emigrants, who were confined directly under it; without air but what came down the crannies, thro' which also the sea poured on them incessantly. For many days together, they could not ly down, but sat supporting their little ones in their arms, who must otherwise have been drowned. No victuals could be dressed, nor fire got on, so that all they had to subsist on, was some raw potatoes, and a very small proportion of mouldy brisket. In this condition they remained for nine days, with scarcely any interval, (good Heavens! poor Creatures) without light, meat or air, with the immediate prospect of death before them; from the last indeed they should have found the only comfort. Their innocent Souls had little to fear from that prospect. This world had been to them a purgatory, and a few short fluttering sighs, with a little struggle, would have finished their pains, and put a period to a life of disappointment and sorrow. They would soon have found a watery tomb and been for ever at rest. But what rest remained for the iron-hearted tyrant, who forced age and infancy into such distress? Could he sleep in peace, who had provided such a cradle for the Babe, and such a pillow for the hoary head? Perhaps he did, but he may be assured that unless he meet that mercy he has not shown, the lot of these despised wanderers is envyable, compared to his. Forgive this, but the scene is before me, and that will excuse me to a heart so feeling as yours.

After several days' confinement to bed, we at last got to the Cabin. During our confinement, we were fed by our honest Indian with a large ham, he had been wise enough to boil, when he observed the storm first begin; together with a little wine and bisket. It was now finished to our no small regret, nor could we in any way supply it, for the weather

was still very squally, and tho' the wind at times inter-
mitted its violence, yet the sea ran so high, that the motion
of the Vessel was intolerable, nor could any fire be made, as
the waves came on board and drowned it out as soon as
lighted. The Emigrants were still confined below the hatches,
and this was really necessary, as they must have been washed
over had they gone on deck, which their misery would have
made them venture. In this wretched situation, a poor young
woman, who had been married only a few months, was so
terrified, that she miscarried. She was supposed for sometime
dead by the women about her, nor could the least assistance
or relief be afforded her. This was a sight for a fond husband; the poor fellow was absolutely distracted, and, breaking thro' all restraint, forced up the hatch, and carried her
in his arms on deck, which saved her life, as the fresh air
recalled her Senses. He then flew to us, and in the most
affecting manner, implored our Assistance, but what could
we do for her? her cloaths all wet, not a dry spot to lay her
on, nor a fire to warm her a drink. I gave her, however, a few
hartshorn drops, with a bottle of wine for her use, and she is
actually recovered.

We had not yet ventured on deck, nor were our dead lights
taken down, when an unforseen accident, had nearly completed what the storm had not been able to effect, and sent
us to the bottom at a minute's warning. Were you a sailor,
I need only tell you our ship broached to, to inform you of
the danger we were in, but as you are not one, I may suppose
you unacquainted with sea terms, and will therefore inform
you, that it is one of the most fatal accidents that can happen
to a ship, and generally proves immediate destruction.
Which, tho' you be no Sailor, you will comprehend, when I
tell you that the meaning of broached to, is, that the Vessel
fairly lies down on one side, but you will understand it better
by being informed of what we suffered from it.

We were sitting by our melancholy Taper, in no very

chearful mood ourselves; my brother (fortunately for him) was within the companion ladder. The Captain had come down to the Cabin to overhaul his Log-book and Journal, which he had scarcely begun to do, when the Ship gave such a sudden and violent heel over, as broke every thing from their moorings, and in a moment the great Sea-chests, the boys' bed, my brother's cott, Miss Rutherfurd's Harpsicord, with tables, chairs, joint-stools, pewter plates etc, etc., together with Fanny, Jack and myself, were tumbling heels over head to the side the Vessel had laid down on. It is impossible to describe the horror of our situation. The candle was instantly extinguished, and all this going on in the dark, without the least idea of what produced it, or what was to be its end. The Capt sprung on deck the moment he felt the first motion, for he knew well enough its consequence; to complete the horror of the scene, the sea poured in on us, over my brother's head, who held fast the ladder tho' almost drowned, while we were floated by a perfect deluge; and that nothing might be wanting that could terrify us, a favourite cat of Billie's lent her assistance. For happening to be busily engaged with a cheese, just behind me, she stuck fast by it, and sadly frighted with what she as little understood as we did, mewed in so wild a manner, that if we had thought at all, we would certainly have thought it was Davy Jones the terror of all sailors, come to fetch us away.

Busy as this scene appears in description, it did not last half the time, it takes in telling. Nothing can save a ship in this situation, but cutting away her masts, and the time necessary for this generally proves fatal to her, but our masts were so shattered by the late storm, that they went over by the Board of themselves, and the Vessel instantly recovered. This second motion, however, was as severely felt in the Cabin as the first, and as unaccountable, for we were shoved with equal Violence to the other side, and were overwhelmed by a second deluge of Sea water. At last however it in some degree settled, and, thank God, no further mischief has happened, than my forehead cut, Jack's leg a little bruised, and the last of our poultry, a poor duck, squeezed as flat as a pancake.

When the light was rekindled, a most ridiculous scene was exhibited, vizt the sight of the Cabin with us in it, amidst a most uncommon set of articles. For besides the furniture formerly mentioned, the two state rooms had sent forth their contents, and the one occupied by the Captain, being a sort of store room, amongst many other things a barrel of Molasses pitched directly on me, as did also a box of small candles, so I appeared as if tarred and feathered, stuck all over with farthing candles.

The Cabin was at last put to rights. A fire was now able to be lighted, and fortunately our Tea Kettle was safe; so Robert with all expedition got us a dish of very bad tea, no milk nor any succedaneum to supply its place, the ham eat out, and every thing else gone to Davy Jones' locker, that is to the Devil. We were now forced to demand the Ship's provisions, for which we had paid very handsomely, and of which I had a splendid list in my pocket from the owner, but it was the man with the bacon and eggs; whatever I asked had been unfortunately forgot, but what else I pleased. At last I prayed them to tell me what they really had on board, and had the mortification to find that the whole ship's provision for a voyage cross the Tropick, consisted of a few barrels of what is called neck-beef, or cast beef, a few more of New England pork (on a third voyage cross the Atlantick, and the hot Climates), Oat meal, stinking herrings, and, to own the truth, most excellent Potatoes. Had our stock escaped, we had never known the poverty of the Ship, as we had more than sufficient for us all. But what must now become of us? Our cabbages, turnips, carrots all gone, except a few Turnips, which provident Robert had placed in such a manner, as to spring and produce us greens and sallad, a delicacy, which you must cross the Atlantick, before you can properly relish as we do.

We now called a general council on this truly interesting and important question, What shall we eat? By the returns made by Robert and Mary, we found we had still a cag of excellent butter, a barrel of flower, a barrell of onions, and half a Cheese, besides a few eggs. As an addition to this the Captain had the humanity to restore us a parcel of *very* fine tusk [*sic*], which he had *accidentally* stowed away. I wish he had likewise let us have a cask of porter, which had the same fate. Of these materials Mary and Robert make us something wonderfully good every day. For example, Lobs-course is one of the most savoury dishes I ever eat. It is com-posed of Salt beef hung by a string over the side of the ship, till rendered tolerably fresh, then cut in nice little pieces, and with potatoes, onions and pepper, is stewed for some time, with the addition of a proportion of water. This is my favourite dish; but scratch-platter, chouder, stir-about, and some others have all their own merit.

But alas our Voyage is hardly half over; and yet I ought not to complain, when I see the poor Emigrants, to which our living is luxury. It is hardly possible to believe that human nature could be so depraved, as to treat fellow creatures in such a manner for a little sordid gain. They have only for a grown person per week, one pound neck beef, or spoilt pork, two pounds oatmeal, with a small quantity of bisket, not only mouldy, but absolutely crumbled down with damp, wet and rottenness. The half is only allowed a child, so that if they had not potatoes, it is impossible they could live out the Voyage. They have no drink, but a very small proportion of brakish bad water. As our owner to save our expence, took the water for his ship from a pit well in his own back yeard, tho' fine springs were at a very little distance, even this scanty allowance is grudged them, and is often due sometime before they are able to get it weighed out to them. Adieu, my friend, I go to dream of you; My soul takes wing the moment its heavy companion is laid to rest, and flies to land, forgetting the watery scene, with which we are surrounded. Yet it is wonderful how sound we sleep; amidst danger, death and sorrow, an unseen hand seals up our eyes, watches over our slumbers, and wonderfully supports and preserves our healths, and I make no doubt, will at last set us safely on sound ground. Adieu, adieu.

Our Ship is a complete wreck. Masts, Sails, and rigging of all kinds, lying on the deck, the ship itself an inactive hulk, lying on the water peaceably, thank God, for the winds and waves seem satisfied with the mischief they have done. They talk of putting up Jury Masts,* but what these are I do not yet know. I have now given you as far as I remember, all that has happened aboard, since I laid my pen down when the storm began, and not having much subject for this day, hope you will excuse my once more introducing my Emigrants to your notice, whose misfortunes seem to know no end.

As soon as I heard they were released from their gloomy confinement, I went on deck to see and to congratulate them on their safety. I was happy to find my number compleat, for I hardly expected to see them all living, but was much concerned to find them engaged in a new scene of distress. When these unhappy wanderers were driven from what they esteemed their earthly paradise, they had gone to Greenock,† in hopes of meeting a Vessel to bear them far from the cruel hand that forced them forth, but most unluckily all the ships were sailed. Having no means to support life another year, they rejoiced to hear of our ship, which, tho' late, was yet to sail this season. With infinite labour and expences from their little stock, they reached Burnt Island. They threw themselves on the mercy of the owner, who was gener-

---

* A jury mast was one rigged for temporary service in an emergency.
† Greenock, at the mouth of the Clyde, is the seaport of Glasgow.

ous enough to take only double, what he had a right to. Their long journey had so far exhausted their finances, that they could only pay half in hand, but bound themselves slaves for a certain number of years to pay the rest.* Lawson bound himself double, to save his wife and daughter. This was too advantageous a bargain for Avarice to withstand, *he* greedily closed with the proposal, but thought only of deceiving us, not of providing for them, so that as soon as they were got on board, with many kind and fair promises, they were shut under the hatches, where they were confined, till the third day we were at sea. In the meantime, all that remained of their worldly wealth, was contained in a timber chest for each family, which were without mercy or distinction thrown into the long boat, and as that was under water for near fifteen days, the consequence was the glue had given way, the chests fallen to pieces, and every thing was floating promiscuously above the water. Notwithstanding all their former misfortunes, this severely affected them; the women particularly could not stand it, without tears and lamentations.

Affecting as the scene was in general, it was impossible not to smile at some Individuals. Besides the company of Emigrants, there was a Smith with his wife, two taylors and a handsome young Cooper. These were voluntarily going to the West Indies, to mend or make their fortune, so had no claim to that pity the others had a right to. The Smith's wife, who ruled her husband with a rod of iron, had made him lay out much money to figure away in a strange country,

---

* The Highlanders had bound themselves to the master of the ship in return for their food and transportation. Thus they had become indentured servants, whose time for four, five, or six years might be sold on their arrival in the colony to whomsoever would buy. The buying of these indentures or contracts was a recognized method of obtaining laborers in nearly all the British colonies in America, West Indian and continental alike. The hardships involved and the extent to which the servants suffered practical slavery differed with the period and the colony.

and had bestowed great part of it on dress for her own person, which had now shared the fate of the others. As she was in perfect despair at her loss, I had a curiosity to see what it was, and found she had provided for her West India dress, a green stuff damask gown, with Scarlet Callamanco cuffs, a crimson plaid, and a double stuff Petticoat, the rest of the dress I suppose in proportion. As we were condoling this Lady, a little fellow came up and with a sorrowful face begged to know, if any body had seen his goose. I supposed his goose had shared the fate of my Duck, which I was very sorry for; but found he was a tailor who had lost his smoothing iron. But while I was amusing myself with the imaginary distress of these adventurers, I observed Mrs Lawson sitting composedly on the deck, with her little family round her, paying no attention to what was going on. "I hope," said I to her, "your things are not there; you appear so calm and easy." "Alas, Madam," returned she, "I am hardened to Misfortunes, all I have in the world is there, but, thank God, my infants are all safe." Just then little Marion came up, with a face full of anxiety, and a lap full of wet cloths. "Oh! Dear Aunt," cried she, "here is every thing ruined, here is your very [best] popline gown all spoiled, and here is my Uncle's new Waistcoat and your best petticoat," continued she, shaking them out as she spoke, and hanging them up to dry. Mrs Lawson took up her little boy, kissed it, and smiled resignation; so leaving little Marion to perform her task of duty and affection, I moved to the Cabin.

Could love be quenched like common fire, surely not a single spark would have remained aboard the Jamaica Packet, yet if we may believe the word of an Abigail, this is far from being the case, and the little deity finds as good sport in shooting our sea gulls as your land pigeons. If I am not mistaken Mrs Mary has herself got a scratch, tho' she was a very prude at land. Love is not a passion (says a philosophic friend of mine) but inspired from situation.

How then can the poor maid be blamed, there are two or three handsome fellows aboard, on one of whom I suspect she has Cast the eye of affection. He is no Joseph, I dare say, and as Mary keeps the keys, I make no doubt she will be successful. It is wonderful how this gentle passion has sweetened her temper, and we think ourselves much obliged to David, for so he is called, for her good humour. We took notice of him first in compliment to her; and soon made him our acquaintance, from a better reason, as my brother finds him the only person that knows any thing of this navigation, he having made the voyage two or three times. He is besides a sensible clever fellow, and much fitter to sail the ship than his Captain. By him we are assured we are a great way out of our course. He shewed my brother a reckoning he privately kept, which was very regular, and much better than that of the Capt. My brother has kept one all along; and has great suspicions of what he is now told.

We were all like to be overset, with our new friend Davy this morning. Scandal, that sad amphibious monster, that can thrive both by land and water, has given much disturbance to poor Mary, who entered the Cabin this morning all in a flutter. "Dear Ladies," cried she, "what do you think; to be sure 'tis no wonder we had such storms; for a judgment must follow such doings, to be sure I make no doubt we will all be cast away." "Pray, Mrs Miller," said I, "what's the matter?" "I intend to tell," said she, "but who would ever have thought it, that handsome man. But now I think he is not handsome a bit, for handsome is, that handsome does." She run on a great while longer, but to relieve you sooner than she did me, I will tell you that she had been informed he had another fair one on Board, to whom he paid more attention than to her, and to add to the injury, the very wine which she gave him, had been converted to the use of this favourite Sultana. He has contrived to make up matters, and she now says that if there were not bad women, there would be no bad men. 'Tis a constant maxim with us always to throw the blame on our own sex, when a favourite Lover is unfaithful, we never fail to discover he has been taken in by art to deceive us.

I hope this fine weather will give me something better worth your reading, but as I write every day, you must sometimes be satisfied with such subjects as this narrow scene affords. We are now in the latitude of Madeira, but what that is, I leave you to consult the map for. I will tell you however that the weather is fine; tho' we have not got into the trade winds. I told you before that my brother suspects the Captain's calculations; this he is daily more convinced of, which does not make us very easy. Our Capt is an excellent practical sailor, very alert, knows all the dutys of a foremast man, is the first to go aloft, and takes his share of the hardest duty; but tho' he would do very well in that station, has had no education to fit him to command a ship; and were not my brother on board, we could not take even an observation with any certainty. We are almost continually on deck, the weather is so fine, and we find great amusement from the sky over us and the water under us. In the first place, we not only build castles, but plant forests, lay out gardens, and raise cities, and wander with much delight thro' hills, groves and valleys. Do not despise these airy Scenes, for pray my friend how much better are you employed in your world? Do not your schemes of happiness change, vary and disappear? Indeed, indeed, by sea and by land we are at best pursuing a cloud which fancy has raised, and your fairest enjoyments are not more durable than our sea landscapes, if I may call them so.

We have had two sharks that followed us all this day. They have stole our beef and spoilt our Lobscourse, but we are busy contriving to be revenged and to eat them. You have them much better described than I can, as only their head and tail are seen above the water. They are very swift Swimmers, and it is said that they have such strength in their tail, that when brought on board, they often damage the deck, by beating it about; so that when they are hooked, the Carpenter stands ready with his axe to cut it off.

As I was pleasing myself this morning, with lying over the side of the ship, and seeing the fishes in pursuit of each other, gliding by, I observed a fine hawk-bill turtle asleep, almost close along side. Oh! how our mouths did water at it, but watered alas in vain; for before any method could be thought of, it waked and dived under the water. I presently recollected, however, that this pride of luxury was too luxurious himself to be many miles from land. This I mentioned to the Captain, but as his reading or observation had not reached so far, he held mine very cheap. We have however laid a bet: he, that we are many hundred leagues from land; I, that we are not above a hundred Miles. He says, twenty four hours will determine the wager, for, if I am right, in that time we will see some land; if not, we will see none till we arrive amongst the Leeward Islands. My brother joins me, tho' he owns he has no other reason, than the same observation I made from seeing the turtle.

The weather is now so soft, that my brother and Miss Rutherfurd are able to amuse themselves with their musick. His German flute is particularly agreeable, and one would think, by the number of fishes that are crouding round us, that he were the Orpheus of the water. If some of the sea-green nymphs would raise their heads and join their Voices, it would be a pretty concert. Some of our fair Shipmates, however, favour us with a melancholy "Lochaber Nae maer," or "heaven preserve my bonny Scotch laddie," sounds that vibrate thro' several hearts.

Pleasant as this evening is, I must leave it for my little state room, and get into bed; which is almost a pity. How sweet it is, the moon shines over us so clear, that it puts me in mind of what I have been told of two lovers who were to part far. They promised that at a certain hour, they would constantly look at the Moon, and have the pleasure to think they were then both admiring the same object. I think I could improve on this. Suppose at a certain hour, we both were to adore the same great power, who rules by Sea and land, and to beg blessings of him for each other. Don't you think, my long loved friend, that in such a moment, our Souls, tho' not our bodies, might meet and mix, we know not how? I go to try the experiment, and hope you also are above this low world to meet me.

I have won my wager; we came in sight of land long before the expiration of the twenty four hours. Just as we were stepping into bed, the Captain came and owned I was right, for that we were along side of land, but what land, he confest, he was utterly ignorant. We presently slipt on our wrapping gowns and with great joy went on deck. The moon was now down, and we could only observe a thing resembling a great black cloud. The Captain swore that he believed after all it was only Cape Fly Away.‡ But we were all positive we smelt the land Air, which on my word I really did. My brother had now got all the maps, charts, Journals, etc., before him, and in a very short time, declared with absolute certainty, that we were among the Azores or Western Islands. The Captain, the Mate and all now agreed in the same opinion. These, I suppose you know, are a set of very fine African Islands, which appertain to the kingdom of Portugal. Mr Schaw further assured us that the one we were now over against, was called Graciosa, a name it had from its extraordinary beauty. The next thing was to get the Captain to ly to, as it was very dangerous for him to proceed on his way, thro' a cluster of Islands, of which he was confessedly ignorant. This being agreed to, we all returned into the Cabin. Read the description of the Island from Salmon's

‡ A cant word for mistaking a cloud for land.

Geographical Grammar.* We're charmed to find it produces every thing we want, Sheep, poultry, bread, wine and a variety of Vegetables, besides the finest fruits in the world. The means to obtain them was the next question, for which purpose my brother wrote three cards, one in Latin to the Superior of the convent, one in French to whoever could read it, and one in English to our Consul, if there was such on the Island.† These set forth that aboard were several people of fashion, particularly two Ladies, that we had lost every thing by the storm, and that the Ladies could not doubt of being properly supplied from the known politeness and gallantry of the Portugueze. As the cards added that the boat would pay whatever price was demanded, there was no doubt but we would have been plentifully supplied with whatever the Island could afford. But our brute of a Captain rendered all this useless, and has fixed us down to finish our Voyage without a single comfort.

After this affair was settled, we went to bed, but our spirits were so elated that we could not sleep, so were again on deck by the first peep of morning dawn. We now saw the Island most distinctly, and must own that it deserves its name, for never did my eyes behold so beautiful a spot. It does not seem in length above five or at most six Miles; its breadth I could not see. In the centre is a large extensive plane, surrounded with hills in form of an Amphitheatre; the ground rises by an easy ascent all the way from the shore, and in the bosom of the hills stands a very noble house, round which is a great deal of fine laid out policy.‡ It fronts the shore, and is entirely open to the Sea, and tho' the Island

---

* Thomas Salmon, *A New Geographical and Historical Grammar*, with a set of twenty-two maps, London, octavo, 1749. Sixth edition, 1758. There were later editions also.

† The knowledge of languages possessed by Alexander Schaw and Miss Schaw's later friend, Archibald Neilson (pp. 218-221), is suggestive of the culture of Edinburgh and other lowland Scottish towns at this time.

‡ A Scottish word meaning the improved grounds around a country house.

is evidently under the power of winter, the beauty of the Verdure is inconceivable; and when the Vines, which are now leafless and cut down, are in foliage and fruit, it is certainly a garden that, had our first parents been sent to repent in, they would soon have forgot their native Eden. The hills behind the plane were covered with pasture or Vineyard, and we observed forts on two of them, but no other house of any note, tho' some hamlets were scattered here and there, and what we took to be Orange groves by the figure of the tree. The Captain however expressly refused to send the boat ashore.

In this resolution he was confirmed by a fright he got in the morning, and which indeed alarmed us all, and with reason; this was the appearance of a ship which was taken for an Algerine corsair, with which these Seas are terribly infested. "O God!" cried the Captain as he entered the Cabin, "we are undone, for we have no Mediterranean pass."* You may guess our situation on this intelligence. But my brother whose presence of mind never forsakes him, asked us in a pleasant way, if we were afraid of being their Sultanas and bade us dress, that our appearance might gain

---

* A Mediterranean pass was a necessary document for all ships, British and colonial, trading in the Mediterranean or along the Atlantic coast, north and south of the Straits of Gibraltar. It was a permit on parchment, partly engraved and partly written, issued by the British Admiralty to protect vessels from attack by the Barbary cruisers, under the terms of treaties previously entered into with the Barbary states. A single pass could be used for more than one voyage. Under Admiralty rules, it was to be endorsed by the British consul at every port entered and when done with to be returned to the issuing office.

The form and wording were as follows:

[King of England, etc.] to all persons whom these may concern greeting.
    Suffer the ship —————— to pass, with her company, passengers, goods, and merchandizes, without any let, hinderance, seizure, or molestation; the said ship appearing unto us, by good testimony, to belong to our subjects, and to no foreigner. Given under our sign manual and the seal of the Admiralty, at the court at ——————, this ——— day of ———, in the year of our Lord, one thousand and seven hundred and ———.
By his Majesty's Command,
[Signature of the Secretary to the Admiralty]   [Signature of the King]

us respect, and the hope of a ransome procure us civil treatment. We immediately obeyed him, but before our task was finished, our fears were happily at an end, by the Vessel sailing from us as fast as she was able. We plied off and on, in hopes that some boats would come off to us, But they are so much afraid of the Algerines that they seldom venture out. The morning was now pretty far advanced, the smoke began to rise from the chimneys of the elegant house, which was full in our view, and my Imagination formed a delightful parlour, where a happy family were saluting each other with the compliments of the morning, and sitting down in comfort to a cheerful breakfast; and I had such an inclination to join this family, that I cannot help thinking I am some how connected with them, and found myself so familiar with them, that I am certain in some future period of my life, I will be on that Island.

We now despaired of boats, so were forced to set sail again with much regret. As we sailed along the Island, we saw every hill covered with Vines or rich pasture. A very fine highway went round the Island, and near the end of it was a large church, and a considerable building which we supposed to be a convent, also a fort which seemed of some strength. The day turned out very clear and fine, but we were not sufficiently near any of the other Islands to see them distinctly. St George stands very high, is rocky and seems a fine Island; St Thomas* is still smaller, but looks very green and seems to have many trees on it. We had a distant view of Pecoa, which appears one high rock formed like a sugar loaf. We now came on Fyall, which is a noble Island; here we wished greatly to put in and refit. We knew this Island carried on a very considerable trade with Britain, that many English resided on it, and above all saw by the Almanack that a Scotch man was Consul. The Captain seemed to yield,

---

* There is today no "St. Thomas" among the Azores; the reference may be to the island of Terceira. "Pecoa" is now Pico.

as he was forced to confess the Vessel was hardly in a state to proceed. But the Supercargo would not be prevailed on. We sailed sixteen or eighteen miles along the Island, but not the side on which the town and harbour stand. We saw however some noble churches and convents, and a prodigious number of Vineyards. This Island is famous thro' the West Indies and America for its wine, which is a sort of weak Madeira; much better than that we have from Teneriff, and I wonder we do not often get it at home, as they tell me it sells amazingly cheap. We have got clear of the Islands, and with a heavy heart once more lost sight of land, and are again to sup on Lobscourse.

I have not had it in my power to take up my pen these five days,* As we have had another terrible tempest after our fine weather. It began about two that morning after we got thro' the Azores; that we were thro', was a most happy circumstance, for had it happened while we were amongst them, I had not now been informing you of it. We have reason however to fear that tho' we are safe, much mischief has happened. I will not give you a minute description of this storm, because it so much resembled the other; with the addition of the most terrible thunder and lightning that ever were seen. All our temporary repairs are destroyed, we have not a stick standing, nor a rag of sail to put up, and we lie tumbling amongst the waves. All hands are employed in making sails, our Smiths and Carpenter busy patching our bitts of timber, so as to make something like Masts, which however were not yet put up. When we were sailing by, the Boyn, a King's ship of seventy four guns, bore down on us to inquire for her consort from whom she was parted in the late storm, and we found she had troops on board for Boston. She is a beautiful ship, but the pleasure of looking at her was all the advantage we gained by the meeting, for tho' she

---

* Five days have elapsed.

saw us in a merchant Ship, belonging to her own country, in the utmost distress, tho' we begged her to let us only have a few spare sticks, of which no doubt she had enough, yet they refused to let us have one, tho' they had every reason to believe that we would never reach our destined port. I know not the Captain's name, but whoever commanded the Boyn in one thousand seven hundred and seventy four, on the third of December, is an exception to the character I formerly gave of Sailors.*

The meeting this Ship has introduced politicks. The supercargo is from Boston a republican and violent American, and tho' we consider him as a very silly fellow, you cannot think how much we feel the ridicule with which he treats our dilatory conduct. God grant that what this fool says may not prove at last too true.

---

* The incident of meeting the *Boyne* offers the only serious difficulty that we have encountered in reconciling the statements of the journal with the evidence from other sources. Miss Schaw says definitely that they met the *Boyne* on December 3, the log of the *Boyne* says with equal definiteness that that vessel "spoke a brigg for Antigo com'd from Leith" on November 17, a discrepancy of more than two weeks. Either Miss Schaw is wrong in her date or the entry in the log concerns another vessel than the *Jamaica Packet*. The former is the more likely explanation, as the *Boyne* "saw Cape Ann," that is, the coast of Massachusetts, on December 7, which would have been impossible had she been seen by the packet on December 3.

The captain of the *Boyne*, whom Miss Schaw so vigorously condemns, was Broderick Hartwell. Had she and others on the packet, particularly that violent republican, the supercargo, though aware that the *Boyne* was taking soldiers to America, foreseen the part that those soldiers were to play in American history, they might have been more lively in their comments. The *Boyne*, the *Asia*, which carried Major Pitcairn, and the *Somerset*, which was the consort referred to, were transporting the marine detachments that fought in the battles of Lexington, Concord, and Bunker Hill. Miss Schaw, without realizing it, had witnessed a significant event in the history of the American Revolution.

Oddly enough, "little Billie" was gazing at a vessel bearing the same name as that on which he was to serve as acting lieutenant in 1794, nineteen years later. The *Boyne* of 1774 was a third-rate of 74 guns and 300 men; that of 1794 was the flagship of Sir John Jervis (afterwards Admiral Earl St. Vincent), a second-rate of 98 guns and 772 men, which was commissioned in 1792 and sailed from England with "little Billie" on board in November, 1793.

We have been all this morning on deck, hard at work with the new sails. I never saw any thing so neat and handy as our Johns. Every man appeared with his clew of thread, his sail needle and his thimble, which he properly terms his palm, as it is worn in the palm of the hand, fastened over the back with a strap of leather. With this he works as cleverly as any sempstress with her needle. We will soon look very clean and neat, but you cannot think how much we are ashamed to enter the Islands with our humble masts, I wish to God we were there however; the appearance we make will give me little pain.

Congratulate me, my friend, we are at length got into the long looked for wind. It met us this morning about four o'clock; what a relief to our poor Sailors, who will now have nothing to do, but dance, sing and make love to the lasses, but let them beware of little Marion; her uncle's eye is never off her, and honest John [Lawson] has an hand that would fell an Ox.

By the observation just taken, we will cross the Tropick [of Cancer] in about thirty hours. We see a number of Tropical birds, and have every reason to believe this calculation just, and as we are now approaching a new World, we have also reason to look for new objects. And indeed the Sea, the Sky, and every thing seem to change their appearance. The moon is ten times more bright than in your Northern hemisphere, and attended by a number of Stars, each of whom may claim a superior title, and pass for sparkling suns. The beauty of the evenings is past all description, and tho' the days are rather warm, yet we feel less inconveniency than one could believe. By the help of an awning we are able to sit on the deck, where I now write. Every moment gives us something to amuse our fancy or excite our curiosity; the colour of the water is now a bright azure blue, and at night all round the Ship seems on fire. This fire is like globules, that tho' larger, bear a resemblance to those produced by

Electricity, and I dare say is an effect of the same kind from the strong salts of this vast Ocean.

The inhabitants of this wat'ry world seem to bid us welcome; the Sea appears quite populous, droves of porpuses, like flocks of Sheep, pass close by us. They have a droll gait and keep a tumbling, as if they proposed playing tricks for our diversion. The dolphin is a most beautiful fish; his skin resembles that of a Mackerel, but the colours more strong, and when he rises out of the water, he appears all over green and like burnished gold. His prey is the flying fish, which, when pursued, rise out of the water, and keep flying while the fins, which answer for their wings, are wet, but the instant that they dry, they drop down, by which means they often fall down on the deck. We have eat some, and I have preserved some for your inspection. We have another fish called pilot fish,* which eats much like our whibers. These greedily take the bait, and we would get them in plenty, had they not such friendships as make them almost superior to the Arts of men; for the moment one is hooked, others come round him, and if you are not very quick they bite and nibble the line, till they break it thro' and let their friend go free. They have never heard our human proverb, 'Avoid the wounded deer and hooked fish.'

We have had an unwieldy companion all this day by the Ship, a Crampus† or small whale. He tumbles about, and when we throw him any thing overboard, he turns on his back, and catches it in a very small mouth.

The effect of this fine weather appears in every creature, even our Emigrants seem in a great measure to have forgot their sufferings, and hope gives a gleam of pleasure, even to the heart-broken features of Mrs Lawson and if we had any

---

* The pilot fish was so called because often seen with a shark, swimming near a ship, from which the sailors imagined that it acted as a pilot to the shark.
† Grampus.

thing to eat, I really think our present situation is most delightful. We play at cards and backgammon on deck; the sailors dance horn pipes and Jigs from morning to night; every lass has her lad, and several chintz gowns have been converted by our little taylor into jackets for the favourite swains. Our handsome cooper, however, has been an unfortunate enamorato. As he fixed his fancy on a young wife, who had a husband she was very fond of, this has produced a commissary trial,* to the no small diversion of every body but the love-lorn youth. It turned out in proof, that for several mornings as soon as the husband was up, this young spark tumbled into his place; this was rather an unceremonious method of declaring his passion, but as he got up the first and second time begging pardon, and laying the blame on accident, the woman said nothing of it, from which I suppose, he concluded, she would not be offended tho' he lay a little longer. In this however he was mistaken. She was enraged at his insolence and flew to her husband with a terrible complaint. This rough fellow had not the patience of our husbands of fashion, he presently went in quest of the lover, and would have used him in a very cruel manner, had he not thrown himself into the protection of the Cabin, and in his own vindication protested that it was accident, for as their beds lay along side of each other, the ship heeld so much, that he was involuntarily thrown into the other bed. It was however remarkable that this never happened when the husband was there, nor during all the bad weather, when it might more naturally have happened.

Last night was most particularly beautiful. I sat on the deck till past twelve. The lustre of the stars, the brightness of the moon, the clearness of the sky, and the Sea washing the side of the Vessel, for we have now no waves, carried my mind beyond itself, and I could not refrain expressing myself

---

* That is, a mock divorce suit. In eighteenth century Scottish law a commissary court was a probate and divorce court.

in the language of the psalmist: "When I look up into the heavens which thou hast made, and unto the moon and stars, which thou hast ordained, then say I, what is man that thou shouldst remember him, or the son of man that thou regardest him." Certainly Man appears but a very small part of the creation, when compared with these grand works, yet that he is the favourite, still greater proofs have been given, than even the creating these glorious Luminaries for his use and pleasure. I think it is not possible to look at these without recollecting what we are told of a new heaven and a new earth; what that is, we cannot conceive, neither could I have formed the least idea of the glory of the firmament that canopies this part of the world.

We have now thrown off our ship-dress and wear muslin Jackets and chip hats: that however is not so wonderful, as our lying under a single Holland sheet, and even that too much. We have got a window cut into our state room from the Companion stair. This is shaded with nothing but a thin lawn curtain, yet is too warm. The people from the Steerage ly on deck, the boys will no longer go into bed, but sleep on the Sea-chests, yet this is the month of December.

We find ourselves greatly the better of bathing which we do every morning in a large cask prepared for the purpose. Tis a very solemn ceremony; when we are to leave the cabin in our bathing dress, all the people quit the deck, and remain below till we return.

My brother is now quite well, and would eat if he could get it; he has lost a good deal of his English beef, but looks very well notwithstanding. Fanny is in great beauty, she has improved amazingly with her Sea-Voyage. This is a long letter and it is time to give both you and me rest.

We are now fairly under the Tropick and are preparing for a farce that is played on this occasion by every ship that goes to or fro under the Tropick. It is, it seems, a sort of Mason word, and till I am admitted in form, I must not appear to know it. I shall therefore only tell you that we have been made to expect a visit from old Tropicus and his ancient dame. He is a wizard and she a witch who inhabit an invisible Island in these Seas, and have a privilege of raising contributions from every Ship that passes their dominions, only however from such as never was that way before. But my account is cut short by the appearance of the Actors, who are dressed for their parts. Tropicus is performed by an old rough dog of a Tar, who needs very little alteration to become a callaban in mind and body, but his wife is played by a very handsome fellow, who is completely transformed. Every body is below waiting, in trembling expectation, and no wonder, for an awful ceremony this Visitation is. Tropick the Island was no sooner seen, than the Jolly boat* was taken down, on pretence of going with the Captain aboard it to meet him, but in fact to be filled full of pump water for a use you shall hear by and by. This being done Tropick is spoke to thro' the trumpet, and with a hollow voice demands what strangers are aboard. All this the people below hear, and tho' many of the Emigrants appear sensible, yet all Highlanders and Islanders are so superstitious, that they may be easily imposed on, in such a thing as this; and they were completely so. The wizard now ordered them to be brought up, one by one blindfolded and their hands bound behind them; such was their fear, that they suffered this to be done without dispute. In this situation, they were to answer certain questions which he put to them; if they spoke strictly truth, then he shaved them, took a small gratuity for his trouble, gave them his benediction, and let them pass.

---

* The jolly boat was generally slung at the stern of the vessel.

Regarding the "awful ceremony," the author of *A Brief Account of the Island of Antigua* (1789), who made the voyage from the Downs to Antigua in 1786, says, "I had almost forgot to observe that on passing the tropic of Cancer, the old custom of ducking and shaving such as have not before crossed it, was performed by the seamen with some humour on one man and two boys. The passengers waved the ceremony by a liquor fine" (p. 5).

But if they disguised or concealed the truth, which he was supposed perfectly to know, then he tumbled them into the Sea, where they perished. Prepossessed with this idea, a poor lad was brought before the infernal Judge: "Answer me," said he sternly, "answer me truth; what made you leave home?" "O troth sir, I dina well ken": "but you must know," said he, "so answer me instantly." "O Dear, O Lord! I think it was, because so many were going, I did not like to stay behind." "And pray what are you good for in this world, to prevent me sending you to the next?" "Trouth, an please your honour, e'en very little." "What," said he, with a voice like thunder, "are you good for nothing?" "O yes, yes, I am no very ill at the small fishing." As this young man did not seem to overrate his own merits, the wizard was satisfied, placed him on the side of the boat, which he believed was the ship, being still blind folded and bound. The wizard began to shave him with a notched stick and pot-black. The sharp notches soon brought blood, and the poor devil starting from the pain, tumbled into the boat amongst the water, and thinking it the sea, roared with terror. And in this consisted the whole wit of the entertainment. He was now unbound and restored to the light and as keen to bring in his neighbours, who one by one, went thro' the same operation. As soon as it was over, custom licences the sailors to treat the officers with every degree of freedom, nor do they fail to take the opportunity. The Capt, mates, supercargo and all were chaced round and round, and drenched in the water from the boat, which they threw at them in bucket-fulls.

We had now got to the Cabin, and believed all was over, when a loud screaming on deck brought us up to see what was the matter, and we found our Capt had begun to act a tragedy after our comedy, and to oblige these poor ruined creatures to pay five shillings for each, or be pulled up to a mast and from that plunged down to the Sea. This was a sum impossible to be raised, and the poor women were running with what remained of their cloths to give in place of it to save their husbands and fathers. Amongst others Marion was going with all speed, with her aunt's popline gown; but it was needless, for John Lawson now stood at bay, his fist clinched and swearing by the great God, that the first man that touched him had not another moment to live, nor was there one hardy enough to encounter a fist, which had not its fellow on board. But this was not the case with others, and they had one man tied, and only waited to see, if his wife had as many moveables as to save his life, for he was a poor weak old man, and would not have agreed with this method of bathing. I never in my life saw my brother in such a passion; he swore solemnly, that the moment he got to land, he would raise a prosecution against the Capt, who pleaded that it was the custom, and only intended as a little drink money to the sailors. If that is the case, replied my brother, let them give up their cloths, and they shall be satisfied.* This was complied with cheerfully, he gave them what they were satisfied with, to which they returned three cheers, as he went to the cabin and serenaded us with the favourite song,

> O grog is the liquor of life
> The delight of each free British tar.

We are now in the constant look out for land; dear hope, how agreeably you fill the mind: yet what do I hope? I have no friend to meet, no fond parent to receive me with joy, no —but away gloomy ideas—why I hope once more to stand on Terra firma, which by the bye, I cannot be said to do on an Island.

I do not find the heat encreases since the first few days. Indeed the constant soft wind cools the air, and renders even the day agreeable. We have discovered that they have

---

* Evidently meaning that if the sailors would give up their claim to the clothes of the emigrants, he (Mr. Schaw) would pay for their grog.

brought a quantity of Bristol beer out for Sale. This they concealed till we were in the West India climate, as they supposed till then we would not give them the price, which is no less than two shillings a bottle, and which we pay with pleasure. We see new birds every day, and observe a greater variety of fishes, but have seen no turtle, since that near the Azores. Every thing flatters us with the hope of Land, yet if you saw our state room, you would suppose we designed to continue in it for years. It is decked out with a toilet, pictures and mirror; so calm is the Sea, that the things never move. How soon are our sorrows forgot; the Sailors that were lately damning the Elements and grudging their duty, now wonder how any man can be such a Luber [lubber], as to stay at land; and I find myself a little in the same way of thinking, and am happy I have come abroad to see the world; tho' God knows I have seen but a small and disagreeable part of it. My travels have been to the moon and stars. The sun is too bright and too warm for me, and as for the earth, I have seen none of it since I left Scotland; I only smelt it off the African Islands. Land, Land, joyful sound, we are in sight of land, the infants are clapping their little hands, and the very cat is frisking about for joy.

Just as we finished supper last night, I was going on deck, when the first thing that struck me was the sight of land, which I should not have known, had I not formerly seen it in the same figure at the Azores. "Is not that land?" said I to the man at the helm, "Yes," said he, squirting out his quid of Tobacco with great composure, "as soon as the mate will come up, I will shew it to him." I did not wait that ceremony, but turning round to the Cabin, exclaimed as loud as I was able, "Land, Land!" Every body run up, such a whistling of joy, and such a shaking of hands. There was no doubt it was Antigua. No body thought of bed, but what will surprize you, Fanny in the midst of this joy was quite melancholy, she never considered herself as really out of Scotland, till now that she was soon to be on another land, and this thought affected her so much, that she is quite sick.

I was already on deck to see the lead thrown, to sound our depths, the colour of the water has already begun to change to a lighter blue, and in a little time became quite green like that at Leith. You remember how much Ossian was criticised for calling the Sea blue and the stars green, but that is truly the appearance they have, when sufficiently distant from land. We soon had a pilot on board, who with his black assistants, brought us round the rocks at the utmost points of Antigua. The beauty of the Island rises every moment as we advance towards the bay; the first plantations we observed were very high and rocky, but as we came farther on, they appeared more improved, and when we got into the bay, which runs many miles up the Island, it is out of my power to paint the beauty and the Novelty of the scene. We had the Island on both sides of us, yet its beauties were different, the one was hills, dales and groves, and not a tree, plant or shrub I had ever seen before; the ground is vastly uneven, but not very high; the sugar canes cover the hills almost to the top, and bear a resemblance in colour at least to a rich field of green wheat; the hills are skirted by the Palmetto or Cabbage tree, which even from this distance makes a noble appearance. The houses are generally placed in the Valleys between the hills, and all front to the sea. We saw many fine ones. There were also some fine walks along the Shore shaded by different trees, of which I am yet ignorant. Will you not smile, if after this description, I add that its principal beauty to me is the resemblance it has to Scotland, yes, to Scotland, and not only to Scotland in general, but to the Highlands in particular. I found out a Dunkeld in one of these walks,*

---

* Dunkeld is a town in Perthshire on the west branch of the Tay. It was formerly the home of the Duchess of Atholl (p. 243) and quite possibly had been at one time the home of Miss Schaw. The scenery, both above and below the town, was greatly admired.

nor do I think the birches there inferior in beauty to the myrtles here.

The other side exhibits quite a different scene, as the ground is almost level, a long tongue of land runs into the Sea, covered with rich pasture, on which a number of cattle feed. At the farther end of this Peninsula is a fort which receives the compliments from the Ships, and has a fee from them. After we passed this point, we saw some very rich plantations, all inclosed by hedges, but of what kind I know not. The next object that engaged our attention, was a high rock, on the sides of which grew a vast number of Oranges and lemons. At the top is a large building, which, our Pilot tells us, is the Old Barracks.* This Barracks is able to contain a thousand Men. But they had now built another, farther up the Island, and one half was gone there. We saw a number of the officers walking among the Orange-trees and myrtles, and I own I thought the prospect was mended by their appearance.

We have cast Anchor at about a mile or little more from the town of St John's, which we have in full view. It lies up a hill, and is certainly a fine town, but the houses are low, and have no chimneys, so that at this distance, it does not make a grand appearance; tho' I dare say it will mend, when we come nearer to it.†

---

* The author of the *Brief Account* says, "The new barracks and military hospital, situated to the eastward of the town, are spacious and healthy and allowed to be the most complete in the islands. There is also a barrack on Rat Island, in St. John's Harbour, but it has been suffered to go to ruin and is now [1786] out of use." The "high rock," to which Miss Schaw refers is Rat Island; the barracks there, built in 1754-1755, were evidently occupied at the time of her arrival, for the new barracks could hardly have been completed in 1774. According to Sir Ralph Payne, governor at this time, the barracks contained four companies of the 2d Battalion of Royal Americans, exceedingly incomplete as to numbers, since they amounted to not more than 87 or 88 effective men. These companies had come to the island in 1772, replacing the 68th Regiment of Foot, which had been there since 1764. The fort is James Fort erected in 1700, now dismantled and used as a quarantine station.

† Antigua is one of the Leeward Islands, forty miles east of Nevis and

My brother and the Captain are gone ashore, the one to enter his ship at the custom house, the other to deliver his letters, and provide decent lodgings for us in the town. Miss Rutherfurd has been extremely ill all the morning; she has not enjoyed nor indeed seen the scene I have been describing, as she was forced to keep below. She is now better, and from the Cabin window has a fine view of the Island, town and shipping, of which a vast number lie round us. I take this opportunity of writing you once more aboard the Jamaica Packet, which I am to quit to morrow, at least for some time.

I hear a boat along side, I hope it is my brother, and that he has brought us something for Supper.

The boat did not bring my brother on board, but a card to let us know he was engaged by company, and could not come aboard that evening. This boat was freighted with the hospitality and politeness of the natives, who no sooner understood there were ladies on board, than they sent us whatever the Island could afford, and which indeed surpasses whatever I saw of the kind. Pine apples, Shadocks, oranges, grapes, guinea fowls and excellent milk. This last was of all others, to my young friends, the highest treat. We drank Tea and supped in luxury; that, you must be five weeks starved, before you can understand. We have been just seven weeks

---

twenty-seven miles from Montserrat. Its chief town, St. John's, was not incorporated until July, 1783.

The best contemporary description of the island is that contained in Sir Ralph Payne's "Answers to Queries," written on June 26, 1774, just three months before the lady's arrival. "Antigua is in its greatest extent about 14 miles in length and in its narrowest breadth about 5 miles. Its highest hills are to the southward, but it is in general by no means a mountainous island. It contains 69,277 acres and 108 square miles and ¼. The soil on the north side is a black mould or marle, and to the southward a strong clay. The body of the island lies in latitude 17" 10' and its longitude from the meridian of London is 60 degrees west. The climate of Antigua as well as of the other Leeward Islands, is between the Tropics under the Torrid Zone, and like the other islands would be insufferably warm, were it not for almost constant breezes that blow chiefly from the eastward, and render it healthy and agreeable" (Public Record Office, C. O. 152:54, no. 17). The number of its white inhabitants in 1774 was about 2590, of blacks 37,308.

on our passage,* so that after all we ought to be satisfied;
for that was no bad passage. This is a delightful evening, I
hope to have a sound sleep, wishing you good night, I will
go to my state room once more.

---

* October 25 to December 12.

CHAPTER II.

Antigua and St. Christopher.

St John's Dec[r] 12th 1774.

I WRITE now on land, but my head is so giddy, that I can't believe I am yet on shore, nor can I stand more than I did on Shipboard; every thing seems to move in the same manner it did there. They tell me however, I will get the better of this in twenty four hours.

My brother came on board this morning with some Gentlemen, and carried us ashore. Every thing was as new to me, as if I had been but a day old. We landed on a very fine Wharf belonging to a Scotch Gentleman, who was with us. We proceeded to our lodgings thro' a narrow lane; as the Gentleman told us no Ladies ever walk in this Country. Just as we got into the lane, a number of pigs run out at a door, and after them a parcel of monkeys. This not a little surprized me, but I found what I took for monkeys were negro children, naked as they were born. We now arrived at our lodgings, and were received by a well behaved woman, who welcomed us, not as the M[rs] of a Hotel, but as the hospitable woman of fashion would the guests she was happy to see. Her hall or parlour was directly off the Street. Tho' not fine, it was neat and cool, and the windows all thrown open. A Negro girl presented us with a glass of what they call Sangarie,* which is composed of Madeira, water, sugar and

---

* Sangaree was a tropical drink, known also to the people of the Carolinas.

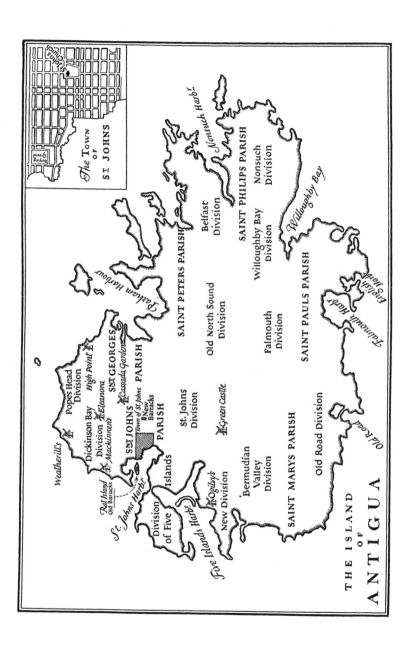

THE TOWN
OF
ST JOHNS

Popes Head
Division

Dickinson Bay
Division
Eleanora

High Point

Weatherill's

Mackinnen's

ST GEORGES

Cassada Gardens

Town of St Johns

New
Barracks

Red Island
Old Barracks

St Johns Harbr

Division
of Five
Islands

Five Islands Harbr

Ogilvy's
New Division

SAINT JOHNS
PARISH

St Johns
Division

Green Castle

Bermudian
Valley
Division

Parham Harbour

SAINT PETERS PARISH

Old North Sound
Division

Belfast
Division

Nonsuch Harbr

SAINT PHILIPS PARISH

Nonsuch
Division

Willoughby Bay
Division

Willoughby Bay

SAINT PAULS PARISH

Falmouth
Division

Falmouth Harbr

English Harbr

SAINT MARYS PARISH

Old Road
Division

Old Road

THE ISLAND
OF
ANTIGUA

lime juice, a most refreshing drink. She had with her two Ladies, the one a good plain looking girl, who I soon discovered was her Niece; but it was sometime before I could make out the other. The old Lady* told us, she had been married to a Scotsman, whose memory was so dear to her, that she loved his whole country. She paid us some very genteel compliments, and with great seeming sincerity, expressed the joy it gave her to have us in her house. She was much prepossessed in my brother's favour, who was now gone out with many of the people in office. "I know," said she, "every body will love you, and that I will be able to keep you but a very little while, but I beg that you will let this be your head quarters, while on the Island." The good Lady said a great deal, but so much benevolence appeared in every look, that I am induced to believe her sincere. I shall be sorry if she is not, for I am already greatly pleased with her.

It was sometime before I was able to make out who the other Lady was, whom we found with Mrs Dunbar, for so she is called. The loveliness of her person, her youth and the modesty of her manners, together with the respect she paid the Old Lady, made me at first take her for her daughter, but I soon discovered that her husband was a member of the Council, and that she waited his return from the Council-board, to carry her to her house, a few miles up the country. There was something in this young Lady so engaging, that it

---

There were other combinations than that mentioned by Miss Schaw, but the ingredients were always liquor, water, and spices. Brandy was sometimes substituted for wine.

* The "old lady" was Mrs. Dunbar, as was also the doctor's wife. There was no relationship between them. Dr. John Dunbar (born 1721), member of the assembly until 1775, graduated at Leyden University in 1742, and married, in Antigua, Eleanor, daughter of Thomas Watkins, who died during the hurricane of August 31, 1772. He married again, July 28, 1773, at St. John's, Sarah Warner, daughter of Samuel H. Warner, deputy provost marshal of the island, a woman much younger than himself, who, however, died before he did, in 1787. The Dunbar plantation of 165 acres was in the Dickinson Bay division, from which the doctor was returned to the assembly.

is impossible not to wish to know her better. Fanny and she appeared mutually pleased with each other. At last I fortunately discovered her to be the wife of my old friend Dr Dunbar, with whom I had been well acquainted in Scotland, and who had resided many months at my father's house. We were now much pleased with our Company. Our Landlady gave us an excellent dinner, at which we had one guest more, a Capt Blair,* a very agreeable genteel young man. My brother did not return, but our young men made up for the long Lent they had kept,† and Mrs Dunbar is charmed with them. I believe they have got into good quarters.

Our dinner consisted of many dishes, made up of kid, lamb, poultry, pork and a variety of fishes, all of one shape, that is flat, of the flounder or turbot kind, but differing from each other in taste. The meat was well dressed, and tho' they have no butter but what comes from Ireland or Britain, it was sweet and even fresh by their cookery. There was no turtle, which she regretted, but said I would get so much, that I would be surfeited with it. Our desert was superior to our dinner, the finest fruits in the World being there, which we had in profusion. During dinner, our hostess who presided at the head of her table, (very unlike a British Landlady) gave her hob and nob‡ with a good grace. I observed the young Ladies drank nothing but Lime-juice and water. They told me it was all the women drank in general. Our good landlady strongly advised us not to follow so bad an example—that Madeira and water would do no body harm, and that it was owing to their method of living, that

---

* Capt. James Blair may have been an officer of the Royal American battalion, but his name cannot be found in any of the printed or manuscript army lists.

† The two boys must have found the greater part of the seven weeks' voyage a veritable Lent.

‡ "Hob and nob" was to drink to the health of the company present. At many colonial dinners it was the custom for the host to drink a glass of wine with everyone at the table.

they were such spiritless and indolent creatures. The ladies smiling replied that the men indeed said so, but it was custom and every body did it in spite of the advices they were daily getting. What a tyrant is custom in every part of the world. The poor women, whose spirits must be worn out by heat and constant perspiration, require no doubt some restorative, yet as it is not the custom, they will faint under it rather than trangress this ideal law. I will however follow our good Landlady's advice, and as I was resolved to shew I was to be a rebel to a custom that did not appear founded on reason, I pledged her in a bumper of the best Madeira I ever tasted. Miss Rutherfurd followed my example; the old Lady was transported with us, and young Mrs Dunbar politely said, that if it was in the power of wine to give her such spirits, and render her half so agreeable, she was sorry she had not taken it long ago; but would lose no more time, and taking up a glass mixed indeed with water, drank to us.

Just as we were preparing for Tea, my brother, Dr Dunbar, Mr Halliday,* the Collector, and Mr Baird, the comptroller, and a very pretty young man called Martin came to us. Here was a whole company of Scotch people, our language, our manners, our circle of friends and connections, all the same. They had a hundred questions to ask in a breath, and my general acquaintance enabled me to answer them.

---

* The Halliday family is of old covenanting stock and has figured in the history of Scotland, county Galloway, since the sixteenth century. John Halliday, the collector, was born in Antigua, a nephew of William Dunbar and a son-in-law of Francis Delap, both prominent residents of the island. He himself had no less than seven plantations in the different divisions, the two most important of which were "Boons" in St. John's parish and "Weatherills" near by. He entered the assembly in 1755, resigned in 1757, and was again returned in 1761. He occupied the position of customs collector and receiver of the four and a half per cent export duty from 1759 to 1777, an office of importance, as the port of St. John's was much superior to its only rival in the island, Parham.

Of Charles Baird, the comptroller, we can give no information beyond that which Miss Schaw furnishes, though his name is to be found in the official list of customs officials and in Governor Payne's "Answers to Queries."

We were intimates in a moment. The old Doctor was transported at seeing us, and presently joined his Lady in a most friendly invitation to stay at his house, which we have promised to do, as soon as we get our things ashore. The Collector has made the same request, and we are to be at his country-seat in a day or two. Mr Halliday is from Galloway, is a man above fifty, but extremely genteel in his person and most agreeable in his manners; he has a very great fortune and lives with elegance and taste. His family resides in England and he lives the life of a Batchelor. Mr Baird is a near relation of the Newbeath family, is above sixty, far from handsome, but appears to be a most excellent creature. I should suppose his connection had rather been with Mrs Baird, he has so much of her manner, her very way of speaking. 'Tis my opinion a mutual passion is begun between him and me, which, as it is not raised on beauty, it is to be hoped will be lasting. Young Martin, our hostess, who is very frank, tells us, is a favourite of the Collector's; that he stays always with him, and that it is supposed he intends to resign in his favour. She moreover informed us, that Mr Martin was much admired by the Ladies, but was very hardhearted.*

---

* Samuel Martin, the "young Martin" here mentioned, was not a son of Colonel Samuel, though he may have been in some way related to him. That there was some family connection seems evident from an agreement entered into in 1775, whereby young Samuel bound himself to pay annuities to certain members of the Martin family (Oliver, *History of Antigua*, II, 245). At this time he may have been twenty or more years of age, and, as Miss Schaw thought would be the case, he succeeded Halliday as collector two years later, serving until 1795, when he was retired. He was followed by Josiah, Colonel Samuel's grandson, who held the office for half a century.

For a woman hater, young Samuel had an interesting matrimonial career. In 1777, the year he was appointed collector, he married Grace Savage, daughter of George Savage of "Savage Gardens" just outside St. John's, and by her had six children. She died, aged 50, in 1810, and in 1812 he married again, a widow, name unknown, by whom he had five children more. Thus he had two wives and eleven children, which is a little unexpected, in view of Miss Schaw's remarks. He died soon after 1825, in England, whither he had gone after leaving the collectorship.

Young Martin's plantation in Antigua was called "High Point" and lay in

Tea being finished, the D^r and his Lady left us, and we surprised the Gentlemen, by proposing a walk out of town.

This was at first opposed, but on our persisting, Mr Baird swore we were the finest creatures he had met these twenty years. "Zounds," said he, taking my arm under his, "I shall fancy myself in Scotland." Our walk turned out charmingly, the evening had now been cooled by the sea breeze, and we were not the least incommoded. We walked thro' a market place, the principal streets, and passed by a large church, and thro' a noble burying place. Here we read many Scotch names, among others, that of poor Jock Trumble* of Curry, who died while here with his regiment. A little above the town is the new Barracks, a long large building, in the middle of a field. I do not think its situation, however, so pretty as that of the old Barracks. A little beyond that we met a plantation belonging to a Lady, who is just now in England; from her character I much regret her absence, for by all accounts, she is the very soul of whim, a much improved copy of Maria Buchanan, M^{rs} O, whose stile, you know, I doated on; her house, for she is a widow, is superb, laid out with groves, gardens and delightful walks of Tamarind trees, which give the finest shade you can imagine.†

Here I had an opportunity of seeing and admiring the Palmetto tree, with which this Lady's house is surrounded, and entirely guarded by them from the intense heat. They are in general from forty to sixty feet high before they put out a branch, and as straight as a line. If I may compare great

the northern part of the island, between Winthrop's Bay and Dutchman's Bay near the entrance to Parham Harbor. He left this plantation to William, born in 1816, his second son by his second wife.

* The "Jock Trumble" here mentioned was probably Lieutenant John Turnbull of the 68th Regiment of Foot, who died in Antigua, October 5, 1767, and was buried on the island. The name "Trumbull" is but a corrupted form of the Scottish "Turnbull," and Scotsmen tell us that the name today is frequently spelled "Turnbull" and pronounced "Trumbull."

† The plantation described is Skerretts alias Nugents, situated about a mile along the road past the barracks.

things with small, the branches resemble a fern leaf, but are at least twelve or fifteen feet long. They go round the boll of the tree and hang down in the form of an Umbrela; the great stem is white, and the skin like Satin. Above the branches rises another stem, of about twelve or fourteen feet in height, coming to a point at the top, from which the cabbage springs, tho' the pith or heart of the whole is soft and eats well. This stem is the most beautiful green that you can conceive, and is a fine contrast to the white one below. The beauty and figure of this tree, however, rather surprised than pleased me. It had a stiffness in its appearance far from being so agreeable as the waving branches of our native trees, and I could not help declaiming that they did not look as if they were of God's making.

We walked thro' many cane pieces, as they term the fields of Sugar-canes, and saw different ages of it. This has been a remarkable fine season, and every body is in fine spirits with the prospect of the Crop of Sugar. You have no doubt heard that Antigua has no water,* but what falls in rain; A dry

---

* "Antigua has but one running stream and that is incapable of the least navigation" (Payne in "Answers to Queries"). Of the water supply the writer of the *Brief Account* says, "This island is almost destitute of fresh springs, therefore the water principally used is rain, which the inhabitants collect in stone cisterns; this water, after being drawn from the reservoir, is filtered through a Barbadoes stone, which renders it free from animalcula, or any disagreeable quality it might have contracted by being kept in the tank. It is exceedingly soft and well flavored . . . as good as any I ever tasted in Europe" (pp. 60-61).

Governor Payne, writing to Lord Dartmouth the October before, gives a description of the island that is equally flattering with that of Miss Schaw. "I have no disagreeable account of any kind wherewith I am to trouble your Lordship, from any part of my government. The crops of the present year which are just finished have in general been very good; and in some of the islands surpass'd the expectations of the planters; and the present propitious weather inspires the inhabitants with sanguine hopes of reaping a plentiful harvest in the ensuing year. There is not in any of the islands under my command any interruption to the general harmony and tranquillity which I have the satisfaction of observing to prevail throughout every part of my government, from my first entrance on my administration"; and in January, 1775, he added, "No mischievous sparks of the continental flame have reached any district of the government. The trade of every island of it is most unseason therefore proves destructive to the crops, as the canes require much moisture.

We returned from our walk, not the least fatigued, but the Musquetoes* had smelt the blood of a British man, and my brother has his legs bit sadly. Our petticoats, I suppose, guarded us, for we have not as yet suffered from these gentry. We supped quite agreeably, but it was quite in public. No body here is ashamed of what they are doing, for all the parlours are directly off the street, and doors and windows constantly open. I own it appears droll to have people come and chat in at the windows, while we are at supper, and not only so, but if they like the party, they just walk in, take a chair, and sit down. I considered this as an inconveniency from being in a hotel, but understand, that every house is on the same easy footing. Every body in town is on a level as to station, and they are all intimately acquainted, which may easily account for this general hospitality. The manner of living too is another reason. They never fail to have a

commonly flourishing. Provisions of all kinds from the continent of America are cheaper and more plentiful than they have been in the memory of man" (Public Record Office, C. O. 152:55).

* The mosquitoes on the American continent as well as in the West Indies were a very troublesome novelty to Europeans. The author of the *Brief Account* says of Antigua, "The mosketos are troublesome, but I defend my legs (which is the part these insects principally attack) with boots" (p. 7). As to the continental colonies, Boucher complained of mosquitoes in Maryland (*Maryland Magazine*, March, 1913, pp. 39-40), Michel in Virginia (*Virginia Magazine*, January, 1916, p. 40), and Beverley of the latter colony once sent for Russian lawn or gauze for four large field beds, "being to let in the air and keep out mosquitoes and flies" (Beverley Letter Book). Peck-over, the travelling Quaker preacher, says that he was "taken with an inflama-tion in my leg" in New Jersey, "occasioned I think by the Muskittos biting me. This is a very flat country and very subject to these insects" (Travels). In North Carolina, mosquito nets were included in inventories and invoices, and in South Carolina in 1744, it was proposed that the merchants in Eng-land send over a large quantity of Scotch kenting for pavilions, as it would come to a good market, "there being at present a great demand for that commodity, the inhabitants being almost devoured by the mosquitos for want thereof:" (*South Carolina Gazette*, June 6, 1744). Even the Pilgrims were "much anoyed with muskeetoes," and some of those who returned before 1624 made them a subject of complaint against the colony. Bradford's *History* (Ford ed.), I, 366, and note.

plentiful table to sit down to. My friend Baird does not love this freedom at all, neither does he admit it at his house. Indeed the custom house people are not considered as on the same footing, and are treated with more respect. I have now given you my first day in the West Indies, part of which is from observation, and part from information. I will go over all the town to morrow, but must now retire and try if I can sleep at land, tho' I really dread the musquetoes. My brother is gone with the Collector to sleep.

We have had a sound sleep in an excellent bed chamber, in which were two beds covered with thin lawn curtains, which are here called musquetoe Nets, but we found it so cool, that we occupied but one bed. A single very fine Holland sheet was all our covering, but we found laid by the side of the beds, quilts, in case we chused them, which by four in the morning we found to be absolutely necessary. A black girl appeared about seven with a bason of green tea for each of us, which we drank, and got up to dress, attended by our swarthy waiting maid, whom we found extremely well qualified for the office. We now descended into the hall where breakfast was set forth with every necessary, but were not a little surprised to see a goat attending to supply us with milk, which she did in great abundance; and most excellent milk it was. Cream, it is impossible to have, as no contrivance has yet been fallen on to keep it sweet above an hour. There are plenty of cows in the Island, but their milk is used only for the sick, while the goats supply milk for every common purpose, and about every house are two or three who regularly attend the Tea-kettle of their own accord.‡

Our things are now brought ashore by Robt, but Mrs Miller absolutely refuses to come to us, which I am not sorry for, as so much ill temper in a servant would make one look silly among strangers, and to dispute the point would render us ridiculous. We have therefore accepted the proffered ser-

‡ This is not in genteel houses however.

vice of Memboe, the black girl, before mentioned, for whose honesty, her M^rs has become responsible, so into her hands we have commited our Wardrobe.

Breakfast was hardly over, when several carriages were at the door, begging our acceptance, to carry us about the town, or where else we chused to go. We accepted one belonging to Mr Halliday; when Mr Martin placed himself between us, and acted the character of Gallant with great address. No Lady ever goes without a gentleman to attend her; their carriages are light and airy; this of Mr Halliday's was drawn by English horses, which is a very needless piece of expence; as they have strong horses from New England, and most beautiful creatures from the Spanish Main. Their Waggons which are large and heavy, are drawn by Mules, many of which passed Mrs Dunbar's window, with very thin clothed drivers, nothing on their bodies, and little any where, which deserves the name of clothing. The women too, I mean the black women, wear little or no clothing, nothing on their bodies, and they are hardly prevailed on to wear a petticoat.

In my excursion this day, I met with some intelligent people, by which means I am become acquainted with a great many particulars, which my stay would hardly be long enough to have learned by my own observation. I have had a full view of the town, which is very neat and very pretty, tho' it still bears the marks of two terrible Misfortunes: the dreadful fire, and still more dreadful hurricane.* Many of

---

* The fire occurred on August 17, 1769, and consumed two-thirds of the town, at a loss of £400,000 Antigua currency.

The hurricane occurred on August 31, 1772. Of this terrible disaster Governor Payne wrote: "On Thursday night, the 27th of August, we had an exceedingly hard gale of wind, which continued for the space of 7 or 8 hours, and then subsided without doing any material damage. On the night of Sunday, the 30th of August, the wind blew fresh . . . and continued increasing till five in the morning when it blew a hurricane from the N. E. . . . a melancholy darkness prevail'd for more than an hour after sun rise. At eight o'clock the fury of the tempest in some measure abated, but it was only to collect new redoubl'd violence, and to display itself, with tenfold terror, for the space of 4 hours . . . Some persons were buried in the ruins

the streets are not yet repaired, but like London, I hope it will rise more glorious from its ruins. The publick buildings are of stone, and very handsome, they have all been built at a great expence, since the hurricane, which happened later, and was attended with more general devastation than the fire. The houses built immediately after this calamity bear all the marks of that fear, which possessed the minds of the Inhabitants at the time. They are low and seem to crutch [crouch], as if afraid of a second misfortune. But by degrees they have come to the same standard as formerly. The town consists of sixteen streets, which all ly to the trade wind in full view of the bay.

The Negroes are the only market people. No body else dreams of selling provisions. Thursday is a market day, but Sunday is the grand day, as then they are all at liberty to work for themselves, and people hire workmen at a much easier rate, than on week days from their Masters. The Negroes also keep the poultry, and it is them that raise the fruits and vegetables. But as I am not yet in the country, I cannot give you so good an account, as I shall do when I have seen a Negro town. We dine this day in town, and to morrow go to Dr Dunbar's. We are much disappointed to find that Sir Ralph Payn* and his Lady are not on the

---

of their houses. Many houses were razed. The doors, windows, and partitions of the Court House were blown in, the interior completely wrecked and most valuable papers destroyed. The barracks are in a deplorable condition. At English Harbour, deemed storm-proof, there was a squadron under Adm^l Parry, whose flagship with others drove ashore and the hospital there was levelled to the ground, crushing in its fall the unfortunate patients and attendants. My new study, with most of my papers, was blown away." Quoted in Oliver, *History of Antigua*, I, cxxi.

There is an old negro adage regarding the coming of hurricanes: "June, too soon; July, stand by; August, come it must; September, remember; October, all over."

* Sir Ralph Payne, governor of the Leeward Islands, with residence in Antigua, was born in St. Christopher, in 1739. He was commissioned governor May 10, 1771, resigned February 17, 1775, and returned soon after to England. "Hardly any West Indian governor," says the author of the *Brief Account*, "ever acquired credit there except Sir George Thomas and Sir

Island, but they are expected to be here by Christmas, as Lady Payn never misses her duty. She has a most amiable character, and is the idol of the whole people. I regret much not having the happiness to see her, as we are particularly recommended to the governor-general and her Ladyship by Lord Mansfield.*

We have just had a visit from two Ladies, Mrs Mackinon and her daughter.† They are two of the most agreeable people I ever saw. We had letters for them, which they no sooner received, than they came to invite us to their house. Mrs Mackinon is an English Lady and but very lately come out; she was much pleased at meeting with some British people. We are engaged to pass some of our time with them:

Ralph Payne. These men were both native West Indians, who knew the disposition of the people they had to govern, and by prudently keeping the arrogant at as great a distance, as the more modest would naturally keep themselves, they had the good fortune to be approved" (p. 166). Lord Dartmouth said that Sir Ralph had "ever shown a zeal and activity that is highly pleasing to the king"; and in August, 1775, after he had left the island and another appointee was under consideration, the general assembly of Antigua presented an address to the king, expressing their gratitude for his having sent them a man of Sir Ralph's character and worth and begging that he would send him back to them again.

Governor Payne had a career in England also. He was an M.P. for Plymouth in 1762, Shaftesbury, 1769, and Camelford, 1774. He was made a K.B. in 1771, and on October 1, 1795, was created an Irish peer, Baron Lavington of Lavington, entering the Privy Council in 1799. He was reappointed governor of Antigua, January 20, 1799, and died in the island, August 3, 1807, aged 68.

* The Right Honorable William Lord Mansfield was the fourth son of David Murray, Viscount Stormont, and brother of the Mrs. Murray of Stormont mentioned later in the narrative (p. 247). He was born at Scone, educated at Perth, and formed part of that Scottish circle of intimates in which Miss Schaw moved. He is frequently referred to, here and elsewhere, as giving assistance of one kind or another to his Scottish friends. His judicial and parliamentary career is too well known to need comment.

† Mrs. Mackinnen was Louise Vernon of Hilton Park, Stafford, who had married William Mackinnen of Antigua in 1757. Mackinnen was an absentee planter for many years, but returned to the island in 1773, and became a member of the council. He went back to England some time before 1798, lived at Exeter, and died in 1809. He was buried at Binfield, Berks, where he had a residence. In Antigua, he had two plantations, "Golden Grove" and "Mackinnen's," the latter, an estate of 830 acres in St. John's parish, is probably the one visited by Miss Schaw. There were four daughters.

We go to church on Sunday, which they tell us is a very fine one, and dine afterwards with Collector Halliday. I must bid you Adieu for the present; my next Letter will be from the Country.

The Eleanora.*

I have heard or read of a painter or poet, I forget which, that when he intended to excell in a Work of Genius, made throw around him every thing most pleasing to the eye, or delightful to the Senses. Should this always hold good, at present you might expect the most delightful epistle you ever read in your life, as whatever can charm the senses or delight the Imagination is now in my view.

My bed-chamber, to render it more airy, has a door which opens into a parterre of flowers, that glow with colours, which only the western sun is able to raise into such richness, while every breeze is fragrant with perfumes that mock the poor imitations to be produced by art. This parterre is surrounded by a hedge of Pomegranate, which is now loaded both with fruit and blossom; for here the spring does not give place to Summer, nor Summer to Autumn; these three Seasons are eternally to be found united, while we give up every claim to winter, and leave it entirely to you.

This place which belongs to my friend Doctor Dunbar, is not above two or three miles from town, and as it is an easy ascent all the way, stands high enough to give a full prospect of the bay, the shipping, the town and many rich plantations, as also the old Barracks, the fort and the Island I before mentioned. Indeed it is almost impossible to conceive so much beauty and riches under the eye in one moment. The fields all the way down to the town, are divided into cane pieces by hedges of different kinds. The favourite seems the

---

* Dr. Dunbar's plantation, "Eleanora," lay about two miles north of St. John's, a mile farther on than that of William Mackinnen. Both were in the Dickinson Bay division.

log-wood, which, tho' extremely beautiful, is not near so fit for the purpose, as what is called the prickly pear, which grows into a fence as prickly and close as our hawthorn; but so violent is the taste for beauty and scent, that this useful plant is never used, but in distant plantations. I am however resolved to enter into no particulars of this kind, till I recover my senses sufficiently to do it coolly; for at present, the beauty, the Novelty, the ten thousand charms that this Scene presents to me, confuse my ideas. It appears a delightful Vision, a fairy Scene or a peep into Elysium; and surely the first poets that painted those retreats of the blessed and good, must have made some West India Island sit for the picture.

Tho' the Eleanora is still most beautiful, yet it bears evident marks of the hurricane. A very fine house was thrown to the ground, the Palmettoes stand shattered monuments of that fatal calamity; with these the house was surrounded in the same manner, as I described the plantation near town. Every body has some tragical history to give of that night of horror, but none more than the poor Doctor. His house was laid in ruins, his canes burnt up by the lightening, his orange orchyards, Tammerand Walks and Cocoa trees torn from the roots, his sugar works, mills and cattle all destroyed; yet a circumstance was joined, that rendered every thing else a thousand times more dreadful. It happened in a moment a much loved wife was expiring in his arms, and she did breath her last amidst this War of Elements, this wreck of nature; while he in vain carried her from place to place for Shelter. This was the Lady I had known in Scotland. The hills behind the house are high and often craggy, on which sheep and goats feed, a Scene that gives us no small pleasure, and even relieves the eye when fatigued with looking on the dazzling lustre the other prospect presents you.

I have so many places to go to, that I fear I will not have time to write again, while on this Island. My brother proposes to make a tour round all the Islands, in which we will bear him company.

My brother has gone to make the tour of the Islands without us. Every body was so desirous of our staying here, and we were so happy, that we easily agreed to their obliging request, nor have we reason to repent our compliance, as every hour is rendered agreeable by new marks of civility, kindness and hospitality. Miss Rutherfurd has found several of her boarding school-friends here;* they have many friends to talk of, many scenes to recollect. This shows me how improper it is in the parents to send them early from themselves and their country. They form their Sentiments in Britain, their early connections commence there, and they leave it just when they are at the age to enjoy it most, and return to their friends and country, as banished exiles; nor can any future connection cure them of the longing they have to return to Britain. Of this I see instances every day, and must attribute to that cause the numbers that leave this little paradise, and throw away vast sums of money in London, where they are, either entirely overlooked or ridiculed for an extravagance, which after all does not even raise them to a level with hundreds around them; while they neglect the cultivation of their plantations, and leave their delightful dwellings to Overseers, who enrich themselves, and live like princes at the expence of their thoughtless masters, feasting every day on delicacies, which the utmost extent of expence is unable to procure in Britain. Antigua has more proprietors on it however than any of the other Islands, which gives it a great Superiority. St Christopher's, they tell me, is almost abandoned to Overseers and managers, owing to the amazing fortunes that belong to Individuals, who almost all reside

---

* It is of course impossible to identify Fanny's boarding school, but the following entry in the *Scots Magazine* (36, p. 392) may well refer to it. "Miss Sarah Young, daughter of Patrick Young of Killicanty, [who] kept a boarding school in Edinburgh for young ladies upwards of thirty years," died on July 30, 1774.

in England. Mr Mackinnon had never been out here, had not his overseer forgot he had any superior, and having occasion for the whole income, had sent his Master no remittances for above two years. He found things however in very good order, as this gentleman for his own sake, had taken care of that. But as his constitution is now entirely British, he feels the effects of the Climate, and is forced to think of wintering at New York for his health. We have seen every body of fashion in the Island, and our toilet is loaded with cards of Invitation, which I hope we will have time to accept, and I will then be able to say more as to the manners of a people with whom I am hitherto delighted. Forgive me, dearest of friends, for being happy when so far from you, but the hopes of meeting, to be happy hereafter supports my spirits.

I was yesterday at church,* and found they had not said more of it than it deserved; for tho' the outside is a plain building, its inside is magnificent. It has a very fine organ, a spacious altar, and every thing necessary to a church which performs the English Service. You know I am no bigoted Presbyterian, and as the tenets are the same, I was resolved to conform to the ceremonies, but am sorry to find in myself the force of habit too strong, I fear, to be removed. The church was very full, the Audience most devout. I looked at them with pleasure, but found I was a mere Spectator, and that what I now felt had no more to do with me, than when

---

* St. John's Church was built in the years 1740-1745, the tower, which had not been erected when Miss Schaw visited the island, being added in 1786-1789. The building occupied a conspicuous position on an eminence in the northeast quarter of the town and was visible from all the country round. It was built of brick and stone, its yard being enclosed by a brick wall, the bricks having been obtained in England and America. On pillars at the south entrance were two well executed figures in Portland stone of St. John the Baptist and St. John the Evangelist, to whom the church was dedicated, and in the tower were a clock and a bell given in 1789 by John Delap Halliday, son of the collector. The organ had been purchased in 1760 and in 1772 an organist, George Harland Hartley, was installed. The rector, whom Miss Schaw so much disliked, was the Rev. John Bowen, 1767-1783 (Oliver, III, 357-359; *Brief Account*, p. 21).

I admired Digges* worshipping in the Temple of the Sun.
This is a discovery I am sorry to make, but if one considers
that the last Clergyman I heard in Scotland was Mr Webster,† and that the last service I heard him perform was that
of a prayer for myself and friends, who were bidding adieu
to their native land, in which were exerted all those powers,
which he possesses in so eminent a degree, his own heart
affected by the subject, and mine deeply, deeply interested.
It was no wonder that those now read from a book by a
Clerk, who only did it, because he was paid for doing it,
appeared cold and unapropos. The musick tho' fine added as
little to my devotion as the sniveling of a sincere-hearted
country precentor, perhaps less; but the beauty, the neatness
and elegance of the Church pleased me much, and in this I
own, we are very defective in Scotland. The seat for the
Governor General is noble and magnificent, covered with
Crimson velvet; the drapery round it edged with deep gold
fringe; the Crown Cyphers and emblems of his office em-
bossed and very rich. Below this is the seat for the Counsel-
lors equally fine and ornamented, but what pleased me more
than all I saw, was a great number of Negroes who occupied
the Area, and went thro' the Service with seriousness and
devotion. I must not forget one thing that really diverted
me; the parson who has a fine income is as complete a Coxcomb as I ever met with in a pulpit. He no sooner cast his
eyes to where we were than he seemed to forget the rest of
the Audience, and on running over his sermon, which he held
in his hand, he appeared dissatisfied, and without more ado
dismounted from the pulpit, leaving the Service unfinished,

---

* For Digges, see below, p. 136.
† Rev. Dr. Alexander Webster (1707-1784) was chaplain in ordinary for
Scotland in 1771 and a dean of the royal chapel. His son, Lieutenant Colonel
William Webster, served in the British army in America and was wounded
at Guilford Court House. Later he died of his wounds and was buried at
Elizabeth, Bladen county, North Carolina.

and went home for another; which to do it justice was a very good one.

We found Mr Martin at the Church door with our carriages, into which we mounted, and were soon at Mr Halliday's Plantation, where he this day dined; for he has no less than five, all of which have houses on them. This house is extremely pleasant, and so cool that one might forget they were under the Tropick. We had a family dinner, which in England might figure away in a newspaper, had it been given by a Lord Mayor, or the first Duke in the kingdom. Why should we blame these people for their luxury? since nature holds out her lap, filled with every thing that is in her power to bestow, it were sinful in them not to be luxurious. I have now seen Turtle almost every day, and tho' I never could eat it at home, am vastly fond of it here, where it is indeed a very different thing. You get nothing but old ones there, the chickens being unable to stand the voyage; even these are starved, or at best fed on coarse and improper food. Here they are young, tender, fresh from the water, where they feed as delicately, and are as great Epicures, as those who feed on them. They laugh at us for the racket we make to have it divided into different dishes. They never make but two, the soup and the shell. The first is commonly made of old Turtle, which is cut up and sold at Market, as we do butcher meat. It was remarkably well dressed to day. The shell indeed is a noble dish, as it contains all the fine parts of the Turtle baked within its own body; here is the green fat, not the slabbery thing my stomach used to stand at, but firm and more delicate than it is possible to describe. Could an Alderman of true taste conceive the difference between it here and in the city, he would make the Voyage on purpose, and I fancy he would make a voyage into the other world before he left the table.

The method of placing the meal is in three rows the length of the table; six dishes in a row, I observe, is the common number. On the head of the centre row, stands the turtle soup, and at the bottom of the same line the shell. The rest of the middle row is generally made of fishes of various kinds, all exquisite. The King fish is that most prized; it resembles our Salmon, only the flesh is white. The Crouper is a fish they much esteem, its look is that of a pike, but in taste far superior. The Mullets are vastly good. These three I think are what they principally admire, but there are others that also make up the table. The Snapper eats like a kind of Turbot, not less delicate than what ye have. They named thirteen different fishes all good, many of which I have eat and found so. They are generally dressed with rich sauces; the red pepper is much used, and a little pod laid by every plate, as also a lime which is very necessary to the digesting the rich meats. The lime, I think, is an addition to every dish.

The two side rows are made up of vast varieties: Guinea fowl, Turkey, Pigeons, Mutton, fricassees of different kinds intermixed with the finest Vegetables in the world, as also pickles of every thing the Island produces. By the bye, the cole mutton is as fine as any I ever eat. It is small, the grain remarkably fine, sweet and juicy, and what you will think wonderful is, that it is thus good, tho' it is eat an hour after it is killed. The beef I do not think equal to the Mutton; it comes generally from New England, and I fancy is hurt by the Voyage. They have just now a scheme of raising it on the high plantations, several of which have begun to wear out, from the constant crops of sugar that have been taken from them. The second course contains as many dishes as the first, but are made up of pastry, puddings, jellys, preserved fruits, etc. I observe they bring the Palmetto cabbage to both courses, in different forms. Of this they are vastly fond, and give it as one of their greatest delicacies. Indeed I think it one of the most expensive, since to procure it, they must ruin the tree that bears it, and by that means deprive themselves of at least some part of that shade, for which they have so much occasion.

I will finish the table in this letter, for tho' I like to see it, yet I hope to find twenty things more agreeable for the Subject of my future letters; yet this will amuse some of our eating friends. The pastry is remarkably fine, their tarts are of various fruits, but the best I ever tasted is a sorrel, which when baked becomes the most beautiful Scarlet, and the sirup round it quite transparent. The cheese-cakes are made from the nut of the Cocoa. The puddings are so various, that it is impossible to name them: they are all rich, but what a little surprised me was to be told, that the ground of them all is composed of Oat meal, of which they gave me the receipt. They have many dishes that with us are made of milk, but as they have not that article in plenty, they must have something with which they supply its place, for they have sillabubs, floating Islands, etc. as frequently as with you. They wash and change napkins between the Courses. The desert now comes under our observation, which is indeed something beyond you. At Mr Halliday's we had thirty two different fruits, which tho' we had many other things, certainly was the grand part, yet in the midst of this variety the Pine apple and Orange still keep their ground and are preferred. The pine is large, its colour deep, and its flavour incomparably fine, yet after all I do not think it is superior to what we raise in our hot houses, which tho' smaller are not much behind in taste even with the best I have seen here, tho' in size and beauty there is no comparison. As to the Orange it is quite another fruit than ever I tasted before, the perfume is exquisite, the taste delicious, it has a juice which would produce Sugar. The Shaddack is a beautiful fruit, it is generally about four or five pounds weight, its Rind resembles an Orange, yet I hardly take it to be of the same tribe, as neither the pulp nor seed lies in the same manner. There are two kinds, the white and the purple pulp, the last is best. There is another fruit as large as a Shaddack, but which is really an Orange; this is called the forbidden fruit, and looks very beautiful, tho' I do not think it tastes so high as the Orange. The next to these is the Allegator pear, a most delicious fruit; then come in twenty others of less note, tho' all good and most refreshing in this climate. The Granadila is in size about the bigness of an egg, its colour is bright yellow, but in seeds, juice and taste, it exactly resembles our large red gooseberry; it is eat with a tea spoon; they say it is the coolest and best thing they can give in fevers.* The grapes are very good, the melons of various kinds as with you, but it were endless to name them; every thing bears fruit or flowers or both.

They have a most agreeable forenoon drink, they call Beveridge, which is made from the water of the Cocoa nut, fresh lime juice and sirup from the boiler, which tho' sweet has still the flavour of the cane. This the men mix with a small proportion of rum; the Ladies never do. This is presented in a crystal cup, with a cover which some have of Silver. Along with this is brought baskets of fruit, and you may eat as much as you please of it, because (according to their maxim) fruit can never hurt. I am sure it never hurts me. When I first came here, I could not bear to see so much of a pine apple thrown away. They cut off a deep pairing, then [cut] out the firm part of the heart, which takes away not much less than the half of the apple. But only observe how easy it is to become extravagant. I can now feel if the least bit of rind remains; and as to the heart, heavens! who could eat the nasty heart of a pine apple. I shall only mention the Guava, which is a fruit I am not fond of as such, but makes the finest Jelly I ever saw. This with Marmalade

---

* "Forbidden fruit" is a small variety of shaddock, so called because it is supposed to resemble the forbidden fruit of the Garden of Eden. The granadilla is the fruit of a species of passion flower (*Passiflora quadrangularis*), often six to eight inches in diameter. Miss Schaw anticipates the modern liking for the alligator pear.

of pine apple is part of Breakfast, which here as well as in Scotland is really a meal.

They have various breads, ham, eggs, and indeed what you please, but the best breakfast bread is the Casada cakes,* which they send up buttered. These are made from a root which is said to be poison. Before it goes thro' the various operations of drying, pounding and baking, you would think one would not be very clear as to a food that had so lately been of so pernicious a nature, yet such are the effects of Example, that I eat it, not only without fear, but with pleasure. They drink only green Tea and that remarkably fine; their Coffee and chocolate too are uncommonly good; their sugar is monstrously dear, never under three shillings per pound. At this you will not wonder when you are told, they use none but what returns from England double refined, and has gone thro' all the duties. I believe this they are forced to by act of parliament, but am not certain.† This however is a piece of great extravagance, because the sugar here can be refined into the most transparent sirup and tastes fully as well as the double refined Sugar, and is certainly

---

* The cassada or cassava is a fleshy root, the sweet variety of which is still used for food. The writer of the *Brief Account* gives nearly the same list of fruits as does Miss Schaw, and of the cassava says, "Cassava (commonly called Cassada) is a species of bread made from the root of a plant of the same name, by expression. The water, or juice, is poisonous, but the remaining part after being dried, or baked on thick iron plates, is both wholesome and palatable, it is eaten dry or toasted, and it also makes excellent puddings" (p. 63; cf. 64-67, 68-72). The Antigua plantation of Abraham Redwood, of Rhode Island, who founded the Redwood Library at Newport, was called "Cassada Garden." It was in St. George's parish.

† There was no act of parliament forbidding sugar-refining in the West Indies, but the British refiners objected strongly to the West Indian planters' entering into competition with themselves (since under the mercantilist scheme they should send to England only raw materials) and endeavored to discourage it in every way possible. Sugar-refining was deemed a form of manufacturing, in which the colonists were not expected to engage. Generally speaking, treatment in the West Indies of the raw juice of the sugar cane went no farther than the Muscovado process, which produced the various grades of brown sugar, with the by-product, molasses. For a description of this process, see Aspinall, *British West Indies*, pp. 171-172; Jones and Scard, *The Manufacture of Cane Sugar*; and for a contemporary illus-

much more wholesome. Many of the Ladies use it for the Coffee and all for the punch. The drink which I have seen every where is Punch, Madeira, Port and Claret; in some places, particularly at Mr Halliday's, they have also Burgundy. Bristol beer and porter you constantly find, but they have not yet been able to have Champaign, as the heat makes it fly too much. They have cyder from America very good. I forgot to tell you that along with the desert come perfumed waters in little bottles, also a number of flowers stuck into gourds. One would think that this letter was wrote by a perfect Epicure, yet that you know is not the case, but this is the last time I shall mention the table, except in general, unless I find some very remarkable difference between this and the other Islands I may be in.

I have been on a tour almost from one end of the Island to the other, and am more and more pleased with its beauties, as every excursion affords new objects worthy of notice. We have been on several visits, particularly to Coll. Martin, but I will say nothing of him till I bring you to his house. He is an acquaintance well worth your making, and I will introduce him to you then in form. As we were to make a journey, we set early off, and for some hours before the heat, had a charming ride thro' many rich and noble plantations, several of which belonged to Scotch proprietors, particularly that of the Dillidaffs (Lady Ogilvy and Mrs Leslie).* We soon arrived at that of Mr Freeman.† This Gentleman who is

tration of a sugar mill, *Universal Magazine*, II, 103. This process is still continued on many West Indian estates, as it is much cheaper than the vacuum process and furnishes the market not only with molasses, but also with the old brown sugar, "sweetest of all and the delight of children for their bread and butter."

* "Dillidaff" is probably phonetic for Tullideph, a well-known Scottish name. Dr. Walter Tullideph of Antigua had two daughters, Charlotte, who married Sir John Ogilvy, and Mary, who married Hon. Col. Alexander Leslie. After leaving St. John's the party rode southward along the coast, turning eastward a mile or so to visit "Green Castle," Colonel Martin's estate in Bermudian Valley under Windmill Hill.

† Arthur Freeman was the eldest son and the heir-at-law of Thomas

remarkable for his learning, is no stranger to the polite Arts, and tho' not a martyr, is a votary to the Graces, as appears by every thing round him. His plantation, which is laid out with the greatest taste, has a mixture of the Indian and European. If your eye is hurt by the stiff uniformity of the tall Palmetto, it is instantly relieved by the waving branches of the spreading Tammerand, or the Sand-box tree. The flowering cyder is a beautiful tree, covered with flowers, and along Mr Freeman's avenue these were alternately inter-mixed with Orange trees, limes, Cocoa Nuts, Palmettoes, Myrtles and citrons, with many more which afforded a most delightful shade, which continued till we arrived at the bottom of a green hill, on which the house stands.

This hill was also shaded with trees, beneath which grow flowers of every hue, that the western sun is able to paint.

Freeman (died, 1736). He was born in 1724 and died January 30, 1780, aged 56. In 1765, when forty-one years old, he eloped with the youngest daughter of the governor, George Thomas, and went to England. Governor Thomas, a native of Antigua and deputy governor of Pennsylvania for nine years, had been appointed governor of the Leeward Islands in 1753. He retired in 1766, was made a baronet in the same year, and died in London, December 31, 1773, aged 79. He was so angry with Freeman for running off with his daughter, at that time not nineteen years old, that he suspended him from the council, giving the following elaborate statement of reasons.

"In defiance of the laws of Great Britain and of this Island, in contempt of the respect due to him as his Majesty's Governor in Chief of the Leeward Islands, and in violation of the laws of hospitality [Freeman] basely and treacherously seduced his daughter, of considerable pretensions, from the duty and obedience due to him as a most affectionate tender father, by pre-vailing on her to make a private elopement from his house, with assur-ances, from his uncommon indulgence, of an easy forgiveness and by bribing an indigent Scotch parson, who had been indebted to the general [Thomas] for his daily bread, to join them in marriage without licence or any other lawful authority, in hopes of repairing the said Freeman's fortune, become desperate by a series of folly and extravagance" (Oliver, I, 266).

The Privy Council in England, deeming the matter a private one, refused to support the action of the choleric old governor and restored Freeman to the council. He returned and took his seat in 1770. Apparently he left his wife in England, where she died in 1797, aged 52, for Miss Schaw's account contains no hint of a wife. He must have gone back later, for he was buried in Willingdon Church, Sussex. For an intimate picture of Governor Thomas in Pennsylvania in 1744, see Hamilton's *Itinerarium* (privately printed, 1907), pp. 25, 33, 35.

Amongst these I saw many that with much pains are raised
in our hot houses; but how inferior to what they are here, in
their native soil, without any trouble, but that of preventing
their overgrowing each other. For as they are the weeds of
this country, like other weeds they wax fast. The Carnation
tree, or as they call it the doble day is a most glorious plant;
it does not grow above ten feet high, so can only be numbered amongst Shrubs, but is indeed a superior one even here.
The leaf is dark green, the flowers bear an exact resemblance
to our largest Dutch Carnation, which hang in large bunches
from the branches. The colours are sometimes dark rich
Crimson spotted or specked with white, sometimes purple in
the same manner. Ruby colour is the lightest I observed.
They are often one colour, and when that is the case, they
are hardly to be looked at while the sun shines on them.
These you meet every where. Another is the passion flower,
which grows in every hedge and twines round every tree; it
here bears a very fine fruit, and as I formerly observed, the
three seasons of Spring, Summer and Autumn go hand in
hand. The fruit and flower ornament the bush jointly. There
is another beautiful shrub, which they call the four o'clock,
because it opens at four every afternoon; this is absolutely
a convulvalous, and they have both the major and minor.
The blue is the finest Velvet and the Crimson the brightest
satin; but allowing for the superiority of colour produced
by the warmth of a Tropick sun, I saw no other difference,
and on this discovery I found out that many more of the
plants were of the same tribes at least with what we have,
but so greatly improved, that they were hardly to be known.
How different is that from the plants of this country, when
they come to our Northern Climate.

My seeing all these in high perfection at Mr Freeman's
plantation led me to describe them here, tho' every place is
full of them; and they are a great hurt to the Canes, tho'
when taken in as he has them, they are most beautiful. His

house, which stands on the Summit of this little hill, is extremely handsome, built of stone. I forgot to tell you that every house has a handsome piazza; that to his is large and spacious. You reach the house by a Serpentine walk, on each side grows a hedge of Cape Jasmine. The verdure which appeared here is surprising, and shews that it only requires a little care to exclude that heat which ruins every thing. The sun was now high, yet it was so cool, that we were able to walk a great way under these trees. I am sorry to add, that I fear the esteemable master is not long to enjoy this earthly paradise. He has been close confined for many months with an illness in his head; one of his eyes is already lost, and it is dreaded, that tho' he were to recover his health, he would be deprived of the pleasure of viewing these beauties I have so much admired. My Brother was often with him and vastly fond of him.

We were next at the plantation of a Mr Malcolm,* a near relation of Mr Rutherfurd's. This Gentleman was bred a physician, but has left off practice, and enjoys a comfortable estate in peace and quiet, without wife or children. But it is inconceivable how fond he was of these relations, whom he caressed as his children, loading them with every thing he had that was good. I shall say nothing of many other places, as I long to bring you acquainted with the most delightful character I have ever yet met with, that of Coll. Martin,† the loved and revered father of Antigua, to whom it owes a thousand advantages, and whose age is yet daily employed

---

* Patrick Malcolm was a surgeon of Antigua, who died in 1785. He had a diploma from Surgeons Hall, London, as had Dr. Dunbar, and was licensed to practice in the island in 1749. That he was on terms of close intimacy with the Martins appears from the mention of his name several times in their wills. His relationship to the Rutherfurds we have not been able to discover. He may have been a brother of George Malcolm of Burnfoot in Dumfriesshire, who married Margaret, daughter of James Paisley of Craig and Burn near Langholm, and so have been connected with the Paisleys of Lisbon (below, p. 214).

† See Appendix II, "The Martin Family."

to render it more improved and happy. This is one of the oldest families on the Island, has for many generations enjoyed great power and riches, of which they have made the best use, living on their Estates, which are cultivated to the height by a large troop of healthy Negroes, who cheerfully perform the labour imposed on them by a kind and beneficent Master, not a harsh and unreasonable Tyrant. Well fed, well supported, they appear the subjects of a good prince, not the slaves of a planter. The effect of this kindness is a daily increase of riches by the slaves born to him on his own plantation. He told me he had not bought in a slave for upwards of twenty years, and that he had the morning of our arrival got the return of the state of his plantations, on which there then were no less than fifty two wenches who were pregnant. These slaves, born on the spot and used to the Climate, are by far the most valuable, and seldom take these disorders, by which such numbers are lost that many hundreds are forced yearly to be brought into the Island.*

On our arrival we found the venerable man seated in his piazza to receive us; he held out his hands to us, having lost the power of his legs, and embracing us with the embraces of a fond father, "You are welcome," said he, "to little Antigua, and most heartily welcome to me. My habitation has not looked so gay this long time." Then turning to Mr Halliday who had brought us his invitation, "How shall I thank you, my good friend," said he, "for procuring me this happiness, in persuading these ladies to come to an old man. Old, did I say? I retract the word: Eighty five that can be sensible of beauty, is as young as twenty five that can be no more." There was gallantry for you. We now had fruit, sangarie and beverage brought us, not by slaves; it is a maxim of his that no slave can render that acceptable Service he wishes

---

* In his *Essay upon Plantership*, pp. 2-7, Colonel Martin deals at length with the proper care of plantation negroes, and expresses opinions similar to those ascribed to him by Miss Schaw.

from those immediately about himself; and for that reason has made them free, and the alacrity with which they serve him, and the love they bear him, shew he is not wrong. His table was well served in every thing; good order and cheerfulness reigned in his house. You would have thought the servants were inspired with an instinctive knowledge of your wishes, for you had scarcely occasion to ask them. His conversation was pleasant, entertaining and instructive, his manners not merely polite but amiable in a high degree. It was impossible not to love him. I never resisted it; but gave him my heart without hesitation, for which I hope you will not blame me, nor was Fanny less taken than myself with this charming old man.

He told us that in compliance with the wishes of his children, he had resided in England for several years, "but tho' they kept me in a greenhouse," said he, "and took every method to defend me from the cold, I was so absolute an exotick, that all could not do, and I found myself daily giving way, amidst all their tenderness and care; and had I stayed much longer," continued he, smiling, "I had actually by this time become an old man. I have had, Madam," said he turning to me, "twenty three children, and tho' but a small number remain, they are such as may raise the pride of any father. One of my sons you will know if you go to Carolina, he is governor there; another, my eldest, you know by character at least."* This I did and much admired that character. He wishes to have his dear little Antigua independent; he regrets the many Articles she is forced to trust to foreign aid, and the patriot is even now setting an example, and by turning many of the plantations into grass, he allows them to rest and recover the strength they have lost, by too many crops of sugar, and by this means is able to rear

---

* The son in Carolina was Governor Josiah Martin; the one in England, whose character Miss Schaw knew, was Samuel Martin, Josiah's half-brother, who attained wide notoriety from his duel with John Wilkes.

cattle which he has done with great success.* I never saw finer cows, nor more thriving calves, than I saw feeding in his lawns, and his waggons are already drawn by oxen of his own rearing.

We were happy and delighted with every thing while there, but as we prepared to leave him, found we had a task we were not aware of; for during the time we stayed, he had formed a design not to part with us. This he had communicated to Mr Halliday and young Martin, who were much pleased with it, as they were so good as to wish to retain us, if possible, on the Island. I shall never forget with what engaging sweetness the dear old man made the proposal, why did he not make another, that would have rendered him master of our fate, of which we ourselves had not the disposal. "You must not leave me," said he, taking both our hands in his, "every thing in my power shall be subservient to your happiness; my age leaves no fear of reputation." "You," said he to me, "shall be my friend, my companion, you shall grace my table and be its mistress; and you," continued he turning to Miss Rutherfurd, "You, my lovely Fanny, shall be my child, my little darling." "I once," said he, with a sigh, "had an Angel Fanny of my own, she is no more, supply her place." Mrs Dunbar joined and begged as if her life had depended on our compliance. "Stay," said the Coll:, "at least till Mr S. be settled,† he will then come for you." It was in vain, go we must, and go we did, tho' my heart felt a pang like that which it sustained when I lost the best of fathers.‡

---

* Colonel Martin was one of those who foresaw the eventual decay of the industry of the island, because of its cultivation, to the exclusion of everything else, of the single staple, sugar. He wished to see some of the cane land converted into pasture for the rearing of sheep and cattle.

† "Till Mr. Schaw be settled," that is, till Alexander Schaw be definitely established in his post as searcher of customs at St. Christopher.

‡ Gideon Schaw of Lauriston, the father of Janet and Alexander, died January 19, 1772 (*Scots Magazine*, 34, p. 51). When he was born we do not know, but he was already married in 1726, for Patrick Walker, in his *Bio-*

Last Saturday was Christmass which we had engaged to pass with Mr Halliday, but our good old hostess Mrs Dunbar had begged so hard that we would pay her a visit, that we took the opportunity of every body being at their devotions to go to her, as her house did not admit of retirement. The old Lady was charmed to see us and we had reason to thank her for Memboe, who had been most exact in her duty. Mr Mackinnon had taken Jack up to his plantation, and was grown so fond of him, that he did not know how to part with him. Billie lives much at his ease between the ship and Mrs Dunbar's. We found Mary had been often ashore, but gave herself no trouble about us. Indeed we had no occasion for her attendance, as Memboe, the black wench, performed her duty in every respect to our satisfaction. Every body who did not attend the service at Church were gone out of town. My brother was not yet returned from his Tour, so we had that night entirely to ourselves. Next morning atoned for this, as every body was with us, and we were carried by Mr Halliday and Mr Martin up to a fine plantation, which belongs to the former. We went out of town pretty early, as Mrs Dunbar with several other Ladies were to meet us.

We met the Negroes in joyful troops on the way to town with their Merchandize. It was one of the most beautiful sights I ever saw. They were universally clad in white Mus-

graphia Presbyteriana (II, 283-284), tells a grewsome tale of the execution and burial near Lauriston at that time of certain condemned persons, in connection with which he mentions both Gideon Schaw and his wife. In 1730 Gideon (or Gidjun) was appointed supervisor of the salt-duty at Alloa, the leading customs port at the head of the Firth of Forth, and there remained until 1734, when he removed to a similar post at Prestonpans, a smaller town below Leith. There he continued to live until 1738, when he was appointed collector of customs at Perth, at the head of the Firth of Tay, serving in that capacity until 1751, when he became assistant to Harnage, the register-general of tobacco in Scotland, with the title of assistant in Scotland to the register-general in England. His appointment was renewed in 1761 (on the accession of George III) and he continued to serve until his death in 1772, residing in Lauriston. His salary, beginning at £30 a year, rose to £150 at the end, an amount not large even for those days. Miss Schaw in her journal frequently refers to Perth, the Tay, and the country about.

lin: the men in loose drawers and waistcoats, the women in jackets and petticoats; the men wore black caps, the women had handkerchiefs of gauze or silk, which they wore in the fashion of turbans.* Both men and women carried neat white wicker-baskets on their heads, which they ballanced as our Milk maids do their pails. These contained the various articles for Market, in one a little kid raised its head from amongst flowers of every hue, which were thrown over to guard it from the heat; here a lamb, there a Turkey or a pig, all covered up in the same elegant manner, While others had their baskets filled with fruit, pine-apples reared over each other; Grapes dangling over the loaded basket; oranges, Shaddacks, water lemons, pomegranates, granadillas, with twenty others, whose names I forget. They marched in a sort of regular order, and gave the agreeable idea of a set of devotees going to sacrifice to their Indian Gods, while the sacrifice offered just now to the Christian God is, at this Season of all others the most proper, and I may say boldly, the most agreeable, for it is a mercy to the creatures of the God of mercy. At this Season the crack of the inhuman whip must not be heard, and for some days, it is an universal Jubilee; nothing but joy and pleasantry to be seen or heard, while every Negro infant can tell you, that he owes this happiness to the good Buccara God,♯ that he be no hard

♯ White men's God.

* The "tenah" was the negro woman's headdress, composed of one or more handkerchiefs put on in the manner of a turban. An excellent description of the market is given by the author of the *Brief Account*. "This market is held at the southern extremity of the town . . . here an assemblage of many hundred negroes and mulattoes expose for sale poultry, pigs, kids, vegetables, fruit and other things; they begin to assemble by day-break and the market is generally crowded by ten o'clock. This is the proper time to purchase for the week such things as are not perishable. The noise occasioned by the jabber of the negroes and the squalling and cries of the children basking in the sun exceeds anything I ever heard in a London market. About three o'clock the business is nearly over." The writer goes on to discuss the obnoxious odors, the drinking of grog, the gambling and fighting, etc., which accompanied the holding of the market (pp. 139-141).

Master, but loves a good black man as well as a Buccara man, and that Master will die bad death, if he hurt poor Negro in his good day. It is necessary however to keep a look out during this season of unbounded freedom; and every man on the Island is in arms and patrols go all round the different plantations as well as keep guard in the town. They are an excellent disciplined Militia and make a very military appearance.* My dear old Coll. was their commander upwards of forty years, and resigned his command only two years ago, yet says with his usual spirits, if his country need his service, he is ready again to resume his arms.

Every body here is fond of dancing, and [they] have frequent balls. We have been at several, very elegant and heartsome, particularly one at a Doctor Muir's,† whose daughters were Fanny's boarding school acquaintance, fine girls, with a most excellent mother, who tho' even beyond Embonpoint began the ball and danced the whole evening, with her family and friends, as did several other Ladies, whose appearance did not promise much strength or agility. Sir Ralph and Lady Payn are now come back, but Lady Payn so ill that she has never been out of bed since her arrival. Every body is melancholy on account of her illness, for by all accounts this amiable creature must soon fall a sacrifice to this climate, if she is not soon removed from it.‡

---

* The militia of Antigua consisted of a troop of horse,—carabineers or light dragoons,—three regiments of foot, known as the red, blue, and green, one independent company of foot, and one company of artillery. Service in the militia was obligatory from 14 to 45. Colonel Martin was at the head of these forces for upwards of forty years. In 1773 Sir Ralph Payne became colonel of the carabineers.

† Dr. John Muir married Eleanor Knight in 1757. He died in 1798. Their daughters were Fanny's boarding school acquaintances in Scotland and must have been about her own age.

‡ Governor Payne's correspondence confirms Miss Schaw's statements in all particulars. The governor left Antigua with Lady Payne, in the summer of 1774, for a tour of the islands under his jurisdiction, and was away when Miss Schaw arrived. He was at St. Christopher in October and soon afterwards at Montserrat, returning to Antigua after Christmas but before the end of the year. As his wife was in poor health, he had already applied to

My brother has been returned these two days, and is so charmed with the other Islands,* that he would persuade us, all I have seen is nothing to them. It will not be easy however to make me believe it possible to excel Antigua. I will not deny I am partial to this delightful spot, and go where I will, my heart will retain a grateful sense of the hospitable reception we have met with, and the numberless civilities we have received from every Individual. He talks much of the advantage they have as to water, a circumstance, in which no doubt this Island is defective, yet their industry has rendered it of less inconveniency, than you who enjoy the roaring streams of Athole could believe. They have not only plenty for domestick use by their attention, and even streams through the cane-pieces, but in our route up the Island, we often met rivers that came up to the horses' belly, and had I not been in the secret, would never have dreamt that they were the work of Art. The cisterns† in which the water for family-use is kept are extremely well calculated to preserve it cool and fresh a great while, and what they use for drink-

---

Lord Dartmouth for permission to go to England and found the secretary's letter of consent awaiting him on his return. In a letter of February 7, 1775, he wrote Dartmouth: "Lord Mansfield's intercession with your Lordship for his Majesty's permission for me to conduct Lady Payne to England, for the reestablishment of her health, does me the greatest honour. I have indeed for a twelvemonth past entertained the most anxious desire of paying a short visit to England, but did [not make application] until the month of last October, when Lady Payne's health appeared to me to have arrived at so dangerous a crisis (and my own was so materially impair'd as to create a despair in me of its reestablishment without the aid of a northern climate) that I determined to submit my domestic situation to your Lordship's humanity" (Public Record Office, C. O. 152:55). He said further that Lady Payne had not quitted her bedchamber twice in the "last six weeks." Dating back from February 7, this would bring the return to Antigua to December 27, two days after Christmas, which accords well with Miss Schaw's remarks.

* Nevis, Montserrat, and St. Christopher.

† The cisterns are thus described by a traveler. "The only water in this country fit for the use of men and animals is that which is collected in tanks or cisterns of mason-work, sunk underground, over which a concave stone or brick cover is usually placed, to collect the rain when it falls, with a hole in the centre for it to run through. They have also on every plantation large ponds lined with clay." (Oliver, I, cxxx.)

ing and table passes thro' a filtering stone into a lead or Marble reservoir, by which means it becomes more lucid and pure than any water I ever saw. This is placed in some shaded corner, and is generally so cold, that it makes one's teeth chatter. It is presented to you in a Cocoa nut shell ornamented with Silver, at the end of a hickory handle. This is lest the breath of the Servant who presents it should contaminate its purity.

At the end of the town of St John's, there is a noble bathing house close on the Sea, where the water is strained thro' many calenders or Sieves to prevent the smallest particle of Sand from entering the baths, the bottoms of which are polished Marble, and every thing done that can render it most deliciously cool. It consists of many large apartments, where you can bathe in what manner you please. These have each a dressing room with every conveniency, and seem the contrivance of luxury itself. It is shaded from the land side with palmetto and cocoa nut trees, under whose umbrage grow a number of European plants, but tho' you would think, this must be one of the most agreeable things in the world, and is indeed of the utmost consequence to health, yet it is very little frequented, and will soon, they say, be given up entirely.

As I am now about to leave them, you, no doubt, will expect me, to give my opinion as fully on the Inhabitants, as I have done on their Island and manners, but I am afraid you will suspect me of partiality, and were I to speak of Individuals, perhaps you might have reason, but as to the characters in general I can promise to write without prejudice, and if I only tell truth, they have nothing to fear from my pen. I think the men the most agreeable creatures I ever met with, frank, open, generous, and I dare say brave; even in advanced life they retain the Vivacity and Spirit of Youth; they are in general handsome, and all of them have that sort of air, that will ever attend a man of fashion. Their address is at once soft and manly; they have a kind of gallantry in their manner, which exceeds mere politeness, and in some countries, we know, would be easily mistaken for something more interesting than civility, yet you must not suppose this the politeness of French manners, merely words of course. No, what they say, they really mean; their whole intention is to make you happy, and this they endeavour to do without any other view or motive than what they are prompted to by the natural goodness of their own natures. In short, my friend, the woman that *brings a heart here* will have little sensibility if she carry it away.

I hear you ask me, if there is no alloy to this fine character, no reverse to this beautiful picture. Alas! my friend, tho' children of the Sun, they are mortals, and as such must have their share of failings, the most conspicuous of which is, the indulgence they give themselves in their licentious and even unnatural amours, which appears too plainly from the crouds of Mullatoes, which you meet in the streets, houses and indeed every where; a crime that seems to have gained sanction from custom, tho' attended with the greatest inconveniences not only to Individuals, but to the publick in general.* The young black wenches lay themselves out for white lovers, in which they are but too successful. This prevents their marrying with their natural mates, and hence a spurious and degenerate breed, neither so fit for the field, nor indeed any work, as the true bred Negro. Besides these wenches become licentious and insolent past all bearing, and as even a mulattoe child interrupts their pleasures and is troublesome, they have certain herbs and medicines, that

---

* "Many of these gentlemen-managers, as well as the overseers under them, contribute, in a great degree, to stock the plantation with mulatto and mestee slaves. It is impossible to say in what number they have such children, but the following fact is too often verified, 'that, as soon as born, they are despised, not only by the very authors, under God, of their being, but by every white, destitute of humane and liberal principles,' such is the regard paid to the hue of complexion in preference to the more permanent beauties of the mind" (*Brief Account*, pp. 45-46).

free them from such an incumbrance, but which seldom fails to cut short their own lives, as well as that of their offspring. By this many of them perish every year. I would have gladly drawn a veil over this part of a character, which in every thing else is most estimable.

As to the women, they are in general the most amiable creatures in the world, and either I have been remarkably fortunate in my acquaintance, or they are more than commonly sensible, even those who have never been off the Island are amazingly intelligent and able to converse with you on any subject. They make excellent wives, fond attentive mothers and the best house wives I have ever met with. Those of the first fortune and fashion keep their own keys and look after every thing within doors; the domestick Economy is entirely left to them; as the husband finds enough to do abroad. A fine house, an elegant table, handsome carriage, and a croud of mullatoe servants are what they all seem very fond of. The sun appears to affect the sexes very differently. While the men are gay, luxurious and amorous, the women are modest, genteel, reserved and temperate. This last virtue they have indeed in the extreme; they drink nothing stronger in general than Sherbet, and never eat above one or two things at table, and these the lightest and plainest. The truth is, I can observe no indulgence they allow themselves in, not so much as in scandal, and if I stay long in this country, I will lose the very idea of that innocent amusement; for since I resided amongst them, I have never heard one woman say a wrong thing of another. This is so unnatural, that I suppose you will (good naturedly) call it cunning; but if it is so, it is the most commendable cunning I ever met with, as nothing can give them a better appearance in the eyes of a stranger.

As we became better acquainted, their reserve wore off, and I now find them most agreeable companions. Jealousy is a passion with which they are entirely unacquainted, and

a jealous wife would be here a most ridiculous character
indeed. Let me conclude this by assuring you, that I never
admired my own sex more than in these amiable creoles.*
Their Sentiments are just and virtuous; in religion they are
serious without ostentation, and perform every duty with
pleasure from no other motive but the consciousness of doing
right. In their persons they are very genteel, rather too thin
till past thirty, after that they grow plump and look much
the better for it. Their features are in general high and very
regular, they have charming eyes, fine teeth, and the greatest
quantity of hair I ever saw, which they dress with taste, and
wear a great deal of powder. In short, they want only colour
to be termed beautiful, but the sun who bestows such rich
taints on every other flower, gives none to his lovely daughters; the tincture of whose skin is as pure as the lily, and as
pale. Yet this I am convinced is owing to the way in which
they live, entirely excluded from proper air and exercise.
From childhood they never suffer the sun to have a peep at
them, and to prevent him are covered with masks and bon-
nets,† that absolutely make them look as if they were stewed.
Fanny who just now is blooming as a new blown rose, was
prevailed on to wear a mask, while we were on our Tour,

---

* Creole is here used in its original meaning of any one born in the West
Indies, irrespective of color. Aspinall says that a child born of white parents
in Barbadoes, for example, was a 'creole' of that island and that the word
is applied to animals and even to produce, it being not unusual to speak of a
'creole' pig or 'creole' corn (*British West Indies*, p. 149). We read also of
'creole' regiments (*Calendar of State Papers, Colonial*, 1702-1703, pp. 440,
441).

† "The ladies, inhabitants of this place, seldom walk the streets or ride
in their wiskys, without masks or veils, not I presume, altogether as a preserv-
ative to their complexion, being frequently seen at a distance unmasked,
but as soon as they are approached near, on goes the vizor, thro' which, by
a couple of peep-holes, about the size of an English shilling, they have an
opportunity of staring in the faces of all they meet. With you, this would
be termed the grossest ill-manners, but here custom has established it, if not
necessary as fashionable. Their dress is generally light, and inclined to
tawdry, and their conversation languid, except when a little of that species
of harmless chat, which ill-nature has called scandal, is busy in circulation,
it is then they are volubile, it is then they are eloquent, it is then they are

which in a week changed her colour, and if she had persevered I am sure a few months would have made her as pale as any of them. As to your humble Servant, I have always set my face to the weather; wherever I have been. I hope you have no quarrel at brown beauty.

The people of Fashion dress as light as possible; worked and plain muslins, painted gauzes or light Lutstrings and Tiffities* are the universal wear. They have the fashions every six weeks from London, and London itself cannot boast of more elegant shops than you meet with at St John's, particularly Mrs Tudhope, a Scotch Lady, sister-in-law to Mr Ross, the writer at Edinburgh, at whose shop I saw as neat done up things as ever I met with in my life. She is a widow of a most amiable character and generally esteemed.

My brother is with the Govr general, but Lady Payn is still confined to bed, so we will not be so happy as to see her, but she has sent us a most polite Message. The time fixed for our departure draws near, and believe me, I feel a most sincere regret at leaving a country and people, where I have been treated with more than hospitality, and for whom I have conceived a real affection. We have promised to return next year, but God knows if ever that may be in my power. No body expresses more regret to part with us than my good friend Mr Baird, who has been constantly with us on all our excursions, and for whom we have a sincere esteem. He has given me a little merry dog, which for its master's sake will be well cared for.

We are now come to town, and to morrow are to leave this charming spot, whose engaging inhabitants are so sorry to part with us, and express their regret in such terms, as is like

---

equal to any women in the world" (*Brief Account*, pp. 35-36). Further comments on marriage, domestic life, abstemiousness, and virtue bear out Miss Schaw's observations.

* Lutestring or lustring was a kind of glossy silk, much worn in the West Indies and the continental colonies. Tiffities or taffetas were a soft fine silk of many colors and varieties.

to break my heart. Mr Mackinnon and good Dr Dunbar have begged us to leave the boys with them, till the ship is cleared to follow us to St Kitt's. Our Emigrants are all disposed of to their hearts contentment, except two families, who, steady to their first idea, persist on going forward to America; one of these is Lawson. I hope we will prevail on our friends to provide for them there. As to those who have stopped here, they are already so entirely changed as not to be known. Our little Tailor, whose whole fortune was his thimble and smoothing iron, is now as pretty, a pert little fellow as one would wish to see; has got four and six pence a day, a good table and as much rum as he can drink. This last article never fails to make room for new adventures. Mr Halliday has taken our Smith,* whose Lady now looks with disdain on her green damask and is providing a garden silk and satin Capuchin.† Those who live will not fail to make fortunes, but the change of living more than Climate kills four out of five the first year. Many of our friends are to be with us this evening, and our little bark is loaded with provisions for many weeks, tho' our Voyage will be over in a few hours, and that on a Sea smooth as a looking glass; but the attention of the hospitable Antiguans knows no bounds. Farewell till I write from St Kitts. The pain I feel at leaving my new friends would be intolerable, were it not alleviated by the hope of meeting others, from whom I have long been parted, the first of whom is Lady Isabella Hamilton, to whom I know my arrival will give sincere pleasure. I wrote her on my landing here; I am sure she has counted every moment since. I shall also meet Miss Milliken, a most amiable girl for whom I had the most sincere affection. And now once more farewell, and ah me! farewell, Antigua.

---

* For "our Smith," see pp. 55-56.
† A cloak and hood resembling the dress of a Capuchin monk.

Basterre St Kitts.*

About three yesterday morning, we got aboard our little vessel, but as we had not a breath of wind, had reason to expect a tedious passage. However we were much pleased with our Transport, which tho' no larger than a Kinghorn boat,† was neat clean and commodious. Our little Cabin was furnished with two neat Settees, a cupboard with Tea-equipage, glasses and punch cups, and indeed with whatever could render it agreeable and convenient. As none of us had got to bed before we left Antigua, we were much fatigued, and willing to forget that we were quitting that charming Island, with its hospitable inhabitants. Fanny and I lay down on the Settees and slept, till we were waked to breakfast, where we found excellent Tea, coffee and chocolate, which were most comfortable in our present Situation. Breakfast over, my brother carried us on deck screened with our Umbrelas, which black Robt held over us, while he, in company with

---

* "Saint Christopher," says Governor Payne, in his "Answers to Queries," "(the southeast part of which is divided from the northwest part of Nevis by a narrow channel of scarcely a league in breadth), lies in latitude 17" 18' north and longitude 62" 40' west from the meridian of London, and contains 68 square miles and 43,726 acres of land. Half of the island or thereabouts is an exceedingly fertile, gravelly and sandy soil; mix'd in some places with a very small proportion of clay, but without marle; and the soil of this nature produces sugar canes. The other half is no where so fertile nor is it at all fit for the cultivation of sugar canes: but in some parts of it are produc'd edible roots, and pulse of various kinds, together with some cotton and a small quantity of coffee and cocoa; and in other places, it is almost inaccessible from its situation on the sides and tops of steep mountains and craggy hills, which produce shrubs and different sorts of woods of little or no value. If any one of the islands deserves a pre-eminent character over the others for the salubrity of its air and the general health of its inhabitants, it is certainly Saint Christopher."

"Neither in Saint Christopher, Nevis, or Montserrat are there any harbours at all and the shipping of all sizes and denominations anchor in open roads and bays. There are at Saint Christopher 1900 white inhabitants, 417 free negroes and mulattoes, and 23,462 slaves."

"The principal port, Basseterre, on the southern side of the island, is divided into two parishes, Saint Peter Basseterre and Saint George Basseterre; the first is on low ground, the second slightly higher, both have less rain and suffer more by the want of it than the other [seven] parishes."

† Kinghorn was a seaport of Fife, a few miles east of Burntisland.

our Capt went a fishing to procure us something from that Element to furnish out our table, while Fanny and myself hung over the side of the Vessel, hardly able to support our languid existence, and you may judge what we must have been suffering under this Tropical heat, where there was not a breeze to ruffle the face of the Sea, in which we could distinctly view our own shadows.

A kingfish was soon caught which was cut into jumps and laid in the Sun, watered with Sea water, which presently became salt on it from the excessive heat, and after having gone thro' the necessary operation of the grid-iron was served to dinner. There is nothing that diverts lassitude equal to eating or even looking at meat, and I have often observed that those people who can neither work nor think are perpetually longing for the next meal, and constantly abusing fashion that has now placed them at such a distance from each other; but as we had no forms to observe, we gave way to our desire of taking the only exercise in our power, that of moving our jaws, as every thing else was listless and inactive. Accordingly we had an early dinner, where our table was once more set forth by the benevolence of our Antiguan friends, which, joined to the produce of our own industry in providing fish, made a most excellent dinner, tho' to say truth, the fruit was the only thing eat with satisfaction, for the heat was become past all bearing. After drinking tea and coffee, Miss Rutherfurd and I threw ourselves again on the Settees, while black Robt with a large fan sat fanning us alternately, till we fell both fast asleep.

How long we slept I know not, but when I waked it was quite dark, and I found myself very dreary, as not an object was to be discerned, nor a sound heard. At least I heard something breathing on the floor of the Cabin, and I ventured to put down my hand to feel what it was, but how much was I shocked to find it no other than my poor brother fast asleep on the bare boards, sweating till every stitch of his cloths were wet thro' with it. Dangerous as his situation was, I could not find in my heart to wake him. Miss Rutherfurd too was as sound as he, tho' fortunately on a better bed; so thinking the only service in my power was to relieve the cabin of the heat of one breath, I crept up as softly as I was able thro' the little hatch, and reached the deck. All was silent as death, not a sound to be heard, except that of four Oars which moved softly on the surface, and scarcely produced a dashing on that vast Sea; it was entirely dark; however I reached about to find a wicker-chair, which I remembered was fixed to the mast. It required some precaution to get safely to it, in which however I succeeded, and tho' not without difficulty seated myself in it. The absence of the sun had diminished the intense heat, and tho' the air still retained a great degree of warmness, it was very sufferable. As I had no external object to entertain me, my eyes naturally turned within, and I soon found amusement from joys that were past, pleasingly mournful to my soul. What would become of me, if I was unacquainted with your three favourite authors David, Job and Ossian? How often do they afford me words when I should find none so apt from myself. If you call this pleasure I will not deny it, but wish rather they could afford me language to serve my present purpose and enable me to describe to you a western sun rising in all his glory, surrounded with splendours that the human eye is hardly able to sustain. No Aurora precedes him, no rosy finger'd Nymphs unbar the doors of the morning and announce his approach, but he bursts from his cloud at once and flashes on you with such a blaze of glory, as recals to the mind Milton's description of the creating power going forth to command worlds into being; and such indeed was the present effect of his appearance, as I instantly found myself not only surrounded by common objects, but by new worlds which seemed at his sight to lift their heads from this unbounded Ocean.

You will easily guess we were now among the Leeward Islands, several of which were in sight at once, and made a most delightful and pleasing appearance. We distinctly saw both Nevise and Montsarat; very fine Islands, but far inferior to St Kitt's, which now appeared crowned with wood-covered Mountains. Noble however as this morning scene might be made in description, it affords not the soft satisfaction that the mind feels from the rising sun on a summer morning in your cool Hemisphere, and tho', to my shame be it spoken, that was one of the Arcanas of Nature, into which my curiosity seldom pryed, yet I now recollected with a pleasing regret the soft dawn, the dew-bespangled lawn, with all that delightful coolness, which I am not to expect under a Tropical Sun.

We soon came to an anchor in the road of Basterre, in which were riding many fine Vessels. From our situation we had an extensive prospect of that side of the Island, which lay next us, which tho' very beautiful is different from the first view we had of Antigua, which rises on you by degrees. As you go up the bay, the plantations on the rising grounds are noble, and the cane pieces wear a superior green to those at Antigua. I was particularly showed the habitation of my friend Lady Bell Hamilton.* It appears magnificent at a distance, and I am assured is not less so when you get to it.

---

* Lady Isabella, or Lady Belle as she was commonly called, was Isabella Erskine, daughter of the 10th Earl of Buchan and sister of David Stuart, Lord Erskine, later the 11th earl, the "fussy and intermeddling" patron of art, letters, and antiquities. Her other brothers were Henry, the lord advocate, and Thomas, the lord chancellor. She was married at Tunbridge Wells, England, January 21, 1770, to William Leslie Hamilton, a prominent planter and attorney of St. Christopher, speaker of the house, member of the council, and attorney-general, 1779. In July of the latter year, on account of dangers attending the American War, Lady Belle returned to England in the *Mary*, Captain Beatty, and her husband followed her the next year. He landed at Portsmouth, October 5, 1780, but died suddenly at London, four days after his arrival, before his wife could reach his bedside (*Gentleman's Magazine*, 1780, p. 495). Her brother, David, was the only member of the family present at the time of his death. On April 3, 1785, Lady Belle married again, the Right Honorable and Reverend John, last Earl of Glencairn, who died

The Parishes of Basseterre.

From a manuscript map of St. Christopher in the British Museum made by Lieutenant SAMUEL BAKER, R.N., in 1753. "Olivees" is the plantation northwest of Basseterre, belonging to Matthew Mills, Esq.

The town of Basterre is scarcely seen from the Sea, and the few houses that are visible give you but a very poor idea of the rest; indeed its very name informs you of its situation.

We landed by a boat* from one of the ships nearest the town, but had a third Voyage to make, which was on the back of Negroes, and tho' there was not a breath of wind, we were much wet and incommoded by the Surge. We soon however reached an excellent Inn, and were welcomed to the Island by a jolly English Landlady, who got us a dish of excellent Tea; my friend the goat attending, and as far as I can see, every thing just the same as at Antigua.

Here we found a gentleman, who by Lady Bell's desire had been several days in waiting: as I had wrote her from Antigua, and made her expect us much sooner than we arrived. He presented me a letter from her Ladyship, which he politely said was his credentials, and entitled him to the honour of attending us to the Olovaze,† where our friends impatiently waited us. Lady Bell's letter was in the style I had reason to expect from so dear a friend. She told me Mr Hamilton had been ill, which prevented her coming down to meet us, but intreated I would let Mr Moor, a near relation and particular friend of Mr Hamilton's, conduct me immediately to her with my other friends. With this request I would have instantly complied, did not some particular busi-

September 24, 1796. She herself died at Boulogne, May 17, 1824, without issue by either husband (*id.*, 1824, p. 177). For "Olivees" and Hamilton's troubles during the war, see Appendix III.

* Davy in 1846 landed at Basseterre in an open boat (*West Indies*, p. 461).

† The name of the Hamilton plantation was "Olivees," the form of the word contained in Lady Isabella's memorial. In the British Museum manuscript it is written "Olovaze" and in that of Colonel Vetch, "Olivese." The word is evidently French in origin and was probably derived from the name of a previous owner. In 1704, Governor Codrington granted to Lieutenant David Dunbar, "for his service in the reduceing the French part of this Island," the plantation of a M. Olivie of 150 acres, lying to the westward of Monkey Hill in Basseterre quarter (C. O. 152:42, no. 1). There can be little doubt that the plantation thus granted was the one which Miss Schaw visited and that the name "Olivees" means simply Olivie's plantation.

ness oblige my Brother to stay in town some hours, part of which time I have strolled about the town with Mr Moor and some other Gentlemen, and am much pleased with it on a nearer inspection. The best houses lie up the town and have an extensive prospect and airy situation; tho' all of wood, they are very neat, and some of them ornamented with carvings on the outside. They in general lie more off the street than those at St John's, and have very pretty parterres* before them and are shaded with cocoa or palmetto trees. I was showed that intended for my brother, which is very handsome, and has not only a parterre in front, but a large orange grove behind it. We were presented with play bills, but I wish I may be able to bear the heat even in the open air. They are strollers of some spirit who have strolled across the Atlantick.

Poor Fanny is so overcome with heat and fatigue, that she has been asleep these two hours. My brother is not yet returned, and I have spent my time in my most agreeable amusement, recounting to you what your partiality to the writer will make interesting. My next will be from the Olovaze, and I hope more entertaining. The Comptroller, Mr Gratehead,† has promised to get this away to morrow.

The Olovaze.

This is the first time you have had reason to accuse me of neglect, for tho' I have been at the Olovaze above a week, this is really the first time I have taken up my pen. All I can say is that had you been in my place, you would not yet have done it.

With what inexpressible pleasure do I again view the unaltered features of my lovely friend. Tho' the lily has far got the better of the rose, she is as beautiful as ever, nor can

---

* Parterres, that is, flower gardens.
† Craister Greatheed was a prominent attorney and politician of St. Christopher, comptroller of the customs and president of the council.

her mind be changed from time. I found in her the same warm affection and as amiable a friend as when we parted. A four years' separation had given us sufficient to say to each other; and would we have indulged our inclinations, we would not have permitted any interruption. But I found a new friend who claimed my attention in every respect—Mr Hamilton the husband of Lady Isabella and one of the most estimable of his sex. A woman never forgets the person of a man, and I assure you Mr Hamilton is well worth the painting. Let it however suffice to tell you that they are the best matched pair I ever saw: his masculine beauty not being inferior to her feminine. He is about twenty six or twenty seven, tall and elegantly made; his shape uncommonly easy, his complexion dark brown-nut, his eyes dark and penetrating, yet soft, his manners at once genteel and manly; far from giving way to pleasure and indolence, he applies with avidity to business. He has raised himself to the first employments and the first business on all the Islands as a Lawyer.

The elegance in which they live is not to be described, and whatever I have said of the table of Antigua is to be found here, even in a superior taste. Never was so agreeable a Landlady; she presides at her table with a degree of ease that gives every thing a double relish, nor does she leave you a wish unfulfilled. Tho' Mr Hamilton's temper has not in it the least levity, yet his conversation is extremely lively, and the brilliancy of Lady Bell's wit seems much improven, as she has it under a perfect command, and never says a thing to give offence. This was not the case when she first came amongst the folk here. She was more lively than what they were accustomed to, and they often mistook her Vivacity, which for sometime made her not so popular as she now is. When I first entered the great hall at the Olovaze, I was charmed with her appearance, but she gave me little time to contemplate that, till she flew into my Arms. Our joy was mutual, as is our affection. She had standing by her a little

Mulatto girl not above five years old, whom she retains as a
pet. This brown beauty was dressed out like an infant Sultana, and is a fine contrast to the delicate complexion of her
Lady. This hall and every thing in it is superbly fine; the
roof lofty, and ornamented in a high degree. It is between
fifty and sixty feet long, has eight windows and three doors
all glazed; it is finished in Mahogany very well wrought,
and the panels finished in with mirrors. This you would believe would render the heat unsupportable, which its situation however prevents, as it stands pretty high up Mount
Misery, which yields a cool and delightful shade to the
back part of the house, while the front has the sea, shipping,
town and a great part of the Island in prospect, and the constant sea-breeze renders it most agreeable. The drawing room
and bed-chambers are entirely fitted up and furnished in the
English taste, but tho' this is esteemed the finest house on
any of the Islands, yet it has a most inconvenient situation
for Mr Hamilton, as he is obliged to be in the court every
morning by seven o'clock, and toil all the day in his chambers, which are neither large nor airy. Besides as the way
from town up to Olovaze is steep and close, it destroys his
horses and fatigues himself in the heat, which he cannot
possibly avoid.

I found Miss Milliken waiting to meet me, and Lady
Isabella has engaged her to stay with us, while I am here. I
was very happy to see this sweet girl, but sorry to find her
health and spirits not what they were, when we were so much
together in Scotland. She introduced me to her friend Miss
Acres, a fine girl, who is soon to be married to a Scotchman*
she has long loved and been beloved by; but I fear their
felicity has been too long delayed to be now of long continu-
ance. She is certainly far gone in a consumption. Lady Bell
left Miss Rutherfurd when she was only a child, and as we

* The Scotchman was Mr. Houston, son of the Alexander Houston mentioned on page 133. Miss Akres was probably a daughter of Aretas Akers
of St. Kitts.

never measure time, she was charmed and surprized to find
her the woman she now is, both she and Mr Hamilton are
vastly fond of her, nor is she less pleased with them.

Crouds of company are here every day, whose visits we
shall return. My brother and Mr Hamilton are mutually
pleased with each other, and are never asunder; he goes down
with him every morning to town and is as much at home as
you can imagine, and intimate with every body. The great
sugar-works of the plantations are just by, and I have viewed
them with much attention. Mr Hughes, the Overseer, who is
a worthy obliging young man a great friend of Mr Hamilton's, has been so good as shew me the whole grand operation, which fabricates one of the prettiest branches of the
British trade. But I shall first finish the Olovaze and then
take a tour with you thro' the Island, and give you every
thing that pleases myself. But writing here, my friend, I
assure you is no easy task; for besides the heat which is great,
I grudge every moment that takes me from the company of
my friends. We live in constant fear of the arrival of our
ship, which will hurry us away, and we have not less than
twenty invitations, and we dance every night for several
hours, from which no person is exempted. All dance from
fifteen to four score, and we are to have a fine ball here a
few days hence, where the whole Island are to be.

I had a walk this morning, that you would hardly believe
me able to have taken, as it was no less than two miles, and
up hill. This was truly a British frolick, and what no creole
would ever dream of. The ascent however is not steep, and
we set off several hours before the sun rose to a high plantation where breakfast was provided for us. The first part of
the way was thro' cane pieces, which are just now in their
greatest glory; but tho' they excluded the sun, they also prevented the breeze from giving us air, and we were a good
deal incommoded, till we reached what is first called the
mountain, which is one of the greatest beauties in nature,

and I will take this opportunity to describe it. Properly speaking the whole Island forms its base, as the ascent begins from the sea and rises from all sides to the top. It is covered with canes for about the third of the way up, then with myrtles, tamarinds, oranges and fruits of various kinds. Above that is a great variety of trees, whose verdure is not inferior to those in Britain, and I am told the climate there approaches to cold; and that further up, the air is so cold, that those who have tried it, were instantly seized with plurisies, and this I can easily believe, for as we were a good deal warmed with walking, the sudden change was very perceptible, and I was shivering with cold all the time we were at breakfast.

I could not however forbear lengthening my walk, by taking a more particular survey of the mountain. My brother and I accordingly walked a good way up alongst one of the streams of water which comes down from it.* It was at present only a scanty rill, but by the appearance of its bed, is at times a large fall. It divides the mountain for a good way up, and resembles one of our highland burns; its source as well as the burns being on the top. But how different is the appearance of its banks, where every thing most beautiful in nature is mixed in delightful confusion. Oranges, limes, shadocks, cherries, citron, papa trees† are all at once covered with flowers and fruit; besides a profusion of vines and flowers out of Number we also saw cotton in plenty, which here is a shrub, as is Coffee. But they are generally raised in

---

* "There are three rivulets of excellent water which flow into the sea on the south west part of Saint Christopher" (Payne's "Answers to Queries"). Taking the island as a whole, however, there are many streams of varying size, the larger of which are called "rivers," the smaller "gutts" (Jeffrey's *West India Atlas*).

† "Papa trees," that is, the pawpaw or papaya tree, a palm-like tree bearing an oblong yellow fruit. "It has a slender and bare stem surmounted by a crown of large leaves, whose milky juice has marked digestive properties. The ripe fruit is a good substitute for the melon" (Aspinall, p. 115). Pawpaw trees are common in the United States, in the Middle West.

cultivated plantations, for tho' they are all indigenous, they are much the better of culture. I formerly said that the seasons were united, which is the case all over the Islands, and just now they are planting, reaping and bruising, in which I include distilling. But tho' perhaps there is no such rich land in the world as in this Island, they use manure in great abundance, and would be as glad of the rakes of Edinburgh streets as the Lothian farmers. No planter is above attending to this grand article, which is hoarded up with the utmost care, and I every where saw large dunghills of compound manure, composed of the ashes from the boiling kettle, the bruised canes, the spilt leaves of the cane, the cleaning of the houses and dung of the stables. These are turned up and kept till proper for use, and no infant cane is placed in its pit without a very sufficient quantity of this to bed and nurse it up.

The Negroes who are all in troops are sorted so as to match each other in size and strength. Every ten Negroes have a driver, who walks behind them, holding in his hand a short whip and a long one. You will too easily guess the use of these weapons; a circumstance of all others the most horrid. They are naked, male and female, down to the girdle, and you constantly observe where the application has been made. But however dreadful this must appear to a humane European, I will do the creoles the justice to say, they would be as averse to it as we are, could it be avoided, which has often been tried to no purpose. When one comes to be better acquainted with the nature of the Negroes, the horrour of it must wear off. It is the suffering of the human mind that constitutes the greatest misery of punishment, but with them it is merely corporeal. As to the brutes it inflicts no wound on their mind, whose Natures seem made to bear it, and whose sufferings are not attended with shame or pain beyond the present moment. When they are regularly Ranged, each has a little basket, which he carries up the hill filled with the manure and returns with a load of canes to the Mill. They go up at a trot, and return at a gallop, and did you not know the cruel necessity of this alertness, you would believe them the merriest people in the world.

Since I am on the chapter of Negroes feelings, I must tell you that I was some days ago in town, when a number for market came from on board a ship. They stood 'up to be looked at with perfect unconcern. The husband was to be divided from the wife, the infant from the mother; but the most perfect indifference ran thro' the whole. They were laughing and jumping, making faces at each other, and not caring a single farthing for their fate. This is not however without exception; and it behoves the planter to consider the country from whence he purchases his slaves; as those from one coast are mere brutes and fit only for the labour of the field, while those from another are bad field Negroes, but faithful handy house-servants. There are others who seem entirely formed for the mechanick arts, and these of all others are the most valuable; but want of attention to this has been the ruin of many plantations. Strange as it may seem, they are very nervous and subject to fits of madness. This is looked on as witchcraft by themselves, and there is a seer on every plantation to whom they have recourse when taken ill. They are also very subject to dropsies, by which they [the planters] lose many of their boilers, who are always the best slaves on the plantation.

To remedy this evil, as much as possible, the boiling houses are very high and lofty, covered with shelving boards that admit the air freely as well as give vent to the steam.*

---

* "The buildings, on a sugar plantation, consist of a wind or cattle mill (sometimes both), a boiling house, a curing house, a house for fermenting the liquor or wash, from which rum is distilled. The great house where the proprietor generally resides, the manager's house, houses for the overseers, store houses for grain, stock houses, and negroe huts. The negroe houses or huts are mostly built of stone, well thatched, and as dry and comfortable as any of that description in England" (*Brief Account*, pp. 85, 88). There is an excellent plan of a sugar plantation in Oliver, II, 308-309.

When one considers the heat that must be produced by four or five kettles which contain not less than a Hogshead apiece, and which requires a strong clear fire to boil the sugar to its proper consistence, it is very wonderful how they contrive to render them so sufferable as they are. Lady Isabella, Miss Rutherfurd and myself were in one of them last night above an hour, when they were boiling to their height, and were very little incommoded by the heat, and much entertained by being shown the process of this great work from the first throwing the canes into the mill to the casking the sugar and rum. But as Mr Hughes is so good as to promise to make it out for me in writing,‡ I will not attempt to give a description from myself from a few slight observations of a business that requires years of study to become perfect in. My Lady had another design, besides satisfying my curiosity in this visit to the boiling house. There were several of the boilers condemned to the lash, and seeing her face is pardon. Their gratitude on this occasion was the only instance of sensibility that I have observed in them. Their crime was the neglect of their own health which is indeed the greatest fault they can commit.

I have paid several visits both in town and country, and have been at church in the town, which tho' not so large nor indeed so magnificently fitted up as that at St John's, has an excellent organ and every thing necessary for the most solemn parts of the church of England-service. We had prayers decently and properly read and an excellent sermon from a Scotch Clergyman. Miss Milliken and her lovely friend were particularly devout, to which the state of health they are both in no doubt contributed, nor did they fail to have an effect on those within whose observation they were placed, even I myself found I could join with this church as a member, and was not to be present as a mere Spectator

‡ Unluckily lost. [But an excellent chapter on sugar-making may be found in Colonel Martin's *Essay upon Plantership*, III.]

when my heart was warmed. And I will venture to tell you, tho' you may laugh at me, that I was much pleased with the discovery I made of myself. For tho' the whole Island is divided into regular parishes, and each has a handsome church, yet there is not the semblance of presbytery, and much as I approve of it myself, 'tis not my talent to make proselytes.

The people in town live very well and are extremely polite and hospitable, as they are every where. The Stores are full of European commodities, and many of the merch[ts] very rich. They are a people I like vastly, and were there nothing to make me wish otherwise, I would desire to live for ever with them. But, oh, my friend! I again repeat that in the midst of these inchanting scenes and amongst a most agreeable people, I would prefer a habitation under a snow-cover'd mountain, were that habitation even a cottage. Do not suppose however that I repent, or in the least regret what I have done—that is far from the case. My heart approves my conduct and that merciful power who has guarded and supported me thro' numberless trials will at last reward that patience and fortitude he has himself inspired. At whatever time we meet, I am certain we will meet with unabated regard, and sufferings past are pleasant on recollection when properly supported. Should we meet no more in this world, what a transporting one will that in the next be, where what is now our misery will become our glory, and where care, anxiety and disappointment are no more. In the mean time I enjoy all the felicity that the friendship and affection of the kindest and best of brothers can give me, and again repeat that I am perfectly satisfied.

Miss Milliken and I took a long drive by ourselves yesterday, and after all I have seen I was surprised at the complete cultivation I met every where. The whole Island is a garden divided into different parterres. There is however a great want of shade, as every acre is under sugar. I mean as to the low plantations, for as to those up the hill, they have sufficient shade from the mountain. She shewed me several fine plantations belonging to Scotch people, who do not reside on them. Amongst these is one belonging to the Milli-kens. It is situated rather high, and goes by the name of Monkey Hill, from which I suppose it more particularly infested by those gentry, from which indeed no part of the Island is entirely free. As I am no enemy to the Pythagorean system,* I do suppose these lively and troublesome com-panions, [are the successors of] the former Inhabitants of this Island,† who you know were French, and truly the difference is so little between one Monkey and another, that the transmigration must have been very easy, and as to the soul, it has undergone no change, but is French in all respects. they grin, they laugh, they chatter and make grimaces. Their frolicks are mischievous, their thefts dextrous. They are subtle enemies and false friends. When pursued, they fly to the mountain and laugh at their pursuers, as they are as little ashamed of a defeat as a French admiral or

---

* Miss Schaw evidently had in mind that part of the Pythagorean system which concerns metempsychosis or the passing of the soul at death into an-other body, either human or animal. Something is wanting in the text here.

† The English colonized St. Christopher in 1623, the French in 1625. By mutual agreement they divided the island into four quarters, the French taking those at the ends, the English occupying those in the centre, with their headquarters at Old Road, Brimstone Hill, Sandy Point, and Palmetto Point. On the east, the French controlled Basseterre (later called by the British "Bastar") and the peninsula towards Nevis, where lay the salt ponds. These they shared with the English, the latter having a path to them through the French grounds. The two peoples lived amicably side by side until 1666, when the French seized the English quarters and only restored them when compelled to do so by the Treaty of Breda. In 1689 they again occupied the English sections, but were driven out in 1690 by Governor Codrington, the elder. The *status quo* was restored by the Treaty of Ryswick in 1697. At the beginning of the war of the Spanish Succession the younger Codrington drove the French completely out of the island, but in 1705-1706, the French fleet reversed the situation and inflicted so much damage upon the planters of St. Christopher and Nevis that parliament appropriated more than £100,000 to cover their losses. The islands were given to England at the Treaty of Utrecht, in 1713, and the French resigned permanently all their claims (For the earlier period see Higham, *Leeward Islands*, 1660-1688).

general. In short they are the torment of the planters; they
destroy whole cane-pieces in a few hours, and come in troops
from the mountain, whose trees afford them shelter. No
method to get the better of them has yet been found out. I
should think strong English dogs the best; as the English is
your only animal to humble your French monkey and settle
his frolicks.

Our Vessel is arrived, my sweet friend in tears, and every
body expressing such concern, that tho' they please my
vanity, they break my heart; but why are we thus disconso-
late? My dear friends, we will meet in a few weeks.* My
dear Miss Milliken says no; she is sure she will no more see
me, till we meet in a better world. Our meeting here was
most unexpected, and she says has beguiled the time like a
pleasing dream; but that now she wakes again to pain and
disappointment. She has taken care of all our paintings, and
my brother has ordered her the use of all his books. I begged
of her to copy those pieces of which she was always particularly fond, and also to let me find at my return some of those
views, which we have so much admired on this Island to
send home to you, to whom she is no stranger. She said she
would try, tho' she feigned she would not succeed, as she
believed her Genius was left in Britain; that even her musick
was not now what it had been, and her pencil had lost the
power of pleasing. Never indeed did I know any thing superior to her in both those Arts, but her taste is too delicate for
those who do not understand them. She has had several good
offers in the way of Marriage, which, however, she has declined. Born to a considerable fortune, and deprived of it by
the folly of a mother, after receiving an education suited to
it, she cannot stoop to be the wife of any one below her early
hope, but if God preserve her, I hope to see her yet happy.†

* Evidently Miss Schaw intended to return with her brother to St. Christopher after leaving the children with their father in North Carolina, though
it is not likely that she intended to remain there for any great length of time.
† The books are manifestly those which Miss Schaw was reading on ship-

Loads of provisions are coming from all quarters for our use: a hundred dozen of limes and oranges, Pine-apples, cocoa-nuts, etc., and my good friend Mrs Acres, an excellent old Lady, with whom I am quite enamoured, has sent in geese, ducks, Turkeys, etc., but this was needless, as the Olovaze had furnished stock for a much longer Voyage. Here is a cart load of Cocoa-nuts for Miss Durham; they are to be sent aboard with Capt Graham for Greenock.* Be so good as to order them with the sweet meats for your Sisters to be taken care of. We are now in Town, and are to embark this afternoon, and every thing but our own persons are on board. Capt Graham waits to take charge of the Packet. Oh thou envied paper! would I could inclose myself within you; my body I cannot, but there goes my soul in that, and that and that kiss.

Aboard the Rebecca of St Kitt's.

My last informed you of the arrival of our Ship and family from Antigua, and that we were to leave our friends

board and which had been brought by Alexander for his use on the ship and at St. Kitts. The reference to the paintings is obscure.

Miss Milliken may have formed a part of the social group in Edinburgh to which both Lady Belle and Miss Schaw belonged and may have shared with them in devotion to literature, painting, and music, accomplishments common to all ladies of quality at this period of Scottish history, when culture in the Athens of the North reached the fulness of its blossoming and exercised its maximum influence. Miss Milliken was probably connected with the Millikens of St. Christopher, possibly with Major James Milliken of "Monkey Hill" plantation (see map facing p. 120), an estate which is still known by that name. She cannot have been related to the "Young Millikin" mentioned on page 302, for the change of spelling indicates a different family. The reference to "a considerable fortune" of which she was deprived "by the folly of a mother" might furnish a clue to her identification, were it worth while to follow it up.

* Captain Daniel Graham was a merchant and sea captain, whose vessel, the *Spooner*, a ship of 200 tons, 16 men, built in Boston, 1765, and registered in Glasgow, 1767, made semiannual trips between Basseterre and Glasgow, carrying sugar and cotton and bringing back general merchandise. The vessel was owned by Alexander Houston & Co. of Glasgow. Captain Graham had a store at the head of Liverpool Row, Basseterre, where he sold dry goods, oatmeal, "jereboams and magnums" of claret, iron hoops and rivets, sad irons, etc. (*St. Christopher Gazette*, March 2, 1776).

at St Kitts and proceed to our American Vessel. As [it happened] next day we enjoyed our friends however a little longer from the most strange and unaccountable conduct in our former Captain, and for which we are yet unable to discover a cause; for no sooner were our provisions, Our Abigail and lap-dog got on board, than he weighed Anchor, set all his sail and went off before the wind, even while my brother aboard a boat was so near as to hail him. Whether Mrs Miller was betrayed herself into this affair, or chused to be the single Lady during this voyage will appear hereafter. In the mean time various circumstances give but an unfavourable idea of her conduct. We have however as yet no cause to regret their flight, as we were soon furnished by our friends with a Vessel from St Kitts, every way indeed the reverse of the Jamaica Packet, for besides that she is neat, clean and commodious, she is as slight as the other was strong, which in our present sailing signifies little; but should we meet a north wester on the coast of America; we will have no great reason to be proud of our light Vessel. At present we appear as on a party of pleasure; far as the eye can reach is one expanse of bright mirror, which reflects not only the sky over us, but even the shadow of our own Ship, which makes a most beautiful picture in the water. This, to be sure, is very fine for the present, but should the scene be deformed with billows, such as I have seen, Heaven, I hope, will take charge of us, as we will not owe our safety to men, the oldest of our sailors, whom we dignify with the title of the man, not being above seventeen and the rest of the crew made up of lovely boys much younger and fit only for such a sea as this. But should storms deform the face of this fair mirror, I fear the winds would pay little regard to youth and beauty, where strength and activity were missing. But we must hope [for] the best and in the meantime, the regularity of the whole renders our situation very agreeable.

The Capt gave us up the cabin and state room, which are

both very neat, and furnished with every necessary. In the State room we found a number of books. They consisted chiefly of Novels and poetry. By this you will guess the commander is not much in years more than his ship's crew, two or three and twenty I suppose, and the mate still younger. The Capt is handsome and genteel beyond what is generally found in those of his profession. He has an air of melancholy that interests one for him; he is often absent and sighs incessantly. The mate told us in confidence that the Captain had got himself so much in love that he was become good for nothing. The Lady is a fair American, and he is now on his way to see and he hopes marry her. For my own part, continued the mate, shruging significantly—but every man to his mind, all's one to me; to be sure I wish him well; but a man's girl, do ye see, is not to be spoke of. No, no, none of your bundlers a' faith for me, a good Scotch lassie for my money. From these hints I fear poor [Captain] Setter has not made a very discreet choice, but as the mate says, every man to his mind.

As we have no Abigail, a fine boy about twelve years old is appointed to the office of our chamber-maid. He is neat, handy and obliging. We make much of the little fellow, and he is quite happy. He has a fine voice and often entertains us with it. In a few hours after we left St Kitts, we landed on St Eustatia,‡ a free port, which belongs to the Dutch; a place of vast traffick from every quarter of the globe.* The ships of various nations which rode before it were very fine, but

---

‡ The Governor to whom we had letters died the day we arrived.

---

* St. Eustatius is a small rocky island, which Henry Laurens once called "that small speck in the ocean," lying but eight miles northwest of St. Christopher, in area somewhat less than seven square miles. It was at this time an open port, free to the commerce of all nations, and hence a flourishing centre of trade, legitimate and illegitimate. The governor who passed away on the day the party arrived was Jan de Windt, 1753-1775, who died on January 19 (*Nouvelles Extraordinaires de Divers Endroits*, commonly called *Gazette de Leyde*, 1775, no. 126, March 31, 1775, p. 4). "On a appris aussi par les Lettres de St. Eustache en date du 20 Janvier, que Mr. Jan de

the Island itself the only ugly one I have seen. Nor do I think that I would stay on it for any bribe. It is however an instance of Dutch industry little inferior to their dykes; as the one half of the town is gained off the Sea, which is fenced out by Barracadoes, and the other dug out of an immense mountain of sand and rock; which rises to a great height behind the houses, and will one day bury them under it. On the top of this hill I saw some decent-looking houses, but was not able to mount it, to look at them nearer. I understand however that the whole riches of the Island consist in its merchandize, and that they are obliged to the neighbouring Islands for subsistence; while they in return furnish them with contraband commodities of all kinds. The town consists of one street a mile long, but very narrow and most disagreeable, as every one smokes tobacco, and the whiffs are constantly blown in your face.

But never did I meet with such variety; here was a merch[t] vending his goods in Dutch, another in French, a third in Spanish, etc. etc. They all wear the habit of their country, and the diversity is really amusing. The first that welcomed us ashore were a set of Jews. As I had never seen a Jew in his habit, except M[r] Diggs in the character of Shylock,* I could not look on the wretches without shuddering. But I was shown two objects that set Christian cruelty in a worse light, than I could have believed it possible. The one, a wretch discovered to be innocent of a crime laid to his charge. While he was stretched on the wheel and under the hands of the executioner, he was taken down with hardly a joint in

Windt, Commandant de cette Isle et des Isles adjacentes de Saba et St. Martin, y étoit mort la veille." We are indebted to Dr. J. Franklin Jameson for this extract.

* West Digges, the actor, 1720-1786, paid frequent visits to Edinburgh, acting there as early as 1756, and Miss Schaw might well have seen him at any time after that date. She is probably referring to the same person on page 94, where she speaks of "Digges worshipping in the Temple of the Sun." There is a brief account of his career in the *Dictionary of National Biography*.

its place, yet the miserable life still remained. He was banished France, as the sight of him was a reproach. He has both his hands and one of his feet fallen off since he came to St Eustatia, where he is treated with much humanity and pity. The other is a man who was eighteen months in the Spanish inquisition, and was tortured till he has hardly the semblance of a human creature remaining. The infernal accuser at last appeared and declared he had mistaken him, for he was not the person they meant, and brought the other to them. As he seemed quite out of his senses, they did not chuse to murder him, but turned him out in the dead of night to the street, where he was found by some Dutch sailors, who being convinced of the truth of his story, and certain that he would either be remanded back to his dreadful prison or immediately murdered, had the humanity to carry him aboard their ship, where their care restored his senses and memory, and they brought him here, where he remains. I was assured of the truth of both these stories by many of the most respectable people of the town, by whose charity they are supported.

From one end of the town of Eustatia to the other is a continued mart, where goods of the most different uses and qualities are displayed before the shop-doors. Here hang rich embroideries, painted silks, flowered Muslins, with all the Manufactures of the Indies. Just by hang Sailor's Jackets, trousers, shoes, hats etc. Next stall contains most exquisite silver plate, the most beautiful indeed I ever saw, and close by these iron-pots, kettles and shovels. Perhaps the next presents you with French and English Millinary-wares. But it were endless to enumerate the variety of merchandize in such a place, for in every store you find every thing, be their qualities ever so opposite. I bought a quantity of excellent French gloves for fourteen pence a pair, also English thread-stockings cheaper than I could buy them at home. I was indeed surprised to find that the case with most of the British manufactures, but am told the merch^{ts} who export them have a large drawback.

We were treated with great hospitality at this place, but they have nothing of the gentility of the neighbouring Islands. I slept or rather lay two nights under the hill, which seemed to threaten me every moment from its Neighbourhood, and the Musquatoes [mosquitos] too are very hearty and strong, so that we had enough of amusement to keep us from sleep, and were not a little pleased to get aboard the Rebecca again. We purchased excellent claret for less than two shillings a bottle, and Portuguese wines of different kinds very cheap. Robt too, who never forgets the table, made several purchases of pickles and sweet meats extremely fine and very cheap. I assure you that by his care and the alertness of a cook that has not yet reached fourteen years old, we live very much at our ease upon four or five good things and well dressed every day, besides a desert of fruits. The Captain does every thing to oblige us and render his vessel agreeable to his passengers, and tho' the sea is quite calm, he makes the ship lie to while we are at meals, so that we eat without the least inconvenience from the motion of the ship; a very agreeable circumstance I do assure you. But these are considerations, that you people who live at home in ease never can properly understand.

As we had not been suffered to provide or put on board any thing for ourselves, I was curious to know what our Sea Store consisted of, and begged the Capt to let me look thro' the Ship, as I had no opportunity of doing so on my former Voyage. This was immediately agreed to, and both Miss Rutherfurd and I were surprised at the neatness of every thing we saw. But what pleased us above all the others was the care that was taken to secure the live-stock in such a way as to keep them safe even in the worst weather, the want of which we had severely suffered for in the Jamaica Packet. This is a place paled in between decks in which were geese, pigs, Turkeys, and sheep. The water too was placed as cool as possible, and that to be used in the cabin was prepared by a filtering stone, such as I formerly described in the Islands. You will think me very attentive to such circumstances; but nothing is of more consequence at Sea both to pleasure and to health.

We had a sheep killed yesterday, and have had a Scotch dinner under the Tropick in the middle of the Atlantick. We eat haggis, sheep-head, barley-broth and blood puddings. As both our Capt and Mate are Scots, tho' long from home, they swore they had not seen such an excellent dinner since they left their native land. We have never yet had a breeze sufficient to curl the Sea, and I really wonder how we move along. Our sails hang like a Lady's loose gown in the most languishing manner, and our poor Capt sighs ready to break his heart at the slow advance he makes to the port that contains his wishes. However he tried to amuse himself. He and my brother are just now gone in the boat a shooting. I see them from where I am writing, it is really pretty to see the little vessel moving on the smooth surface of that vast ocean, a perfect world of water. They are just returned and have been very successful; but the greatest entertainment they have had, was painting the Ship on the outside. Our mate who is really a man of taste, hath ornamented her with many festoons of flowers and various figures very neatly. But only think of the softness of our sailing, when he can row round her for hours and hold the pots of paint in one hand, while he uses the brush with the other.

Our life is so uniformly calm, and placid, that we are glad to meet any thing, that has the air of an Adventure to vary the Scene, and which yesterday afforded Jack Rutherfurd, (who is continually on the look out, and to say the truth, has more observations than we have all,) the sight of somewhat floating on the water, but at such a distance that he could only see it was very long, and from that concluded it might be a boat belonging to some Vessel. All the glasses were presently out, and as every body observed it, various conjectures were formed. In a moment it was a wreck, it was a whale, it was an island. For my part I liked the wreck best, as it was likely to afford most entertainment. The Captain however ended all disputes by sending off the boat, which soon returned loaded with fishes, and brought us certain advice that it was a tree of immense size, blown off the American coast, and which had lain on the water, till covered over with barnacles, and round which fishes of all kinds crouded, so that they had only to put over their hands and bring them into the boat. All hands were now pressing to go. The Capt, my brother and the Rutherfurds got presently into the boat, and the Captain ordered the ship to bear down to it, that we might share in the sport. The expedition had almost proved a fatal one however, for two of our youthful sailors landing on Log-island, as they named it, tumbled over, and were very near becoming the prey of a Shark, which lurked hard by it. They were fortunately saved, and no more attempts were made to land. They brought on board a surprising quantity of fish, but all flat, of the turbot and flounder kind, and some, I am sure, are the same with our Soles. We have many alive in tubs filled with Sea water; a great number are salted, and hung amongst the shrouds by the lads for their own use. We had at first some little objection to eating them, as the fishes of these seas are at a certain season unwholesome, and some are even poison; but this is owing to their being near Copper Islands, which is not the present case. A dollar was put in the kettle with them; it came out pure, and all was safe, and our young cook and Robt dress them nicely, and they are truly good.

Last night the air changed, and tho' the wind did not in the least increase, yet it became very chilly on deck, and this morning is so cold, that we are not able to leave the Cabin. I plainly find we are out of the warm climates, and fast approaching the coast of America. I am sick at heart, my spirits fail me, but I will not give way to resentment. We are now actually on the American coast, and it is so cold that I am not able to go on deck, tho' the Capt invites me to view the woods, as he assures me, they are in sight. I can hardly hold the pen, I left June and found December.

At last America is in my view; a dreary Waste of white barren sand, and melancholy, nodding pines. In the course of many miles, no cheerful cottage has blest my eyes. All seems dreary, savage and desert; and was it for this that such sums of money, such streams of British blood have been lavished away? Oh, thou dear land, how dearly hast thou purchased this habitation for bears and wolves. Dearly has it been purchased, and at a price far dearer still will it be kept. My heart dies within me, while I view it, and I am glad of an interruption by the arrival of a pilot-boat, the master of which appears a worthy inhabitant of the woods before us. "Pray, Sir," said I to him, "does any body live hereabouts?" "Hereabouts," returned he in a surly tone, "don't you see how thick it is settled." He then pointed with his finger to a vast distance, and after some time, I really did observe a spot that seemed to be cut amongst the woods, and fancied that I saw something that resembled smoke. On this acknowledgment, he answered with a sort of triumph, "Ay, ay, I told you so, that there is Snow's plantation, and look ye there; don't you see another? Why sure you are blind, it is not above five miles off." I confessed I was short-sighted at least, for I really did not see it, and as he was now attending the casting the lead and reckoning our soundings, I troubled him with no more questions, but retired to the Cabin, not much elated with what I had seen.*

---

* Miss Schaw and her party had now entered the Cape Fear River and were approaching the town of Brunswick, after a voyage of twenty-four days. When the captain pointed out Snow's plantation, they must have been in the river channel, nearly opposite Fort Johnston, for the plantation lay about half way between Brunswick and the fort, on the northern side of

We are now opposite to the fort* which guards this coast, and the Capt has gone to it to show his credentials and pay certain fees which constitute the salary of an officer, who is called Governor.† In figure and size this fort resembles a Leith timber-bush, but does not appear quite so tremendous, tho' I see guns peeping thro' the sticks. If these are our fortresses and castles, no wonder the Natives rebel; for I will be bound to take this fort with a regim^t of black-guard Edinburgh boys without any artillery, but their own pop-guns. I now write on shore, but will finish my journal of the Rebecca, before I say any thing of my present situation here.

I told you the Capt had gone to the fort, but forgot to tell you there is an old sloop of war that lies here,‡ which, like

Snow's Creek, Sturgeon's Point, the terminus of the road running north on that side of the river. It is shown on Jeffrey's map in *The American Atlas* and on Collet's map printed in 1770. Its owner is referred to in the following entry from the Brunswick records of date 1766. "As Robert Snow and his now wife find it impossible to live together with that harmony which the married state requires and have therefore for their mutual ease agreed to relax as far as they can that obligation which they cannot totally dissolve," they enter into a formal indenture as to the division of the property (Brunswick County Records, Book A, Wills, Conveyances, and Inventories, pp. 67, 69). Snow was a church warden of St. Philip's; hence a separation rather than a divorce.

* The fort, of which Miss Schaw speaks with so little respect, was Fort Johnston, eleven miles from the mouth of the river. It was built of "tapia," consisting of equal parts of lime, raw oyster shells, sand, and water, forming a paste or "batter," as the negroes called it, which was poured into boxes, much as liquid concrete or cement is poured today. The fort was constructed in 1740 and rebuilt in 1764, with a wall of tapia and a lower battery and fosse (*North Carolina Records*, VI, 1028, 1099, 1183). Governor Tryon, in commenting on its condition in 1766, said: "The proportions observed in the construction are as miserable as are the materials with which it is built. There is so great a proportion of sand that every gun fired brings down some of the parapet. I think the fort a disgrace to the ordnance his Majesty has placed in it" (*ib.*, VII, 246). Compare Dobbs's statements, 1754 (*ib.*, V, 158), 1756 (*ib.*, V, 595), 1761 ("Answers to Queries," *ib.*, VI, 614-615).

† The reference here is not to the governor of the province but to the governor of the fort, at this time Captain John Collet. Captain Seater on passing the fort would have to pay five shillings, a perquisite that went to the officer in command, "for giving the masters of vessels their product bill" (*North Carolina Records*, VII, 249).

‡ The *Cruizer.*

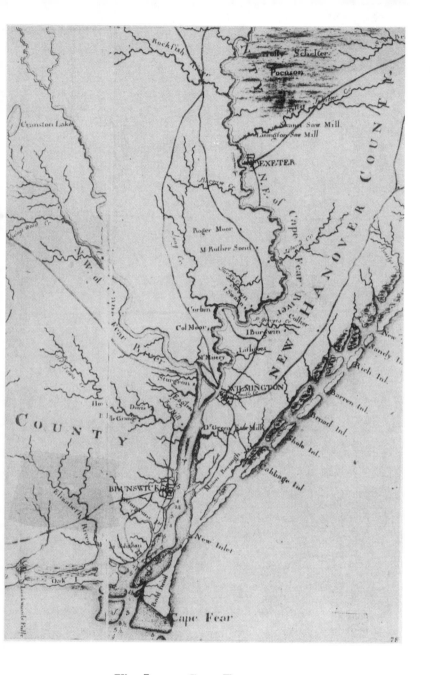

The Lower Cape Fear: 1770.

From John Collet's manuscript map of North Carolina
in the British Museum.

the log before commemorated, has lain till all covered over
with barnacles. From this vessel an officer came alongst with
our Captain to view our men.* But as we had in fact but
one man,‡ we had hid him with great care under the bed of
our state-room, and stuffed round him all the dirty linens
which were not few, so that the situation of Sir John Falstaff
in his buck-basket was airy, when compared to that of this
poor Sailor, and which was rendered unsupportable by the
politeness of the officer, who absolutely refused to enter our
apartment, but sat down in the cabin with us, and seemed
so much pleased with his company that he showed not the
least design to leave us. He had drank enough to render him
very loquacious, and we not only had the history of Carolina,
but of himself, and the very officers aboard the sloop, on
which he dwelt so long, that I made not the least doubt, but
the poor devil under the bed would be smothered, and was
ready to die myself with apprehension. At last we found the
only way to get quit of him was to go with him, leaving
Robert† to deliver the poor prisoner, who, I dare Swear, will
not soon wish for the honour of being hid in a Lady's bed-
chamber. Adieu, yours by sea and land.

‡ He had deserted from the Sloop.

* Evidently the lieutenant from the *Cruizer* was on the hunt for deserters
or else was engaged in impressing men for the royal navy.

† This is the last mention of Alexander's Indian servant, Robert. Where
he was from this time until Alexander sailed for England in July we do not
know. Probably he returned to England with his master.

CHAPTER III.

Residence in North Carolina.

Brunswick.*

WE got safe on shore,† and tho' quite dark landed from the boat with little trouble, and proceeded thro' rows of tar and pitch to the house of a merch^t, to whom we had been recommended.‡ He received us in a hall, which tho' not very orderly, had a cheerful look, to which a large carron stove‖

* Except for the ruins of St. Philip's Church and a few disinterred fragments, the town of Brunswick has today entirely disappeared and the site is included within the boundaries of Orton plantation. See Appendix IV.

† In Appendix V is printed Alexander Schaw's description of North Carolina, written in London and dated the October after his arrival in 1775. It supplements his sister's account written in quite a different vein.

‡ One of the most agreeable incidents connected with the editing of Miss Schaw's journal has been the discovery of the exact entries of the arrival of the *Jamaica Packet* and the *Rebecca*, in an old Brunswick customs book of entrances and clearances kept by William Dry, the collector. This book, containing the entrances from 1773 to July, 1775, and the clearances from 1763 to 1775, was discovered by Mr. James Sprunt of Wilmington, "in the ruins of a house, said to have been the residence of Nathaniel Rice," and is now in his possession. We are greatly indebted to Mr. Sprunt for the privilege of examining this sadly mutilated but invaluable manuscript. The entries are as follows:

"January 31, 1775, Jamaica Packet, Thomas Smith Captain, Brig, 80 tons, no guns, 8 men, built in Mass. 1772, registered Kirkaldy, 22 Oct. 1774, George Parker owner, ballast from Antigua, [signed] Thos Smith."

"February 14, 1775, Rebecca, Hugh Seater, Brig, 50 tons, no guns, 6 men, built in Mass. 1764, registered Basseterre, 29 Dec. 1774, Richard Quince owner, ballast, from St. Kitts." This entry is not signed, but one later, of July 2, 1775, when the *Rebecca* returned from another voyage to St. Kitts, bringing sugar and rum, is signed "Hugh Seater."

‖ A Carron stove was one made at the Carron Iron Works on the Carron River in Stirlingshire, Scotland. The works were started in 1760 and are

Entries of the *Jamaica Packet* and the *Rebecca*
in the old Register kept by William Dry.

filled with Scotch coals not a little contributed. The night was bitterly cold, and we gathered round the hearth with great satisfaction, and the Master of the house gave us a hospitable welcome. This place is called Brunswick, and tho' the best sea port in the province, the town is very poor— a few scattered houses on the edge of the woods, without street or regularity. These are inhabited by merchants, of whom Mr Quense [Quince]* our host is the first in consequence. He is deeply engaged in the new system of politicks, in which they are all more or less, tho' Mr Dry,† the collector of the customs, is the most zealous and talks treason by the hour. The arrival to day of my brother Bob‡ and Mr Murray‖ of Philiphaugh gives us great pleasure. Bob is really a handsome fellow. I did not know how much I was complimented, when told I was like him. Mr Rutherfurd is some hundred miles up the country, so it will be several weeks before he hears his children are arrived, which is no small disappointment to them.

We have found our Captain with his Vessel here before us. Mrs Miller is up at my brothers. It turns out that the Capt left St Kitts in a drunken fit, in which he fancied he was affronted by the Capt of the king's yacht. As to Mary, I will take her innocence for granted, for fear it turn out otherwise; in which case I would be much at a loss, for what can I do with a poor creature in this strange land, I must and will take care of her, tho' God knows her conduct does not en-

---

described by the traveller Pennant, who visited them in 1769, as "the greatest of their kind in Europe," employing 1200 men (Hume Brown, *Surveys of Scottish History*, p. 113). The name "Carronade" for a piece of ordnance comes from the same source.

* Richard Quince would naturally be Miss Schaw's first host, as he was the owner of the *Rebecca*, the vessel upon which she had just arrived. For his biography, see Appendix XI.

† For William Dry, see Appendix XI.

‡ For Miss Schaw's brother Robert, see page 21, note, and for additional details, Appendix XII.

‖ For the career of James Murray, see Appendix VIII.

courage me. The Captain knows his fate is in my brothers hand, who, I make no doubt, will forgive him, and meet with as ungrateful a return as possible.

Schawfield March 22ᵈ 1775.

We have been these three or four days here, but this is the first time it has been in my power to write, but I have now sat down to bring up my Journal from leaving Brunswick;* which we did last Friday, under the care of a Mʳ Eagle,† a young Gentleman just returned from England and who owns a very considerable estate in this province. The two brothers were to follow and be up with us in a few miles, which however they did not. We were in a Phaeton and four belonging to my brother, and as the roads are entirely level, drove on at good speed, our guide keeping by us and several Negro servants attending on horse back. During the first few miles, I was charmed with the woods. The wild fruit trees are in full blossom; the ground under them covered with verdure and intermixed with flowers of various kinds made a pleasing Scene. But by and by it begins to grow dark, and as the idea of being benighted in the wilds of America was not a pleasing circumstance to an European female, I begged the servant to drive faster, but was told it would make little difference, as we must be many hours dark, before we could get clear of the woods, nor were our fears decreased by the stories Mʳ Eagle told us of the wolves and bears that inhabited that part of the country.

Terrified at last almost to Agony, we begged to be carried

---

* Miss Schaw, according to the chronology of the narrative, remained at Brunswick from February 14 to March 17, and it is therefore strange that she should have given us no account of her life there. Possibly portions of the narrative have been lost. All we know of the month's experience is that during that time Miss Schaw was without a "dish of tea," a fact that may have political significance in view of the anti-British attitude of the provincial group which lived at Brunswick.

† For Joseph Eagles, see Appendix XI.

to some house to wait for day-light, but we had drove at least two miles in that situation before Mr Eagle recollected that a poor man had a very poor plantation at no great distance, if we could put up with it and venture to go off the road amongst the trees. This was not an agreeable proposition; however it was agreed to, and we soon found ourselves lost in the most impenetrable darkness, from which we could neither see sky, nor distinguish a single object. We had not gone far in this frightful state, when we found the carriage stopt by trees fallen across the road, and were forced to dismount and proceed thro' this dreary scene on foot. All I had ever heard of lions, bears, tigers and wolves now rushed on my memory, and I secretly wished I had been made a feast to the fishes rather than to those monsters of the woods. With these thoughts in my head, I happened to slip my foot, and down I went and made no doubt I was sinking into the centre of the earth. It was not quite so deep however, for with little trouble Mr Eagle got me safe up, and in a few minutes we came to an opening that showed us the sky and stars, which was a happy sight in our circumstances.

The carriage soon came up, and we again got into it. I now observed that the road was inclosed on both sides, and on the first turning the carriage made, we found ourselves in front of a large house from the windows of which beamed many cheerful tapers, and no sooner were we come up to the gate than a number of black servants came out with lights. Mr Eagle dismounted, and was ready to assist us, and now welcomed us to his house and owned that the whole was a plan only to get us to it, as he feared we might have made some objections; he having no Lady to receive us. I had a great mind to have been angry, but was too happy to find myself safe, and every thing comfortable. We found the Tea-table set forth, and for the first time since our arrival in America had a dish of Tea. We passed the evening very agreeably, and by breakfast next morning, the two brothers joined us. Mr Eagle was my brother Bob's ward, and is a most amiable young man. We stayed all the forenoon with him, saw his rice mills, his indigo works and timber mills. The vast command they have of water makes those works easily conducted. Before I leave the country, I will get myself instructed in the nature of them, as well as the method of making the tar and turpentine, but at present I know not enough of them to attempt a description.

We got to Schawfield* to dinner, which is indeed a fine plantation, and in the course of a few years will turn out such an estate, as will enable its master to visit his native land, if his wife who is an American will permit him, which I doubt. This plantation is prettily situated on the northwest branch of the river Cape Fear. Every thing is on a large Scale, and these two great branches of water come down northeast and northwest, and join at Wilmingtown. They are not less in breadth than the Tay at Newbrugh, and navigable up a vast way for ships of pretty large burthen.

Mr Eagle, who is still here, appears every day more worthy of esteem. He is not yet Major, yet has more knowl-

---

* "Schawfield" or "Sauchie," as it was sometimes called by its owner, Robert Schaw, Miss Schaw's elder brother, was situated on the southwestern side of the Northwest branch, but a few miles above Wilmington. The northern part of the plantation was bought of James Moore and Ann his wife in 1772 and covered an area of 500 acres. The following is a description of that part of the property: "Beginning at the mouth of Indian Creek running up the river to the lower line of a tract or parcel of land, containing 500 acres, conveyed by deed to George Moore, Sr. by Maurice Moore, Jr. by Maurice Moore dec'd, thence west 400 poles thence south 80 poles to Indian Creek to the first station." The plantation also contained another tract of 400 acres, purchased by Robert Schaw of Benjamin Stone, shipwright, June 19, 1773, "beginning at a stake at an elbow on the old northwest road leading from Mt. Misery ferry, running along the lower side of said road south 15 degrees west 14 poles, thence along the said road 88 degrees west 120 poles, thence north 65 degrees west to back or westernmost line of the aforesaid lands, thence along the said line north to Indian Creek, then down the various courses of said creek to the mouth, then down the NW River to the first station" (Brunswick County Records, Conveyances, B, 300). Thus Indian Creek, the first creek above Mt. Misery on the other side of the river, ran through the middle of the plantation, which lay between the old northwest road and the river.

edge than most men I have met with at any age. He left his country a child, and is just returned, so is entirely English, as his father and mother were both of that part of our Island and his relations all there. He very justly considers England as the terrestrial paradise and proposes to return, as soon as he is of age. I would fain hope his good sense will prevent his joining in schemes, which I see plainly are forming here, and which I fear you at home are suffering to gain too much ground from mistaken mercy to a people, who have a rooted hatred at you and despise your mercy, which they View in a very different light. We have an invitation to a ball in Wilmingtown, and will go down to it some day soon. This is the last that is to be given, as the congress has forbid every kind of diversion, even card-playing.*

This morning a fine wood was set on fire just by us, and tho' I was informed of the reason and necessity of it, yet I could not look at it without horror; before it could be extinguished twenty thousand trees at least must have been burnt. I wish you had them and the ground they stand on. We had yesterday a curious tho' a frightful diversion. On a visit down the river, an Alligator was observed asleep on the bank. Mrs Schaw was the first who saw it, and as she is a notable house-wife was fired with revenge at the loss of many a good goose they have stolen from her. We crept up as softly as possible hardly allowing the oars to touch the water, and were so successful as to land part of the Negroes before it

---

* According to clause eight of the Continental Association, adopted by the Continental Congress, October 20, 1774, all "expensive diversions and entertainments" were discountenanced and discouraged (*Journals of Congress*, I, 78). Acting upon this recommendation, the Wilmington Committee of Safety, on January 28, 1775, resolved "that Balls and Dancing at Public Houses are contrary to the Resolves of the General Congress" (*North Carolina Records*, IX, 1118), and on March 1 warned a Mrs. Austin of the town to withdraw the plans made for a ball at her house (*ib.*, 1136). A few days later the same committee issued a general warning, declaring as its opinion "that all persons concerned in any dances for the future should be properly stigmatised" (*ib.*, 1150). The ball to which Miss Schaw refers was to be given after this last warning, perhaps by some arrangement with the Committee of Safety.

waked, which it did not do till all was ready for the attack. Two of the Negroes armed with strong oars stood ready, while a third hit him a violent blow on the eye, with which he awaked and extended such a pair of jaws as might have admitted if not a Highland cow, at least a Lowland calf. The negroes who are very dextrous at this work, presently pushed the oars down his throat, by which means he was secured, [but not] till he received thousands of blows which did him no harm, as he is covered with a coat of Mail, so strong and compact, that he is vulnerable no where but in the eye, and a very small opening under the throat and belly. His tail is long and flexible, and so are his huge arms. With these he endeavoured to catch at his assassins, but the superior arts of man are more than a match for his amazing strength. Was superior reason never used to a more unworthy purpose it were well; for he is a daring Villain, an insolent robber, who makes war on the whole animal creation, but does not man do the same? Even worse, for this monster does not devour his fellow-monsters.

But let me proceed to his destruction, which was not accomplished with ease, and had he had his full strength, it is my opinion, he would have baffled all our arts. But they are one of the sleepers and retire into the swamps during the winter, from which this one had come earlier than common, and not having had breakfast after his five months nap he was too weak to make the resistance he would otherwise have done. He is indeed a frightful animal of which a lizard is the miniature, and if you can raise a Lizard in your imagination fifteen foot in length with arms at least six feet and these armed at the end with hands and claws resembling the talons of the eagle and clothe all with a flexible coat of mail, such as is worn on the back of a Sturgeon; if you have strength of imagination for this, you have our Alligator, which was at last overcome by pushing out his eyes and thursting a long knife into his throat. After all I could not see this without horror and even something that at least resembled compassion. The sight joined to the strong smell of musk that came from him made me sick, and I was very glad when they left him and pushed the boat from the shore, out of which by the bye neither Miss Rutherfurd nor I landed during the execution which seemed excellent sport to every one else, even to my tender-hearted brother.*

I have now been above a month in this country, and have not lost a day in endeavouring to find out something or another worth your attention, tho' I am far from being certain of my success. Yet I am sure if you was on the spot, you would not be one hour without something to engage your curiosity or amuse your fancy, which is the case with your friend. I never saw so general and so extensive a genius as he [Joseph Eagles] is possessed of. Trees, plants, flowers and all the vegetable world fall under his particular observation: nor is inanimated nature his only study. The animal creation from the small reptile up to what is here dignified with the title of man engages his attention, and if I am happy enough to afford you any entertainment, you may thank him for it, as it is he who points out to me a thousand objects that I should overlook. He makes me walk with him for hours in the surrounding woods, which indeed are full of subjects to amuse the mind and please the fancy of such as have the least pretensions to taste or curiosity, and it is impossible to converse with him, and not gain a degree of both.

I think I have read all the descriptions that have been published of America, yet meet every moment with something I never read or heard of. I must particularly observe that the trees every where are covered over with a black veil of a

---

* There was an Alligator Creek on Eagles Island, but apparently Miss Schaw's alligator hunt was in the Northwest branch of the Cape Fear. Hugh Meredith, in his account of the Cape Fear section, contributed to the *Pennsylvania Gazette*, May 6-13, 1731, says, "Alligators are very numerous here, but not very mischievous; however, on their account swimming is less practos'd here than in the northern provinces."

most uncommon substance, which I am however at a loss to describe. It is more like sea weed than any vegetable I ever saw, but is quite black and is a continued web from top to bottom of the tallest trees and would be down to the ground, were it not eat up by the cattle. But as it is full of juice and very sweet, they exert their whole strength to obtain it, in which they receive no assistance from their Masters, tho' they own it is excellent feeding, but they are too indolent to take any trouble, and the cattle must provide for themselves or starve.* The women however gather it at a certain season, lay it in pits as we do our green lint, till the husk rot. It is made up of small tubes, within each of which is a substance, which exactly resembles that of the baken hair with which we stuff chairs, matrasses, etc, etc. and which answers pretty well with a very little trouble and no cost.

The trees that keep clear from this black moss (as it is called) are crowned with the Mistletoe in much higher perfection than ever you saw it, and as it is just now in berry looks beautiful. Indeed all the trees do so at this Season. The wild fruits are in blossom and have a fine effect amongst the forest-trees. Amongst the various trees that grow here, none seems so fit for the Cabinet maker's use as the red Mulberry. Its colour is infinitely more beautiful than the mahogany and it is so hard and close as to resist vermine, and grows large enough to afford planks of any size, yet it is only used to burn or for the most common purposes. It grows spontaneously every where, and the White Mulberry is also found in every place, which points out that the making of silk in this part of the country could be done with great ease.

---

* "As far as cattle and stock are concerned, it is purely their care to see to it how they get through the winter; with horses it is no better. If they survive it, they survive it. Hay they have none for there are no meadows and corn fodder and tops do not go far. Thus in winter the people have no milk at all, and when spring comes the cows are so nearly starved out as to be of little benefit till harvest. This may be the reason that their horses are not much larger than English colts, and their cows the size of their yearlings" (Diary of Bishop Spangenburg, 1752, *North Carolina Records*, V, 2).

But tho' I may say of this place what I formerly did of the West India Islands, that nature holds out to them every thing that can contribute to conveniency, or tempt to luxury, yet the inhabitants resist both, and if they can raise as much corn and pork, as to subsist them in the most slovenly manner, they ask no more; and as a very small proportion of their time serves for that purpose, the rest is spent in sauntering thro' the woods with a gun or sitting under a rustick shade, drinking New England rum made into grog, the most shocking liquor you can imagine. By this manner of living, their blood is spoil'd and rendered thin beyond all proportion, so that it is constantly on the fret like bad small beer, and hence the constant slow fevers that wear down their constitutions, relax their nerves and infeeble the whole frame. Their appearance is in every respect the reverse of that which gives the idea of strength and vigor, and for which the British peasantry are so remarkable. They are tall and lean, with short waists and long limbs, sallow complexions and languid eyes, when not inflamed by spirits. Their feet are flat, their joints loose and their walk uneven. These I speak of are only the peasantry of this country, as hitherto I have seen nothing else, but I make no doubt when I come to see the better sort, they will be far from this description. For tho' there is a most disgusting equality, yet I hope to find an American Gentleman a very different creature from an American clown. Heaven forefend else.

Wilmingtown.*

I have been in town a few days, and have had an opportunity to make some little observations on the manners of a people so new to me. The ball I mentioned was intended as a civility, therefore I will not criticize it, and tho' I have not

* For Wilmington, see accompanying plan and the description in Appendix VI.

the same reason to spare the company, yet I will not fatigue
you with a description, which however lively or just, would
at best resemble a Dutch picture, where the injudicious
choice of the subject destroys the merit of the painting. Let
it suffice to say that a ball we had, where were dresses, dancing and ceremonies laughable enough, but there was no
object on which my own ridicule fixed equal to myself and
the figure I made, dressed out in all my British airs with a
high head and a hoop and trudging thro' the unpaved streets
in embroidered shoes by the light of a lanthorn carried by a
black wench half naked. No chair, no carriage—good leather
shoes need none. The ridicule was the silk shoes in such a
place. I have however gained some most amiable and agreeable acquaintances amongst the Ladies; many of whom
would make a figure in any part of the world, and I will not
fail to cultivate their esteem, as they appear worthy of mine.

I am sorry to say, however, that I have met with few of
the men who are natives of the country, who rise much above
my former description, and as their natural ferocity is now
inflamed by the fury of an ignorant zeal, they are of that
sort of figure, that I cannot look at them without connecting
the idea of tar and feather. Tho' they have fine women and
such as might inspire any man with sentiments that do
honour to humanity, yet they know no such nice distinctions,
and in this at least are real patriots. As the population of the
country is all the view they have in what they call love, and
tho' they often honour their black wenches with their attention, I sincerely believe they are excited to that crime by no
other desire or motive but that of adding to the number of
their slaves.

The difference between the men and the women surprised
me, but a sensible man, who has long resided here, in some
degrees accounted for it. In the infancy of this province, said
he, many families from Britain came over, and of these the
wives and daughters were people of education. The mothers

took the care of the girls, they were train'd up under them, and not only instructed in the family duties necessary to the sex, but in those accomplishments and genteel manners that are still so visible amongst them, and this descended from Mother to daughter. As the father found the labours of his boys necessary to him, he led them therefore to the woods, and taught the sturdy lad to glory in the stroke he could give with his Ax, in the trees he felled, and the deer he shot; to conjure the wolfe, the bear and the Alligator; and to guard his habitition from Indian inroads was most justly his pride, and he had reason to boast of it. But a few generations this way lost every art or science, which their fathers might have brought out, and tho' necessity no longer prescribed these severe occupations, custom has established it as still necessary for the men to spend their time abroad in the fields; and to be a good marksman is the highest ambition of the youth, while to those enervated by age or infirmity drinking grog remained a last consolation.

The Ladies have burnt their tea in a solemn procession,* but they had delayed however till the sacrifice was not very considerable, as I do not think any one offered above a quarter of a pound. The people in town live decently, and tho' their houses are not spacious, they are in general very commodious and well furnished. All the Merchants of any note are British and Irish,† and many of them very genteel people. They all disapprove of the present proceedings. Many of them intend quitting the country as fast as their affairs will permit them, but are yet uncertain what steps to take. This town lies low, but is not disagreeable. There is at

---

* Miss Schaw may refer here to the Edenton tea party of October 25, 1774, but more probably she has in mind some Wilmington tea party of which, as far as we know, no record exists. At Edenton the tea was not "burnt;" and as at Wilmington the proceedings at this time far exceeded in violence those in the quiet Albermarle section, it is quite likely that Miss Schaw is recording a fact that has hitherto escaped observation.

† That is, Scots Irish. "British" is evidently intended to include "Scottish," as Scotland at this time was called North Britain.

each end of it an ascent, which is dignified with the title of the hills; on them are some very good houses and there almost all my acquaintances are. They have very good Physicians,* the best of whom is a Scotchman,† at whose house I have seen many of the first planters. I do not wish however to be much in their company, for, as you know, my tongue is not always under my command; I fear I might say something to give offence, in which case I would not fail to have the most shocking retort at least, if it went no further.

The ports are soon to be shut up,‡ but this severity is voluntarily imposed by themselves, for they were indulged by parliament and allowed the exclusive privilege of still carrying on their trade with Europe, by which means they would not only have made great fortunes themselves by being the mart for the whole continent, but they would have had the power to serve the other colonies by providing them in those commodities, the want of which they will ill brook, and which is a distress they themselves must soon suffer, as European goods begin to be very scarce and will daily be more so, as the merchts are shipping off their propertys, either to Britain or the West Indies. I know not what my brother proposes to do with himself or me; for if he stays much longer, he will find himself in a very disagreeable situation. He is just now up the country at a town called Newbern, where Govr Martin‖ resides, whose situation is most terrible. He is a worthy man by all accounts, but gentle methods will

---

* As early as 1736 there was a physician, Dr. Roger Rolfe, in New Liverpool, as Wilmington was then called. Two others, Drs. Mortimer and Green, died in 1772. At the time of Miss Schaw's visit Dr. Cobham and Dr. Tucker were those whose names are most frequently met with.

† For Dr. Thomas Cobham, see Appendix XII.

‡ The most important feature of the Continental Association was a nonimportation agreement, to go into force (by an extension of time from December 1, 1774) on February 1, 1775. The Association was not formally adopted in North Carolina until April 5, 1775 (*N. C. R.* IX, 1180-1181), so that Miss Schaw must have written her account a few days before that date.

‖ For Governor Josiah Martin, see Appendix II, "The Martin Family."

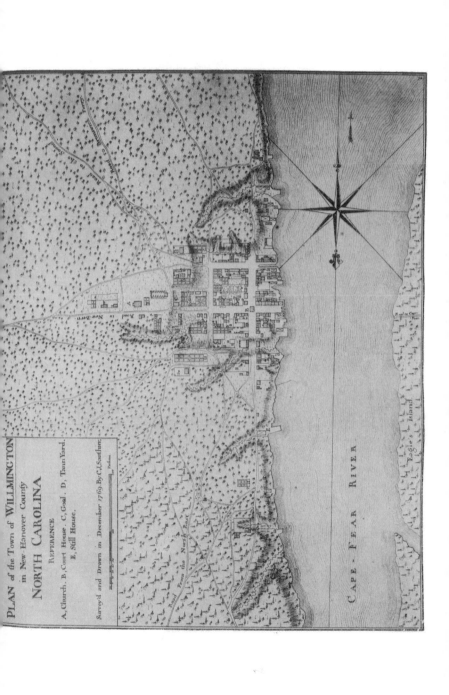

PLAN of the Town of WILLMINGTON
in New Hanover County
NORTH CAROLINA

REFERENCE

A, Church. B, Court House. C, Goal. D, Town Yard.
E, Still House.

Survey'd and Drawn in December 1769 By C.J.Sauthier.

Perches

CAPE - FEAR - RIVER.

Eagle Island

not do with these rusticks, and he has not the power to use more spirited means. I wish to God those mistaken notions of moderation to which you adhere at home may not in the end prove the greatest cruelty to the mother country as well as to these infatuated people; but I am no politician, as yet at least, tho' I believe I will grow one in time, as I am beginning to pay a good deal of attention to what is going on about me.

You will rejoice with me to hear that your young friends, Miss Rutherfurd and her brothers, have got a very considerable accession to their fortunes, by a gift of an old lady,* their father and mother's great friend, and whose death is hourly expected, as she has long been in a dropsy that now seems at a height. Mr Rutherfurd is as much in love with his daughter as I expected he would be, and so fond of the boys, that I fear they will be quite spoiled. I am as yet indulged with their company, but find the old Lady wishes to have Fanny with her, which is very right, tho' I am in pain for her with an old woman not of the best character or most amiable manners, and in so lonely a situation. But her gratitude and good sense will do much to please her. I inclose this and leave it behind me to go by the first ship. Mrs Schaw is impatient to get home, nor can I blame the anxiety of a mother for her little ones† in such brutal hands as the Negroes to whose care she is forced to leave them in her absence. Perhaps my next may be from St Kitts, but in

---

* The "old lady" whom Miss Schaw describes as "not of the best character or most amiable manners" was Mrs. Jean Corbin, who married, first, Colonel James Innes, of Braddock's campaign (died 1759), and second, in 1761, Francis Corbin, Lord Granville's agent in North Carolina (Appendix VIII). She made her will on February 10, 1775, and died probably toward the end of the next month. The will was probated on April 3 and the inventory completed on the thirteenth. Of her history nothing else is known, neither who she was—though "Jean" is manifestly a Scottish name—nor when she was first married. For the bequest, see Appendix X.

† Evidently referring to Mrs. Schaw's two youngest children, Alexander and Robert, sons of the second husband, Miss Schaw's brother Robert (below, p. 160).

this I suppose my brother will be directed by Govr Martin, if he can be of any use, I am sure he will willingly run every risk, as I can answer for it, the king has not a more sincere or loyal subject. Farewell, my dear friend, that God may deliver us from this, and preserve you, is the prayer of a mind not much at its ease.

Schawfield.

After I put my last packet into a safe hand, I left Wilmingtown and returned to Schawfield by water, which is a most delightful method of travelling thro' this Noble country, which indeed owes more favours to its God and king than perhaps any other in the known world and is equally ungrateful to both, to the God who created and bestowed them and to the king whose indulgent kindness has done every thing to render them of the greatest utility to the owners. Well may the following text from the prophets be applied to this people, and with very little alteration may be addressed to them. "My beloved has a vineyard in a very pleasant land, he Dig'd it, he planted it, he hedged it round, and built a winepress in the midst thereof, but when he looked for grapes, they brought forth wild grapes. Judge I pray you between me and my vineyard, what could I do more for it than I have done, yet when I looked for grapes, behold it brought forth only wild grapes. Go to, I will tell you what I will do to my vineyard, I will take away the fence thereof, I will break down the wine press in the midst thereof, and I will leave it as I found it a habitation to wolves and bears." Such is the fate it deserves, but both its God and its king are merciful. May they be inspired to seek it before it be too late.

Nothing can be finer than the banks of this river; a thousand beauties both of the flowery and sylvan tribe hang over it and are reflected from it with additional lustre. But they spend their beauties on the desert air, and the pines that wave behind the shore with a solemn gravity seem to lament that they too exist to no purpose, tho' capable of being rendered both useful and agreeable. For those noble trees that might adorn the palaces of kings are left to the stroke of the thunder, or to the annihilating hand of time, and against whom the hard Sentence (tho' innocent of the crime) may be pronounced, why cumber ye the ground? As that is all that can be said of them in their present state that they cover many hundred, nay thousand acres of the finest ground in the universe, and give shelter to every hurtful and obnoxious animal, tho' their site is a most convenient situation both for trading towns and plantations. This north west branch is said to be navigable for Ships of 400 tons burthen for above two hundred miles up, and the banks so constituted by nature that they seem formed for harbours, and what adds in a most particular manner to this convenience is, that quite across from one branch to the other, and indeed thro' the whole country are innumerable creeks that communicate with the main branches of the river and every tide receive a sufficient depth of water for boats of the largest size and even for small Vessels, so that every thing is water-borne at a small charge and with great safety and ease.

But these uncommon advantages are almost entirely neglected. In the course of sixteen miles which is the distance between these places and the town, there is but one plantation, and the condition it is in shows, if not the poverty, at least the indolence* of its owner. My brother indeed is in some degree an exception to this reflection. Indolent he is

---

* The word "indolence," here and elsewhere used by Miss Schaw, was frequently employed by critics of the southern colonies, who, accustomed as many of them were to the careful husbandry of the Old World, were often roused to indignant protest against the slipshod methods of agriculture in vogue in America and the idleness which was encouraged by an all too bounteous nature (cf. *N. C. R.* V, 314, 640; VI, 1040). We may not wonder that the impressions which Miss Schaw received of North Carolina were unfavorable or that she should have expressed her opinions so frankly. She was writing to a private correspondent and not for the press. She had come

not; his industry is visible in every thing round him, yet he also is culpable in adhering to the prejudices of this part of the world, and in using only the American methods of cultivating his plantation. Had he followed the style of an East Lothian farmer, with the same attention and care, it would now have been an Estate worth double what it is. Yet he has done more in the time he has had it* than any of his Neighbours, and even in their slow way, his industry has brought it to a wonderful length. He left Britain while he was a boy, and was many years in trade before he turned planter, and had lost the remembrance of what he had indeed little opportunity of studying, I mean farming. His brother easily convinced him of the superiority of our manner of carrying on our agriculture, but Mʳˢ Schaw† was shocked at the mention of our manuring the ground, and declared she never would eat corn that grew thro' dirt. Indeed she is so rooted an American, that she detests every thing that is European, yet

from Scotland, by way of Antigua and St. Kitts, to a frontier country, which was still in large part a wilderness and where agriculture was still undeveloped. Her impressions were similar to those of many a New Englander who visited the Middle West in the early nineteenth century, or of those English men and women who made tours of the United States before 1840. In a more limited field she was a forerunner of Mrs. Trollope, whose *Domestic Manners of the Americans* pictures more elaborately, but with equal vigor, some of the cruder aspects of early American life. Unlike Mrs. Trollope, however, she was influenced in her criticisms by a dislike of democracy and a profound distrust of radical activities.

* Robert Schaw acquired "Schawfield" in 1772 and 1773.

† Though we have not been able to trace Mrs. Robert Schaw's connections with any degree of certainty, it is fairly clear that she was related, either nearly or remotely, to the "best people in the country," as Miss Schaw says. Miss Schaw would not have used this phrase without ample knowledge of that whereof she wrote. If Mrs. Schaw, who was Anne Vail before her marriage with her first husband, Job Howe (elder brother of Robert), belonged to the family of John and Jeremiah Vail of Perquimans and Craven counties, she was related to the Swanns, Ashes, Lillingtons, Moseleys, Hasells, Porters, and Moores—the "best people" in very truth, and engaged, most of them, as Miss Schaw says later, in the revolutionary movement.

Mrs. Schaw died in 1788, leaving her property to her two sons, William Tryon Howe and Alexander Schaw, with a bequest of six negroes to Isabella Chapman, who, we suspect, was a daughter of Barbara Rutherfurd (John's sister) and Alexander Chapman of Wilmington. The fact that she made be-she is a most excellent wife and a fond mother. Her dairy and her garden show her industry, tho' even there she is an American. However he has no cause to complain. Her person is agreeable, and if she would pay it a little more attention, it would be lovely. She is connected with the best people in the country, and, I hope, will have interest enough to prevent her husband being ruined for not joining in a cause he so much disapproves.

I have just mentioned a garden, and will tell you, that this at Schawfield is the only thing deserving the name I have seen in this country, and laid out with some taste. I could not help smiling however at the appearance of a soil, that seemed to me no better than dead sand, proposed for a garden. But a few weeks have convinced me that I judged very falsely, for the quickness of the vegetation is absolutely astonishing. Nature to whose care every thing is left does a vast deal; but I remember to have read, tho' I forget where, that Adam when he was turned out of paradise was allowed to carry seeds with him of those fruits he had been suffered to eat of when there, but found on trial that the curse had extended even to them; for they were harsh and very unpalatable, far different from what he had eat there in his happy state. Our poor father, who from his infancy [alternative reading, from his first creation] had been used to live well, like those of his descendents, was the more sensible of the change, and he wept bitterly before his beneficent Creator, who once more had pity on him, and the compassionate Angel again descended to give him comfort and relief. "Adam," began the heavenly messenger, "the sentence is passed, it is irrevocable; the ground has been cursed for your

<hr/>

quests also to the daughters of Joseph Leech of New Bern, strengthens the belief that she was related to Jeremiah Vail, who was of the same town. In her will she names as one of her executors "John Rutherfurd" (Clerk's Office, Wills, C, p. 396). If she means the father it is strange that she should not have known that he had died five years before. She may mean the son, who in 1787 would have been twenty-four years of age.

sake, and thorns and briers it must bring forth, and you must eat your bread with the sweat of your brow, yet the curse does not extend to your labours, and it yet depends on your own choice to live in plenty or in penury. Patience and industry will get the better of every difficulty, and the ground will bear thistles only while your indolence permits it. The fruits also will be harsh while you allow them to remain in a state of uncultivated nature; because man is allowed no enjoyment without labour; and the hand of industry improves even the choicest gifts of heaven." Adam bowed in grateful acknowledgment, and his heavenly instructor led him forth to the field, and soon taught him that God had given him power over the inanimate as well as the animate part of the creation, and that not only every beast and every bird was under his command, but that he had power over the whole vegetable world; and he soon proved that the hand of industry could make the rose bloom, where nature had only planted the thistle, and saw the fig-tree blossom, where lately the wild bramble was all its boast. He taught him that not only the harsh sourness of the crab was corrected, but the taste and flavour of the peach improven; by the art of ingrafting and budding the pear became more luscious, and even the nectarine juice was poor and insipid without this assistance. Adam had no prejudices to combat, he gave the credit due to his heavenly instructor, and soon saw a new Eden flourish in the desert from his labours, and eat fruit little inferior to those he had left, rendered indeed even superior to his taste by being the reward of his honest Industry.

As I cannot produce my Authority, perhaps you may suspect I have none, but that it was coined for the present purpose, should you think so, I cannot help it, but should Gabriel himself assure the folks here that industry would render every thing better, they would as little believe him, as they would your humble servant. Truly the only parable they mind is that of the lily of the Valley, which they imitate as it toils not, neither does it spin, but whether their glory exceeds that of Solomon is another question, but certain it is they take things as they come without troubling themselves with improvements. I have as yet tasted none of their fruits, but am told that notwithstanding the vast advantages of climate, they are not equal in flavour to those at home in our gardens,—on walls which indeed they have no occasion for. Wherever you see the peach trees, you find hard by a group of plumbs so fit for stocks, that nature seems to have set them there on purpose. But her hints and the advice of those who know the advantages of it are equally unregarded. There are also many things that are fit for hedges, which would be a vast advantage, but these straggle wild thro' the field or woods, while every inclosure is made of a set of logs laid zagly close over each other.*

On our arrival here the stalks of last year's crop still remained on the ground. At this I was greatly surprised, as the season was now so far advanced, I expected to have found the fields completely ploughed at least, if not sown and harrowed; but how much was my amazement increased to find that every instrument of husbandry was unknown here; not only all the various ploughs, but all the machinery used with such success at home, and that the only instrument used is a hoe, with which they at once till and plant the corn. To accomplish this a number of Negroes follow each other's tail the day long, and have a task assigned them, and it will take twenty at least to do as much work as two horses with a man and a boy would perform. Here the wheel-plough would answer finely, as the ground is quite flat, the soil light

---

* The fence here mentioned is the "zigzag" or Virginian fence, found sometimes in southern New England, and frequently in the Middle West, where it is known as the "snake fence" or "log fence." The rails, usually split, are laid zigzag fashion, one upon another, without posts, but generally with bracing of some sort at the angles. It is a slovenly affair; though easy to make and convenient for removing. Its height runs from three to five feet.

and not a stone to be met with in a thousand acres. A drill too might easily be constructed for sowing the seed, and a light harrow would close it in with surprising expedition. It is easy to observe however from whence this ridiculous method of theirs took its first necessary rise. When the new Settlers were obliged to sow corn for their immediate maintenance, before they were able to root out the trees, it is plain no other instrument but the hoe could be used amongst the roots of the trees, where it was to be planted, and they were obliged to do it all by hand labour. But thro' this indolence some of them have their plantations still pretty much incumbered in that way, yet to do justice to the better sort, that is not generally the case. Tho' it is all one as to the manner of dressing their fields, the same absurd method continuing every where. If horses were hard to come at or unfit for labour, that might be some excuse, but far is it otherwise. They have them in plenty, and strong animals they are and fit for the hardest labour.*

The little time I have been here and the little of the country I have seen hardly admit of my sending you such particular accounts. The truth is, I should not in many years be able to give you so much merely from my own observation, but I have been much indebted to other people, particularly an old Gentleman, who has been many years in this country, and did not leave his own till he was arrived at a time of life to remember it perfectly and draw proper comparisons; for this he was perfectly qualified, as he was both a scholar and a man of sense. He left his country on account of some un-

---

* Had Miss Schaw visited the middle and northern colonies where the staples were similar to those of Mid Lothian, she would have found agricultural conditions more to her liking. Both manuring and grafting were known and their value understood in Pennsylvania, New York, and New England, and though farming devices and appliances were inevitably crude, they were not so far behind those of Scotland as were the contrivances of the plantation colonies. Probably Miss Schaw did not herself realize how comparatively recent were the improvements in agricultural methods employed by the East Lothian farmers, whom she so greatly admired.

happy affair, which is needless to relate; spent several years in Holland, every part of which he seems to have studied with accuracy. He has a very good idea of farming in all its parts, is an excellent Mathematician and has no bad smattering of Mechanicks; he has studied Physic and Botany; of the last he is particularly fond, and this country affords him ample gratification for that study, as there is hardly a medicinal herb or plant produced in any climate that he has not discovered something here to answer its purposes. Add to this that his manners are those of a Gentleman and his deportment such as may render age respectable; his conversation agreeable and instructive, and his good nature most extensive. Would you not imagine this man would be prized and courted? that the young would refer to his experience, and those of riper years apply to his superior knowledge. That however is far from the case. He has found but one man who had sense enough to understand him, and whose friendship he has cultivated. Who this man is you may know hereafter; sorry I am it is not my brother.

With this friend he lives a pleasant tho' obscure life; as the Gentleman is fond of retirement himself, he easily indulges his old friend. They both love reading, and are better provided for that amusement than all the rest of the province put together.* I am fond of conversing with him, and happy in fancying he is pleased with my curiosity. He is always willing to answer my interrogatories, nor is prolixity displeasing, as it shows me how willing he is to explain every thing to me that I wish to know. He told me, that when he came here, like other projectors, he hoped to improve the country; that he had brought many seeds out with him, particularly all the different kinds of grass-seed, to try what

* Evidently John Rutherfurd is the man referred to (see below, p. 184). That Miss Schaw should occasionally indulge in exaggerations is not surprising. She is certainly wrong in her remarks about books in the province, just as she is wrong in saying, on page 194, that there were not five men of property in Wilmington who favored the revolutionary movement.

would best answer this soil and climate, as he was thought no despisable gardener at home. He tried it here and soon had a very good garden where he first settled, but being in no situation to defend his property, his fruit, his vegetables and every thing else became the prey of the neighbouring Negroes, who tore up his fences, carried off what they could eat and destroyed the rest. He then accepted the invitation of a planter of fortune in the Neighbourhood, and endeavoured to return his civility by being useful to him. There he laid out a very neat garden, which soon produced every thing he wished, but this did not long continue, his neighbours laughed at him for it. He first became sulky and then rude to poor H——, refusing him a negro to work, and bidding him raise his damned European stuff with his own hands. He left this savage and as the Gentleman in whose family he has long resided had seen and admired him, he directly begged to be favoured with his company, where he has ever since been as happy as he wishes to be. It is evident he was once no stranger to the haunts of men, and that he has formerly known better days, but unless he voluntarily comes on the subject I will not ask his adventures. He asked me if I had not heard that poultry was here in vast plenty, and that there were more Turkeys raised here than in any part of the world. I owned I had been told so, but did not observe it to be the case, as in most farmers' yards at home I saw more domestick poultry than here about the houses of the planters. This he said was true, but that they all believed they exceeded, and would be very much affronted if I said otherwise; that they certainly had opportunity of doing so, as the rice and Indian corn were fine feeding, but that now the season was advancing, I would see how bad their method of managing them was. This I have now been an eye witness to; not a tenth part of what is hatched ever coming to perfection, tho' those that do escape their nursing come on prodigiously fast.

I am here in the country; my brother is not yet returned and Miss Rutherfurd is gone to attend her old friend, who is just dying. The sooner the more agreeable to me, as I do not approve of her situation.

We had company to day, amongst others a brother-in-law of Mrs Schaw a Robt Howe,* or as he is called here Bob Howe. This Gentleman has the worst character you ever heard thro' the whole province. He is however very like a Gentleman, much more so indeed than any thing I have seen in the Country. He is deemed a horrid animal, a sort of a woman-eater that devours every thing that comes in his way, and that no woman can withstand him. But be not in pain for your friend, I do assure you they overrate his merits, and as I am certain it would be in the power of mortal women to withstand him, so am I convinced he is not so voracious as he is represented. But he has that general polite gallantry, which every man of good breeding ought to have, and when he meets with those who receive it as he deserves, I will answer it goes no further, but if it has particular effects on any one, I make not the least doubt, but he will be as particular as they please, but that, as they chuse, you know. He is at present a candidate for the command of the army that is now raising, for an army certainly is raising, fancy to yourselves what you please. I am sure he came to speak to my brother on the subject, but was too polite to introduce politicks. I wish he may get the command with all my heart, for he does not appear to me half so dangerous as another candidate, a Coll: Moor,† whom I am compelled at once to dread and esteem. He is a man of a free property and a most unblemished character, has amiable manners; and a virtuous life has gained him the love of every body, and his popularity is such that I am assured he will have more followers than any other man in the province. He acts from a steady tho' mistaken

* For Robert Howe, see Appendix XI.
† For James Moore, see Appendix XI.

principle, and I am certain has no view nor design, but what he thinks right and for the good of his country. He urges not a war of words, and when my brother told him he would not join him, for he did not approve the cause, "Then do not," said he, "let every man be directed by his own ideas of right or wrong." If this man commands, be assured, he will find his enemies work. His name is James Moor: should you ever hear him mentioned, think of the character I gave him.‡

I will not give you any account of the culture of the rice, as you have it very distinctly in Miller's dictionary,* and it is still the same method. I am much out of the way of any thing here; as my brother keeps himself much retired to avoid solicitations, which are at present both disagreeable and dangerous. But as I am really tired of this Style, I will go down to town to amuse myself, and you will not have any more letters till then. Adieu.

Point Pleasant.

I recollect I closed my last with a promise of writing you from Wilmingtown, and should not have failed, had not sundry events prevented me till now, when I once more resume my Journal. Early next morning after I got to town, I was waked by the sweetest chorister that ever I heard in my life, and of whose uncommon talents I had no warnings. It pitched on a Mulberry tree, close to the window of the

‡ He afterwards opposed Parker and Clinton and defeated the Loyalists.

---

* Philip Miller, *The Gardener's Dictionary*, 1731, eight editions. Of Miller the *London Chronicle* printed the following obituary notice. "Died, aged upward of 80, Dec. 18, 1771, Mr. Philip Miller, F.R.S., gardener to the Apothecaries Company, at their physic-garden at Chelsea [founded by Sir Hans Sloane], to which office he succeeded his father about fifty years ago, but lately resigned on account of advanced age. He was allowed to be the best writer on gardening in this kingdom and was honoured with the acquaintance and correspondence of the connoisseurs of that science all over Europe and America. The universal good reception of his Dictionary and Calendar, the esteem in which they are still held, and the various editions they have passed through will be a lasting monument to his memory."

apartment where I slept and began with the note of our thrush so full, that I never doubted it was our sober suited songstress, but presently I heard those of the black bird, which was succeeded by the shrill note of the lark, and after a few warbles, I heard the well known notes of our Linnet and Goldfinch. I could not believe that these various birds were here, yet to suppose that all the musick of a British grove was poured from one little pipe was not less surprising. I got up and opened the window-shutter to take a peep at my musician, but softly as I unbarred it, he was scared, and I just saw on wing what they call here the mocking bird. He is of a bluish colour on the back, his breast and head white about the size of our thrush, and by no means pretty. He is very improperly named; for as he never heard one of the birds I mention, he cannot be said to mock or imitate them. The red bird which is very pretty has but a few notes and these form only a chirp, which he never mixed with his Notes. He is not much regarded and they tell me will not live in a cage.

It was very early when this little serenader roused me. I sat down to write while it was yet cool and pleasant, and no yelping Negroes with their discording voices to grate my ears and disturb my thoughts, which often obliges me to lay down my pen, but neither they nor the sun were yet up, and I had wrote some time in peace and quiet, when an outcry like that of a score of hogs going to the shambles to be slaughtered made me tear my paper and fly down stairs, where I saw the unhappy occasion of this uproar was no less than the whole court of offices belonging to the house of my agreeable hostess Mrs Heron* in flames and making hasty steps to the

---

* Mrs. Alice Heron was the widow of Captain Benjamin Heron, one of the most active and influential men of the province. The name "Heron" was well known in Scotland and in England, where Captain Heron had a brother, Charles, an apothecary and surgeon at Corhampton in Hampshire. Mrs. Heron also had a sister, Peggy, in England. Captain Heron, as lieutenant in the royal navy, had taken part in the Cartagena expedition, and afterwards,

destruction of her whole property; as the fire had already caught hold of a pailing that joined to the house. Tho' there were upwards of 500 blacks and whites by, yet her house and perhaps the whole town had been burnt,* had not some British sailors come to their assistance, and by pulling up the pailing, left a sufficient void, by which means the houses already on fire burnt out of themselves. Evident as this manoeuvre must have appeared to every bystander, yet the inactivity of the white people, and the perverseness of the Negroes would not do it. As to the amiable widow she behaved with remarkable presence of mind, and tho' a considerable loser expressed her thanks to providence for what was saved in a most becoming manner.

It would not have been easy to resume my pen after this alarming business; but had I even designed it, another event put it again out of my power; for I just then got a letter from Fanny begging me to come to her as the old Lady was so ill, she could not survive another day, and she had no female friend with her. On my arrival next morning, I found the old Lady had taken her departure, and my friend very much

---

as master of a sailing vessel, was accustomed to go back and forth between England and the colony. He served the government as deputy auditor, deputy secretary, and clerk of the pleas and of the crown, an office with extensive patronage and perquisites. He was also for some years a member of the council. He died in 1771.

By his will he left to his wife the house and furniture in Wilmington, where were the offices named in the narrative; to his daughter, Mary, his plantation, "Mulberry," on the Northwest; to his daughter, Elizabeth, his plantation "Mount Blake" or "Heron's" on the Northeast; and to his son, Robert, lands on the Sound next to those of Job Howe.

* The Wilmington town and borough records show that fires were a source of much trouble and a cause of much legislation in the early history of the town and borough. As early as 1749 the possession of buckets and ladders was made compulsory and in 1751 it was ordered that any one whose chimney got on fire should pay a fine of twenty shillings. Chimneys were to be built at least three feet above the ridgepole. In the year 1756 a serious conflagration took place and consequently a water engine was ordered from England, hose was provided, and an engine house was built. This engine got out of repair, and in 1772 was deemed too small and a larger one was bought. When a fire was discovered the bell on the courthouse was rung to arouse the inhabitants.

shocked and affected at witnessing a scene at once so new and solemn, and which had the addition of one of the Negroes shooting another almost in the same moment his late proprietor expired. For my own part I could find no regret that a tedious and disagreeable attendance had not been necessary, and that there was no fear of her revoking what she had done in their favours.

Mr Rutherfurd had my two brothers and some other Gentlemen with him, and every thing prepared to lay her in the grave* in a manner suitable to her fortune, and the obligations he had to her friendship. Every body of fashion both from the town and round the country were invited, but the Solemnity was greatly hurt by a set of Volunteers, who, I thought, must have fallen from the moon; above a hundred of whom (of both sexes) arrived in canoes, just as the clergyman was going to begin the service, and made such a noise, it was hardly to be heard. A hogshead of rum and broth and vast quantities of pork, beef and corn-bread were set forth for the entertainment of these gentry. But as they observed the tables already covered for the guests, after the funeral, they took care to be first back from it, and before any one got to the hall, were placed at the tables, and those that had not room to sit carried off the dishes to another room, so that an elegant entertainment that had been provided went for nothing. At last they got into their canoes, and I saw them row thro' the creeks, and suppose they have little spots of ground up the woods, which afford them corn and pork, and that on such occasions they flock down like crows to a carrion.

They were no sooner gone than the Negroes assembled to perform their part of the funeral rites, which they did by running, jumping, crying and various exercises. They are a noble troop, the best in all the country; and the legacy, in

---

* Mrs. Corbin was buried at "the bottom of the lawn" on the "Point Pleasant" plantation, between her husbands, James Innes and Francis Corbin.

every part, turns out more considerable than was even at first thought. God rest her soul, and for this one good deed, let all her evil ones be forgiven. She sleeps between her two husbands at the bottom of the Lawn, in a very decent snug quarter. Mr Rutherfurd will be obliged to go up the country soon; so I will remain sometime here with my sweet friend whose good fortune affects me more than it does herself, on whom it has wrought no change. All the country has been to visit her, and they all pretend to be pleased; but as many had form'd hopes, you may easily believe they are not all sincere. She is busy inventoring her new effects, which in furniture, plate, linen, jewels and cloths, are very considerable. The house is very handsome and quite on a British plan. The place is a peninsula that runs into the river and is justly called Point Pleasant.* It stands on a fine lawn, with the noblest scattered trees in the world thro' it. But here is more company, and I must lay down my pen. Adieu, Adieu.

Mr Rutherfurd and my brother set out for Newbern some days ago. Mr Rutherfurd is an active member of the Assembly [that is, of the Council],† and has gone to do his duty, tho' he expects much trouble, which has prevented most of the others from venturing up at this time, as they hear from

---

* "Point Pleasant" was the plantation of Colonel James Innes and was situated on the Northeast, on the south side, at the bend of the river. The location is shown on Wimble's map of 1738 and was, as Miss Schaw says, on a peninsula jutting northward into the stream. Mrs. Corbin had only a life interest in this plantation, which at her death was to go to support a free school at Wilmington. What she left to the children was as much of the Innes property—lands, personal possessions, and negroes—as was hers to dispose of according to the terms of her marriage settlement with Francis Corbin (Register's Office, Conveyances, E, 89-94). These together with certain annuities due her under that settlement were to be cared for by "her good friend" John Rutherfurd for the maintenance and education of Fanny and the boys. The dwelling house and other buildings on the "Point Pleasant" plantation were destroyed by fire shortly before the year 1783 (North Carolina State Records, XXIV, 512).

† Rutherfurd was a member of the council, not of the assembly proper. The session opened on April 4, the council meeting for the first time on April 6. Rutherfurd was present.

undoubted authority that the provincial congress is also to meet at the same time without any regard to the presence of the Govr or members of the Assembly. This is also the time when Mr Rutherfurd should receive and settle the quit-rents, as he is a receiver-general of the province, and every year should settle the Acc^ts and have them signed by the Govr.* This he has reason to believe cannot be done, yet is still resolved to perform his duty to the last. My brother attends the Govr, by his orders, as he wishes to have as many friends to the Government near him, as he can assemble. His situation is every way to be pitied. He is a man of spirit as well as a loyal subject, and will ill brook having an unlawful convocation† sitting openly in the same town, controverting every Act that he and the lawful assembly propose, yet he must submit, as he has no power to do otherwise, and an attempt to support his own and the authority of the assembly might be attended with many bad consequences, and could render the King no sort of service. I am vastly anxious and will be most uneasy till they return. Good Heavens! what had we to do here.

The weather now begins to be very warm, and tho' the thermometer never rises to the same height as in the West Indies, yet the want of air makes it quite intolerable. The

---

* For Rutherfurd's connection with the quit-rents, see Bond, *The Quit-Rent System in the American Colonies*, pp. 305-308; and for a brief biography and estimate, Appendix VIII. Martin wrote, July 29, 1774, to the Treasury, that he was convinced a much larger collection of this revenue could be made by a proper exertion on the part of the receiver-general, and said that the deficiency in the fund was due largely to Rutherfurd's neglect. He said further that he had done all in his power to urge on that official and had in fact prevented formal complaint of his conduct from being laid before the board, not wishing to take advantage of his "extreme good nature" and "distressed circumstance" (Public Record Office, Treasury 1: 505, fo. 317).

† The "unlawful convocation," mentioned by Miss Schaw, was of course the Provincial Convention at New Bern, April 3, 1775. This convention consisted of the members of the assembly sitting as a convention, without authorization from the governor, and so without sanction of law. The same men, in the same quarters, sat the next day as a lawful assembly. See below, page 181.

evenings however are very fine, and we go out in Mr Rutherfurd's phaeton thro' the adjoining woods, and tho' the lightning flashes round us in these airings, yet it is a lambent flame, that we know will not hurt us. It is only the red lightning which sets the trees on fire, which is not so frequent, and is always attended by loud explosions and heavy rains. But the lightning I speak of is a blue flame, resembling that of spirits on fire, and is so common that no body pays the least attention to it. But the other is more dreadful than any thing I ever saw at home; it sets whole woods on fire and shatters the largest trees from top to bottom, and is followed by a storm of wind and rain, that of itself is terrible. But this is a necessary evil, and makes that circulation, which alone can purify the putrid air that rises from bogs and swamps. The fruits are now ripe,* and I find the truth of my old friend's observation. I have never yet seen a peach, that either from colour or flavour was superior to those we have at home. As to the Nectarine or Apricock I have seen none, nor any plumb, a small red one excepted, such as we find growing red and yellow thro' our hedges, but which the fine climate makes better-tasted. The water-melon, of which they are so fond, I do not like, but perhaps that may be owing to my taste, not yet being accustomed to them. I have seen but few vegetables, and those very poor of their kinds. This too is their own fault, for the fine light soil is intirely fitted for them, and roots of all kinds would be excellent here, but their indolence makes them prefer what herbs they find growing wild to those that require the least attention to propagate, and one is really grieved to see so many rare advantages bestowed on a people every way so unworthy of them. I do assure you that every gift of nature is here. Not Italia, Spain

---

* This section is misplaced. Fruits were not ripe at this time. Miss Schaw could hardly have tested a watermelon between February and May, and certainly could not have found "grapes dangling over our heads in large bunches" before August or September.

or Portugal produce an Article that might not be had in
higher perfection, wine and oil not excepted. Finer grapes
cannot be met with than are to be found every where wild,
more particularly on the banks of the rivers, and up all the
creeks, a proof of which I had a few days ago. On a sail we
took up a creek, we found the grapes dangling over our heads
in large bunches, particularly a red grape, whose berries are
very large. The Negroes landed and filled the boat and we
had them bruised and set to ferment, and this day we tasted
the wine, which is already excellent, and in time will be as
good as any of the common Portuguese wines, and yet the
vines are perfectly uncultivated. How much better would it
be, if any care were taken of them. There is a great variety
of white as well as red, but they do not even make tarts of
them. What they use for that is a huckle berry, which has a
faint resemblance to our black or blue berry, but not equal to
the crane berry.

The congress has forbid killing Mutton, veal or lamb,* so
that little variety is to be had from the domestick animals;
but indulgent nature makes up for every want, by the vast
quantities of wild birds, both of land and water. The wild
Turkeys, the wild pigeon, a bird which they call a partridge,
but above all the rice-bird, which is the Ortalon in its highest
perfection, and from the water the finest ducks that possibly
can be met with, and so plenty that when on wing sixteen or
eighteen are killed at a shot. The beauty of the Summer-duck
makes its death almost a murder. The deer now is large, but
not so fat as it will be some time hence; it is however in great
plenty, and makes good soup. The rivers are full of fine fish,
and luxury itself cannot ask a boon that is not granted. Do
not however suppose by this that you meet elegant tables,

---

* The Continental Association of 1774 contained a clause (VII) binding
the colonists not to export or kill sheep "especially those of the most profit-
able kind." It is likely that Rutherfurd accepted the terms, but equally probable that he did not adhere to them very strictly.

far from it; this profusion is in general neglected. The gentlemen indeed out of idleness shoot deer, but nothing under
a wild turkey is worth a shot. As they are now on the eve of a
War, or something else I dare not name, perhaps they save
their powder for good reasons; but at Mr Rutherfurd's there
is a huntsman, with as many assistants as he pleases,* and
every day provisions are brought home of those Articles I
have mentioned. Besides as he pays no great regard to the
orders of the congress, he wants neither mutton [n]or lamb
in their turn.

They have the true vulture here, with the bald head,
which they call Turkey buzard, as he is little less than a turkey.† The bears are exceeding troublesome and often carry
off the hogs. I have got a whelp, which was only a day old
when its dam was killed. Miss Rutherfurd is fond of it, but
tho' only a fortnight old, it is too much for her already. We
have also a fawn, which is much more beautiful than any
I ever saw at home and tame as a dog. The Negroes are the
only people that seem to pay any attention to the various
uses that the wild vegetables may be put to. For example,
I have sent you a paper of their vegetable pins made from the
prickly pear, also molds for buttons made from the calabash,
which likewise serves to hold their victuals. The allowance

---

* The huntsman and assistants were probably negroes. Both in North
Carolina and South Carolina it was necessary for a negro to have a license or
ticket to carry a gun. Therefore it was common for their masters to enter
the names of such negroes as they wished to be licensed on the records of
the county court and to offer security according to law. For instance, as
early as 1740, Edward Moseley entered as "hunters on his sundry plantations" the names of four negroes. In 1764 Thomas Halloway "prayed for a
ticket for a negro man named Burgaw Billy to carry a gun at Burgaw Plantation," and John Rutherfurd did the same for a negro named Mingo at
Rocky Point, with his friend Benjamin Heron as security. After Rutherfurd
acquired "Hunthill" he must have obtained a number of such licenses for
his negroes.

† The turkey buzzard is one of the varieties of the American vulture,
differing structurally from the vultures of the Old World. It is not considered, however, a true vulture any more than are those of Europe. Nevertheless Miss Schaw was well up in her ornithology.

for a Negro is a quart of Indian corn p^r day,‡ and a little piece of land which they cultivate much better than their Master. There they rear hogs and poultry, sow calabashes, etc. and are better provided for in every thing than the poorer white people with us. They steal whatever they can come at, and even intercept the cows and milk them. They are indeed the constant plague of their tyrants, whose severity or mildness is equally regarded by them in these Matters.

Wilmingtown.

We came to town yesterday by water, and tho' it was excessively warm had a pleasant sail. Mr Rutherfurd has a very fine boat with an awning to prevent the heat, and six stout Negroes in neat uniforms to row her down, which with the assistance of the tide was performed with ease in a very short time. The banks of the North east are higher than those of the North west, but produce the same trees, flowers and shrubs. There are two plantations on the banks, both of which have the most delightful situations that it is possible to imagine, one of them in particular has a walk of above a mile long just on the top of the bank, which nature has formed with the most beautiful exactness, and left nothing for Art but that of cleaning away the luxuriancy, which generally attends her works. This however is too much for the listless hands of indolence and this beautiful place is overgrown with brambles and prickly pears, which render it entirely useless, tho' a few Negroes with their hoes could clear it in a week. The master of this fine place is rich and uncumbered by a family. Something like a glimmering of taste inspired him about a dozen years ago to build a house on a good plan and near this a fine walk, and a most delightful situation it must have been. The outside was accordingly finished, and even a part of the windows put in, when the

‡ An infant has the same allowance with its parents as soon as born.

hot months, I suppose, destroyed this temporary Activity, which has never yet returned, and he and his wife live in a hovel, while this handsome fabrick is daily falling into decay and will soon cease to exist at all.

In a few miles farther and very near the town, I found another* and must confess that in all my life I never saw a more glorious situation. It fronts the conflux of the north east and north west, which forms one of the finest pieces of water in the world. On this there is a very handsome house, and properly situated to enjoy every advantage. But the house is all, for I saw nothing neat done about it; tho' Nature has blocked out a fine lawn for them; down to the river it is overrun with weeds and briers. They tell me however that the M^{rs} of this place† is a pattern of industry, and that the house and every thing in it was the produce of her labours. She has (it seems) a garden, from which she supplies the town with what vegetables they use, also with

---

* The first of the two plantations to which Miss Schaw refers we have not been able to identify, but the second was "Hilton," the home of Cornelius Harnett, one of the leaders of the revolutionary movement in North Carolina. It was situated but a short distance north of Wilmington. It was at "Hilton" that Josiah Quincy held conferences with Howe and Harnett in 1773, where "the plan of Continental correspondence [was] highly relished, much wished for, and resolved upon as proper to be pursued." For a description, see *North Carolina Booklet*, II, no. 9, p. 71, and Connor, *Cornelius Harnett*, pp. 201-202.

† The maiden name of Mary, wife of Cornelius Harnett, is unknown. Her identification as a Grainger is wrong. She lived at "Hilton" but died in New York City, April 19, 1792. Her will is still preserved (Wills, AB, 486-488). Miss Schaw's later comment on Harnett as a "brute" may have only a political significance, but more probably it refers to his personality. If so the remark is not surprising, for despite Harnett's great services to the cause of the Revolution, he was not a man of either delicacy or refinement. The fact that he had an illegitimate child must be judged according to the moral standards of that day: Robert Halton, Francis Nash, and Matthew Rowan each had the same, and no one seems to have thought less of them on that account. But both Harnett and Howe were men of a fibre less fine and sensitive than that of James Moore, for example, and Miss Schaw was easily impressed by such distinctions. George Hooper's characterization of Harnett, drawn up many years later, though the tribute of one with loyalist antecedents and a Bostonian, is almost too flattering an estimate to be convincing. Certainly in Miss Schaw's day Harnett was not "beloved and honored by the

mellons and other fruits. She even descends to make minced pies, cheese-cakes, tarts and little biskets, which she sends down to town once or twice a day, besides her eggs, poultry and butter, and she is the only one who continues to have Milk. They tell me she is an agreeable woman, and I am sure she has good sense, from one circumstance,—all her little commodities are contrived so, as not to exceed one penny a piece, and her customers know she will not run tick,* which were they to be the length of sixpence, must be the case, as that is a sum not in every body's power, and she must be paid by some other articles, whereas the two coppers [that is, halfpence] are ready money. I am sure I would be happy in such an acquaintance. But this is impossible; her husband is at best a brute by all accounts and is besides the president of the committee and the great instigator of the cruel and unjust treatment the friends of government are experiencing at present. There are a few plantations forming near town, but so much in their infancy, that I can say little of them.

I rose this morning with a violent headache. The Musquetoes, tho' not yet so troublesome as at Point Pleasant, are swarming in town, which stands on a sandy soil, and is rendered from that situation intolerably hot. What they do in the low parts of the town, heaven knows. We are just now at

adherents of monarchy," as Hooper says (Connor, *Cornelius Harnett*, pp. 202-203).

Miss Schaw formed sudden likes and dislikes and acknowledges herself as prejudiced. This is shown in the case of the emigrants and of Neilson, both of whom, as she found, improved on acquaintance. Perhaps the same might have been true in the case of Harnett, Howe, and other American radicals, had she known them longer and under different circumstances.

* To "run tick" was, and still is, to give credit. Mrs. Harnett's practice was unusual, for charge accounts or book debts were very common in colonial days, when small change was difficult to obtain. Inasmuch as Mrs. Harnett was able to enforce her rule, coppers must have been more plentiful in 1775 than they were under Dobbs or Tryon. The former in 1755 wanted the British government to issue a copper coinage for North Carolina (*N. C. R.* V, 155, 324-325), and the latter in 1764 suggested that North Carolina's share of the parliamentary appropriation be sent over either "in the copper coin of

the house of Doctor Cobham which is the best house and
much the airiest situation, yet it is hardly possible to breathe,
and both Miss Rutherfurd and myself appear as in the
height of the small-pox; but terrible as this is, I will stay till
I learn something of what is going on both here and at Newbern.‡ I have sent to Mr Hogg and Mr Campbell, both
Merchts of eminence;* from them I will hear truth not
always to be met every where. My friends have been with
me, by them I learn things are going on with a high hand. A
boat of provisions going to the king's ship has been stopped,
and Mr Hogg and Mr Campbell, the contractors, ordered to
send no more. Good God! what are the people at home
about, to suffer their friends to be thus abused. Two regiments just now would reduce this province, but think what
you will, in a little time, four times four will not be sufficient. Every man is ordered to appear under arms. This the
town's folks have been forced to comply with, tho' determined to go no further in a cause they so much disapprove.
Melancholy clouds every honest face, while ferocity and
insolence blaze in those of their enemies. Heaven grant them
deliverance, for much they are to be pitied. Miss Rutherfurd
and I intended going up the North West to Schawfield, but
have changed our design, as we find the boys very unhappy
at the house where they are boarded. Jack naturally despises
a Schoolmaster,† who knows not half what he does himself,

‡ Newbern town where the Congress meets.

Britain or in such coin as his Majesty may be pleased to order to be coined
in the Tower of London" (ib., VI, 1219-1220).

* The firm of Hogg & Campbell was one of the leading mercantile and
contracting houses in Wilmington, doing both a wholesale and a retail business. In the Cape Fear Mercury, December 29, 1773, we read, "For London,
the ship Good Intent will be ready to sail; part freight secured, for remainder apply to Hogg and Campbell." The firm was composed of Robert Hogg
and Samuel Campbell, prominent men of known loyalist sympaties. That is
why Miss Schaw felt that she could turn to them for such information and
advice as she was not likely to obtain elsewhere. For biographical data concerning these men, see Appendix XII.

† On the arrival of Miss Schaw in the province, the boys were probably

so we carry them up to Point Pleasant and return next Monday to see the review of all the troops raised in this province. I will leave this letter to be sent, tho' I risk tar and feather was it to be seen. Perhaps it may be the last I will ever write you at least from this part of the world.

Point Pleasant.

The evening I came back here, my brother arrived from Newbern, having left Mr Rutherfurd at his plantation thirty miles from this. He had with him a young man* of so agreeable an appearance, that tho' I believed him an American, I could not help owning he had the look of a Gentleman, yet I was pre-determined not to be pleased with him. His wan meagre looks disgusted me, his white hands gave me great offence, as I could not help thinking he displayed them ostentatiously. His gravity, for he was vastly grave, frightened me, yet after all, the creature was tame and genteel enough, made a bow, as if he had once known what it was to enter a decent apartment, spoke with a voice that seemed humanized and entered into conversation very much like a rational being.

I now learned what had passed at Newbern meeting, where both the Govr. and assembly had been treated with great insolence, and those friends that dared own their principles had been abused in a most shocking manner,† and that

sent with Mrs. Miller to "Schawfield," where they remained about two months. They were then put to board with a schoolmaster in Wilmington, where they were so unhappy that Miss Schaw took them away and carried them off to "Point Pleasant." Very likely they remained there until the final departure from North Carolina.

* This was Archibald Neilson, who arrived at "Point Pleasant" about June 1 and remained there, off and on, until August 25. See Appendix XIII.

† The situation at New Bern was unique and we may not wonder that it aroused Miss Schaw to wrathful comment. Mr. Connor, in his *Cornelius Harnett* (pp. 83-84), has described the circumstances as follows. "It was, indeed, a pretty situation. One set of men composed two assemblies, one legal, sitting by authority of the royal governor and in obedience to his

the provincial congress had come to a resolution and had it signed by its whole members to unite with and obey the grand continental congress in all their resolutions. I send you inclosed a copy of Govr Martin's speech, the protests taken by some of the members of the assembly, and also a paper wrote by a M^r McNight,* for which he has been obliged to fly the province of Carolina. Our Stranger Gentleman turns out a man of family in Scotland and of rank here, from the office he holds under the crown; and as I view him now divested of prejudice, he makes quite a different figure from what he did; sorry I am to say however that his wan looks continue, and I fear will while he is in this climate, as he is under the power of an Ague, whose fits shake him to pieces. He is certainly not vain of his hands however white, and as far as I can observe is neither a savage nor a coxcomb. He is really an agreeable young man, has seen the world and knows a great deal. If he does not go up the country again, he will prove an agreeable accession to our little party.†

We have a most obliging invitation from the Govr and Mrs Martin, to go up and stay with them and celebrate the king's birth-day, which is not now far off, and this we will not fail to do. The heat daily increases, as do the Musquetoes, the bugs and the ticks. The curtains of our beds are now supplied by Musquetoes' nets. Fanny has got a neat or rather elegant dressing room, the settees of which are canopied over with green gauze, and on these we lie panting for breath and

---

writ; the other illegal, sitting in defiance of his authority and in disobedience to his proclamation. The governor impotently called on the former to join him in dispersing the latter. The two assemblies met in the same hall and were presided over by the same man. 'When the governor's private secretary was announced at the door, in an instant, in the twinkling of an eye Mr. Moderator Harvey would become Mr. Speaker Harvey and gravely receive his Excellency's message.' "

* For the case of Thomas Macknight, Loyalist through circumstance and against his will, see Appendix XII.

† Archibald Neilson plays an important part in Miss Schaw's narrative from this time on.

air, dressed in a single muslin petticoat and short gown. Here I know your delicacy will be shocked, and I hear you ask, if our young man bear us company in this sequestrate apartment. Oh yes, my friend, he does, but he is too much oppressed himself to observe us. This serock [sirocco] has the same effect here as Briden* tells us it has in Sicily; it has ruined all vivacity, as my pen shows you, and renders us languid in thought, word and deed.

My Journal now meets many interruptions, and all I can do, is, to take notes and join them as I have opportunity. Mʳ Neilson, our new friend, is gone up the country again and we are to follow in a few days, and pass some time at Newbern. I find [feel] the loss of his company: he is that sort of man, who is of all others the fittest companion for us at present. He has seen a great deal of the world; his manners, naturally soft, give him a sort of Melancholy, that is far from displeasing any where, but here is particularly agreeable. I am told he is in love,† and I make no doubt that is true. I should be glad to be acquainted with the Lady, for from what I am able to discover of his sentiments she must have something more than mere beauty to recommend her to his regard, dif-

---

* Patrick Brydone, *A Tour Through Sicily and Malta, in a series of Letters to William Beckford, Esq.* Two volumes, London, 1773. The account of the "Sirocc" or Southeast Wind is in II, 104.

† Writing from her plantation "Chinese Temple," August 25, 1775, Mrs. DeRosset says: "It is thought Mr. Nelson's suit at Point Pleasant will end in matrimony—by his frequent stay there. For as Bevil (in Conscious Lover) says—'A denial is a favor every man may pretend to, and if a Lady would do honor to herself, she should never keep a gentlemen in suspense, if she knows she can't like him.'

"As Miss [Rutherfurd] appears to be a sweet, innocent young creature, I think she won't seem to encourage what she disapproves, and she is too sensible to trifle away his time without approbation. In general people in love look mighty silly, but I do assure you Mr. Nelson is more chatty and agreeable than ever—even before his mistress. I should not wonder if Fanny loved him. Do you remember how you looked when you were in love? Nay, do not give such a sigh, or I will never speak to you again of the Ladies of Cedar Grove [the DeRosset plantation]: They are all well—as much yours as ever, even little Fanny" (*James Sprunt Historical Monographs*, no. 4, p. 23).

ferent from the men of this country; I should hope she will be satisfied with the lot assigned her. But, good heaven! think of my talking in that way of a poor fellow that is chaced from place to place, and uncertain of his life. In the present situation, love does not admit of the various cares that press him; friendship however may be a consolation to him, and as he appears worthy, I dare say you will approve of my affording him as much esteem as is fit for me to bestow, or as he will ever desire of me.

I have been at a fine plantation called Hunthill belonging to Mr Rutherfurd.* On this he has a vast number of Negroes employed in various works. He makes a great deal of tar and turpentine, but his grand work is a saw-mill, the finest I ever met with. It cuts three thousand lumbers (which are our dales [deals]) a day, and can double the number, when necessity demands it. The woods round him are immense, and he has a vast piece of water, which by a creek communicates with the river, by which he sends down all the lumber, tar and pitch, as it rises every tide sufficiently high to bear

---

* John Rutherfurd had a plantation "Bowland" at Rocky Point, which he held until the sale of his properties in 1772. Sometime before Miss Schaw's arrival he acquired in trust for his children a large group of nine tracts, 4084 acres, on the east side of the Northeast, between Holly Shelter Creek and New Exeter, thirty miles from Wilmington and ten from Rocky Point. Four of the pieces bore distinctive names, "Stony Brook," "Bear Garden," "Price's Neck," and "Arthur's Neck." North of the plantation was Holly Shelter "pocósin," a term that Brickell defines as signifying wet and low lands "where large cypress trees grow." We even find the phrase "pocósin swamp." This pocósin may be the "vast piece of water" referred to by Miss Schaw.

Rutherfurd's fondness for his Scottish connections appears in the names which he gave to his plantations. The first he called "Bowland," after his father's estate in Scotland, which had some years before passed into the hands of the Pringles; and the other "Hunthill," the name of the estate of his Scottish relative, Henry Rutherfurd, which lay on the right bank of the Jed, extending north to the neighborhood of Jedburgh. His New York cousin, Walter Rutherfurd, showed the same liking, for he named his summer home in New Jersey near Boiling Spring (now Rutherford) after the family estate in Scotland, "Edgerston Manor" (Supplementary Notes to *Rutherfurds of that Ilk and their Cadets*, printed but not published, pp. 26-36).

any weight. This is done on what is called rafts, built upon a flat with dales, and the barrels depending from the sides.*
In this manner they will float you down fifty thousand deals at once, and 100 or 200 barrels, and they leave room in the centre for the people to stay on, who have nothing to do but prevent its running on shore, as it is floated down by the tides, and they must lay to, between tide and tide, it having no power to move but by the force of the stream. This appears to me the best contrived thing I have seen, nor do I think any better method could be fallen on; and this is adopted by all the people up the country.

There is a show of plenty at Hunthill beyond any thing I ever saw, but it is a mere plantation. He has not so much as a house on it, yet he has a fine situation for one which he proposes to build. Here the old Gentleman I formerly mentioned resides with him, and I assure you they keep a good house, tho' it is little better than one of his Negro huts, and it appeared droll enough to eat out of China and be served in plate in such a parlour. He has however an excellent library with fine globes and Mathematical instruments of all kinds, also a set of noble telescopes, and tho' the house is no house, yet the master and the furniture make you ample amends. But I must tell you he built a bed-chamber for our reception, by no means amiss. This will be a fine plantation in time of peace, as he is able to load a raft once a fortnight —the plantation not only affording lumber, but staves, hoops and ends for barrels and casks for the West India trade, and he has a great number of his slaves bred coopers and carpenters. Every body agrees that it is able to draw from twelve to fifteen hundred a year sterling money.

---

* The following extract from the county court records of Brunswick (1737-1741, p. 81) illustrates the raft system. "Large rafts of lumber are frequently brought down the river and by stress of weather are broke and lyable to be lost. Persons picking up the scattered lumber, boats or goods are to advertise the same in public places." The Scottish "dales" are the English "deals," that is, sawn boards or planks.

We had a Tarrapin dressed there for turtle. They have really an excellent cook and she made it as good at least as any I ever eat in Britain. We are now preparing to go up the country, but we dread the heat, which every day increases. This place is one of the coolest, as the reflux of the tide ebbing and flowing every twelve hours forces a circulation of air; notwithstanding of which, we are hardly able to breathe even here. What must it be when more inland? for even at my brother's, tho' on the banks of the river, I was not able to exist, and had been in the fever and ague before this, had I remained there, as he has most of his ground in rice, which renders the air perfectly putrid. Of this he is very sensible, and has made a purchase down on the sound* for his children to live at, but times just now put a stop to every thing.

This letter was begun several days ago,† but was to have been finished before I went up the country, where now I will never be. Mr Rutherfurd and Miss Rutherfurd had set out for Newbern, and my brothers, myself and another Gentleman were to follow. There are no inns on the road, so we could only travel in such companies as could be accommodated in private houses. They had been gone two days, and I was at Schawfield ready to set out, when to my no small surprise Miss Rutherfurd returned, and came to me there. The reason of which was, that they had met an express from Mr Neilson, informing them and us that the Govrs house had been attacked, himself obliged to get down to the man-of-war, and send off his wife, sister and children in a little

---

* Lands or plantations "down on the sound" were those along the western side of the shallow waters enclosed by the sand bars and islands of the Atlantic coast. Many planters, Heron, Howe, Hasell, Grainger, Mason, Hooper, Harnett, Lillington, Maclaine, Gabriel Johnston, and Porter, had lands or plantations there and resided on them for all or a part of the summer season. The waters, extending for miles along the coast, "not being freshened by rivers and constantly receiving the tide from the sea," were later experimented with as affording "a good surface" for evaporating salt.

† The journal was resumed sometime after May 24.

vessel, with directions to land them in the first safe port. What renders these circumstances the more affecting is that poor Mrs Martin is big with child, and naturally of a very delicate constitution, yet even this is better than her staying here, where she would be rendered constantly miserable with fear.*

On the Govr's first coming down, the people at Wilming-town sent aboard to him, desiring him to come on shore, and he would be safe. But he had luckily got information that a guard and ship were ready to carry him off to the congress.†

Field days are now appointed, and every man without distinction ordered to appear under arms and be drilled. Those who will not comply, must fly out of the country, and leave their effects behind them to the mercy of these people, whose

---

* Governor Martin escaped from New Bern on May 24 and by June 2 had taken up his residence at Fort Johnston. Before leaving he despatched his wife and children in a small vessel to New York, where they found refuge with his father-in-law at "Rockhall," Long Island. Later, in 1776, one James Green carried his furniture and baggage in a sailing vessel to the Cape Fear, but arrived after he had left and consequently the property was seized by the Americans.

Martin remained at Fort Johnston until its destruction and then took up his residence on the ships of war, going to Charles Town in May, 1776. In July he left the *Peggy*, upon which he had been living in Charles Town harbor, and went to New York, arriving there August 1, but for a month was unable to join his family, only twenty miles away, on account of the manœuvres preliminary to the battle of Long Island. With that battle won by the British (August 27, 1776) the way was made clear and he probably went at once to "Rockhall." His daughter Augusta was born there on September 5.

† There were three attempts made to capture Governor Martin: one at New Bern, one at Fort Johnston, and one on the *Peggy* in Charles Town harbor. Probably that to which Miss Schaw refers was the attempt at Fort Johnston, which resulted in the seizure and destruction of the fort, but not in the capture of the governor. Robert Howe was the instigator of this attempt, and was also concerned in the project to take Martin at Charles Town, the following spring, in order to prevent him from bringing Cornwallis upon the colony. The Americans believed that Martin, while at Charles Town, was endeavoring to persuade Cornwallis to attempt the invasion of the colony by way of the southern coast, with the idea of joining the Highlanders in an attack upon Wilmington. See the letters from Howe to Charles Lee, "Lee Letters," *Collections*, New York Historical Society, 1871, I, 398, 401. Cf. *N. C. R.* X, 43.

kindness is little to be trusted. Fanny insists on my going again to Point Pleasant, and I am myself very willing, for I think it much more agreeable, as my brother [Alexander] is gone down to the Govr, and will probably stay with him aboard, and poor Bob, my other brother, is very much at a loss how to act, and dares not speak on the subject.* Mrs Schaw's whole connections are engaged. Mr Howe, who I told you was a candidate for the command of the army here, has got a reg^t and Moor is general. My brother has been offered every thing, but has refused every offer, and I tremble for his fate, but any thing rather than join these people. I will write you from Point Pleasant, and I will leave this as we pass Wilmingtown† to catch the first safe opportunity.

Point Pleasant.

On our return here, we found Mr Rutherfurd and poor Neilson, whose situation is very deplorable, but whatever he suffers for himself, he feels more for his friend the governor, whom he loves and esteems as much as man can man. When one considers the fate of this young fellow, it is impossible not to be greatly affected. Had this unlucky affair not happened, he had been in as fine a way as any man in the province, and as he had turned all his attention to this line, it will not be easy for him to carry it to another. His health too is much worse, which is an addition to his distress, as it prevents his being so active as he wishes to be. I laugh at him and use every little Art in my power to make him view things in a more cheerful light, but he knows better than I do, and tho' his good nature and politeness make him appear to be

---

* James Murray wrote in 1777, "Billy and Sam C[ampbell] and Bob Schaw will be obliged to leave Carolina for not taking the oaths to the states, and so must several Scotch for the like crime" (*Letters*, p. 266).

† In taking the longer and more roundabout route by water from "Schawfield" to "Point Pleasant," Miss Schaw would have to pass Wilmington. Apparently this is what she means by her remark.

diverted with my foolings, I am sensible they do not amuse his melancholy. Mr Rutherfurd has got the gout, but he does not mind it; he is a most cheerful companion. However it is prudent in him to keep out of the way, and he has gone to Hunthill. Notwithstanding Mr Neilson's anxiety, he is a great help to our spirits. He reads, walks and goes out on the water with us; but he leaves us in a day or two and goes down to the man-of-war. I keep scribbling on, tho' I have nothing now to say, unless I tell you I have seen a number of snakes, but have had no opportunity of taking them under consideration.

Mr Rutherfurd left us yesterday, and we go to town to see a review of the troops that remain after sending a little army to South Carolina. You at home know nothing of the power of this country, nor will you believe it till you find it with a witness. I yesterday crushed an Alligator with my foot that in six months hence would be able to devour me. Six months ago a very little force would have done here, and even yet a proper exertion would do much towards resettling peace in these Southern provinces, tho' I am far from believing that the case with those further North.

Wilmingtown.

Good heavens! what a scene this town is: Surely you folks at home have adopted the old maxim of King Charles: "Make friends of your foes, leave friends to shift for themselves."

We came down in the morning in time for the review,*

---

* Though no specific reference is elsewhere made to this review, which so excited Miss Schaw's derision, it was probably connected with the drilling of the militia in the spring and summer of 1775, under the direction of Robert Howe, against which Martin so vigorously protested (*N. C. R.* IX, 1157; X, 149-150). This particular review took place early in June. We know of no troops sent to South Carolina at this early date, although recruiting officers from that colony came to North Carolina about this time. Martin, writing on June 30 and speaking of these recruiting parties, said that he hoped they

which the heat made as terrible to the spectators as to the soldiers, or what you please to call them. They had certainly fainted under it, had not the constant draughts of grog supported them. Their exercise was that of bush-fighting, but it appeared so confused and so perfectly different from any thing I ever saw, I cannot say whether they performed it well or not; but this I know that they were heated with rum till capable of committing the most shocking outrages. We stood in the balcony of Doctor Cobham's house and they were reviewed on a field mostly covered with what are called here scrubby oaks, which are only a little better than brushwood. They at last however assembled on the plain field, and I must really laugh while I recollect their figures: 2000 men in their shirts and trousers, preceded by a very ill beat-drum and a fiddler, who was also in his shirt with a long sword and a cue at his hair, who played with all his might. They made indeed a most unmartial appearance. But the worst figure there can shoot from behind a bush and kill even a General Wolfe.

Before the review was over, I heard a cry of tar and feather. I was ready to faint at the idea of this dreadful operation. I would have gladly quitted the balcony, but was so much afraid the Victim was one of my friends, that I was not able to move; and he indeed proved to be one, tho' in a humble station. For it was Mr Neilson's poor English groom. You can hardly conceive what I felt when I saw him dragged forward, poor devil, frighted out of his wits. However at the request of some of the officers, who had been Neilson's friends, his punishment was changed into that of mounting on a table and begging pardon for having smiled at the reg^t.

would be "disappointed in their expectation of great succour from hence" (*ib.*, X, 48). Miss Schaw may have been mistaken in saying that "a little army" had been sent to South Carolina, but as she was on the spot and wrote down what she heard at the time, her statement cannot be rejected as impossible.

He was then drummed and fiddled out of the town, with a strict prohibition of ever being seen in it again.

One might have expected, that tho' I had been imprudent all my life, the present occasion might have inspired me with some degree of caution, and yet I can tell you I had almost incurred the poor groom's fate from my own folly. Several of the officers came up to dine, amongst others Coll: Howe, who with less ceremony than might have been expected from his general politeness stept into an apartment adjoining the hall, and took up a book I had been reading, which he brought open in his hand into the company. I was piqued at his freedom, and reproved him with a half compliment to his general good breeding. He owned his fault and with much gallantry promised to submit to whatever punishment I would inflict. You shall only, said I, read aloud a few pages which I will point out, and I am sure you will do Shakespear justice. He bowed and took the book, but no sooner observed that I had turned up for him, that part of Henry the fourth, where Falstaff describes his company, than he coloured like Scarlet. I saw he made the application instantly; however he read it thro', tho' not with the vivacity he generally speaks; however he recovered himself and coming close up to me, whispered, you will certainly get yourself tarred and feathered; shall I apply to be executioner? I am going to seal this up. Adieu.

I closed my last packet at Doctor Cobham's after the review, and as I hoped to hear of some method of getting it sent to you, stayed, tho' Miss Rutherfurd was obliged to go home. As soon as she was gone, I went into the town, the entry of which I found closed up by a detachment of the soldiers; but as the officer immediately made way for me, I took no further notice of it, but advanced to the middle of the street, where I found a number of the first people in town standing together, who (to use Milton's phrase) seemed much impassioned. As most of them were my acquaintances,

I stopped to speak to them, but they with one voice begged me for heaven's sake to get off the street, making me observe they were prisoners, adding that every avenue of the town was shut up, and that in all human probability some scene would be acted very unfit for me to witness. I could not take the friendly advice, for I became unable to move and absolutely petrified with horror.

Observing however an officer with whom I had just dined, I beckoned him to me. He came, but with no very agreeable look, and on my asking him what was the matter, he presented a paper he had folded in his hand. If you will persuade them to sign this they are at liberty, said he, but till then must remain under this guard, as they must suffer the penalties they have justly incurred. "And we will suffer every thing," replied one of them, "before we abjure our king, our country and our principles." "This, Ladies," said he turning to me, who was now joined by several Ladies, "is what they call their Test, but by what authority this Gentleman forces it on us, we are yet to learn." "There is my Authority," pointing to the Soldiers with the most insolent air, "dispute it, if you can." Oh Britannia, what are you doing, while your true obedient sons are thus insulted by their unlawful brethren; are they also forgot by their natural parents?*

---

* On March 6, 1775, the Wilmington Committee of Safety formally accepted the Continental Association and voted that all its members should go in a body and wait upon the housekeepers in town, requesting their signatures to the same or receiving from them their reasons for refusing to sign, in order "that such enemies of their country may be set forth to public view and treated with the contempt they merit." Nine merchants and planters and two tailors (among the nine was Dr. Cobham) at first refused to sign (*N. C. R.* IX, 1166) and were placed under a boycott, but later, another opportunity being given, Dr. Cobham took advantage of it.

John Ashe, who had declined a reappointment as colonel of militia under Martin, took command of a body of some four or five hundred men and appearing in Wilmington threatened "the people above mentioned with military execution, if they did not immediately sign the Association dictated by the committee, and being interrogated for his authority pointed to the men he had assembled." "His cowardly intimidations of these individuals

We, the Ladies, adjourned to the house of a Lady, who lived in this street, and whose husband was indeed at home, but secretly shut up with some ambassadors from the back settlements* on their way to the Govr to offer their service, provided he could let them have arms and ammunition, but above all such commissions as might empower them to raise men by proper authority. This I was presently told tho' in the midst of enemies, but the Loyal party are all as one family. Various reasons induced me to stay all Night in the house I was then at, tho' it could afford me no resting place. I wished to know the fate of the poor men who were in such present jeopardy, and besides hoped that I should get word to my brother, or send your packet by the Gentlemen who were going to the man-of-war. In the last I have succeeded, and they are so good as [to] promise to get it safely there to my brother or the Govr who would not fail to send it by first opportunity to Britain. Indeed it is very dangerous to keep letters by me, for whatever noise general warrants made in the mouths of your sons of faction at home, their friends and fellow rebels use it with less ceremony than ever it was practised in Britain, at any period.

Rebels, this is the first time I have ventured that word, more than in thought, but to proceed.

(writes Martin) so far answered the purpose that they were obliged to sign what their consciences revolted at and abhorred." In another letter Martin adds, "The Scotch merchants at Wilmington who so long maintained their loyalty have lately (August, 1775) been compelled ostensibly to join in sedition by appearing under arms at the musters appointed by the committees, although they are still at heart as well affected as ever" (*ib.*, X, 48, 170-171, 236). In the *Cape Fear Mercury* of August 25, 1775, among the items is this: "Lt. Col. Cotton & Saml and Jacob Williams stopped, having been eight days on board the Cruizer with Gov. Martin. They signed the association."

* The "ambassadors from the back settlements" were of course Highlanders, one of whom was Captain Alexander McLeod, late an officer of marines, who had been in the colony about a year. With whom he was closeted in Wilmington we are not informed, but eventually he made his way down the river and had an interview with the governor (*N. C. R.* X, 326).

The prisoners stood firm to their resolution of not signing the Test, till past two in the morning, tho' every threatening was used to make them comply; at which time a Message from the committee compromised the affair, and they were suffered to retire on their parole to appear next morning before them. This was not a step of mercy or out of regard to the Gentlemen; but they understood that a number of their friends were arming in their defence, and tho' they had kept about 150 ragamuffins still in town, they were not sure even of them; for to the credit of that town be it spoke, there are not five men of property and credit in it that are infected by this unfortunate disease.

As I had nothing further to do in town, I came up to Schawfield, where Fanny met me, and we will go to Point Pleasant again in a day or two, as I find this place so warm, that I shall certainly have a fever, if I stay. It is beautiful however, the garden is in great glory, tubby roses so large and fragrant, as is quite beyond a British idea, and the Trumpet honey-suckle is five times as large as ours, and every thing else in proportion. I particularly name these two as their bell seems the favourite bed of the dear little humming birds, which are here in whole flocks. The place altogether is very fine, the India corn is now almost ready, and makes a noble appearance. The rice too is whitening, and its distant appearance is that of our green oats, but there is no living near it with the putrid water that must lie on it, and the labour required for it is only fit for slaves, and I think the hardest work I have seen them engaged in. The indigo is now ready; it looks very pretty, but for all these I refer you to Miller's description, which, on comparison, I find perfectly just. Tho' the water melons here are thought particularly fine, I am not yet reconciled to them. My brother brought some cantalup melon seed, which was sown here; tho', by what accident I cannot tell, they were all torn up while green. They must have been exquisite, but every melon except the water melon, is indiscriminately called musk melon and despised, which is a pity, for our good ones must be a great treat here. The cotton is now ripe,* and tho' only annual grows to a little bush. It seems extremely good, and is very prolifick. They complain much of the trouble it requires, as it must not only be weeded, but watched while green, as the bears are very fond of it in its infancy. It also is troublesome to gather and to clean from the husk, so that few house-wives will venture on the task, and I am glad they do not; for under proper management, it would be an Article of great consequence. Two or three score of our old women with their cards and wheels would hurt the linnen Manufactories. But were I a planter, I would send a son or two to be bred to the weaving and farming business, who might teach the Negroes, and I would bring out a ship loaded on my own account with wheels, reels and Looms, also ploughs, harrows, drills, spades, rakes, etc. And this may all happen, when Britain *strikes home.* We set off this afternoon for the Point and travel by land, so I will be able to give you some account of our journey in that way, as we must go by the great road that leads into South Carolina the one way and Virginia the other.† Adieu.

---

* This section is surely misplaced. Cotton cannot have been ripe in the first week of July. It may have been in flower, but not in boll before the latter part of September.

† The plan was to go to "Point Pleasant" by land instead of by water, taking the road out of Wilmington that led north toward Heron's bridge and from that point along the west side of the river on into Virginia. This road, known as the Duplin road, was the main thoroughfare into the up-country in the direction of Hillsboro and the Dan. It seems to have been possible to go to New Bern also by this route, turning just below Holly Shelter Creek, at New Exeter (a town that never grew up), and eventually joining the regular New Bern road. Craig's army, after taking Wilmington in 1781, marched on New Bern and returned to Wilmington by this route, stopping at Rutherfurd's plantation for four days on the way.

But Miss Schaw would not go as far as Heron's bridge. Passing behind "Hilton," she would turn off a short distance beyond the "Hermitage" and "Castle Haynes" and ride four miles west through the woods to "Point Pleasant," which lay on the south bank, at the bend of the river. Even in 1801 the road out of Wilmington up the Northeast branch "was narrow and

P. S. This will be delivered to you by my brother, who has just stole up from the Sound to bid me, farewell. He has not an hour to stay: he goes home with despatches from the Govr. I am lost in confusion, this is unexpected indeed—oh heavens! Farewell.

Thank God, my brother got safe aboard the King's ship and sailed with Capt Talmash in his frigate that same afternoon for England.* It was very fortunate he had the precaution to venture thro' the woods under the guidance of a single Negro, for tho' his coming up from the Sound, as well as his intended expedition were concealed with the utmost care, yet his leaving the frigate just as Capt Talmash arrived had been known and raised such suspicions that the roads were guarded to watch his return and seize him. Of this his friend at the Sound was informed and was in the utmost distress. It would not however have been an easy matter to make him yield, as he had an invincible aversion to the tar-

---

led through a pine forest." "We thought we were in a lane," writes Caroline Burgwin, who had just come from England to take charge of the "Hermitage," her father's home, "and expressed to our astonished driver our fears of an attack by wild beasts" (Burr, *The Hermitage*, 1885).

* On July 5, Governor Martin wrote to Lord Dartmouth, "I have engaged Mr. Alex^r Schaw, whom I have had the honour to introduce to your Lordship, to charge himself with this letter. This gentleman is qualified by his intelligence, his candour, and his accurate observation, during some months that he has resided in this colony, to give your Lordship every information that you can desire relative to its present condition and circumstances. Mr. Schaw is an officer in the customs in the Is. of St. Christopher's, from which he has been absent by leave on his private concerns, and was preparing to return to it, when Capt. Tollemache's arrival presented me with so fair an occasion to employ him advantageously for his Majesty's service that I could not resist it" (Public Record Office, C. O. 5:318).

Schaw sailed with Captain Tollemache on the *Scorpion*, July 6 or 7. The *Scorpion* had left Charles Town shortly before for Boston, touching at the Cape Fear to deliver despatches from Gage to Martin and to receive anything that Martin might wish to send. Schaw transshipped at Boston to another vessel for England, arriving there sometime in September or October. He had not reached London by September 15, but was there on October 31. His letters to Dartmouth are dated October 31 and November 8. For his expenses Governor Martin advanced him £100, which sum was afterwards included in Martin's statement of account with the British government (Public Record Office, Declared Accounts, 1259, 139).

pot, and as he carried a pair of pistols in each pocket, he would have tried these in the first instance; but it is much better as it is. I have a letter from him after he got on board Capt Talmash, where he desires me to take the first opportunity of going to St Kitts and carrying with me my young friends. And that I might be able to do so in comfort, he sends me an order to his man of business to put into my hands, whatever belonged to him on the Island, and pay me his Salary till I can hear from him about my return to Britain* and begs Mr Rutherfurd to agree to his proposal, and Mr Rutherfurd says it must come to that or worse, and seems satisfied. But poor Fanny has so lately found a father that she is loath to lose him again so soon, so that for the present the scale of fate hangs doubtful.

Mr Neilson came here some days ago, he looks worse than ever, and his ague more severe. He has anxiety painted on his looks. He makes light however of his own distresses, but seems to suffer perfect agony on the Governor's account, whom he cannot mention without feeling that anguish, which is too strong for his constitution. May God deliver him and all our distressed countrymen from the present situation. A few months ago the task would have been easy; it is still possible, but (God make me a false prophetess) it will not be long so. The inclination of this country is however far from being generally for this work. Indolent and inactive, they have no desire to move, even where their own immediate interest calls them. All they are promised is too distant to

---

* Schaw was appointed searcher of customs at Basseterre, St. Kitts, March 31, 1774. When there in January, 1775, he obtained leave of absence for twelve months from March 6, but never went back. That he intended, when he left North Carolina, to return to St. Christopher from England, and that his friends expected him to do so, when he parted from them in July, appears from the act of his brother Robert, who six months later, on December 10, 1775, transferred to "Alex^r Schaw, Senior, of the Island of St. Christopher, Esq." a certain negro woman named Lucy, for the "maintenance and education" of his own son, Alexander Schaw, Jr. (Brunswick County Records, Conveyances, B, 299).

interest them; they suffer none of those abuses they are told of and feel their liberty invaded only by the oppressive power of the Congress and their Agents, who at this Season are pressing them from their harvest, for they know not what purpose. But tho' they show at first a very great degree of reluctance to go, yet they believe there is no retreat, after they have been once under arms and are convinced that from that moment they fight for their lives and properties, which by that act are both forfeited to their blood-thirsty enemies. You may therefore be assured they will not fail to exert all the activity and courage they are able to muster up, and, once engaged themselves, are willing to draw in others.

It is a most unfortunate circumstance they have got time to inculcate this idea. Three months ago, a very small number had not any thing to apprehend; a few troops landing and a general amnesty published would have secured them all at home. For I do not suppose them of such a martial spirit as voluntarily to have joined Cother's standard. At present the martial law stands thus: An officer or committee-man enters a plantation with his posse. The Alternative is proposed, Agree to join us, and your persons and properties are safe; you have a shilling sterling a day; your duty is no more than once a month appearing under Arms at Wilming-town, which will prove only a merry-making, where you will have as much grog as you can drink. But if you refuse, we are directly to cut up your corn, shoot your pigs, burn your houses, seize your Negroes and perhaps tar and feather your-self. Not to chuse the first requires more courage than they are possessed of, and I believe this method has seldom failed with the lower sort. No sooner do they appear under arms on the stated day, than they are harangued by their officers with the implacable cruelty of the king of Great Britain, who has resolved to murder and destroy man, wife and child, and that he has sworn before God and his parliament that he will not spare one of them; and this those deluded people believe more firmly than their creed, and who is it that is bold enough to venture to undeceive them. The King's proclamation* they never saw; but are told it was ordering the tories to murder the whigs, and promising every Negro that would murder his Master and family that he should have his Master's plantation. This last Artifice they may pay for, as the Negroes have got it amongst them and believe it to be true. Tis ten to one they may try the experiment, and in that case friends and foes will be all one.

I came to town yesterday with an intention of being at church this day, where I was informed there was to be service performed by a very good clergyman. In this however I was disappointed, for I found the whole town in an uproar, and the moment I landed, Mr Rutherfurd's negroes were seized and taken into custody till I was ready to return with them. This apparent insult I resented extremely, till going up to Doctor Cobham's, I found my short prophecy in regard to the Negroes was already fulfilled and that an insurrection was hourly expected.† There had been a great number of them discovered in the adjoining woods the night before, most of them with arms, and a fellow belonging to Doctor Cobham was actually killed. All parties are now united

---

* By "King's proclamation," Miss Schaw means the proclamation issued by Governor Gage of Massachusetts, Boston, June 12, 1775, as a broadside, offering "His most gracious Majesty's pardon to all persons who shall forthwith lay down their arms and return to the duties of peaceable subjects, excepting only from the benefits of such pardon, Samuel Adams and John Hancock," etc. It corresponds to a similar pardon issued by Clinton offering amnesty to all in North Carolina, except Harnett and Howe. Martin calls Gage's proclamation "a proclamation of the King" and it was generally so interpreted.

† It was believed in the province that Martin had planned to arm the negroes and to proclaim the freedom of such of them as would join the King's standard. John Stuart, in his letter to Dartmouth, of July 21, 1775, mentions a report which had spread through the Carolinas that the negroes were immediately to be set free by the government and that arms were to be given them to fall upon their masters. In consequence of these rumors, the Wilmington Committee ordered that all negroes be disarmed. During June and July the conditions which Miss Schaw describes characterized the life of the town (*N. C. R.* X, 43, 94-95, 112, 118).

against the common enemies. Every man is in arms and the patroles going thro' all the town, and searching every Negro's house, to see they are all at home by nine at night. But what is most provoking, every mouth male and female is opened against Britain, her King and their abettors—here called the tories,—tho' the poor tories are likely to suffer, at least as much as any of them, and who were as ready to give their assistance to quell them as any independents amongst them. But whatever way this end, it will confirm the report I formerly mentioned to you past all contradiction.

As I was afraid to venture up with only the Negroes, I despatched the boat with them, and a letter to Fanny, begging her to secure all their arms and come herself down to town. She is far from well: her father is as yet at Hunthill. Mr Neilson came down with me and presently went off to the Governor, so she has no white person with her, but our two Abigails. I expect her every moment. I go to sup with my friends on the hill, and return to sleep at the Doctor's. I change my quarters every time I am in town, to please all my friends. To do the whole justice, they are very hospitable. Good evening to you. I will write again to morrow. I have an excellent apartment, and every body is too much engaged about themselves to mind what I am doing.

After a sleepless night, to which the musquetoes contributed more than my fears of the Negroes, I am sat down by the first peep of day to inform you of what further happened yesterday. I told you I was going to sup at the hill, which is at the other extremity of the town. Here I found the affair of the Negroes justly attributed to the cause I formerly mentioned, vizt that of falsifying the King's proclamation, for tho' neither they nor I had seen it, we were convinced it was in a style the reverse of what was given out. Our time passed so agreeably that it was now too late to venture so far without some male protector, and as all the Negroes were locked up, I therefore waited till the Midnight patrol arrived, the commander of which was a tory, and my particular acquaintance. Under his protection therefore I marched off at the head of the party stopping at the different houses in our way to examine if the Negroes were at home. For God's sake! draw a picture of your friend in this situation and see if 'tis possible to know me. Oh! I shall make a glorious knapsack-bearer. You have formed a very wrong idea of my delicacy; I find I can put it on and off like any piece of dress. But to proceed with my Mid-night march. While the men went into the houses, I stayed without with the commander of the party, who took that opportunity to assure me, he believed the whole was a trick intended in the first place to inflame the minds of the populace, and in the next place to get those who had not before taken up arms to do it now and form an association for the safety of the town. What further design they had, he could not tell, but made not the least doubt it was for some sinister purpose this farce was carried on. That poor Cobham had lost a valuable slave, and the poor fellow his life without the least reason, he was certain; for that it was a fact well known to almost everybody that he met a Mistress every night in the opposite wood, and that the wench being kept by her Master, was forced to carry on the intrigue with her black lover with great secrecy, which was the reason the fellow was so anxious to conceal himself; that the very man who shot him knew this, and had watched him. My hypothesis is however that the Negroes will revolt. I bade my friend good night and found Mrs Cobham in a terrible huff, from the idea I was not to come back that night. She is so much affected by the fate of her Negro, that she is almost as great a tory as her husband, which was not lately the case.* But here comes the Coffee, farewell. If Fanny come down, I will write again from this.

---

*Mrs. Cobham was probably a native of the province. Her first husband was John Paine of Brunswick county and she was married to Dr. Cobham sometime in the late sixties.

Point Pleasant.

Fanny could not come down, and my fear of the Negroes
being over, I returned in the Phaeton she had sent down for
me and travelled off by the great road, which I believe I have
never mentioned to you. I am indeed extremely inaccurate,
but you must pardon me. I do the best to obey your commands and keep my own promise, to both of which I am in
duty bound. This road begins at Wilmingtown and goes clear
across the country to Virginia on one side and South Carolina
on the other, and as its course lies across the river, it is
crossed by a bridge, which tho' built of timber is truly a noble
one, broader than that over the Tay at Perth. It opens at the
middle to both sides and rises by pullies, so as to suffer Ships
to pass under it.* The road is sufficiently broad to allow
fifty men to march abreast, and the woods much thinner of
trees than anywhere I have seen them. The pasture under
these trees is far from bad, tho' the hot season has parched
it a good deal. Off from this wood lie many plantations,
which however are hid amongst the trees from the view of
the road, and not easy of access from it. Point Pleasant lies
about four miles off from it—part of the way is thro' the
woods, where the path is devious and uncertain to those that
are unacquainted with it. About a mile or little more from
Point Pleasant, begins a most dismal swamp thro' the middle
of which there is a road made with infinite labour, raised on
piles covered with branches, and over all sods; and it is by
no means comfortable to drive a carriage over it, as the
swamps on each hand appear unfathomable, and I would

---

* As far as we know Heron's bridge was the only drawbridge in the
colonies. There had been a ferry at that point over the Northeast until 1766,
when Captain Heron, who owned land there on both sides of the river, was
authorized by act of assembly to build a bridge. This bridge was to "have
one wide arch of thirty feet for rafts and pettiauguas to pass through and
six feet above high-water mark, and be made to draw up occasionally for the
navigation of vessels of larger burthen." The ferry was abolished and Heron
was authorized to erect a gate and take tolls (*N. C. State Records*, XXV,
506-507). Miss Schaw's description of this bridge is interesting.

RESIDENCE IN NORTH CAROLINA

really believe them so, did not the noble Magnolias, the bays and a thousand Myrtles convince me it had a bottom from which they spring.

For a description of the Magnolia, I refer you to Miller, tho' they are infinitely more beautiful than he describes them, and carry the flower twice a year on trees as large and full spread as our Oaks, and you may conceive the Glory of a full spread oak covered with white roses, for both in smell and look that is the flower they resemble. The Myrtle thro' all this swamp is the candle-berry-myrtle, which makes the green candle you have seen at home. They give a very pleasant light, and when placed in a silver candle-stick, look extremely pretty. And here for a moment let me lead you to admire what Nature has done for the inhabitants of this country. This is an Article which every house-wife grudges the expence of—here they have it for nothing, if they would only accept of it. The cotton is in plenty growing every where for the wick, if they would take the trouble to spin it. The berries hang to the hand, and seem to beg you to gather them, but they generally beg in vain, not one out of fifty will take the trouble to make them into candles. The poorer sort burn pieces of lightwood, which they find without trouble, and the people of fashion use only Spermaceti, and if any green wax, it is only for kitchen use. I have seen it prepared however, and its process is the most simple you can imagine. When the berries are gathered and picked from the stalks, they are thrown into a kettle of Water, which is set to boil, and kept boiling for a few hours, in which time the berries melt almost away. It is then set to cool, and when cold, you find the grosser parts have sunk to the bottom of the kettle, while the pure wax forms a cake on the top. To have it fine, it requires to go thro' several boilings, and then it will become so transparent as to be seen thro'. All that is further to be done is only to melt it, and pour it into proper moulds, when it will afford the most agreeable light a candle can give.

As soap and candle are commonly a joint manufacture, I will now mention that article, which they have here very good, as they have the finest ashes in the world. But when you have occasionally to buy it, however, you meet only with Irish soap, and tho' some house-wives are so notable as to make it for themselves, which they do at no expence, yet most of them buy it at the store at a monstrous price. They are the worst washers of linen I ever saw, and tho' it be the country of indigo they never use blue, nor allow the sun to look at them. All the cloaths coarse and fine, bed and table linen, lawns, cambricks and muslins, chints, checks, all are promiscuously thrown into a copper with a quantity of water and a large piece of soap. This is set a boiling, while a Negro wench turns them over with a stick. This operation over, they are taken out, squeezed and thrown on the Pales to dry. They use no calender; they are however much better smoothed than washed. Mrs Miller offered to teach them the British method of treating linens, which she understands extremely well, as, to do her justice, she does every thing that belongs to her station, and might be of great use to them. But Mrs Schaw was affronted at the offer. She showed them however by bleaching those of Miss Rutherfurd, my brothers and mine, how different a little labour made them appear, and indeed the power of the sun was extremely apparent in the immediate recovery of some bed and table-linen, that had been so ruined by sea water, that I thought them irrecoverably lost. Poor Bob, who has not seen a bleaching-washing since a boy, was charmed with it, and Mrs Miller was not a little pleased with the compliments he made her on it. Indeed this and a dish of hodge podge she made for him have made her a vast favourite, and she has promised him a sheeps' head. But as she rises in the Master's esteem, she falls in that of the Mistress, who by no means approves Scotch or indeed British innovations.

Some days ago we were informed that Gen¹ Moor with 1500 or 2000 men had marched down the country, having resolved to take the fort, and with the cannon they expected to find in it, take also the Cruiser, the Govʳ and the whole covey of tories he had with him. The fort indeed was no hard conquest;* but the Govʳ some how or other having a hint of the design, had taken out the cannon, which with the garrison, vizᵗ Capᵗ Collet† and his three servants, were now aboard the Cruiser. However they did burn this mighty place of strength, together with the houses belonging to it; but not stopping there, they wantonly destroyed the corn and burnt the houses of several planters, who had at times been useful to those aboard the frigate. This we were informed of by a Gentleman who was making his escape from the country, and called on us in his way.‡ He further informed us, that he and the other Gentlemen who had armed and formed themselves into two companies for the defence of the town, had been ordered out on this duty of burning the fort, but that they having all refused, were now ordered to stand trial for mutiny and desertion, but had refused to submit. This, he said, was all done in consequence of a letter received from the grand congress, in which they were accused of having done nothing to show the side they had espoused. I therefore make no doubt every step will be taken to show (at least) their zeal by the abuse of their fellow-subjects. But as every

* The fort was attacked and burned July 19, 1775. Governor Martin's account of this event can be read in his letter to Dartmouth, of July 20; that of the Wilmington Committee in their resolution of July 21 (*N. C. R.* X, 107-109, 113-115. Cf. 140). The two versions show how hopeless was any prospect of a reconciliation between the contending parties at this time.

† For Captain Collet, see Appendix XIV.

‡ The gentleman referred to was Robert Hogg, who left Wilmington in July (see Appendix XII). One of those who had been ordered out "on this duty of burning the fort" was his partner, Samuel Campbell, whose statement before the Loyalist Claims Commission confirms what Miss Schaw says here (see below, p. 324).

body is getting off as fast as possible, they will not have many objects to vent their fury on.

Mr Neilson was so ill that he was again forced to come ashore for a few days to recover a little. He has no place to sleep in aboard, but lies on the quarter-deck in his hammock, as do many more Gentlemen, as it is quite crouded. He left us this day. Mr Rutherfurd sometimes comes down, but seldom, nor stays above a day or two, which is very prudent every way. His daughter has not been well to day, and been forced to keep her bed. I fear she is in for the fever and ague. She is now asleep, and tho' it is struck one, I will watch by her till she waken, as I am not a little anxious about her. Farewell, I go to my charge.

Never was any thing more fortunate than poor Neilson's leaving this [place] yesterday, had he remained, I have reason to believe his sorrow and anxieties would by this [time] have been over, a circumstance of much less consequence to himself than his friends, in which number I must ever rank myself, or be a most ungrateful wretch, as he has been to me as a brother, ever since we became acquainted. Judge then what I must have suffered to have seen a man of so much worth murdered before my eyes for doing his duty to his King, his country, and if any thing can be above these sacred names, his friend. I wrote you in a former packet that some Scotch Gentlemen had come down from the back settlements with offers to the Govr of raising a considerable number of men, provided the Govr could obtain for their use, arms and ammunition, and that he would give such commissions as empowered them to act in it with safety. This last part was immediately agreed to, and as to the first, he sent off an express to the commander in chief, and makes no doubt the request will be complied with, and with these assurances the Gentlemen returned to their friends.

The commissions were prepared as fast as possible, also a copy of the King's proclamation with an additional one from the Govr,* offering pardon to whoever would return, and reward to whoever joined the Royal party. These finished, an English groom, who was the same that had escaped the tar and feather, and who was a most expert rider, was mounted on a fine English hunter, the commissions put into the travelling bags before him, under cover of his own linens, and fixed to the crupper; in a leather case were the two proclamations. He had made out two days journey very safely, when on the third he happened to pass by a house where a set of officers and committee-men were baiting their horses, as they were so far on the way to Hillsburgh, where they make their paper-money for the use of the army. The beauty of the English mare took their fancy, and discovering who the fellow was, were resolved to become masters of her. But he no sooner observed he was pursued, than he quitted the road and struck into the woods, where trusting to the superior swiftness of his mare, he put her full speed, and in a few moments would have left his pursuers far behind, but, alas, he was not on New Market course.† A tree struck her or rather she a tree so violent a blow, that she fell to the ground, and threw her unfortunate rider with the bags, and before he could get hold of the bridle, scampered off most unluckily, carrying with her the two proclamations, which were fixed to the saddle. The fellow however had the presence of mind to bury the commissions in the sand, then running to a distant part of the wood, he let the bags lie on the ground, as if thrown by the mare, and laid himself down as half killed by the fall.

---

* Martin issued four proclamations in 1775: one on March 1, from New Bern; a second on April 3, also from New Bern; a third on June 16, from Fort Johnston; and a fourth on August 8, from on board the *Cruizer*, the "fiery" proclamation ordered by the Wilmington Committee to be burned by the hangman. The last is the one to which Miss Schaw refers. It used to be said in Scotland, in the days of religious controversy, that when a treatise was difficult to answer the most convenient method was to have it burned by the common hangman.

† Newmarket is a town in central England, on the border line between Cambridgeshire and Suffolk, long famous for its horse racing.

He was now questioned and threatened, but would give no further account of his business, than that he was on his way to quit the country and begged them to let him go; and it is probable they might have agreed, had not some of the party gone in search of the booty, which they caught and found on her this dreadful treasonable paper. There was now no denying, so the poor wretch lost all courage, and begged they would not punish a poor servant that was forced to obey his master. He fell on his knees before his inexorable judges and executioners, for such they would have been had they not hoped to force more from him, or at least pretend they had. To give a face to their proceedings, he was now brought to Wilmingtown, and the proclamation taken to the Committee, where it was read, and such was the indignation it raised in the members, that they burnt it with their own hands, publishing another for themselves; in which they set forth the bloody design forming against them by Britain and Governor Martin. As to the prisoner, he was suffered to escape; as a further inquiry might have cleared up those points they had a mind to hide from the multitude under very false colours. Besides they had got the Mare, which was a main Article.*

The fellow came here in his retreat, where he is taken care of, and gave me the above particulars. But he was Neilson's servant; the mare was also his property, and to crown all, the Governor's proclamation was found to be his hand writ-

---

* The incident narrated by Miss Schaw illustrates admirably Martin's remark in his letter of August 28. "The same ill fortune has attended my latest attempt to counteract the design of a Convention at this time assembled at Hillsborough, by a Proclamation of which your Lordship will receive a copy forthwith, the messengers employed to circulate it in the country having been all intercepted, which I the more lament as I think it might have produced good effects upon the minds of the people, and that I have much reason to apprehend the difficulty of communication which becomes daily greater and greater, will totally cut me off from all intercourse with the interior parts of it hereafter until I am able by force to lay it open" (N. C. R. X, 231-232).

ing. On this about a dozen of the greatest brutes they had, with two or three of the most worthless of the scoundrels received a commission to go to Point Pleasant and search for the person of Arch^d Neilson, with full authority to put the law in execution in what way they saw proper. By this time they were all drunk, and set out about twelve at night on this humane expedition. Fortunately however they were such a set, as were not in use to visit at this house, so were strangers to the way, after they quitted the great road,* and rambled down on other parts of the wood, which brought them on the plantation of a Gentleman, who tho' engaged in their own party was by no means easy at these Midnight Visitors. They however explained the mistake sufficiently to convince him, that they were very improper people to pay a visit, where they were likely to behave in no very delicate manner. He therefore readily gave them the drink they demanded of him, and they were soon in no condition to leave his house, and therefore transferred their commission to him, which he faithfully promised to execute before morning, and accordingly I was beckened out, Miss Rutherfurd being still asleep, and found a Gentleman he had despatched, as soon as he could, to give us information, and to carry Neilson, if there, to the committee with him; who as they would by this time be come a little to themselves, would not hurry his fate. He expressed great pleasure however at hearing he was gone, for the truth of which he took my word, without further search, assuring me honestly, that had these people got him, he had never got out of their hands alive, so enraged were they at his conduct.

---

* The "great road" was that already noted from Wilmington up the Northeast and on to Virginia, via Heron's bridge. "Point Pleasant" was west from the road, four miles toward the river. The plantation referred to in the text was probably "Rose Hill," the owner of which, Parker Quince, son of Richard Quince, was living there at the time and must have been the gentleman who, according to Miss Schaw, did not take kindly to these midnight raids. In his will (1785) Quince left "Rose Hill" to his son. He died in England and was buried in Ramsgate, the home of his fathers.

Coffee was brought in, and during breakfast, he frankly confessed, they had got some news that had not been agreeable, which had been transferred [transpired, *sic*] by the arrival of a ship from Boston. This was a battle having happened on a place called Bunkershill, where some of the lines had been forced by the English. He believed however they had suffered more than the Americans. I am glad however to find that we had any advantage, tho' not a little uneasy to hear more particulars.

Miss Rutherfurd is now quite well; an emetick, which was far too strong, has however removed every symptom for the present. I shall not be easy till I go to town to inquire the particulars of this battle, which before this you are perfectly acquainted with. I have now been in town, which is intirely deserted by the Tories, some of whom are out in the country, and others gone out of the way, till this hurry of passion be a little settled. I have seen a newspaper published by the committee's order, where the whole story of the battle is denied, tho' it is said that the Americans had made an attack on us and killed many of our officers, amongst others they mentioned Major Pitcairn. I hope it is not the Pitcairn that was married to a Miss Dalrymple, as I know many of her relations.* But tho' 'tis all false together, I hope the publisher will be hanged, for they have vexed me, tho' I do not believe them.

Aboard the Cruizer, his Majesty's Frigate of war.†

Rejoice with me, my friends, to find me safe this length. You suppose I have fled from the tar-pot. In truth I am not

---

* Major John Pitcairn, who was killed at Bunker Hill, married Elizabeth, daughter of Robert Dalrymple of Annfield (or Annefield) in Dumfriesshire (Anderson, *Scottish Nation*, III, 291). So Miss Schaw's worst fears were realized. A petition from the widow, Elizabeth Pitcairn, is in Adm. 1. 486.

† It was in September or October that Miss Schaw, Fanny and the boys, and Mrs. Miller took refuge on board the *Cruizer*. All apparently crossed the

sure what might have happened, had I stayed much longer, for the ill humour was come to a very great height.

Our coming here, for we are all here, is the most extraordinary thing that has yet happened, and was so sudden and surprising, that I am not yet sure, if I am awake or in a dream. But I hope it is no dream that I have found here a large packet from you, which I sincerely thank God did not fall into the hands of the Committee, as your last did, and I am most happy to find that I am obeying you by leaving this unhappy country.

Before I begin to fill up the blanks in my Journal, which is no less than a whole month, suffer me to take one look back to the unhappy people I have left, and on whose conduct I can now calmly reflect, tho' on reflection it appears still more extraordinary. We have often met this sort of madness in individuals, who, surrounded with prosperity, have yet resolutely determined to be wretched. Poor Lady —— was a strong instance of this; who never would believe she was happy, till misery forced her to know the state she had forfeited. Many indeed are the instances of that ingratitude to divine providence in single persons, but that a whole empire should be seized by such a delirium, is most amazing. Yet I take the view too wide, it is not a whole empire, but some self-interested wretches, who are endeavouring to ruin this royal first-rate [vessel] on purpose to steal from the wreck materials to build themselves boats with. But farewell unhappy land, for which my heart bleeds in pity. Little does it signify to you, who are the conquered or who the victorious; you are devoted to ruin, whoever succeeds. Many years

ocean together, but as there is no mention of Mrs. Miller and the boys in the account of the Lisbon sojourn, it is probable that they remained on the *George*, which seems to have been chartered for the use of the party and so to have waited in Portuguese waters until the Lisbon visit was over. That the boys went back to Scotland with Miss Schaw and the others is pretty clearly proved by the remark on page 253; and if they did so Mrs. Miller must have gone back with them.

will not make up [for] these few last months of depredation, and yet no enemy has landed on their coast. Themselves have ruined themselves; but let me not indulge this melancholy. I at present require all my spirit to carry me thro' many difficulties.

I shall therefore without preface begin an account of how I am so unexpectedly here, for so it was even to me, however much I wished it. As I write much at my ease, and am in no dread of having my letters seen, I would probably tire you with my own reflections; but there is a ship just ready to sail, in which we endeavoured to have taken our passage, but it is crouded beyond any thing that ever was seen with people flying from this land of nominal freedom and real slavery. There is however a fine Vessel just come in,* which we have secured, but she will not be able to sail for some time, as she has obtained leave to land the Emigrants. They are all out of her however, and we have got her, and will sleep in her every Night, tho' we stay all day aboard the frigat, where we meet the utmost friendship and kindness. My brother and Mr Rutherfurd are both with us, and our ship affords them all accommodations. I shall write as much as I can, as this packet will go by the other vessel, and I am certain will find its way safe to you. It shall be addressed to the custom house.

About a fortnight ago, the Govr issued out an order for the members of the assembly to meet him on board the frigat. Mr Rutherfurd was then in a fit of the gout, yet went without a shoe to obey the summons, and was indeed the only member that made his appearance.† This he thought his

---

* Under date October 22, the master's log of the *Cruizer* says, "Came in the ship George belonging to Glasgow with passengers." The captain's log reads "with emigrants from Scotland," and Will Cruden in his letter to Dartmouth speaks of the *George* as returning to Glasgow "after landing emigrants from Scotland" (Feb. 20, 1776, Dartmouth Papers). There is no other reference to this particular company of emigrants, but doubtless they were Scottish Highlanders, of the same class as those already described by Miss Schaw.

† Miss Schaw seems easily to confuse council and assembly. Of a council

duty, tho' he made no doubt of the consequence that would attend it. On his return he was ordered by the Committee to give up his seat in the assembly [Council], and also to resign into their hands his commission as Receiver general of the quit-rents, and hold that office in future of the Congress. As he was resolved to do neither, he became very anxious in regard to his children, whom he feared he would not long be able to protect. My brother too had the same cause to wish me away safely. They had appointed him from the first Quarter Master general with a Colonel's rank. He had put off giving any positive answer, till now that they were forming camps, where his duty was necessary, and he was commanded to attend. His plan is to send Mrs Schaw and her children amongst her friends and get out of the way himself. But this was not a way to secure me. Mr Rutherfurd and he therefore agreed to our going down to the Sound, and waiting the first opportunity either to the West Indies, Britain or indeed any place of peace and safety. Of this we were not told, till the very night before it was to be put in execution, for had we been making the least preparations, I would have been forced to find bail for £500, for the expence of the war, which my brother wished to avoid. As to Fanny and her brothers, they left sufficient behind them. My brother applied to the Committee for himself and some company to go in his boat on a fishing party to the Sound, which was agreed to, so in it we set off and went down in this boat and two canoes, above fifty miles on a river, as broad, for part of the way, as the Queensferry.* It was very rough and the wind so high,

---

meeting at this time (about October 8 or 10) there is no trace. If held it could have left no official record, as there would not have been a quorum, since Rutherfurd was the only one present besides the governor.

* Queensferry is a small seaport on the Firth of Forth, eight miles west of Edinburgh. South Queensferry is in Linlithgowshire and North Queensferry in Fifeshire. A ferry at that time and until 1890 connected the two places. The distance is a mile and a half, covered now by the famous Forth bridge.

as to toss us about at a sad rate, and I do own, that at that moment I felt my spirits ready to forsake me entirely; but no sooner found myself amongst friends and in a snug birth, than they returned, and I hope will not again play truant. Poor Fanny however feels severely at again leaving her father. As to the young rogues, they are perfectly happy. My heart suffers a severe pang in parting with my poor brother Bob. Our acquaintance has been but short, but I sincerely love him, and the situation I leave him in adds greatly to my concern.

We have had a terrible work to get some hard money. We durst not try for it in town. We had indeed several hundred pounds of paper, but that could serve for no more use, than as so much brown paper, nor durst the folks aboard the frigate part with any that they had got, as they expected daily to sail, when our paper would be of no use to them. To our great joy we find Mr Neilson is to bear us company, and he got a message privately sent up to town, and several of our friends have come on board and brought us as many dollars and Joes,* as have filled my dressing box, of which I am made keeper. At our own request the George, which is the name of our Vessell goes by Portugal. I have promised Mrs Paisley a visit ever since she was married, and this is a fine opportunity. But Capt Deans calls for this. Adieu, shall

---

* The paper money which Miss Schaw had was probably the old legal tender of North Carolina, still in circulation, as no bills of credit had been issued since 1761. Its exchange value with sterling at this time was in the ratio of 181-177 to 100, so that a pound currency would buy only a little more than half as much as a pound sterling. As a rule colonial bills circulated but little outside the colony which issued them. In going to Lisbon Miss Schaw would need either bills of exchange or hard money. There was no time to get the former and the latter she secured with difficulty. What she finally did obtain were Spanish silver dollars and Portuguese gold Johannes, that is, "dollars and Joes." The Spanish dollar was worth four shillings and six pence sterling, the double Jo., seventy-two shillings, the single Jo., thirty-six shillings, and the half Jo., eighteen shillings sterling. The Jo. and half Jo. were among the commonest of the gold coins in actual use among the continental colonists.

I really see you and dear Scotland once more? My head turns giddy at the thought. I am ready to faint. Oh my God! 'tis a sort of feeling I have long been a stranger to.

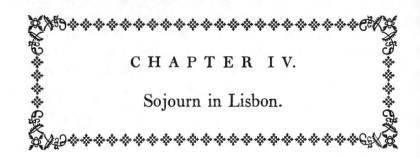

CHAPTER IV.

Sojourn in Lisbon.

Out at Sea.

WE are now fairly over the bar and once more launched on the vast Atlantick.* We have every reason to hope a prosperous Voyage, and every thing has been done to render it an agreeable one. I know not if I ought to rejoice that we have Mr Neilson for our companion, as want of health has forced him to leave the continent, and what sits heavier on his spirit, his friend Govr Martin, at a time when he wishes to be near him, but in his present state of health, must be a trouble not an assistance. I have been greatly obliged to that Gentleman, ever since he became my acquaintance. His attention has been that of a kind brother, and my gratitude is that of a much obliged sister. Should he get soon better, he will (as far as possible) supply my brother to me on this voyage. His conversation is entertaining and instructive, and if he recover his health, I hope he will recover his spirits and gain the fortitude necessary to his present situation, which is truly a hard one, as he had very considerable emoluments in

---

* The *George*, Captain Deans, sailed for Glasgow, via Lisbon, on November 10, 1775, as recorded in the log of the *Cruizer*. The only contemporary reference to Miss Schaw's departure is contained in a letter from Mrs. De-Rosset to John Burgwin. "Mr. Tom Hooper," she writes, "went to Scotland in a vessel with Miss Shaw and Miss Rutherfurd, on the way to England" (*James Sprunt Historical Monographs*, no. 4, p. 28).

America, and still higher prospects, which I fear will not be his again for a long time. But he is a vast philosopher and often uses your expression "it will be all one a hundred years hence."

Mr Rutherfurd and my brother Bob saw us over the bar— a bitter parting, I do assure you, it was on all sides; poor Mr Rutherfurd with all his family, and my brother with a lately found and much loved sister. I fear the Adieu is for ever and for ever. Poor Fanny was hardly able to support it, nor has she yet recovered from the shock. I should think less of myself than I do, did I not feel severely for those I leave behind; tho' in hopes of soon meeting Objects dear to my heart as life; objects indeed that can only endear life to me. Our schemes for the present are frustrated, yet let us not think we are the sport of fortune. Dark as my fate seems I sincerely believe that mercy ever triumphs over evil, and that a powerful hand controls what we call fate. To him then let us submit, and only pray for that fortitude, whose basis is trust in his goodness and omnipotence. I do not suppose this voyage will furnish any thing new, but if it should, it is not in my power to keep a journal of it, as my brother begged my stock of writing-materials, there being none to be had for love or money. The few sheets I now have I will keep, till we arrive at Portugal, when I will begin again to write, not to inform you of what you know so well already, but a journal of my own thoughts, ideas and apprehensions, where every thing is new to me.

Mr Neilson is very ill; Miss Rutherfurd not very well; the boys in good health, as I am. We have brought many pets, of which number is the bear. We were afraid he would join his brethren of the congress, and as he has more apparent sagacity, than any of them, he would be no small addition to their councils. Our Captain is a plain, sensible, worthy man, plays cribbage and backgammon dexterously, and when our poor Messmates are better, we are provided for

Whist. Our cabins and state-rooms are large and commodious, our provisions excellent and our liquor tolerable; but I long for a drink of Scotch two penny, and will salute the first pint-stoup I meet and kiss the first Scotch earth I touch. A weight however hangs on my heart. Adieu, you shall hear from me first opportunity. Adieu, may our meeting be happy.

Decem^r 4th 1775* Aboard the George in the bay of
St Tubes.

Between ten and eleven at night, we were hailed by a pilot-boat, which the Sailors called a bear-cod, as it exactly resembles one. By the Master we were told that we were then just opposite to Lisbon, and tho' it was extremely dark, I was directly for going aboard the boat, and making for the place, where my friends all resided, but was not a little surprised to be informed, that if the boatman carried me ashore, he would be hanged for his pains, and that it was not easy to answer what would become of myself. This brought on an explanation of all we must go thro' before we landed, and I was most terribly mortified that tho' so near our port, it would yet be several days before I could step on terra firma. The Capt also recollected that we had got no bill of health, and we dreaded the horrours of a Lazaretto;† but Neilson happily was the very officer, from whom we should have had our certificate, so having the seal of office in his trunk,‡ he made no scruple to antedate it a month and some

---

* Probably "December 4th" should be December 12. According to Miss Schaw's statement, the voyage lasted thirty-two days ("a month and some days," she says elsewhere), which, reckoned from November 10, the date of sailing, would bring the arrival at St. Tubes to December 11 or 12. As the party remained at St. Tubes only a few days and reached Lisbon on the 19th, it may be that the date of arrival should be put as late as the 14th.

† A lazaretto was usually a pest-house for smallpox and other contagious diseases, but here is used for quarantine.

‡ Neilson had been appointed naval officer by Governor Martin only a month or so before. It is curious that he should have had the seal of his office

days, and to write out a long certificate in very handsome Latin, which our faces bore witness to.

Our fears of a quarantine were at an end, and we slept that night in quietness; as we hoped to be in port by breakfast. But the wind coming against us, it took up most of the day to get forward, and we did not get on the coast till the afternoon, which luckily proved very fine, and here I had the pleasure of viewing an Italian sky, the beauty of which you have so often described to me, and at which I looked with uncommon delight, because it brought back to my memory, what you have said to me on this and many other Subjects. Nor was I entirely engaged with the heavens; the earth claimed part of my attention, and the hills, the rocks, the dales, all joined to please an eye that had been long deprived of such delightful variety, and confined to a dead level or nodding black pines equally disagreeable. The verdure just now is most lovely and meets the eye every where. Tho' this is by no means the sort of country I took it for, as I have fancied to myself a West India Island as large as a world, I was vastly pleased to behold the noble buildings as we sailed along the coast, till I was informed by our pilot, that they were, in general, bastiles—oh sound of horror and fear to a British ear.

At last we reached the bay, where we anchored within less than a mile of the Town of St Tubes.* The scene altogether was very lively and animating, particularly when joined to the idea of being once more in Europe. The evening was fine, the sun gilding the horizon and giving additional beauty to the green hills. The sky was placid and serene—above fifty ships were lying at Anchor, and above a hundred boats en-

in his trunk. Were the seals deemed, as were the papers, the private property of the incumbent? It is more likely, however, that his possession of the seal was something of an accident, since he had never actually entered upon the duties of the office.

* The name of the seaport is Setubal, called by the French St. Ives and by the British St. Tubes or St. Ubes.

gaged in the sardine fishing and chanting Vespers. The town was full in prospect and many windmills going above it, which I think a very cheerful object. The coast is extremely bold and the hills and high grounds, covered with wheat or pasture, looked so fresh that they perfectly cheered the senses.

But while we were busy admiring this pleasing scene, a boat approached, which was presently known to be from the custom-house. There were three or four tide-waiters in her, the sight of whom set our Johns to such cursing and muttering, that I could not conceive what ailed them, till the Capt told me these vermine were come to take their Tobacco, and would not leave them a single quid in their pouches. I could not wonder at their distress or rage on this occasion, nor be offended when they declared that America was dam—ly in the right to keep clear of these land rats. These however were only the guards come to prevent any being carried ashore. The others came in the morning. We have got figs, grapes and most charming wine on board, at which we are sipping at no allowance. I am charmed with the bells—there goes one just now as like our eight o'clock bell as it can be—*clink*, *clink*—dear me 'tis heartsome. Good Night.

There has been a general search for Tobacco, our Johns laid down there quids with a sneer that fully convinces me they have not lost all their comfort that way. Tho' the people who came on board made but a scurvy personal appearance, I found a vast difference between their manners, and those in the same station at home. They were actually distressed when they saw Ladies and made a thousand apologies. As Mr Neilson speaks every European language, we were informed of whatever we wished to know thro' his means. But tho' he made the tour of Europe a few years ago, he never was in Portugal, so is a stranger to their customs. He is particularly distressed about getting ashore, which, these people say, cannot be for three or four days.

I plainly see he is to take such a charge of us, as will tease his life—Lord help him, he little knows how perfectly easy I am, and more inclined to laugh than cry at the little accidents we meet with on this journey. Oh my friend! that I had no more to distress me—but let us not repine nor quarrel with the wise œconomy we ought to adore. 'Tis in our own breasts that the events of fate must take their colour. The reception they meet with and the turn they take there, constitute them good or evil. One thing I am at least sure of, that if you are happy, I never can be miserable.

I was interrupted by a message informing me that the officers of health and of the holy Inquisition were just coming aboard—also that the Proconsul begged the honour of waiting on the English Ladies. Tho' the Inquisition has now lost its sting, there is still an horrour in the sound, and, Miss Rutherfurd says, I grew pale at the name. I had no reason however. In place of a stern Inquisitor, came a smiling young Priest, who, I fancy, would render penance pretty easy for some of us, were he chosen Father confessor properly. Our healths were taken for granted, and our chests tho' opened, were not searched. On opening my chest, I observed a piece of excellent self-attention in Mrs Miller, who had been told, that if a Bible was found, the person who owned it, would be sent to the Inquisition. She had one in folio, which she had transferred to our chest, and taken no care to conceal it. However it was taken no notice of. The proconsul spoke very good French, and our priest conversed with Mr Neilson in Italian. They drank tea with us, and after making the Capt sign to a set of most curious articles for himself and his crew, they left us at full liberty to go ashore when we pleased, and to carry our trunks (which they marked) unmolested by further search. I made Neilson translate the Articles signed by the Capt, mate and himself, some of which were as follows. That the said officers or none of the crew shall insult any female they chance to meet. Item, that they shall take off their hats to the clergy, and not affront them in any way; that they shall kneel at the elevation of the host; that they shall in no way insult the cross, whereever set up, by making [water], but however urgent their Necessities may be, shall retain the same, till at a proper and lawful distance. Many more equally important were set down and signed.

Neilson, who went on shore with our Visitors, has returned and informs us he has by their means got us excellent lodgings, and that we are to eat meat to morrow on shore, tho' this is a season of strict fasting. He has given us a most ludicrous account of the Lady who is to receive us; a Senora Maria, who has said so many handsome things to him, that he is quite afraid of her. He has told her however he is married, and his wife comes ashore with him. I fancy he found this necessary, and I am to take him under my protection.

They assure me the packet will sail from Lisbon in a few days, and I will get this sent you. You will see by my writing, we had a good voyage, tho' I forgot to tell you so. We were just thirty two days, the blinds were never up, nor were we incommoded, tho' we had a fresh breeze thro' the whole Voyage.

We dined yesterday with Senora Maria, a squat sallow dame between forty and fifty, but such an Amarosa in her manner, that Neilson required the presence of his supposed wife to save him from the warmth of her caresses, which, to say the truth, she bestowed on us all, embracing and clasping us till we were half suffocated. But this was not the worst of it: she brought her maid to pay her compliments. She was just Don Quixote's Maratornious [Maritornes],* with her

* The description of Maritornes in Don Quixote (ch. xvi) reads as follows: "An Asturian wench, broad faced, flat-headed, with a little nose, one eye squinting and the other not much better. It is true, the elegance of her form made amends for other defects. She was not seven hands high; and her shoulders, which burdened her a little too much, made her look down to the ground more than she would willingly have done." Hogarth gives us a

jacket and rouff-eye; have not seen such an animal. She would measure half as much again round, as from head to foot. Her bushy black hair was frizled up, which with her little winking eyes and cock-nose made a most complete appearance. I trembled for her embraces, as the effluvia of the kitchen were very strong, but happily she was more humble than her dame, for she squatted down and clasped us round the knees, kissing our feet, which we permitted her to do without raising her to our arms, as it seems we ought to have done. Senora took much pains to inform us she was no publican, only kept a house of accommodation for her friends, in which number she did us the honour to consider us. This would have surprised an Englishman, but I, who had been used to such friendships, thought it not stranger than that of the bridge of Tay, with many more in your country, where I have been treated as a friend with very little ceremony, and paid very decent or rather indecent bills for meat and drink, of which I had the smallest share.

Dinner over, we went to view the town, which has been once magnificent, but is now almost entirely a ruin, partly owing to the dreadful earthquake,* and partly owing to the still more horrid effects of despotism. Here I beheld the remains of the palace of the Duke de Alvara, a most noble ruin. His fate you know well, and I dare say we both join in thinking that he and his son the Marquis deserved every severity; for it is past a doubt, that they made an attempt on the life of their sovereign—a crime that admits of no palliation.† Yet as Voltaire most justly observes, there is no crime

---

picture of Maritornes in one of his scenes illustrating Don Quixote. Miss Schaw may have seen this print.

* The great earthquake occurred on November 1, 1755, just twenty years before Miss Schaw's arrival.

† The Duke of Aveiro (Joseph Mascareñhas), 1708-1759, with the marquess and marchioness of Tavora, their two sons, and four or five others, were executed in 1759 for an attempt on the life of King Joseph I, September 3, 1758. The duke and the marquess were broken on the wheel, their bodies consumed by fire, and their ashes thrown into the sea; the marchioness

however great, but we lose sight of, when the punishment is extended beyond the limits of humanity. Thus the memory of these two parricides would have been held in utter detestation, had they alone suffered death; but when we see the venerable Dutchess, the two amiable youths not yet eighteen years old suffering the same dreadful fate, tho' entirely innocent, nature revolts, and will no longer term it justice, but diabolical barbarity. Nor does it appear less shocking to find the impotence of power extend to objects incapable of feeling or understanding punishment—one infant daughter rendered infamous and shut up in a convent to [serve in] the lowest offices; ashes strewn in the air; one palace torn down and the ground salted, another entirely ruined, tho' the walls yet remain so far as to let you observe how great this unhappy family once were, and whose fate is silently regretted by their country. You know the exclusion of the Jesuits followed this affair, and with them fell the power of the Inquisition.*

We visited several churches, which are now decorating for

was decapitated, the ducal palace pulled down, and the family and even the name of Tavora obliterated as far as possible. The cruelty of the sentences and the torture which accompanied the execution of the principal conspirators, as well as the "grand affair" itself, made a great stir at the time and the details must have been well known to Miss Schaw. No one who has ever read the contemporary accounts of the scene at the scaffold at Belem, as printed, for example, in the *Universal Magazine*, XXIV, 96-99, which Miss Schaw might well have seen, can ever forget the harrowing details of the spectacle. There were two palaces, one at Setubal and the other at Lisbon. From Miss Schaw's account neither would seem to have been entirely destroyed.

* A recent historian of Portugal says of the plot, "Whatever the real origin of this plot may have been, it resulted in the king being waylaid and wounded, and in the execution of some of the most prominent nobles of Portugal. It seems not impossible, in view of the repetition of the incident ten months later that Pombal [see page 236, note] by these 'popish plots' was killing his two birds with one stone, so as to strengthen his influence with the king by disgracing the great nobles who were jealous of his power and by discrediting the Jesuits, whose reputation and record would certainly render them responsible. In 1759 the Society's estates were confiscated and its members expelled" (*Portugal, An Historical Study*, by George Young, p. 195).

Christmas—the Virgin is dressing out, and is sometimes very pretty, tho' at other times most gloriously ridiculous. Some of the churches are truly fine, but the images are in general paltry and no fine paintings in any of those I have seen. But we have an invitation to a convent of Missionaries to morrow, where they tell me every thing is noble, and they are rich tho' beggars by profession. It will not be easy for the sailors to observe strictly the articles of not affronting the cross, for they [the crosses] are so close on each other, that it will hardly be in their power to keep clear of offence. Indeed the profusion of emblems of the most sacred of all subjects shocks me greatly. You find it over the doors of places for the vilest uses. You see the most horrid violation of it, wherever you turn your eyes, and one would think it was set up by Turks or Jews, as a standing ridicule and reproach on a religion they despised and disbelieved. It is not here I would be converted to the Catholick faith, as it is no better than a puppet show.

I must tell you an anecdote of our hostess Maria. As she carried us thro' a very disorderly and dirty house, we at last arrived at a sort of lumber room, where stood a large cloth press. She put on a solemn look, and bade Neilson inform us we were in her private chapel, that she was not rich, but what she had to spare she bestowed on her God. I approved of the object of her liberality, but could observe nothing in her chapel worthy the acceptance of a much lower person. But on opening the above mentioned press, we were struck with a view of the Virgin and her son in figures, not much above the length of my middle finger, attended with a croud of Lilliputian saints, who were gayly dressed, and stood on each side in decent order. A folding up altar was then let down, on which was displayed every utensil necessary for devotion in minature, the whole making a very pretty baby house. Senora Maria kneeled and crossed herself most devotely, in which the good breeding of Mr Neilson accompanied her.

I made a slight obeisance, but Fanny viewed the whole with the utmost contempt. No sooner was it shut up, than the Vivacity of Senora returned, and pulling out the drawers under this model of a Romish Church, she displayed her Wardrobe, of which she was not a little vain, then making us a present of some artificial crosses, she led us to the further corner of the chapel, where was fitted up a great number of wicker baskets for sale, extremely pretty, of which we purchased several. Were I sufficiently in cash, I could buy many things here vastly cheap. Some money I will venture to lay out; as at Lisbon I am sure of credit. But were not that the case, I should feel a pang every time I unlocked my little cash-chest, which contains a large sum for a poor refugee, and of which I never dare lose sight, having no very high idea of Portugueze honesty. The bed-chambers at Maria's were so dirty that we could not stay in them. Neilson indeed was so resolute to have us go on board to sleep, that I could not help thinking, he was afraid to be from under my *protection* at that season [that is, at night], when I could not so cleverly keep up the character of wife.

We leave St Tubes to morrow morning, and are to proceed to Lisbon—but tho' no great journey, the manner of our travelling has been a work of no little trouble to Mr Neilson, whose goodness and attention knows no bounds. What must have become of us without him? I think it would have been impossible to have gone on. Yet I am often vexed at his anxiety, for as he is hurt by our smallest inconveniency, he is for ever uneasy, as such accidents must constantly occur in our present situation. Our mode of travelling has been a source of great distress, as no other carriage was to be had, but that of a pack-saddle fixed on the back of either an ass or a mule. For my part I had just been contemplating the ease with which a set of market women was moving along and admiring their mounterrara caps,* when he entered the

* Mounterrara caps, Spanish *montera*, were hunting caps made of cloth,

room, and in the greatest vexation told me, he believed I would not get to Lisbon. On being informed of the wherefore, I assured him that should not prevent my Journey, as I thought the pack saddle as pretty a method of travelling as any I had seen. What! Miss Rutherfurd and me on pack saddles! Be it ever so easy a method, he would not submit to see us in such a style. I begged him to consider that we had no dignity to support at St Tubes, and that the disgrace of the pack saddle would be entirely washed away before we got to Britain. Nothing could reconcile him to it however, and telling me adventures did better in theory than practice, he went off with a priest, who soon procured him the calash of a noble Lady, who is banished from court to this place, for having privately married without the King's consent a brave officer, who is confined in one of the Neighbouring bastiles, and it is supposed he will be put to death. As her relations are very powerful, she has offered to shut herself up in a Monastery, and make over all her fortune to the court, if they will pardon him. Oh Britons, Britons, little do you know your own happiness!

This affair settled, we went round the churches, which are this day finished. The new dresses of the Virgin are all in the British taste, white and silver, and blue and silver are the favourites. But at one church she had on a tie-wig—but why am I describing to you what you are so perfectly acquainted with; yet allow me to say that I could not have believed it possible to have turned the plain, the noble and rational worship ordained by its blessed Author into such a farce, as is acting here at this moment, nor can I believe the Actors are not in general laughing at themselves. We have made several acquaintances with priests, whom I like very well, and one of them is so much pleased with our company, that he has not found the way to his convent since our

which, though originally used by mountaineers, came to be the common head-gear of the peasant people of Spain.

arrival. He stays at a M^r G—'s, an English merchant, who politely carried us to his house, and introduced us to his sister, who tho' married to a Portugueze husband, takes all the liberties of a British wife.* We have found her however a very good companion, and as she knows every body are much the better for her. Our pére Francis is a jolly round-faced, round-belly'd father in grace. A certain young American engages however his attention at present as much as his holy Mistress; not that he neglects his duty to her, far from it—he gets up every now and then even from cards, and running to a lamp and Mass-book, which lie ready, he re-peats his Ave Marias as fast as possible, and then returns to the object of his present adoration, and begging her pardon, shrugs up his shoulders, saying these things must be done. This father, whose vows tie him down to poverty and morti-fication, wears his robes round his middle very gracefully, his cowl hangs back in a careless manner, and shows a jolly, comely countenance. He eats monstrously and drinks a tumbler of wine to wash down every three or four mouthfuls, and by the time dinner is over, is fit for any frolick you please. Yet he has a sort of decency of manner, and in the midst of a very foolish conduct, has a sobriety in his looks, which is not the case with them all.

One in particular at whose convent we yesterday paid a visit, is a perfect light-headed Oxonian. He was so trans-ported at seeing us at the convent, that he lost sight of his character, fell on his knees and embraced ours, to our no small surprise and confusion. He then ran for the superior, with whose looks I was indeed quite charmed, and involun-

---

* To take all the liberties of a British wife meant a good deal in Portu-gal, where at this time the wives of the better classes rarely left their homes to appear in public places or to share in the social life of the men. Pombal tried to relieve women somewhat of their ennui, due (as was commonly said) to masculine jealousy, but even he failed in his main object and was obliged to contrive pleasures that could be enjoyed by the women alone among themselves.

tarily paid him that respect, I could not believe any of his order could have deserved. Nay, so much reverence did this old man of seventy nine inspire, that I seriously begged his benediction, and found myself affected by the benevolent solemnity with which he bestowed it on me. Our gay priest provided a collation for us, which he produced and placed without ceremony on one of the low altars that adorned this church, which is indeed a very fine one, and has some good paintings and images, particularly one of our Lady of Sorrow, placed under a large crucifix, which I think as affectingly beautiful as the fancy of any Artist could produce. But the image on the cross, appears more calculated to inspire horror than either love or devotion. Nor are you ever shown this amiable pattern of all human perfection from his childhood, till he appears in the attitude of agony and extreme misery. This is doubtless owing to the dark superstition peculiar to the people of this country, where religion is held as a whip over slaves, and every individual has a court of Inquisition within his own breast. They figure the merciful father of his creatures, dark, gloomy and inexorable as the first Inquisitors. That this does not prevail in every Roman Catholick country is certain; of which the fine paintings I have seen copied are a proof, where we see that divine figure often delineated in the act of pardon and mercy, with a countenance that inspires the beholder with love, gratitude and adoration—in those there might be danger, but in nothing I have seen here.

We slept last night in an apartment in the Duke de Alvara's palace. Luckily we did not know where we were till the morning, otherwise that most unfortunate noble family would have haunted our dreams. Tho' the place where we were is part of the vast building, yet it seems to have been only apartments for the domesticks, as it enters differently from the palace, but has been itself most magnificent, and is now occupied by the English Gentleman, whom I before mentioned, and he is making it very neat. But the grand apartments where the family resided are under the sentence of infamy, the windows built up and no one suffered to enter. The earthquake did it no harm, and there still remains a noble balcony covered with lead round the whole, which is longer than our Abbey of Holyrood house. Also the ruins of a vinary at least a thousand feet in length, where they had grapes all the year. The gardens and fish-ponds have been noble and extensive, they are now turned into vineyards, and let out to tenants. Tho' treason is a crime of so high a nature as to admit of no palliation, yet we must regret that such a family committed a crime to deserve such punishments. Adieu, till I write from Lisbon, which I certainly will the first packet. I have just got a letter from Mrs Paisley in return to one I wrote her. It is impossible to say whether her pleasure or surprise is strongest. Her affection however is most expressive, and I am sure my heart feels it.

Lisbon Decemr the 20th

We got here last Night thro' many adventures, and are now as happy as the most amiable and most affectionate of friends can make us. But I will go on in proper form and begin with our journey, which proved a perfect comic-tragedy, and I was often at a loss, whether to cry or laugh. We set out in the calash of the noble Lady, which was really a neat one, drawn by two excellent Mules and conducted by a postilion, whose head would be an object of envy to the first Macaronie in Britain. But our excellent governor [Neilson] was so happy at getting us properly accommodated, that he forgot to take care of himself, and left it to a Muleteer to provide three Mules—one for our baggage, another for a scoundrel of a chetsarona [cicerone] and a third for himself, begging only that he might get a common saddle not a pack one. He got a saddle indeed, but not a common one, for it was an old French pique, that had not felt the air for fifty years, with a rusty stirrup at one side and a wooden box at the other to thrust his foot in.

The muleteer placed the baggage on the best mule. Our chetsarona had the next choice, while the old pique was placed on the back of a mule, which to his natural perverseness had added the positive humours of at least five and twenty years experience, and guessing we were about to ascend the mountain, absolutely refused to move. In vain did his unfortunate rider make his back resound with kicks; he was insensible to every remonstrance. The day was shockingly hot, Mr Neilson had run about to have every thing convenient for his female charge, till he had got a return of his fever, with a violent head-ache. No wonder his philosophy was staggered. His courage indeed was so far spent, that he was on the point of yielding the Victory to his Antagonist, when the Muleteer came to his assistance, and with three or four hearty blows of a cudgel across the rump of his stubborn property, he thought fit to move at last, but with the most untoward motion, and stopping every now and then, till the correction was repeated, went off with a jerk, which made our poor friend feel all the defects of the old saddle. This was a bad remedy for a head-ache, nor was it mended by the noise of the bells, which hung round the baggage mule, and which I insisted on having in view, having no very high idea of the honesty of a Portugueze Muleteer. A light-headed young Portugueze officer, being on the parade when we went into the calash, took a fancy to attend us, tho' a perfect stranger, and observing Mr Neilson's distress, he politely begged to have the honour of whipping up his beast. Neilson by this time was so heartily tired, that he did not care if the Devil was to whip him up, and readily accepted the offer, when the ridiculous creature began a scampering round our carriage, mounted on a fine Spanish horse, smacking his whip over the mule, and hollowing *diable mulla, mulla.* There was no resisting laughing, in which the sufferer himself joined in spite of his head-ache.

I was exceedingly vexed however at this accident, as it was likely to deprive us of Mr Neilson's company the whole way, thro' a glorious country, diversified beyond description, every now and then a noble building attracting our attention, but of whose use or names we could get no information, our postilion speaking only his native language, our Chetsarona not come up, and our best instructor kept off by his confounded brute and light-headed companion. How often did I wish for my brother who would have enjoyed this scene to the full, and rendered it many degrees more agreeable to us by his judicious remarks. Quite impatient, we at last resolved to leave the calash, and ascend the remaining part of the Mountain on foot, which was now become so steep, that it was all our mules were able to pull up the carriage. The whole road was covered with mules and asses, carrying wine in skins to the waterside. Mr Neilson found no regret in relieving his stubborn pad of his burthen, and by the assistance of his arm, we got on tolerably, but not without many stops, not only to breathe, but to take a survey of the charming prospects that presented themselves to us on all sides.

As we advanced nearer the summit, we left behind St Tubes, the sea, the shipping, the large salt-works, the fine ruins, and a country beautifully green with corn and rich pasture-ground. Before us we had the river, Tagus, with the town of Lisbon and all the adjacent country on the opposite shore. On our left hand we had a scene nobly wild and beautifully romantick. The mountains presented us with rocks and woods, thro' which flowed many a rapid stream, which fell down in noisy cascades thro' the valleys below. But tho' these valleys boasted their cultivation and invited us to admire vine-yards, orange-groves and olive orchards, yet that where Nature alone held dominion entirely engaged our attention, and we traced the wildness of the mountains, as far as our eyes could penetrate thro' the trees or over the rocks. While we were making different observations, Miss Rutherfurd said it recalled to her mind a description she had often admired, that of the scene when Don Quixote met the unhappy Gentleman deprived of his senses.* We had all agreed in the justness of the observation, when at the very instant, as if by design, the scene was completed by the appearance of an unhappy wretch in the very situation in which the unfortunate count is there represented. Tho' a deep valley divided the two mountains, he was directly opposite to us, and so near, that we both heard and saw him distinctly. He was almost naked, his hair hanging loose about his shoulders, while the swiftness with which he leaped from rock to rock too plainly indicated the situation of his mind, and as he approached the precipice, I trembled lest he would go headlong over. However he stopped just on the utmost point, and falling on his knees seemed to implore us (with uplifted hands) in a supplicatory voice, which however was soon converted into that of the greatest wildness, and his actions were quite frantick. He beat his breast, tore his hair, and by his gestures seemed to be imprecating curses on us, after which with terrible cries, he returned behind the rocks, and we saw him no more. We were vastly affected at this view of the greatest extremity of human misery, and which our Chetsarona told [us] he had been reduced to by the infidelity of a wife he adored; that he had killed her lover, and taken refuge in the convent just before us, but was soon deprived of his senses. However the fathers humanely took care of him, tho' he often escaped to the woods and rocks. That every female he saw, he took for his wife, and always at first addressed them with softness, but soon with such rage, as made it very dangerous to be near him.

---

* The scene referred to is in Don Quixote, Book III, ch. xxiii.

We were so much affected with this melancholy scene, that we walked in silence up the mountain, and had reached the summit before we were aware, and found ourselves just under the convent of Palmella, which gives its name to a very pretty village just by, remarkable for a small pleasant wine produced on the Valley and rising grounds to our right hand. Whether the hurry of the former scene had prepared us to look with peculiar delight on one that appeared the perfect valley of contentment, I know not, but it certainly conveyed to the mind a strong idea of rural felicity; and the same thought struck all our company. It was one continued vineyard, with a number of hamlets scattered thro' it, the neatness of which could not be exceeded, and the whole scene looked like humility and safety. A nearer view might have shown our mistake. We left both the town and the convent without stopping, tho' much pressed to take refreshment. Our mules however drank at an elegant marble fountain for the relief of travellers. We got into our Calash, Neilson mounted his mule, which seemed more reconciled to his rider, and descended the other side of the mountain in perfect safety, and to my no small surprise, I found a heather moor above three miles long, and at the end of it came on a flat, very unpleasant tho' a cultivated country, and got to Mytoe [Moita], which is in the kingdom of Lisbon, about four o'clock.* Our guide conducted us thro' a narrow lane,

---

* In going from Setubal to Lisbon, the party would have to ride over the Sierra da Arabida and sail across the Tagus. Southey has described the reverse journey, from Lisbon to Setubal, in terms which may well be compared with those of Miss Schaw. He crossed the Tagus to Moita, rode thence on mules (at a "cruzado novo" apiece) up the hill of Palmella, through the pines, with flowers scattered on every hand amid the heather and sand, and found at the entrance to Palmella a fountain "with the arms of the town and an inscription, in which (he says) I was sometime amused at seeing S. P. Q. P., by the idea of the Senate and People of Palmella." He then descended on the other side of the sierra with a prospect before him "the most beautiful I ever beheld" and entered Setubal, which he describes at some length (*Letters written during a Short Residence in Spain and Portugal*, pp. 320-321).

where we saw wrote over a door an *Anlish hot for man and bost*. This we entered, but did not find it did much credit to England. Our Chetsarona however had been aware of this, and we had every thing brought with us for dinner, and found we had only to pay for leave to eat our own meat.

The Tagus like our Firth can only be crossed at the tide. Mr Neilson had secured the first boat for ourselves, and we were just stepping on board, when two or three men interposed, and told us we were prisoners to the state and must return. Our guide took much pains to assure us that it was nothing, but I by no means liked the Adventure. We were taken to the house of a judge, who received us in his Library, but seemed very little pleased with this interruption to his studies. Tho' the regard paid to our sex by every man in this country obtained us civility, our judge or rather jailor was a little spare old body, wrapt in a great cloak with a woollen coul on his bald pate, which however he uncovered, nor could be prevailed on to cover his head or resume his seat, while we were standing, which we did, till Neilson was carried off to the Governor, from whom a message came to let us know that we were at liberty, but the Gentleman a prisoner. This favour I absolutely refused, and declared I would remain, till I could send to my friends at Lisbon for redress.

No sooner had Neilson left the judge than he made us be seated, and I dare say he paid us many compliments, as he accompanied all he said with a most obliging air. We understood he offered us fruit, which however we did not accept, but returned bow for bow in silence for above an hour, during which time, our postilion, our guide and Muleteer had been under examination in regard to us, and had given such answers as convinced the Governor, who fortunately was not an idiot, that we had no design either on the King's or Marquis of Pombal's life.* Two men then came and took an

* Joseph I, 1750-1777, son of John X, married Maria Anna, daughter of Philip V of Spain. His daughter, the princess of Brazil, married his youngest

inventory of our features, our complexion, the colour of our
hair, and made us take off our hats to see we had not wigs.
This being done, a certificate was attested and delivered to
Mr Neilson, and we were set at liberty. We were forced
however to pay no less than Nine shillings and ninepence a
piece for this certificate, and we had lost the tide and were
forced to return to our paltry inn, till the next arrived.*

Now for the first time, since I set out on my expedition,
my temper fairly forsook me. The Night was cold and a
drizling rain had come on. It was also so dark, that I lost all
the pleasure I hoped for on the Tagus. Tho' we had hired
the boat entirely, it was half full of dead hogs, fish and a
variety of articles for Market, and we were hardly set off
from the shore, when the crew began chanting their Vespers,
and had the dead swine which lay by them joined their
grunts to the concert, it could not have rendered it more
disagreeable.† But farewell, the Captain of the Packet calls,
and is to take charge of this, and one for my brother himself.
Adieu, Adieu.

---

brother, her uncle Peter. After Joseph's death in 1777, she and her husband
reigned as Maria I and Peter III, he until his death in 1786, she after that,
alone, until her death in 1816, when she was succeeded by her son John VI,
the great-great-grandfather of the late Carlos I. See below, p. 251.

Sebastian Joseph de Carvalho e Mello, Marquess of Pombal, was the
greatest statesman that Portugal ever produced. Not only did he rebuild
Lisbon after the earthquake but he endeavored also to win independence for
Portugal from the political dominance of Spain, the commercial dominance
of Great Britain, and the religious dominance of the Inquisition and the
Jesuits. (The most accessible life of Pombal is by J. Smith, Count of Carnota,
Memoirs of the Marquess of Pombal, 1843, but though a scholarly work it
stands in great need of revision.)

* This adventure happened at Moita, which though located today some
distance from navigable water, was then the place of departure on the
southern shore of the Tagus for those wishing to go to Lisbon.

† Southey returned to Lisbon and in crossing the Tagus from Moita had
much the same experience as had Miss Schaw. He made the trip in a boat
"used for carrying dung," the moisture of which "oozed through upon us."
"Half a dozen ducks, who made part of the passengers, amused us (he
writes) with their music, and the men stunk so abominably that even Manuel
complained. We preferred being wet to this pestilential atmosphere and
reached Lisbon after a passage of five hours" (pp. 331-332).

Friendship is a plant of slow growth in every climate, and of so delicate a Nature, that the person who can rear up a few, may think himself happy, even where he has passed his early years and has had his most constant residence. Travellers in passing thro' foreign countries have no right to expect friendship, and if they meet its resemblance in politeness and civilities, ought to be perfectly satisfied. But how much greater reason have I to be pleased, who have met the real genuine plant, a heart that beats time to my own, and enjoys all the happiness she bestows, and participates all the pleasures and civilities that on her account and by her means are hourly heaped on us. You cannot have forgot the lovely and amiable Christy Pringle. You have heard me speak of her a hundred times, and never without the sincerest regret for her absence. That affection, that began while she was in the nursing, is not lessened, and has proved to me a source of infinite satisfaction. Mr Paisley, whom she married some years ago, adds dignity to the name of a British merchant, a title that conveys more in my idea than that of Duke or Lord in any other part of the world. He carries on an extensive commerce to the East and West Indies, the African Islands, the Brazils and indeed to every quarter of the globe. His success has been what he justly merited, and I believe he is not now second to any in our British factories. He lives with the Magnificence of a prince and the hospitality of an English merchant. He is a French-man in politeness, which his benevolent actions daily show to a number of obliged and grateful connections, who by his means are put in the way of becoming independent and happy.

We were received by him with that openess of manner, that did not suffer us to feel we were strangers, and he soon gave us every reason to think ourselves at home with our nearest relations. The evening after our arrival, we were visited by a number of the British of both sexes. Amongst

these was General McLean, Govr of Lisbon* and commander
in chief of the land forces. His name informs you of his
country. He is indeed a fine highland looking fellow, and
tho' not now a boy is still a great favourite with the Ladies.
His Aid de Camp, Major Scott,† is from Mid Lothian, Scott
of Mollinie's eldest son, who has been so long abroad, that
he has entirely gained the manners of a foreigner, and tho'
a most worthy man and much beloved here, if ever he returns
to his country, will not fail to be called horribly affected.

But of all the men I have yet seen, I prefer Major Lindsay,‡ also a Scotchman. This Gentleman who is universally
and justly admired, is brother to Lindsay of Wormiston in
Fife. Never did I see in my life a more agreeable figure, or
more amiable manners than he possesses; he looks and moves
the Gentleman. I am never so happy as when attended by
him. His conversation is elegant, polite and entertaining, his
taste is refined, his remarks judicious. He has such an accurate manner of explaining the present objects and describing
the absent, that I am at a loss to discover with which of the
two I am most pleased. My brother would doat on him. He
is the man entirely to his taste. I am never happy when he is

---

* The General Maclean mentioned by Miss Schaw as "governor of Lisbon," was Francis Maclean of the Macleans of Blaich, who was a lieutenant
in the army of Cumberland at the siege of Bergen-op-Zoom in 1747, served
with Wolfe at Quebec in 1759, and accompanied the expedition against
Belleisle in 1761. His extraordinary position in Lisbon was due to the fact
that when in 1762 France and Spain combined against Portugal, England
offered her assistance and sent Maclean to organize the military defences of
the country. He was appointed in 1762 governor of Almeida and later, as
major-general, governor of the province of Estremadura and the city of
Lisbon, serving in that capacity until 1778. On his departure he was presented
by Peter III with a sword and by his consort Maria I with a ring. During
the next two years he was with the army in America as brigadier-general. He
died in 1781 (*Historical and Genealogical Account of the Clan Maclean*,
1838, p. 293).

† The "Major Scott" mentioned here was John Scott of Mallony, who in
1742 married Susan, granddaughter of the Marquess of Tweeddale. Their
eldest son, Thomas, served with distinction in America, Holland, and India.

‡ "Major Lindsay" was probably Major Martin Eccles Lindsay, son of
Henry of Wormiston, though the identification is not certain.

not with us, and could attend to him the day long. Yet I view him as a superior being, as he is on the utmost Verge of Mortality, and in a few weeks at farthest will join his kindred angels. He knows this is the case and waits his fate with the fortitude of a man and the resignation of a Christian. It has ever been my lot to pay days of sorrow for hours of pleasure, and my heart tells me I will sincerely regret this blasted bud of friendship—indeed the subject already pains me, so I will say no more.

I ought to have begun my list of civilities with Sir John Hort,* our British consul, as he was the first who waited on Mr Paisley on our arrival and politely invited us to a ball at his house the day following, an offer, which scarcely we knew how to accept, as we are perfect Goths in the article of dress, so much has fashion altered since we left Britain. Our friends Mrs Paisley and her sister Charlotte Pringle however exerted themselves so successfully, that we really made a decent figure; to me it appeared a most surprising one, as a French frizler and Portugueze comber exalted my head to a height I did not believe it capable of attaining, and between flowers, feathers, and lace, I was perfectly metamorphosed. It did not cost much to make Miss Rutherfurd fit to appear. At her age every thing does well; then either the magnificence or simplicity of dress is equally admired. Mrs Paisley was always remarkable for the last, and tho' dressed up to the fashion, still contrives to have it in that style, which is indeed suitable to her character, which tho' polite to the height of good breeding, is yet admired for the most gentle and native simplicity that can adorn the sex in any age or in any station.

The labour of the toilet over, we arrived at Sir John's, where we found a most superb entertainment for a brilliant

* Sir John Hort was the second son of Josiah Hort, archbishop of Tuam, and married Elizabeth, daughter of the Honorable William Fitzmaurice, brother of the 20th Lord Kerry. He was appointed British consul-general at Lisbon in 1767, was created a baronet in the year, and died October 23, 1807.

company. To me it appeared particularly so; to me who have not seen any thing of the kind for so long a time. Here we were presented, or more properly to speak as a Lady, had presented to us all the foreign Envoys and residents and one ambassador, but I forget from what court. The Ladies were all British or French, as no Portugueze Ladies appear in publick. The King is just now at a palace about 12 or 14 miles off,* and has with him many of the first Nobility. However there were several, and I thought them genteel-looking people. The house is large and there was a number of apartments lighted up, which received great Addition from the manner in which all the fine rooms are furnished here, which is up to the surbase, where our rooms are painted, with a sort of china-tiles, as we do the inside of chimneys in England. These are often very fine, and so nicely fitted as to form complete landscapes. Add to this that they use the most brilliant cut crystal in Lusters, so that take it altogether, a Portugueze visiting room is not inferior to the first drawing room in Europe. We were served in the genteelest style I have seen. The table was very much on the plan of a West Indian entertainment, but every thing was hid under the profusion of Artificial flowers, which cover every thing in this place. Sir John is said to be very formal in his manners, but to do him justice, I cannot say he appeared so to me. Mr Paisley says indeed he never saw him so easy as that Night.

Our Envoy, Mr Walpole,† has invited the whole company to his house; but the day is not fixed. He is a cheerful

---

* The royal palace at Cintra, some sixteen or seventeen miles away.

† Robert Walpole was the son of Horatio Walpole, diplomat and auditor-general of the plantation revenues, nephew of Sir Robert Walpole, and cousin of Horace, the wit and letter writer. He served as clerk of the Privy Council in extraordinary, 1748-1764, in ordinary, 1764-1768, on diplomatic business in France, 1768-1770, and as envoy extraordinary and minister plenipotentiary to Portugal, 1771-1800. He married at Lisbon, May 10, 1785, Miss Stert, daughter of Richard Stert, a merchant there, and died in 1809. His relative Thomas, son of Horace, was a member of the Ohio Land Company in 1773 and one of the Vandalia petitioners in 1774.

pleasant man, but tho' he was vastly polite to our company, I could not help observing he is fond of a certain species of wit, to which he was too much encouraged by some Ladies he talked to. This I can easily see is considered as taste, yet it certainly affords no great triumph, as of all others it is what is practised by the lower class with greatest success. I know you will tell me there is a vast difference between vulgar language and a delicate double entender. But I deny that there can be a delicate method of treating indelicate subjects, and that all the difference is no more than Tweedle dee and Tweedle dum. My friend told me on our return, that I had missed a great deal by not understanding the Portugueze, which it was her misfortune to do. By the bye I must tell you a very polite piece of attention in Sir John: finding Mr Neilson did not stay at Mr Paisley's tho' he saw him there, he waited on him next morning and gave him his invitation in person.

Such a succession of new scenes presents itself to me every day, nay every hour, that I am at a loss where to begin, and seem to want subject, by having too many at my command. All travellers are fond of ruins, and Lisbon can shew as pretty a set as any Modern city need boast of. Yet I do not find they afford me such infinite satisfaction as one might expect. The disagreeable idea that what has been may be again often intrudes on my Imagination, and I view churches, Monasteries, palaces and even the Inquisition in ruins with a sort of reverential awe, and tho' a staunch protestant, cannot help reflecting on the words of our Saviour, which certainly exclude the daring insolence of pronouncing what are his Judgments, "Think ye these on whom the tower of Siloam fell were sinners above all others? I say nay," These however were not the sentiments of a good Lady, whom I had the honour to call Grandmother, and who had lived at the period when miracles and Judgments were greatly the fashion. This affair of Lisbon gave strength to her doctrine, and tho' she pretended to pity, I really believe she privately rejoiced at an event that seemed to confirm all she had said (which was not little) on the subject. She sincerely believed that this vast Magazine of dreadful materials had been treasuring up in the bowels of the earth from the foundation of the world to catch the priests and their votaries at this very nick of time, when, to use her own words, they had no cloak for their sin. And she used to ask with a sort of triumph, did any protestants fall in this, I trow not. This always finished the whole. For none of her young audience knew more of the matter than what she told them. Let us not therefore confine the spirit of persecution alone to popery. This Lady, who wanted neither sense nor good Nature, was not sorry for any misfortune that befel a Papist.*

I have often been told that Lisbon resembled Edinburgh. This to me is not very apparent. It is true they are both built on high ground, but it would require you to bring the Calton hill into the middle of the city to give a strong resemblance. The houses built on the hill in Lisbon are finely situated for air, and have one of the finest prospects in the known world, that of an extensive country, covered with vineyards, intermixed with churches, Villas, and one of the King's palaces called Belleim.† This luxuriant prospect is at once under your eye, and joined to it that of a water scene, no less magnificent of its kind, as the Tagus is here large as a Sea

* If the reference in the text be to Miss Schaw's grandmother on her father's side, her first name was Anna. She is mentioned as living at Lauriston in 1726 and must have survived until after the earthquake in 1755. It would be interesting to know more about this old lady, who, in characteristic Scottish Presbyterian fashion, "was not sorry for any misfortune that befel a Papist."

† Belem was a suburb of Lisbon, extending three or four miles southwest along the Tagus, from a mile and a half to five miles distant. It is sometimes called the Westminster of Portugal, because containing two royal palaces and a royal monastery founded in 1490. One must distinguish between the palace d'Ajuda and the Belem palace (the Paço de Belem), sometimes called the Botanical Palace. The former was not built at this time, so that it was the latter which Miss Schaw visited.

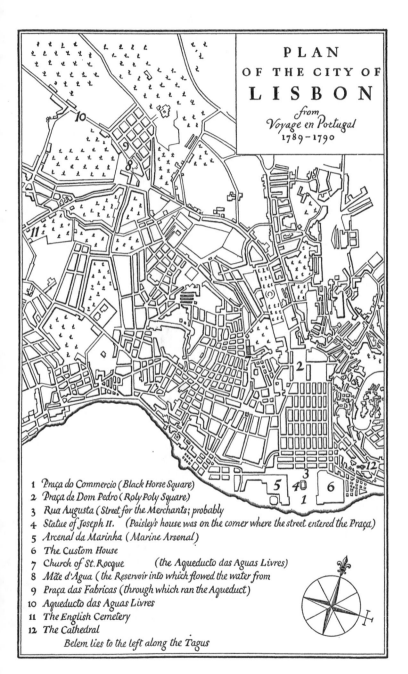

PLAN
OF THE CITY OF
LISBON
from
Voyage en Portugal
1789–1790

1 *Praça do Commercio (Black Horse Square)*
2 *Praça de Dom Pedro (Roly Poly Square)*
3 *Rua Augusta (Street for the Merchants; probably*
4 *Statue of Joseph II.   (Paisley's house was on the corner where the street entered the Praça)*
5 *Arcenal da Marinha (Marine Arsenal)*
6 *The Custom House*
7 *Church of St.Rocque   (the Aqueducto das Aguas Livres)*
8 *Mãe d'Agua (the Reservoir into which flowed the water from*
9 *Praça das Fabricas (through which ran the Aqueduct)*
10 *Aqueducto das Aguas Livres*
11 *The English Cemetery*
12 *The Cathedral*
       Belem lies to the left along the Tagus

and covered with a vast number of ships as well as the King's galleys. Every thing appears busy. I cannot help considering commerce as a chain to link all the human race to each other, by mutually supplying each other's necessities. I was much pleased with the prospect I have been describing, but no pleasure is without its alloy, for I viewed it from the sick chamber of my old friend Colin Drummond, brother to your friend the Dutchess of Athole.* He is come to Lisbon as the Denier resort, and tho' he affects to think himself better, told me privately, it was all over. This his physician confirmed, adding with some warmth that the people of Britain loved mightily to be buried at Lisbon, as they seldom come there, till just ready to step into the grave.† I stayed with him all day. He took my visit very kindly, and his spirits grew much better, while I remained with him. This however was by no means the case with my own. The unexpected meeting and the situation he was in very much affected me and recalled to my remembrance the agreeable circle in which I was accus-

---

* The Duchess of Atholl (second wife of James, 2d Duke of Atholl) was Jean, daughter of John Drummond of Meginck, Perthshire. Colin Drummond was her brother. It is odd that Miss Schaw should speak of her as the "Dutchess of Athole," because on September 2, 1767, she was married to Lord Adam Gordon, of the 66th Regiment of Foot, who had just returned from a long tour through the American colonies (journal printed in Mereness, *Travels in the American Colonies*). Her first husband died in 1764. As she had first married in May, 1749 (*Universal Magazine*, IV, 239), she must have been about forty-five in 1775.

† For many years Englishmen and Scotsmen had made Portugal a British winter resort. Mr. George writing of the eighteenth century says, "The new trade in tourists was just beginning with those whose health made a winter in England a worse hardship than crossing the seas; and Fielding's account of his journey to Portugal as a luxurious invalid late in the eighteenth century, shows what hardship then meant. The moist mild climate of Lisbon was considered suitable for consumptives by the science of the day, and all who could afford or survive the journey went with Fielding to fill the British cemetery at Lisbon" (p. 185).

The land for a cemetery was ceded to England in 1655, in accordance with the XIV article of the treaty of 1654 ("and finally, that a place be allotted them fit for the burial of their dead"). The most famous persons who lie buried there are Henry Fielding and Dr. Philip Doddridge, but scores of others also found in the British cemetery their final resting place.

tomed to converse with him, almost all of whom are now no more.

I was that evening at a very brilliant assembly given by the factory,* and tho' there were many fine women, my partiality gave it for our own three friends Mrs Paisley, Charlotte Pringle, and my own Fanny. I found the men in general of my opinion, and was informed that some of them had given a strong proof of their preferences, as Miss Charlotte would soon be Mrs Main, a Gentleman equal in every way to what I formerly said of Mr Paisley, and in the same line, as well as connected by the strictest bond of friendship. I hope it is true.

I saw mass performed one day in the great church of St Rock,† where all the nobles of Lisbon were prostrate on the ground, covered with their vails. The English seldom or never enter the churches, but particularly avoid them on high festivals. However one of Mr Paisley's young Gentlemen went with us. For tho' Miss Pringle had been a considerable

* To understand the reference to the "factory" and the presence of so many English and Scottish merchants in Lisbon, one must remember that since the treaties of 1642 and 1654, the marriage treaty of 1661, which confirmed the earlier arrangements, and the famous Methuen treaty of 1703, Portuguese commerce had come practically under British control. British merchants established themselves in Oporto and Lisbon, receiving and selling imported merchandise to the Portuguese, either for home consumption or for export to Brazil, and for this purpose erected buildings which were used as warehouses and agencies, for the storing and selling of goods. In a sense Portugal became in the eighteenth century Great Britain's commercial vassal, and the Portuguese merchants rarely rose above the level of shopkeepers and retail traders. It was this condition of commercial subordination that Pombal wished to alter by restoring trade to the natives and making them importers and wholesale dealers in foreign goods. He was unsuccessful in his effort.

The terms "factor" and "factory" were used as the equivalent of "agent" and "agency." Evidently the buildings served not only as commission houses and places for storage, but as residences also and centres for entertainment.

† The Church of St. Roque was erected by the Jesuits in 1561. It is "exteriorly a building of the meanest architectural pretensions," but contains a beautiful chapel, that of St. John the Baptist, constructed of costly marbles, jasper, and lapis lazuli. Apparently Miss Schaw and Fanny were so taken up with the altar and the wardrobe that they did not see this work of art, the usual object of interest to visitors.

time there, she had never been in any of the churches. I was much disappointed in the highest part of this showy religion. I had formed to myself a very grand idea of it, but perhaps it was owing to the particularity of their church, where the great altar is never displayed, nor used but when a Bishop or a Cardinal performs the Service. Two priests were immediately sent to take charge of us, and they made us step without ceremony over the very backs of the people, who were on the ground almost quite flat on their faces, and by a private door landed us behind on the great altar, where they let us see the Service below by drawing up the crimson velvet curtain, and I own (God forgive me) that viewing it as I then did, it appeared little more solemn than my friend Senora Maria's cloth-press. But the altar is very superb, and adorned with the finest Mosaic work I ever saw, which forms four beautiful pieces of painting. We now repaired to the Wardrobe, where we saw some gorgeous dresses for the Cardinal. But the fine Brussels point took Miss Rutherfurd's fancy so much, that I think the only method to convert her would be to bribe her with a present of the prettiest shirt. They showed us two altar-pieces of solid silver, but more to be coveted than admired, as their richness was their only merit. We had a very elegant rout at the Paisleys in the evening, and are engaged for every evening for a week.

I had just got this length, when Mr Paisley came to inform me that a Gentleman was in the visiting room, who was just setting out for England. I send this by him, as I will miss no opportunity. I am an easy correspondent, however as I can expect no answer. Adieu, I hope to see you before you can receive another, tho' I will write again by the King George Packet. Adieu.

I was yesterday at Belleim, the winter palace of the King; tho' they are just now spending their Holydays at one further in the country. The house is by no means fine, and did not the garden and other appurtenances atone for it, it would

hardly be worth the trouble of going to see, but those indeed
are well worthy of a traveller's Notice. This garden contains
within it variety enough almost to satisfy a Sir William
Chalmers,* and had I not read his account of what a garden
ought to be,‡ I should not venture to express all I saw under
that single appellation, but tho' it is far from being so extensive as his plan, yet it contains a great deal more than his
three natural notes of earth, air and water, water, earth and
air. As this palace is intended for a winter residence, every
thing has been done to render it agreeable for that season of
the year. The walks are covered with the finest gravel and
sheltered from the cold by hedges of ever-green. They are so
contrived as to stretch your power of walking to a considerable length, every now and then opening into orange-groves
and shrubberies of various winter plants and flowers.

Nor is unanimated Nature all you have to amuse you.
While we were admiring a row of cape jessamine, which
even now is covered with flowers, a huge elephant laid his
proboscis over the wall against which it was planted. I confess I was startled at the uncommon salutation, tho' I had no
reason. This unwieldy novelty was very well secured, and
on mounting the stair of an adjoining summer house, we had
a full view of him in safety. What a pigmy is man, when
compared to such an animal as this, and yet is vain enough to
pretend dominion over him. A little further on we met a com-
partment entirely the reverse of the last. This is an Aviary
which contains five hundred singing birds, all exquisite in
their plumage, tho' I could not hear their notes. These are a
yearly tribute to the queen from the Brazils, the Madeira,
and indeed from all the dominions where they are to be had.
Their apartment is large and well contrived, of an oval form
and grated over the top. It is planted round with orange-

‡ His description of an Asiatick garden.

* Sir William Chambers, *A Dissertation on Oriental Gardening*, 1772.

trees, Myrtles, and a variety of evergreens, and in the middle
is a piece of water, which receives a constant supply from the
hands of a Hebe placed at the upper end, and runs off from
the bottom, so as to be always fresh, while a small grate prevents the little gold and silver fishes from being carried off,
and they look very pretty frisking about in it.

A little further on, we found Indian fowls of all denominations, some of them very beautiful and others very much
the reverse. It were impossible to name them all, but they are
well represented on the Indian papers we get home. One
however I took more particalar Notice of, as I had often
admired her figure on the gold medal which hung at M^rs
Murray of Stormont's breast,* and which empowered her to
keep in decent order those Misses and Masters, whose heads
and heels were equally light. You will guess I mean the
pelican, which is the badge of her authority as Lady direct-
ress of our assembly. Her power both you and I have felt,
tho' much oftener her goodness and even partiality. This
tender mother is not however in fact lovely, tho' of good
report. There were several other compartments filled by the
feathered race of different kinds, but it would be tedious to
mention them all. We now entered a field, at the further end
of which was a whole street of small houses, which we found
were occupied by animals of the most noxious natures, such
as pole cats, weasels etc. One in particular was inhabited by
rats of Brazil, of a very large size. They all came peeping
thro' their grates, just like so many nuns, and if they were
to confine only such as they think would do mischief to
society, if free, they were in the right. Behind this we found
a very noble menagerie, in the form of a court. Here are lions,
leopards, panthers, bears and wolves. Both the lioness and

---

* Nov. 7, 1777. "Died at Edinburgh, Hon. Mrs. Helen Nicholas Murray,
daughter of the deceased David, Viscount of Stormont, aunt of the present
Viscount of Stormont, and sister of the Earl of Mansfield" (*Scots Magazine,*
1777, p. 627).

the panther have whelps. The last has the most beautiful kittens it is possible to conceive. I forgot the tiger, which has also a young family. Tho' there is a number of officers to attend this ferocious court, they are not kept neat, and the smell is intolerable.

Leaving this, we found ourselves again in the garden, and presently arrived at another court, which I may venture to pronounce magnificent. This was the menage and the royal stables. These contain above three score of the finest horses in the world. The absence of my brother on this occasion, converted my pleasure into pain, as I could not help bitterly regretting his not enjoying this satisfaction, and the more I was charmed with these lovely animals myself, the more sincerely I lamented his Missing that, which of all other sights would have pleased him most. But I hope on some future occasion it may be in his power. The elegance of these creatures is past description, and I admired them so long, that I had scarcely time for the next sight, which is just behind them, and indeed makes part of the same buildings. This is no less than thirteen Zebras. But as you have often seen the Queen's ass, I need not describe them, for they are exactly the same. They have been endeavouring to break them to draw in the Kings carriage, which would look very pretty, but tho' several grooms have been maimed and some even killed in the attempt, they are as untamed as ever, and tho' many of them have been colted in the stables, and began as early as possible, it has had no effect. They are infinitely stronger as well as taller than the common breed of asses, and I should think mules bred from them would both be useful and much handsomer than those they at present have.*

---

* Southey visited the same gardens and his account of conditions twenty years later supplements admirably that of Miss Schaw. The collection of birds he considers "the richest I ever saw," but the menagerie was "ill managed and ill supplied." "I was almost sickened," he writes, "at the pestilential filth in which the beasts are confined. The fine old elephant of John V was put upon a short allowance of cabbages, but as those who diminished his

Good night, it is very late and I write by the light of a lamp, as they use no candles in bed-chambers here.

The King George packet sails to morrow, and I am set down to finish the last letter to you from the continent. My hopes are now on the wing, and I trust that goodness which has hitherto protected me, will carry me safely to the end of my long voyage, and let me find my friends as much mine as ever.

We were yesterday a considerable way in the country, where the depredations of the earthquake are very visible; but our principal object was the fine aqueduct, on which it was able to make no impression. So compact and firmly are the stones united, and so indissoluble is the composition with which they are cemented, that tho' many years have passed since the water first began to flow thro' it, it is not the least impaired. It has its beginning sixteen miles up the country and comes over many high mountains in its way to Lisbon. The arches on which it rests are for that reason very unequal; on the mountains not exceeding three or four feet, and in the valleys often rising to above two hundred, as I am informed, for my eye is not exact enough to judge of heights. The pillars which support these arches are plain, but strike the Imagination with an idea of the greatest possible strength. The aqueduct seems to be from forty to fifty feet in breadth, but the water does not take up above twelve or fifteen feet of it. A walk is raised on each side, and the roof appears about sixteen feet high. At the distance of every fifty feet is an opening, which admits the light and the air, but is so contrived as to exclude rain. These look like little towers on the

food could not lessen his appetite, the poor animal died. There are only three zebras remaining; they [were] bred in this country and some attempts were made to break them in. The late Don Jaze de Menezes, son of the Marquis of Marialva [the friend of William Beckford] actually drove them in an open carriage, till they broke two or three carriages for him, and some of them had killed themselves by struggling" (pp. 314-316).

outside.* I have been particular as to this fine piece of Architecture, as I do not recollect ever to have read a description of it, nor indeed of Lisbon by any hand, who has done it justice. Mr Twiss† says a great deal, but his travels seem only a journal of his own bad humours, prejudices and mistakes, for I believe he would not willingly tell a falsehood, but I am at a loss to think where he found the dirty scenes he describes. I have been at no pains to avoid them, yet have met with no such thing.

After our return from the country, we took a whole round of the town, which tho' spacious, I do not like so well as Edinburgh. Their principal street (the Rua Augusta) is neither so broad, nor near so long as our High street, and tho' the people live over head of each other as we do, the buildings are not so high, nor appear so well built, and the

---

* The Church of St. Roque and the aqueduct were the usual "sights" for visitors to Lisbon at this time. The latter, whose "stupendous height" filled Southey "with astonishment," brought water into Lisbon from springs ten miles away, as far as Chellas, spanning a valley upon huge arches, the highest of which was over 250 feet in altitude. This structure, the Aqueducto das Aguas Livres, was built under John V by Manuel da Maia, and so well built that it escaped injury from the earthquake. It has 127 arches in a single row, with pointed openings.

Of this famous work Beckford, the author of *Vathek*, writes, "I sat down on a fragment of rock under the great arch and looked up at the vaulted stone-work so high above me, with a sensation of awe not unallied to fear; as if the building I gazed upon was the performance of some immeasurable being endowed with gigantic strength, who might perhaps take a fancy to saunter about his work this morning, and, in mere awkwardness, crush me to atoms" (*Letters*, II, 36).

† Richard Twiss, *Travels through Portugal and Spain in 1772 and 1773*, London, 1775.

From all accounts the Lisbon of this period was dirty and unsanitary, Miss Schaw to the contrary notwithstanding. Southey says that Lisbon at the end of the eighteenth century was notorious for its dilapidation, insecurity, and dirt. "The filth of the city is indeed astonishing. Everything is thrown into the street and all the refuse of the kitchen and dead animals are exposed to the scorching sun" (p. 213). And Byron—

"The dingy denizens are rear'd in dirt;
Ne personage of high or mean degree
Doth care for cleanness of surtout or shirt,
Though shent with Egypt's plague, unkempt, unwash'd, unhurt."
Childe Harold's Pilgrimage, I, xvii.

jalousies* on the windows give them all a look of prisons. In this street is the arsenal, which is a fine building. The town is fast getting the better of her Misfortunes. Many of the streets are rebuilding in a handsome and modern manner, and one noble square is finished, in a corner of which is Mr Paisley's house.† Here is a statue of the present King and the favourite Minister, the Marquis of Pombal. It is no easy matter to form an opinion of the character of this statesman, either as a private man or a minister, one party extolling him, and another abusing him. He is hated by the princess of Brazil,‡ in proportion as he is loved by her father, and the moment the king dies he will find all the weight of her resentment. She is said to be very bigoted in matters of religion, and gloomy and vindictive in her temper. The moderation of the minister, and the lenity with which he is supposed to have inspired the king towards hereticks give great offence to her and the clergy, while the nobility in general are his enemies from his endeavours to lessen their exorbitant power,

---

* Jalousies were iron or wooden shutters, with fixed slats sloping upwards from the outside. They could, as a rule, be raised or lowered, at the will of the person within, enabling her to look out without being seen.

† The portion of the city that was rebuilding was the lower town (Cidade Baixa) near the river. The Praça do Commercio, the "noble square" of the text, was the centre of its business life. From this square running back along the higher ground was the Rua Augusta, connecting it with the Praça de Dom Pedro, with its wavy pavement, called Roly-Poly Square by the British sailors. Along the Rua Augusta were the commercial houses and on the north-west corner of the Praça do Commercio, extending west along the Arsenal street, was the huge Arcenal da Marinha, which Miss Shaw wrongly locates on the Rua Augusta. (See plan of the city in *Voyage en Portugal, 1789-1790*, 1797.) In the centre of the Praça do Commercio was the equestrian statue of Joseph I, erected only the year before, from which later came the name, Black Horse Square, given by the British. On the south front of the pedestal was a bust of Pombal. This bust was removed in April, 1777, after Pombal's fall, and the city arms in bronze substituted. It was restored in 1833. Mr. Paisley's house was on a corner of the Praça do Commercio.

‡ Joseph I's eldest daughter, Maria Francesca, Princess of Brazil, married her uncle, Dom Pedro, his youngest brother. They succeeded to the throne in 1777, but as a consequence of continued in-breeding were too feeble-minded to rule with any regard for the welfare of Portugal. Maria was fanatically religious and Pombal was overthrown by a combination of a court camarilla and the clerics.

and reduce them to the laws of their country and of humanity. Nor does he gain much approbation from the middle and low class, who unused to liberty, know not how to make it sit easy. The severity with which he has punished the crime of murder, particularly assassination in the streets, has been attended with such success, that the streets of Lisbon are now as safe as those of any town in Europe, tho' they are still entirely dark.

I was at a play a few Nights ago and saw an actress, who had been mistress to a Marquis, whose Jealousy on her account had made him murder no less than three suspected rivals. For the last he was banished, and would have been broke on the wheel, notwithstanding his high rank, had not the princess of Brazil obtained him the liberty of retiring. The playhouse is not fine, the scenes paltry and the play unintelligible from the action at least.* I wished to see the Portugueze manner of dressing, and had no other way than this, as they are ordered to keep strictly to the mode. They have a very good Italian opera when the court is at Lisbon, but no ladies are admitted. This they say is owing to the Queen, who is extremely jealous of her Royal consort, and if we credit

---

* The theatre was in the Rua d'os Condes, and the employment of men for the female parts aroused ridicule and disgust among French and British travellers. "Comme il est interdit," writes the author of the *Voyage en Portugal*, "aux femmes depuis quelques années de monter sur le theâtre, les hommes sont obligés de jouer leur rôles. Rien de plus ridicule ni de plus dégoûtant à la fois que de voir sous les habits d'une femme un homme à larges épaules et menton barbu," etc. (II, p. 44). Beckford writes, "The play afforded me more disgust than amusement; the theatre is low and narrow, and the actors, for there are no actresses, below criticism. Her Majesty's absolute commands [that is, of the former Princess of Brazil, see preceding note] having swept females off the stage, their parts are acted by calvish young fellows. Judge what pleasing effect this metamorphosis must produce, especially in the dancers, where one sees a stout shepherdess in virgin white, with a soft blue beard, clutching a nosegay in a fist that would almost have knocked down a Goliath, and a train of milk-maids attending her enormous footsteps, tossing their petticoats over their heads at every step. Such sprawling, jerking, and ogling I never saw before, and hope never to see again" (II, 71-72). The royal opera house of São Carlos was not built until 1792-1793.

report, not without reason. Tho' the natural character of the men is that of jealousy and suspicion, there is no place where the women are held in such estimation and treated with such respect. Every wish is gratified except that of liberty, and even the husband who confines his cama with bolts and jalousies, never approaches her, but with the respect and adulation of a passionate lover. Indeed the violence of his love is his only excuse. I have been in the parlour of several of the genteelist monasteries, and conversed with many nuns of the first fashion. They are however very hard of access, and it requires no small interest to see some of them. They appeared very much pleased with us, particularly with Fanny, whose person and manners they highly complimented. They never suffered us to leave them, without presenting us with some little mark of their approbation, and we have got as many artificial flowers as would dress a whole Assembly.

I will have no other opportunity of writing from hence. My next letter will be from Greenock. Had it not been our care for the boys, we would have returned by the way of France, and Mr Neilson is perfectly acquainted with the route. This would have been very agreeable, nor were we restrained on account of our finances, as Mr Paisley offered us an unlimited credit to draw on him from every town that was in our route. Indeed his friendship and attention are not to be described, and I consider it as no small acquisition to have gained his acquaintance, tho' my travels had afforded nothing more.

And now, my friend, adieu to our epistolary correspondence, which I hope ends here, as I sincerely hope we may never be again as long parted, and that our travels shall mutually serve to amuse our winter evenings, when we shall travel them over again in the friendly circle of a cheerful hearth. I have wrote my brother under cover to Lord T—d, Ld C— B, C—M,* and if he is in Britain he will not fail to

---

* "T——d" is manifestly Lord Townshend, in all probability George,

get some of them. Be sure to have a letter for me at Greenock, to the care of your old correspondent George Neil, who
is land-waiter there. How many of your letters has he had
charge of! Let me know about my brother. I will positively
say Adieu, Adieu.*

Marquess Townshend, 1724-1807, who had the boys under his protection in
1776-1778. The identification of the others is unimportant.

* It is not easy to determine from the internal evidence of the narrative
just how long the Lisbon visit lasted or just when the party sailed for Scotland. As nearly as can be made out the duration of the visit was somewhat
less than four weeks, so that the departure could not have been earlier than
the middle of January. It might have been later. In any case Miss Schaw,
Fanny, the boys, and Neilson could hardly have reached Greenock before the
end of the month or early in February, 1776. It is strange that in the narrative no mention is made of Christmas or New Year's festivities, for the
visit included both of these festal days.

APPENDICES

APPENDICES

I. The Highland Emigration.

IT is a curious coincidence that among the many experiences of her journey, Miss Schaw should have come into contact with a phase of that highland emigration which is a conspicuous feature of Scottish-American history just before the Revolutionary War. Between 1763 and 1776 there left Scotland many thousands of her people—the total number is not known—who had lived in towns, valleys, and islands of North Britain, from the southwest to the uttermost north, including the Hebrides, the Orkneys, and the Shetland Islands. They represented nearly all grades of the population—tacksmen, farmers and other tenants, and laborers, and covered many gradations of wealth, from the substantial and prosperous chief tenants to the very poor, unable to maintain themselves and their families. These people, migrating at different times and under different conditions, seem all to have been attracted by the fertile and cheap lands of the New World and by the opportunities these lands offered of making a living. They went to nearly all the colonies, but chiefly to Nova Scotia, New York, and the Carolinas.

The causes of this movement have never been adequately explained, although there is a great mass of evidence, printed and in manuscript, upon which a thorough study might be based. In general it was due to the breaking up of the clan organization and the transition from tribal to civil power and authority, constituting a veritable revolution in Scottish highland life in the eighteenth century. Three results followed: an increase of anarchy and crime; a substitution of money payments for payments in kind in rents and other transactions; and an increasing pressure of population upon the food supply. The landed proprietors or their chief tenants, the tacksmen, began to absorb small farms into large ones, evict tenants or raise rents, and harry the lesser folk with exactions and heavy oppressions, whereas the latter, bred to a farming and stock-raising life, were unable to find new forms of livelihood. The old linen manufacture was in decay, while the redundancy of population rendered stock and cattle raising and the time-honored methods of agriculture a precarious and insufficient means of subsistence. By witness of all whose testimony has been recorded, the chief cause of the movement was the rise of rents, and the difficulties of subsistence due to the enhanced cost of provisions and other necessaries of life. The situation was in many ways not unlike that which accompanied the enclosure movement in England in the sixteenth, eighteenth, and nineteenth centuries.

The emigrants complained of all of these conditions as making it impossible for them to remain in Scotland. "It is a grief to our spirits," said one, "to leave our native land and venture upon such a dangerous voyage; but there is no help for it. We are not able to stand the high rents and must do something for bread or see our families reduced to beggary." But just who were responsible for the situation is not so easy to determine. A recent writer has called attention to the fact that one cause of the emigration was the "tacksman system." The tacksmen were chief tenants, often men of wealth and social standing, who held their lands of the proprietors or lords of the soil on long leases and were accustomed to "subset" these lands to undertenants. Both classes suffered, for while some of the tacksmen were among the oppressors, others, confronted with the prospect of heightened rents and lowered social position, themselves joined the movement and came to America, bringing with them not only much wealth, but also many of their lesser tenants, who followed them partly from motives of clan loyalty and partly in the hope of bettering their condition (Miss Adam, in *The Scottish Historical Review*, July, 1919).

Among those who were driven from Scotland because of the increase of lawlessness and crime was James Hogg, who came to North Carolina in 1774. He agreed that "others complain, with too much justice, of arbitrary and oppressive services, of racked rents and cruel taskmasters," but declared that in his case he and his family were compelled to leave because of "the barbarity of the country," meaning thereby the theft and pilfering of his crops and stock by the people of the neighborhood, the burning of his house and other buildings, and the threats which were made against his own life. "A list of the murders, robberies, and thefts," he wrote, "committed with impunity there during my residence in Caithness, would surprise a Mohawk or a Cherokee. The loss of so many people and the numbers they may in time draw after them will probably be missed by the landholders, but let them learn to treat their fellow creatures with more humanity. Instead of looking on myself as an enemy to my country in being accessory to the carrying off so many people, I rejoice in being an instrument in the hand of Providence to punish oppression which is by far too general, and I am glad to understand that already some of those haughty landlords now find it necessary to court and caress those same poor people, whom they lately despised and treated as slaves or beasts of burden" (*Scots Magazine*, 36, pp. 345-346).

Miss Schaw's fear that the emigration of so many able-bodied men would have a bad effect on recruiting was realized during the American War, when the obtaining of soldiers from Scotland, always a fertile field for the recruiting sergeant, became exceedingly and increasingly difficult.

II. The Martin Family.

COLONEL SAMUEL MARTIN, of whom Miss Schaw gives an engaging account, was well called the "Father of Antigua," for he was born on the island in the last decade of the seventeenth century, and except for three trips to England, covering probably less than ten years in all, lived continuously there until the very eve of the Revolution. Thus his long life of more than eighty years was coincident with the most important period in the history of the colony, and touched at many points its industrial, social, and political development.

The Martins came originally from Ireland, some of its members migrating early to Surinam and the West Indies, and settling finally, in the seventeenth century, in Antigua. Many of the later members returned to England, and as officials under government or officers in the army and navy rose to eminence in their professions, a few attaining the honors of knighthood. Others went to the American continent, to Boston, New York, and North Carolina, becoming representative men of their communities, and acquiring, as a rule, ample wealth, wherewith to maintain social positions commensurate with their prominence. The family as a whole got widely scattered during the colonial period, but its members never lost their regard for Antigua, retaining property there, and manifesting interest in its welfare and a desire to be of service to its people whenever the occasion arose. In England the most prominent sons of the family dwelt in or near London, in Surrey, Dorset, Herts, and Berks, where, supported in part from the income of their Antigua plantations, they possessed country seats and lived the lives of country gentlemen. Wherever Martins resided, whether at "Green Castle" in Antigua, "Rockhall" in Long Island, or in England at Ashtead in Surrey, Great Canford in Dorset, or "White Knights" near Reading, they were of more than ordinary influence and importance. Some of them rose to positions of high distinction, particularly in the navy.

Because of the meagre records of the time, the various members of the family are not always easy to identify, and, in consequence, much confusion has resulted among those who have endeavored to deal with the family genealogy. In three generations there were five Josiahs, and in four generations, six Samuels; and in addition there were others bearing the same names, who do not appear to have belonged to this particular Martin line at all. Even with all the available evidence before us, there are still some difficulties that cannot be surmounted.

Colonel Martin's father, also a Samuel, was the son of Samuel Martin of Dublin county, Ireland, fourth in descent from a Josiah Martin of the same place (Debrett, *Baronetage*, ed. 1840, p. 374). He was probably born in Surinam, but appears in Antigua as early as 1678. He soon became one of the conspicuous men of the island, an ensign and major in the militia, a member of the assembly, of which he was speaker in 1689, a councillor, treasurer and collector of imposts, and, toward the end of his life, member of a committee to compile a body of laws. In 1699 he is spoken of as "of great estate, good sence, and repute." That he lacked the urbanity and instinctive kindliness of nature which Miss Schaw noted in his son, appears from the severity of his attitude toward his slaves, by whom he was murdered on Christmas Day, 1701. "We have lost a very useful man in Major Martin," wrote Governor Codrington. "I am afraid he was guilty of some unusual act of severity or rather some indignity toward the Coromantes, the best and most faithful of our slaves."* Though the

---

* *Calendar of State Papers, Colonial*, 1701, pp. 720-721 ; 1702, p. 167. The murder was a shocking affair and caused wide alarm throughout the island. Whether the "Major Samuel Martyn" of Antigua mentioned in 1698 as engaged in illicit trade and called "a great villain" by an enemy of doubtful

young Samuel was but a child when this tragic event took place, he must have been deeply impressed by its significance, for Miss Schaw presents a pleasing picture of the large troop of healthy negroes upon the "Green Castle" plantation—numbering about three hundred at this time—cheerfully performing the tasks imposed by a kind and beneficent master, a prince of subjects rather than an owner of slaves. Many of them had been freed, as Miss Schaw says, and others were freed later by Martin in his will.

Of Colonel Martin's life we have but a slender outline. He was born about 1690—the exact date being uncertain, because statements differ as to the age at which he died—and he died in Antigua in November, 1776, a little less than two years after Miss Schaw's visit. His early career is obscure, owing to the presence of more than one Samuel Martin on the island, but he seems to have been the Samuel of "Five Islands" plantation, who was major of militia in 1707 and of the troop of mounted horse or carabineers in 1712. In 1716 he was elected to the assembly and, except for a trip to England in 1716-1717, continued to serve either as deputy or speaker until he again left the colony in 1729. He married, before 1714, Frances Yeamans, daughter of John Yeamans, the deputy governor (1693-1711), but she died and he married, as his second wife, Sarah Wyke, the daughter of Edward Wyke, deputy governor of Montserrat, and widow of William Irish of the same island. His fourth child, Henry, the second son by his second wife, was born in Dorset, England, in 1733, so he probably remained in England on his second visit for a number of years. Soon after his return he must have been commissioned a colonel of militia, for Miss Schaw tells us that in 1772 he had been head of the militia "upwards of forty years." In 1750 he was again elected to the assembly and chosen speaker at its first session. From this time forward, living on his "Green Castle" plantation in New Division, which was picturesquely located in Bermudian Valley under Windmill Hill (Davy's *West Indies*, p. 408), he led an increasingly peaceful and prosperous life, resigning his place as speaker in 1763, and his seat in the assembly in 1768. At the urgent request of his children, three of whom, Samuel, Jr., Henry, and William Byam, had been living there for a number of years (a nephew, William, was a business man in London), he went to England, when nearly

character is our Major Samuel we cannot say. It is likely, though the charges need not be taken at their face value. Charges and counter-charges were common enough in all the colonies at that time. Nevertheless the elder Samuel would appear to have been a man of a vigorous personality and somewhat irascible temper. *Ib.*, 1697-1698, pp. 194, 195-197, 338.

eighty years of age, doubtless with the expectation of spending his declining years there. But as he told Miss Schaw, he could not stand "the dreary climate." He spent his time partly in Surrey and partly in Dorset, and at the former place, August 13, 1773, made his will, adding codicils and generally settling his affairs. He must have returned to Antigua soon afterwards, glad to get back, as he himself said, to the "warm sunshine" of his semitropical island. He died on the island, where he had been born, and where he had spent more than three score and ten of the more than four score years of his life. His only venture into the field of authorship, as far as we know, is a pamphlet entitled *An Essay upon Plantership, humbly inscribed to his Excellency George Thomas, Esq., Chief Governor of All the Leeward Islands, As a Monument to Ancient Friendship,* which was written in Antigua and first published there about 1755. A third edition was issued in London in 1763, and a fourth, a work of sixty-two pages, in 1765. The treatise shows Colonel Martin to have been a model planter and a high-minded, considerate master.

Colonel Martin, according to his own statement, had twenty-three children, but of this number it is impossible to give the names of more than seven: Samuel, Jr., and Henrietta, children by his first wife, and George, Henry, Josiah, William Byam, and Fanny, children by his second wife. That many of his children died young is probable, and that others may be found among the many Martins whose names appear in the records of Antigua and neighboring islands, is equally likely.

Samuel, Jr., his eldest son, was born in Antigua, September 1, 1714. He went to England when but a lad, possibly accompanying his father on the latter's second trip in 1729, in order to be educated, as there were no educational facilities in Antigua. He was entered at the Inner Temple about 1740, and became a bencher in 1747, continuing in residence until 1761. From 1742 to 1744 he served as deputy agent for the colony, while his cousin, John Yeamans, appointed agent in 1727, was absent on leave in Antigua; and in 1744 he was recommended by Yeamans as his successor, but the recommendation was not acted on by the colony. He became a member of parliament from the borough of Camelford in Cornwall, 1747-1768, and from the Cinque Port Hastings, 1768-1774, both controlled boroughs, and he took some part in parliamentary business. His most important post was that of first secretary to the Treasury Board, to which he was appointed in 1756, serving until 1762, and in which he must have had a great deal to do with the distribution of the money appropriated by parliament to recompense the continental colonies for their services and expenditures in the French and Indian War.* He became treasurer to the Princess Dowager of Wales, possibly after the death of the prince in 1751, and continued to serve in that capacity until the death of the princess in 1772, "a long service," he calls it in his will. In the latter year, possibly to compensate for the loss of his office, he was granted an annuity of £1200 out of the four and a half per cent duty, until a grant in reversion of the office of usher of H. M. Exchequer, a post paying about £4000 a year, should take place. But he died before he could profit from the emoluments of the office, which had been enjoyed since 1738 by Horace Walpole, the wit and letter writer, who survived him by nine years. He does not appear to have held any government position during the years after 1772; but we occasionally get glimpses of various business activities, by means of which he may have added to an income already large. He had a small estate, "Marshalswyck," near St. Albans, Herts, where he was living in retirement in 1780, when sixty-six years of age; and another in Dorset, possibly near Great Canford, about two miles southeast from Wimborne minster on the south side of the river Stour. While in London, after 1761, he lived in Queen Street, Westminster, until 1777, and afterwards at 84 Pall Mall. He died November 20, 1788, and was buried in Great Canford churchyard, where there is a tablet of white marble, placed by his executors, his brothers Henry and William Byam, and his intimate friend Ralph Willet of Merly, with the inscription, we "loved him when living and lament him now dead" (Hutchins, *Dorset*, III, 310).

When Colonel Martin, the father, said to Miss Schaw, "my eldest son you know by character at least," and Miss Schaw in reply expressed her admiration for that character, both were probably referring to Samuel's chief claims to the remembrance of posterity—his duel with John Wilkes and his friendship for Hogarth, who painted his portrait.† Though Hogarth's biographers mention the portrait,

---

* There is a letter from Jared Ingersoll to Martin in the *Fitch Papers*, II, 131-134, which deals with Connecticut's claims for repayment of expenses for provisions furnished in 1757. The letter is dated June 29, 1761.

† In the *Gentleman's Magazine*, 1805, Pt. I, 113, a correspondent sends a portrait of Martin, with the following letter: "The celebrity of Samuel Martin, Esq., some time secretary to the Treasury and for several years member for Camelford, and the memorable event of his duel with Mr. Wilkes may render the annexed plate, engraved from the last portrait painted for him, an acceptable present to collectors and to those who wish to illustrate the works either of Wilkes or Churchill. It is well known that in 1772 Mr.

none of them have identified Martin or have been able to give any of the circumstances under which it was painted. Hogarth retained the portrait during his lifetime, and left it to Martin in his will, and Martin in turn left it to his brother, William Byam. The date when it was painted is uncertain and its present whereabouts are unknown. It is probable that the duel with Wilkes grew in some way out of Martin's acquaintance with Hogarth and the latter's quarrel with Wilkes and Churchill, 1762-1764, for it took place at the same time, although its immediate cause was Wilkes's attack upon Martin in the *North Briton* (March, 1763), in which he stigmatized him as "a mean, abject, low-lived, and dirty fellow" (Bleackley's *Life of Wilkes*, pp. 132-133, and for the duel, pp. 135-137).

During the period after 1772, Martin performed a number of services for his Antiguan and North Carolinian friends and was useful in furthering the claims of some of the Loyalists before the commission. Thomas Macknight applied to him with letters from his brother, Governor Josiah Martin (Dartmouth Papers, letter of July 24, 1781), and there is a paper in the Public Record Office bearing Samuel's comments on Josiah's own claims for compensation and a pension. In these comments, Martin suggested that the Treasury grant Josiah a post in the recently organized government of Bengal. Though nothing came of the suggestion, it is interesting to note that Josiah's son, Josiah, born in North Carolina in 1772, was afterwards appointed register of the court of appeals at Benares, a post that he was filling at the time of his death in 1799 (*Gentleman's Magazine*, 1799, p. 1087).

Samuel's half-brother Henry, second son of Colonel Samuel by his second wife and the progenitor of the present English line, was born in England in 1733, and as far as we know never visited Antigua. He early rose to prominence in naval circles, being for many years naval commissioner at Portsmouth. In 1790 he was appointed comptroller of the navy, one of the four principal officers of the Navy

---

Martin declined an alderman's gown, and that he was a frequent speaker in parliament between the years 1782 and 1786 is evident from the ample notice you have taken of him in your parliamentary debates for those years."

The last part of this letter is quite incorrect, as Martin was not a freeman of the City of London and so could have had no opportunity to refuse an alderman's gown (the person so refusing was one Joseph Martin), and he was not in parliament during the years from 1782 to 1786. The portrait reproduced in the magazine cannot be that painted by Hogarth, who died in 1764. A correspondent would hardly have called a picture painted twenty-five years before a man's death his "last portrait."

Board, an office which he retained until his death. He was knighted July 28, 1791, and died August 1, 1794. He lived in Harley Street, London, but died apparently in Dorset, possibly at Great Canford. He inherited "Green Castle" from his father, and had lands also in Ireland and England. He had four sons and four daughters: the eldest son, Samuel, died in 1782; his second, Sir Henry, who attained no special distinction, died in 1842; his third, Josiah, was collector of customs in Antigua, succeeding the "Young Martin," mentioned in the text, and died in 1849; his fourth, Thomas Byam, afterwards Sir Thomas, who became an admiral in the navy and whose biography is given in the *Dictionary of National Biography*, died in 1854. The members of this family in no way concern us here.

Colonel Samuel's fourth son was Josiah, the governor of North Carolina, who played an important part in the events leading to the Revolution, and is mentioned a number of times in Miss Schaw's narrative, though it is doubtful if she ever met him personally. To North Carolina historians he has been but a fleeting figure, and they have been but little concerned to find out whence he came or whither he went after he left the colony. It is worth while, therefore, to give a sketch of his life, as far as the details can be recovered.

Josiah was born in Antigua in 1737 and was probably named for his uncle, whose daughter he afterwards married. He joined the local militia in 1754, at the age of seventeen, but in 1757 entered the regular army as ensign of the 4th Foot. In November, 1758, he was commissioned lieutenant and on August 11, 1761, was bracketed with Charles Lee, of unsavory reputation, as major in the 103d or Volunteer Hunters. The next year, 1762, he was commissioned lieutenant colonel of the 22d Foot, afterwards Gage's regiment, but in 1764 was transferred to the 68th, which was located in Antigua from 1764 to 1772. On account of ill health, he sold his commission in 1769 and retired from active military service. Just where he was stationed during these years is not easy to ascertain, but he must have spent part of his time in Long Island, where he married his wife; part in London, where Miers, a London jeweller and portrait painter, painted his portrait (a miniature); and part in Antigua, whither he went in 1764. There he was appointed by Governor Thomas a member of the council, in place of Arthur Freeman, whom Thomas had suspended for running away with his daughter, and he retained that position, nominally at least, until Freeman's return from England in 1771. In 1761 he married his cousin Elizabeth (apparently five years his senior), the daughter of his uncle Josiah by his first wife, a Mrs.

Chester, and probably both before and after that event lived at "Rockhall," Josiah's countryseat in Long Island. He must have resided there again after resigning his commission in 1769, perhaps for two years. On December 14, 1770, he was named governor of North Carolina, through the influence of Governor Tryon, and on May 1, 1771, received his commission and instructions from England, through Lord Dunmore. He was delayed in Long Island by continued ill health and did not reach the province until July 11 of that year, holding the first meeting of his council on August 12. Samuel Johnston of North Carolina wrote to Thomas Barker, June 10, 1771, "We are in daily expectation of Mr. Martin our new Govr, and as we hear a very amiable character of him are not uneasy at the approaching change" (Letter in North Carolina Historical Commission files).

Josiah was resident governor of North Carolina until 1776. He made a tour of the colony with his family and retinue in 1772, reaching Hillsboro in July, and although he endeavored to adjust the difficulties arising out of the Regulators' War, he was only moderately successful. Temperamentally he was not well fitted to deal with the unrest of the period, and has always been harshly judged, not only by North Carolina historians, but also by all whose sympathies are with the revolutionary party. He was energetic, conscientious, and loyal to the cause which he upheld, but he lacked wisdom and the spirit of compromise, and saw in the colonial movement, as did Miss Schaw herself, only an exhibition of contumacy and sedition. His letters are long and his style is turgid and tiresome. He adhered inflexibly to the constitutional rights of the prerogative, and, believing that force was the only remedy to apply in the case, he suffered the fate of those who endeavor to coerce rather than to control an uprising based on legitimate grievances. He showed unquestioned ability and laid his plans with shrewdness and skill, but the breaks in the game went against him. When his first efforts to obtain military assistance failed, he fled before the rising storm, and somewhat to the discredit of his valor, if not of his discretion, escaped from New Bern on May 24, 1775, and took refuge, first at Fort Johnston (June 2), and then on board the *Cruizer* in the Cape Fear River (June 18 or 19). He remained in the province (on the ships of war) "for the sake of correspondence with the friends of government," and not only organized a corps of Highlanders for an attack upon Wilmington (*N. C. R.* XXII, 616-617), but also formulated elaborate plans, which in the autumn of 1775 he sent to Lord Dartmouth in England, by Miss Schaw's brother, Alexander—plans providing for a combined attack of land and sea forces for the purpose of reducing to subjection the Southern colonies. On January 10, 1776, he removed from the *Cruizer* to the *Scorpion*, and from that vantage point inaugurated the highland campaign, which ended in the defeat of the Highlanders at Moore's Creek bridge on February 27, 1776. In March he changed to the transport *Peggy*, and when Sir Henry Clinton and Admiral Warren, who arrived during the spring, decided that further effort was useless, he accompanied them to Charles Town and remained there on the transport during June and most of July. With his departure from the province his governorship came to an actual, though not a legal, end. In his memorial presented to the Loyalist Claims Commission, he said that he never acted as governor after his flight from New Bern; but we know that he issued a proclamation from Charlotte in October, 1780, when he was with Lord Cornwallis's army (Connor, *History of North Carolina*, I, 469) and that he continued to receive his salary until October, 1783 (*The Royal Commission on the Losses and Services of the American Loyalists*, Roxburghe Club, p. 290).

Toward the end of July, 1776, anxious to see his family, and knowing that for the time being there was nothing more for him to do in the South, Martin went to New York on the *Sovereign* and "for the sake of rendering immediate service" remained there for nearly three years, living with the family at "Rockhall." During this time his property in North Carolina, real and personal, was sold by order of the congress at New Bern, February 6, 1777. What his employments were during this period we do not know. He was certainly not the "Lt. Col. Martin" who presided at a court-martial in New York, March 27, 1778 (*Order Book of the Three Battalions of Loyalists commanded by Oliver DeLancey*, 1776-1778), for he was no longer of military rank; but he was the "Josiah Martin" appointed a member of the Board of Associated Loyalists in October, 1780 (*American Manuscripts in the Royal Institution*, II, 198), though he can have had little or nothing to do with the work of that board. In the autumn of 1779, he accompanied Clinton on the latter's second expedition to South Carolina ("at the desire of Sir Hy Clinton, who proposed to make him governor of S. Carolina when conquered but found his commission did not enable him to do so," Public Record Office, C. O. 5:318) and the next year (August, 1780) he joined Cornwallis's army and served as a volunteer until April, 1781. He made a number of efforts to return to military command, but without success. Those of his former highland regiment who served under Cornwallis endeavored to raise a regiment of their country-men, of which Martin was to be colonel, but the results were unsatis-factory, as only about a hundred men returned to the colors, and these, in two companies, under Captain Forbes at Charles Town in 1781, and Captain McArthur at Fort Arbuthnot in 1782, were compelled to remain on guard duty (Ross, *Cornwallis Correspondence*, I, 54; Loyalist Muster Rolls, MSS., 1777-1783).

Cornwallis thought well of Martin and spoke highly of his ser-vices. "In opening up channels of correspondence with our friends in North Carolina," he wrote to Lord George Germain, "I have been greatly assisted by Gov. Martin, from whose abilities and zeal for the service I have on many occasions derived great advantage" (August 20, 1780). "Gov. Martin became again a military man," he wrote to the same after the battle of Camden, "and behaved with the spirits of a young volunteer" (August 21, 1780). "I have constantly received the most zealous assistance from Gov. Martin during my command in the southern districts," he again wrote (March 17, 1781). "Hoping that his presence would tend to incite the loyal sub-jects of this province to take an active part with us, he has cheerfully submitted to the fatigue and dangers of our campaigns; but his deli-cate constitution has suffered by his public spirit, for, by the advice of the physician, he is now obliged to return to England for the recovery of his health" (Ross, *Cornwallis Correspondence*, I, 489, 494, 509).

In April, 1781, after the battle of Guilford, Martin, suffering from increasing ill health, left Cornwallis's army and returned to his family at "Rockhall." There he spent a part of the summer, after which, with his wife, a son, and three daughters, he set sail for Eng-land. In London he presented his claims to the American Loyalist Claims Commission, and in memorials—one of which was supported by the "observations" of his brother Samuel,*—and in evidence given personally in the presence of the board, he made statements of his

---

* In a letter to Lord George Germain, October 12, 1780 (Public Record Office, C. O. 5:157, p. 395), Samuel writes: "I received very lately a letter from my brother Gov. Martin acquainting me that he had besought your Lordships patronage to obtain of his Majestys goodness an equitable relief for the losses he sustained by the depredations of the Rebels on the eruption of Rebellion in North Carolina, where he was then acting and he trusts doing his duty as a Governor commissioned by the King. . . . My brother long ago desired me to submit his case and humble petition to the King's ministers, but I discouraged him, urging my own privacy, insignificance, and want of strength for an effectual support of such an application."

losses. His salary, he said, with the perquisites of the governor's office, was worth from £1700 to £1800 a year; his furniture he valued at £2400 to £2500, his books at £500 to £600; and his horses, two carriages, and the lands which he as governor had granted to himself and his children (10,000 acres) were worth altogether £3500. The Treasury had been paying him his salary of £1000 since July, 1775, and a temporary pension of £500, but the board decided that as long as the salary was paid the allowance should cease. Until October, 1783, therefore, Martin had his salary, but after that date the £500 allowance seems to have been his only payment from the British Exchequer, except the compensation for losses, which was placed at £2100. In 1785, Martin reported that he had received only £840 of that amount (Audit Office Papers).

There is nothing to show that Martin engaged in any occupation under government or in any way concerned himself with public affairs after he returned to England. Probably his health forbade active work. He performed useful services in behalf of members of the highland regiment that he had raised in 1775-1776, and he wrote recommendations and appeared before the board personally in behalf of their claims. In 1782 he was living in South Molton Street (off Oxford Street) and later resided at 56 James Street and in New Norfolk Street (Grosvenor Square). He died intestate* at the latter place in March, 1786, at the age of forty-nine, and was buried in St. George's, Hanover Square. Miers, as has been noted, painted his miniature some time before 1771, for which Martin said that he sat fifty times (*Copley-Pelham Letters*, p. 128). It cost him thirty guineas, and Copley, who saw it, told Henry Pelham that he thought it well worth the money. Copley himself in 1771, going from New York to "Rockhall" specially for the purpose, painted a portrait of Mary Elizabeth, Martin's eldest daughter, at that time eight or nine

* Letters of Administration, dated June 20, 1786, and February 17, 1789, may be found among the records of the Prerogative Court of Canterbury, in the Admonition Act Books for those years. Sarah, Alice, and Josiah Martin are the beneficiaries in both grants, Mary Elizabeth having renounced all claim to a share in the estate. The latter's position at this time is not a little puzzling. In the grant of 1789 she is mentioned as "now residing at Black Rocke in North America." Can this represent an attempt to say that she was residing at "Rockhall" in 1789? She was considerably older than the other children and had been left £200 by her grandfather, Josiah, in his will in 1773, the only one of the children to be so favored, and it is not impossible that, after the death of her mother and father, she lived with the Long Island family. Hers is the portrait painted by Copley. (Josiah's will is in *Collections*, New York Historical Society, 1900, Wills, IX, 55.)

years old, with a dog, a picture that is not included in Bayley's list of Copley paintings. This portrait was originally painted on canvas and set in the chimney piece over the mantel in the back parlor, but Mr. Hewlett, who bought "Rockhall" in 1824, had it taken out and framed lest it be injured by damp and mould (letter from Mr. Hewlett's granddaughter, Louise Hewlett Patterson). All together Martin had eight children, Mary Elizabeth, born in Long Island, 1762, two daughters born either in Long Island or in Antigua between 1762 and 1769, Sarah, born in Antigua about 1769, Alice, born in Long Island about 1770, Samuel, born in Long Island, 1771, Josiah, born in North Carolina, 1772, and Augusta, born in Long Island, 1775. Little Sammy and two unnamed daughters died in North Carolina, and Augusta died in England before 1788. The others were all living in 1795, Josiah dying unmarried in 1799. Of the mother's death we know certainly but little.* Payson says that she died at the age of forty-four, in October, 1778, a month before her father (Oliver, *Antigua*, III, 441; *New England Historical and Genealogical Register*, Jan., 1900).

Colonel Samuel's next younger brother, Josiah, the uncle of Governor Josiah, with whom he has frequently been confounded, was born in Antigua in 1699. He lived in the island during his earlier years and from his rank in the militia was often known as Major Martin. If, as the records of St. George's parish, Hempstead, seem to show, his daughter Elizabeth was born in Long Island in 1732, two facts, not otherwise known, come to light. First, that Elizabeth was the daughter of his first wife and so half-sister to his other children; and second that Josiah himself must have gone with his wife to Long Island as early as 1730-1732.† If he was present in Long Island before 1732, he must have returned soon to Antigua, for his marriage to his second wife, Mary Yeamans, a niece of his brother's first wife, on May 8, 1735, is to be found in the register of St. Paul's parish, and in the same year he was appointed a member of the council there. He must have acquired land in Long Island early, for "Major Martin's lands" are mentioned in the Hempstead Records in 1742. He was a justice of the peace and notary public in Antigua in 1741 and

---

* Josiah was a widower when he died. That fact is stated in the letters of administration. Sarah, Alice, and Josiah Henry were all minors in 1789, that is, under the age of twenty-one. Therefore the birth of the elder, Sarah, cannot have been earlier than 1769.

† In the parish register of St. Peter's, Antigua, is to be found entry of the baptism of Lidia, daughter of Mr. Josiah Martin, February 3, 1727. It is impossible to say whether this is our Josiah or not (Oliver, II, 250).

president of the council from 1743 to 1746. In 1749 he was given twelve months' leave of absence, and at that time must have made up his mind to leave the island permanently. His name appears in the Hempstead records in 1751, as subscribing £20 for erecting a gallery in the parish church (Onderdonk, *Antiquities of the Parish Church, Hempstead*, p. 11; *Annals of Hempstead*, p. 76). He purchased land in 1761 at the head of Cow Bay (Far Rockaway) and there must have erected his mansion, "Rockhall," soon after.* In 1755, he was recorded as possessing six slaves, the largest number but one in a list of that date, and it is probable that he was a man of wealth, though holding no remunerative official post or engaging, as far as we know, in any business other than that of a country gentleman.

In the very few biographical statements that have been made regarding Josiah Martin the elder, we are told that he was aide-de-camp to Lieutenant Governor DeLancey in 1757, but that is wholly unlikely, as he was fifty-eight years old at the time, and the reference must be to Josiah Martin the younger. We are also told that he was on the council of the governor of the province of New York from 1759 to 1764, and that statement is probably correct, for he is called "Hon." in the notice of his death, a title indicating membership in the council, and in the legislative journal the name is entered followed by "Esq.," a style that would hardly have been used had the Josiah Martin in question been an officer in the regular army. Yet the matter is made perplexing by the fact that in the Privy Council Register he is spoken of as no longer of the council because he had "settled at Antigua" (*Acts of the Privy Council, Colonial*, IV, 493), and it was the nephew, not the uncle, who went to Antigua in 1764. Whichever it was, this particular Josiah Martin was not of much use as a councillor, for he was present at but five meetings of the council in five years (*Journal of the Legislative Council*, II, 1371, 1372, 1402, 1417, 1428). He died, November 21, 1778, at "Rockhall" and was buried in the chancel of St. George's Church, of which he was long a member. His will mentions six children, Samuel, Charles Yeamans, William, Elizabeth, Alice, and Rachel, and we know that he had one other son, Josiah, who died in 1762, after graduating at the College of Philadelphia (University of Pennsylvania), A.B.

* There is an account of "Rockhall" in Bellot's *History of the Rockaways*, pp. 76-77, but it is full of inaccuracies. Its most important feature is the reproduction of an old photograph of the house as it was in 1874, showing "Quokko House," the slave quarters, which was removed in 1881. This photograph (and others of a similar character) is in the possession of the descendants of Mr. George Hewlett.

1757, A.M. 1760, and after he had been entered at the Inner Temple, London. His wife died in 1825, having lived during her later years in a house left her by her son in his will and which stood on the site of the Astor House in New York.*

The eldest surviving son of Josiah the elder was Samuel, born in 1740 (baptized, October 14, in St. George's Church, Hempstead), who became a doctor, but from what medical school he obtained his diploma we do not know. He was a loyalist and in 1776 was implicated in a plot to overthrow the revolutionary government in New York. On February 17, 1776, he was compelled to give a bond of £500 to behave peaceably and refrain from harboring Tories in his house. Later his name was placed on the list of suspects, and in June he was summoned before the committee for hearing and trying disaffected persons. When interrogated he said that he had never done anything against the country and was not an enemy to America; that he always meant to remain as peaceable and inactive as he could. On being asked whether the British parliament had a right to tax America, he replied that in his opinion it had no right to levy internal taxes on the colonies. On being further asked what he meant by an internal tax, he answered a land tax, not a personal tax, which was not unconstitutional if for the regulation of trade, but, he added, he was not a politician and had confined his studies to his profession. Asked if he would give security, said that he would and named his father living on Long Island. The committee resolved unanimously that Samuel Martin was not a friend to the American cause, but after a further interrogation on June 26 accepted his parole and did not molest him during the war (Force, *American Archives*, VI, 1776, ff. 1153, 1160, 1175, 1176).†

Martin continued to live at "Rockhall," serving for many years as vestryman of St. George's Church, and exercising considerable local influence. In 1773 he was recommended by the Royal Society "to make researches and collections in the branches of Natural His-

---

* Payson in Oliver's *Antigua*, III, 441, and in *New England Historical and Geneological Register*, January, 1900, says that Josiah's wife died August 30, 1805. His evidence is the parish record of death. She is mentioned in Samuel's will of August 13, 1802, administered in 1806. If she died in 1805, then Alice probably occupied the New York house.

† In a "list of persons charged as enemies to America," following the date June 20, 1776, appears the following:

"——— Martin from Antigua. Dwells in Obd. Mills house opposite the Meeting House at a high rent. He associates chiefly with James Depeyster" (Force, *op. cit.*, f. 1158). We cannot identify this particular Martin. Josiah, Jr., was not there at that time. The Mills house was in Jamaica.

tory in America" (*Home Office Papers*, 1773-1775, §127) and so must have acquired something of a reputation in England. He never married. His death took place on April 19, 1806, and he was buried under the chancel of the old St. George's Church. When the first church was burned and its successor placed on a slightly different site his grave remained unmarked. At his death Samuel left instructions that all the family papers should be sent to his brother Charles in England. Whether or not they are still in existence we do not know.

III. "Olivees" and the Hamiltons.

Miss Schaw visited the Hamiltons at the height of their happiness and prosperity, before the clouds of the American War had begun to cast their ominous shadows and darken the scene. Her account possesses great charm and vivacity and presents a delightful picture of "Olivees" at its best, glowing with hospitality and life. There, as elsewhere, Miss Schaw was aroused to an enthusiastic appreciation of all that she saw and enjoyed, and was manifestly impressed by the reception she met with from old and new friends alike. Undoubtedly these circumstances added vastly to her pleasure and led her at times to indulge in roseate views of the islands that are not always borne out by the accounts of others, though none deny that West Indian plantation life, in the heyday of its existence, was socially of a luxurious and convivial character.

Lady Isabella Erskine and William Leslie Hamilton were married in England in 1770, and immediately afterwards sailed for the West Indies, where the latter, receiving his legal education at the Middle Temple, had been admitted to practice as a lawyer in 1767. He must have been older than Miss Schaw thought he was, for if he were but twenty-six or twenty-seven in January, 1775, he would have been but twelve or thirteen when entered at the Middle Temple in 1761, but eighteen or nineteen when called to the bar in 1767, and less than twenty-five when chosen speaker of the house. Such precocity is possible but hardly credible. Immediately upon arrival the bride and groom took up their residence at the splendid plantation "Olivees," belonging to Hamilton's sister, who allowed them to occupy the estate rent free, and to enjoy without charge the services of the negroes and (within certain limits) the products of the plantation.* The latter lay pleasantly and coolly situated on the high ground a mile from Basseterre, two or three hundred feet above the level of the sea. It stood "on a well raised stone terrace, paved with marble and had spacious open galeries and verandahs." The "great hall," of which Miss Schaw speaks, was a large, finely proportioned room, which ran the entire length of the front, with a handsome deep cornice and ample doors, both of dark mahogany, and a paneling of the same wood. It constituted the great reception and dining-room, the scene of lavish entertainment and hospitality. In addition the house had a drawing-room and bedchambers finished and furnished in English style. The estate comprised 283 acres, 151 of which were cane land and 132 pasture, and taken as a whole was esteemed the finest in all the West Indies. In later years it fell very much into disrepair, and Davy reported in 1846 that the whole might then be bought for £3000, which was less than the original cost of the house (*West Indies*, p. 463).

Until 1777 the Hamiltons lived at "Olivees" in affluence, the social leaders of the southern part of the island; but in the same year they removed to Basseterre that Mr. Hamilton might the more efficiently perform his duties as the deputy solicitor-general of the islands. There they remained, burdened with the increasing expenses of town life and the obligations which the war of the American Revolution imposed, until, in 1779, Lady Belle left the island and returned to England; and the next year, Mr. Hamilton, broken in health, obtained leave of absence and followed her, but died in London, in October, 1780, four days after his arrival. Their last years in St. Kitts were a time of anxiety and financial embarrassment. As deputy solicitor-general and afterwards attorney-general, Hamilton

* From a pamphlet in the British Museum, entitled *An Account of the late dreadful Hurricane which happened on the 31st August, 1772*, we learn that "Olivees" was the property of Peter Mathew Mills, son of Mathew Mills of St. Christopher, who died in 1753. The latter's name is entered on the map of Basseterre and its surroundings (above, p. 120) as the owner of a plantation, which is probably "Olivees." If so, the sister who allowed the Hamiltons to occupy the plantation, rent free, must have been Peter Mathew Mills's wife, so that Mills and Hamilton would be brothers-in-law. We have not been able, however, to establish the connection. The first name of Mills's wife was Catherine, but her family name is unknown. As Mills and his wife were living in London at the time of the Hamiltons' marriage, they might well have turned over the plantation in St. Christopher to the newly wedded pair.

was responsible for the peace and good order of the islands and in consequence became involved in many important and expensive undertakings for the purpose of thwarting the revolutionary influence. There was a powerful radical party in St. Christopher, which Governor Burt characterized as "factious, disappointed, and Gallo-American principled," for (he adds) the president of the council, Craister Greatheed, "suffered them to do in a manner as they pleased and escaped [trouble]. By two years' relaxation of government and acquiescence (1775-1777), distraction and American principles and attachments took head. I had them to combat; your Lordship may rest satisfied I will eradicate these monsters or fall in the contest" (letter of Nov. 25, 1778). In the same letter he speaks of the extremes to which the madness of the assembly had gone, and reports that some say "the King's instructions are not binding on them." Later (Oct. 25, 1780) he writes: "The disposition of that assembly, as well as of others in this part of the world, having caught the infection from America and [being] deeply tinged with the principles of Republicanism, attempt bringing all to a level and assume privileges to which I cannot think them constitutionally, I am certain they are not from the mode of government hitherto, entitled."

Such were the conditions, undoubtedly much exaggerated by Governor Burt, under which Hamilton performed his duties, first as the deputy solicitor-general and then as the attorney-general of the Leeward Islands. Had Miss Schaw visited St. Christopher two years later (she was there in January, 1775), she might have had a different tale to tell, a tale not unlike that which she told for North Carolina. Hamilton was called upon to repress the trade in arms which was taking place between the North American colonies and the Dutch island of St. Eustatius; for, as Burt wrote, the Dutch governor, De Graaff, did all in his power "to support and countenance the Rebels and French" and connived at trade in munitions of war and the fitting out of privateers (cf. also *American Historical Review*, VIII, 693-695).* As Governor Burt had no available fund for this purpose, Hamilton's purse was resorted to on all occasions, and his money used for the carrying on of correspondence with the governor, the

---

* In the Public Record Office is an autograph letter from Hamilton to Governor Burt regarding the capture of two vessels with Danish property, in which is enclosed an extract of a letter from the principal owner "earnestly asking his friendship in getting these brigantines clear" and adding "there will be £200 sterling at your service, i.e., £100 each." To this Hamilton replied that no temptation would ever influence him to betray the public trust bestowed on him (C. O. 152:58).

hiring of vessels, the securing of information, and the furnishing of aid to the commanders of the British fleet in West Indian waters. Hamilton was also frequently required to entertain officers of the squadron, at one time receiving the wife of Admiral Cumming as a member of his family for more than a year (1777-1778), and in other ways becoming involved in expenditures which seriously depleted his fortune. He suffered also heavy losses. The expense of living at Basseterre was considerably more than at the plantation, and on account of his official duties he was obliged to give up his private practice, thus incurring a total loss of income amounting to £9000 sterling. Before leaving the island in 1780, he shipped to England goods—clothing, tea, Nankin china, plate, etc.—worth £2500, but the vessel was captured by the French and his property seized as prize of war. Lady Belle, in one of her memorials, says that a part of the plate was seen afterwards on the sideboard of the Marquis de Bouillé (French governor in the Antilles), "Mr. Bingham,* the American agent, winking at the outrage." Some of the tea and china, she says further, was sent to Mrs. Washington; and later in London when she entertained Mr. Bingham at her table and reminded him of the stolen property, he acknowledged the obligation and in recompense offered her land in America.

All together Hamilton's losses were estimated at £15,000, a sum which apparently did not include the value of the property captured by the French.† In the years from 1803 to 1809, Lady Belle, then Countess of Glencairn, petitioned the government for compensation. She presented several memorials and a number of statements from persons familiar with the circumstances, among them two from William Knox, who testified that when undersecretary of state he knew of Hamilton's services and could say that no remuneration had been given. Nelson, who had been with the fleet in the West Indies in 1777-1778, visited the countess at Mollard's Hotel, Dover Street, in

---

* This was William Bingham, in 1778 American agent at St. Pierre, Martinique (*Journals of Congress*, XI, 837; XII, 147, 150, 153), afterwards senator from Pennsylvania, who died at Bath, England, in 1803. His daughter married Lord Ashburton.

† In 1779 Governor Burt said of Hamilton, "I have in many years been intimately acquainted with him. His Majesty has not in all his dominions a subject more firmly attached . . . a more steady warm and zealous promoter of his service or one who would with more cheerfulness stake life and fortune for H. M. against all the factions set on foot by the Gallo-American party." In a later letter he adds that Hamilton was a considerable sufferer from the loyal part he had taken, losing in a few years near £15,000 sterling (C. O. 152:60).

September, 1805, just before leaving England for the last time, and there approved of her claim and testified to the value of Hamilton's information and help to the naval commanders. Lord Thurlow, the lord chancellor, "who honoured Lord Glencairn and myself with his particular regards," also rendered assistance in determining the amount of the claim. Unfortunately Lady Belle was unable to make out accurate accounts of disbursements, because all of Hamilton's papers were lost, when the ship on which they were despatched foundered at sea. (Governor Burt's letters and accompanying papers are in the Public Record Office, C. O. 152:58-60; the memorials of the countess and corroborative statements in the same series, volumes 84, 94.)

Hamilton's case shows that the Loyalists on the American continent were not the only ones who suffered in the American revolution.

IV. Brunswick.

THE town of Brunswick, which lay about twelve miles within the bar of the Cape Fear River, was located on the lands of Maurice and Roger Moore, upon high ground along the western bank. Maurice Moore, the chief promoter, had come from South Carolina in 1719, had settled at first in Chowan county on Albemarle Sound, and in 1722 had taken up lands on the Cape Fear. In 1725 he "caused a plot or plan containing 360 acres of land to be admeasured and laid out in lots, which 360 acres is but part of a larger tract or parcel of land containing 1500 held by patent thereof" of the proprietors. Forty of the 360 acres were added by Roger Moore "to make the said town more regular" (*N. C. State Records*, XXIII, 239). The terms of settlement were that a house, 16 by 20, should be built on each lot sold or "in such size as shall seem habitable" within eight months (Register's Office, Conveyances, A, pp. 71-72). The lots contained half an acre each and were numbered, the numbers running to 350. In 1731 it was said that the town was "like to be a flourishing place by reason of its excellent situation for the trade of those parts" (*N. C. R.* III, 261), but Hugh Meredith, writing in the same year, reported that it was "but a poor, hungry, unprovided place, consisting of not above 10 or 12 scattering mean houses, hardly worth the name of a village," but, he added, "the platform is good and convenient, and the ground high considering the country" (*Pennsylvania Gazette*, May 6-13, 1731). Because of the slow growth of the place, a bill was passed in 1745 by the provincial assembly organizing a town government and settling and securing the titles to the land. Possession of the soil was vested in a board of commissioners, of which Richard Quince and William Dry, 2d, were members. There is no certainty as to how many lots were sold or how many houses were built, though the owners of about fifty can be identified. We read of "Front Street," the "Street on the Bay," and the "Second Street on the Bay." Other streets were probably laid out, but may not have been named.

A little north of the centre, placed according to the true meridian and occupying one block, was St. Philip's Church (76 ft. by 54 ft.), the walls of which, two feet nine inches in thickness, are still standing. Until 1762 or 1763 the only place of worship in Brunswick had been an "old chapel" with but 15 actual communicants (*N. C. R.* VI, 730); but in that year the church, which had been begun in the early fifties, was finally and after long delay roofed in (*ib.*, V, 158, VI, 235, 237), and must have been used for services soon after. There was no parsonage. On the north of Brunswick was the plantation Russellboro, named for its first owner, Captain Russell of H. M. S. *Scorpion*, an estate of about fifty acres, which afterwards became the home, first of Governor Dobbs and then of Governor Tryon. The site of the Tryon house has recently been located and suitably marked (Sprunt, *Chronicles of the Cape Fear*, 2d ed., pp. 103-106). On the south was York plantation, belonging to Nathaniel Moore.

The town contained at least one ordinary, known as Roger's tavern, and probably many more. Except as a port of entry and clearance, and a residence of sea-captains, merchants, and storekeepers, it was never conspicuous, though courts were held there, business was transacted, physicians practiced, missionaries labored for many years without glebe, church, or salary, and neighborly intercourse was carried on of a social and friendly character. Disorder and crime prevailed also, for as early as 1739-1740 we learn that both court house and jail were greatly needed (New Hanover County Records, 1737-1741). There lived the Drys, the Moores, the Quinces, and others of the better sort who constituted the provincial group of those who opposed many of the policies of Governor Gabriel Johnston and his friends, and who resisted with vigor the governor's efforts to develop Wilmington at the expense of Brunswick. They had invested money in lands and buildings there and hoped that from its lucrative trade in naval stores, lumber, and rice it would in time become a great city. Burrington had said as early as 1736 that it would be a place of very great trade as soon as it became well peopled (*ib.*, IV, 169). But all were destined to be grievously disappointed. With the rise of Wilmington, Brunswick steadily declined; and even in 1775 Miss Schaw could describe it as but a poor town "with a few scattered houses on the edge of a wood," and her brother could call it "but a straggling village." See also Appendix VI.

V. Description of North Carolina by Alexander Schaw.

"IN the province of North Carolina there are several rivers, which run a considerable way into the country. Upon the south is Cape Fear river, which is navigable for ships of large burden as far as a shoal which they call the Flats, about seven miles above Brunswick town, which is situated twelve miles within the bar. In consequence of this impediment, vessels which have a draught of above nine and a half feet of water cannot go up to Wilmington, which is the next port above and the most considerable town on the river, even at spring tides, till they are lightened to that draught. Above, or rather at Wilmington, the Northeast and Northwest branches of the river join. The Northwest is the least considerable, and upon the whole extent there is no town, tho' its banks are very well settled. The first town is Cross Creek, about 100 miles above Wilmington. Here the whole trade with the back settlers is carried on for a great way round.

"From Fort Johnston at the mouth of the river to Brunswick is twelve miles. From Brunswick to Wilmington there are two roads: one goes up the right side of the river upon which Brunswick stands and crosses two ferries opposite to Wilmington, occasioned by the river being there divided by a large swampy island, through which there is a very bad road of a mile and a half. The length of this road is reckoned sixteen miles. To go by the other road, one must cross a ferry at Brunswick of a mile over, from whence to Wilmington it is about ten miles. Every part of these roads is more or less sandy. Some of them for miles together is very deep, as the surface often is a pure white sand, without a particle of soil to bind it together. This is the case with almost every part of the province near the sea.

"The roads on both sides of the river cross a few water runs, which in the country are called creeks; they are generally swampy along the sides, which are crowded with trees, bushes, vines, and brambles. Over all these creeks are wooden bridges. Wherever the land is dry, there is little or no brush. The woods in general are in the style of open groves in England, except in such places as have once been cleared and afterwards abandoned. These are always covered with brush. The roads upon the Northwest branch of the river grow more solid every mile above Wilmington, and long before they reach Cross Creek are very hard. The only making they bestow upon the roads in the flat part of the country is cutting out the trees to the necessary breadth, in as even a line as they can, and where the ground is wet, they make a small ditch on either side. The roads through swamp land are made by first laying logs in the direction of the road and covering them cross ways with small pine trees, layd regularly together over sod, with which the logs are previously covered.‡ The roads run constantly thro' woods, which tho' they are generally pretty open, yet objects at any considerable distance are intercepted from the eye, by the trees crowding into the line of direction as the distance increases.

"The next navigable river to the northward is the Neuse, upon which Newbern, the Governor's residence, is situated, about forty miles from the Sound. This river can admit only of small vessels.

"Albemarle sound is the inlet to Roanoke River, upon which Edenton is situated, sixty miles within land, and about 140 miles further up the river is Halifax, which carries on considerable trade. In the neighborhood of Halifax they have a good breed of horses; to the southward the horses are smaller, but spirited and handy.

"The lower parts of the province are subject to agues, pleurises and bilous complaints; the people of the back counties are not subject to these disorders.

"The rivers in the lower parts of the country have no fords. Their banks are in general covered with impenetrable swamps and bottomless morasses, a very few spots excepted, upon which generally plantations are settled. But in the back country, they have good fords.

"The settlements upon the lower part of Cape Fear river do not

‡ "Causeways, they call them."

produce grain enough, particularly wheat, to answer their own demand. Large quantities are therefore sent down from Cross Creek in row boats, which in return carry up whatever goods are wanted for the use of the back settlers.

"Every proprietor of ever so small a piece of land raises some Indian corn and sweet potatoes and breeds some hogs and a calf or two, and a man must be very poor who walks on foot.

"Brunswick county contains fewer of the lower class of country people than any part of the whole province, particularly near the sea.

"There is no specie in the province and there never was a person who could command a sum of any consequence even of their paper currency. Nothing in the stile of a banker or money merchant was ever heard of.

"Governor Tryon left the province very soon after the submission of the Regulators, and when Colonel Martin succeeded to the Government, their wounds were still bleeding and they had received no protection from the oppression of the pettyfogging attorneys, whose rapacity had been the original cause of the rebellion. Governor Martin arrived in the province at this very critical time. He made a progress through his Government; and when he was in this part of the country his attention to the relief of these poor people was such as won him their highest confidence and esteem.

"There is now a numerous body of the sons and grandsons of the first Scotch highland settlers, besides the later emigrants who retain that enthusiastic love for the country from which they are descended, which indeed scarce a highlander ever loses, that they will support its dignity at every risk. The Governor has attached them strongly to him, as well as the later emigrants by many services he has had opportunities of doing them. Many highland gentlemen are now in that country, several of whom have been officers, and still retain their influence among the people.

"Many of the people of the largest property in the country, tho' they now languish under the hand of oppression, will instantly join to support the Constitution, upon the first appearance of a chance of support.

"The low country people in general have fire-arms. I never was in a house without seeing one or more muskets. Indeed the militia laws required them. The highland emigrants carried few arms with them and the Regulators delivered up the greater part of theirs to Governor Tryon.

"The town of Brunswick, which is indeed but a straggling village, is twelve miles within the bar. At low water there is ten feet of water upon the bar; at spring tides there is from 19 to 20 feet, so that in fine weather ships of deeper draught can easily go in. The water, both below and above the flats is deep enough for any vessel. Vessels can run from the bar to Brunswick in three or four hours with the tide, with almost any wind.

"There is good anchorage within half a musket shot of the town. The bank is pretty high for this country and the woods are cut down a good way round the town. This is the only town on the west side of the river. Brunswick county is thinly settled, consequently cattle and horses are few." (Alexander Schaw to Lord Dartmouth, written from Orange Street, London, October 31, 1775. Dartmouth Papers.)

An earlier and more particular account of the province can be found in Governor Dobbs's "Answers to Queries" of December, 1761, *N. C. R.* VI, 605-623; and another and contemporary account in *American Husbandry* (1775).

VI. Wilmington.

THE beginnings of Wilmington are to be found in John Watson's grant of 640 acres, Michael Higgins's and Joshua Grainger's purchase of fifty of these acres, and James Wimble's purchase of the remainder at the forks of the Cape Fear about 1733 (Wilmington Town Records, pp. 3-4). There were altogether seven grants upon which the modern Wilmington rests and at first separate names seem to have been given by the grantees to some of their particular tracts. The earliest settlement was called New Liverpool, probably because of Liverpool merchants, Dunbiben, Jenkins, Blundell, and Marsden, for example, who resided there, but in 1733 the name "New Carthage" appears, which was probably nothing more than a paper name for the James Wimble tract lying in the southern section (Register's Office, Conveyances, AB, 6; C, 196-196A). Later the whole area was called New Town or Newton. This name is met with as early as March, 1735, but New Liverpool continued in occasional use until toward the end of 1736. In 1740, the name Wilmington, already in use for four years, was formally adopted out of compliment to Spencer Compton, Viscount Pevensey and Earl of Wilmington, Governor

Johnston's patron, and the village of Newton become the town of Wilmington.

John Watson, Joshua Grainger, Michael Higgins ("innholder," "victualer," "tavern keeper," and "merchant," as he is variously called), and James Wimble ("mariner, late of Newton, now of Boston," 1737*) were the chief owners of the land on which Wilmington now stands, and in April, 1733, they joined in laying out the town after a plan similar to that of Brunswick. Half-acre lots were sold on condition that the purchaser build "a tenementable house," 16 by 12, within two years after date of sale and pay a quit-rent. Before the end of 1736, Market Street, Front Street, Dock Street, Mulberry Street, Chestnut Street, Red Cross Street, King Street, Queen Street, and Nun[ns] Street were already in existence. Settlers came from England, Scotland, New England, Brunswick, the Albemarle, and the Channel Islands, and the town grew rapidly. The inhabitants were mostly mariners, artisans, merchants, innkeepers, with a physician or two and a clergyman. Unlike Brunswick it had at first few residents who combined the pleasures of town and country and who possessed, in addition to their houses in town, plantations along the banks of the Cape Fear. Though in 1765 it contained less than eight hundred people, it had been for some years dubbed "our metropolis" (*South Carolina Gazette*, Sept. 23, 1748), and before Miss Schaw's arrival had become the leading town in the province.

Wilmington's rapid advance to this position of prominence was due less to Governor Johnston's efforts than to the natural advantages of its location. Brunswick was too near the mouth of the river and as a port was too open to the sea. The situation exposed it to storm and the attacks of pirates and rendered it dangerous as a mooring ground for rafts of lumber and lighters of naval stores which were the leading staples of that part of the province. It had no adequate back-country as an area of supply, was not readily accessible from the north, for the river at that point was too wide for easy and rapid ferriage, and in general was too remote from the other main thoroughfares of the province. Wilmington, on the other hand, had a secure and sheltered harbor, of fresh water free from the sea-worms which destroyed ships lying in salt water, was readily reached from other ports of the province, and fitted in admirably with the

---

* James Wimble was the author of a *Chart of his Majesty's Province of North Carolina*, which was engraved and printed according to act of parliament in 1738. It was sold by Mount & Page in London and by "the author in Boston, New England." On this map Wilmington is represented as a much larger town than Brunswick, perhaps with intent.

demands of the postal system, which after 1740 was extended south-ward from Virginia. Peter du Bois wrote of it in 1757, "I have not yet had time to take a minute survey of this town, but from what I have yet seen it has greatly the preference in my esteem to New Bern. I confess the spot on which its built is not so level nor of so good a soil, but the regularity of the streets are [*sic*] equal to those of Philadelp[hi]a and the buildings in general very good. Many of brick, two and three stores high with double piazas, wch make a good appeara[nce]" (Hayes Collection).

Wilmington was a town under commissioners elected by the free-holders until 1760, when by royal charter under the provincial seal, dated Brunswick, February 25, 1760, and signed Arthur Dobbs (Borough Records, pp. 92-97, and at the end), it was erected into a borough. Town government and borough government continued side by side, the liberties and precincts of the latter including Eagles Island and an area stretching two and a half miles on all sides from the court house. It was given the usual powers of a borough—a mayor's court, markets, fairs, and a court of piepowder. Its govern-ment consisted of a mayor, a recorder, and eleven aldermen, and these with the freeholders constituted the Common Council, which made by-laws. The earliest mayors (each dubbed "His Worshipful") were John Sampson, Frederick Gregg, Caleb Mason (who declined the office), and Moses John DeRosset; the earliest recorders were Mar-maduke Jones and William Hooper, the latter a graduate of Har-vard. In 1766 Cornelius Harnett was chosen to represent the borough in the provincial assembly (*ib.*, pp. 99, 103, 107, 127, 128).

The "regularity" of which Du Bois speaks was due to design. There appear to have been three consecutive plans for laying out the town: that of Higgins *et al.*, already mentioned; that of Michael Higgin-botham ("late of Newton, mariner," 1737); and that of Jeremiah Vail, who in 1743 was employed to resurvey the town and draft a plan. This plan, mentioned in the Wilmington Act of November 30, 1745 (*N. C. State Records*, XXIII, 234-237), was accepted as offi-cial by a final Wilmington Act of 1754 (*ib.*, XXV, 237-263), and, with slight changes and allowances for increase of territory, remains the official plan for the present city.

The town was built on uneven ground, rising from the lowest level at the river end of Market Street, where were the wharves and the town house (under which was the town market), east and south to lands higher than they are today, constituting in the main the resi-dence districts. The "hills," as Miss Schaw calls them, were the elevations toward Third or Broad Street, in one direction, and the "Boundary," now Wooster Street, in the other. There were few houses beyond these points, which lay in a sense outside the town proper. Even Third Street is represented on Sauthier's plan of 1769 as little more than a country road, but in the five or six years before Miss Schaw's arrival, it had become a residence street. Near the Market Street corner, on the east side, was Mrs. Heron's house, with piazza, brick cellar, and steps on the street; across Market Street, below the jail, were the houses and lots of Duncan and Dry, and farther down, the house of George Parker. Dr. Tucker occupied a shop on Front Street; Dr. Cobham's house, with piazza and steps, was between Princess and Chestnut streets; and the house in which Rutherfurd lived until he removed to "Bowland" may have been that lying west of William Dry's, "above the Market House," which he transferred to Ancrum & Schaw in 1768 and finally gave up to Murray of Philiphaugh in 1772 (Register's Office, Conveyances, F, 11). The matter is, however, rendered uncertain by the fact that he and his wife sold some Wilmington property before buying "Bowland" (*ib.*, E, 1), and this property may have included their dwelling house.

Wilmington had at this time a public whipping post, a ducking stool, a burying ground which lay to the rear of Mrs. Heron's property on Third Street, and two water engines or fire engines with hose, the first of which was bought by Captain Benjamin Heron in 1756 through his brother in England (Alexander Duncan serving as keeper in 1759, for which two of his family were exempted from working on the streets); and the second purchased in Philadelphia by Ancrum & Schaw in 1772 (Wilmington Town Records, pp. 34, 41, 56, 64, 68, 73, 159, 163, 179).

VII. James Innes and Francis Corbin.

James Innes.

IN the year 1751 there sat at the council board of North Carolina Governor Gabriel Johnston and seven councillors, among whom were James Innes, Francis Corbin, James Murray, and John Rutherfurd, friends and associates, standing to each other on varying terms of

intimacy. Though Johnston and Corbin had been political antago-
nists, nevertheless the five men belonged to a common group. Innes and
Murray were very intimate, for, next to Thomas Clarke, Innes was
Murray's best friend in the colony; Murray and Rutherfurd, as we
shall see, came to the Cape Fear together and worked together for
twenty-five years. Innes and Corbin were in constant touch personally
and officially, and Mrs. Corbin was the "great friend" of Rutherfurd
and his wife, named one of her slaves "Rutherfurd," and left her
property to the Rutherfurd children. It is a curious fact that two of
the men who sat at the council board, Corbin and Rutherfurd, should
have married eventually the widows of two of the others, Innes and
Johnston.

Colonel James Innes, the first husband of Jean Corbin,—the old
lady mentioned in the Journal,—was a Scotsman, born in Cannesby,
county Caithness, a far-away region in northern Scotland, from which
others also migrated to North Carolina. He probably came to the
colony with Governor Johnston in September, 1734, and with his
wife, whom in his will he calls "the companion of my life," settled on
the Cape Fear. He early became prominent in the province, holding
many offices of trust, civil and military, and winning the esteem of
his contemporaries as an honorable man and an honest and efficient
public servant. He served as captain of the Wilmington company of
North Carolina troops in the expedition against Cartagena in 1740
(Connor, *History of North Carolina*, I, 262), and was appointed
after his return colonel of militia in New Hanover county. In 1754
he was spoken of as an old and experienced officer. His military service and close intimacy with Governor Dinwiddie of Virginia—they
called each other by their first names—led to his being selected to lead
the provincial troops in the Braddock expedition. His connection with
that campaign is well known.

Innes played a prominent part in civil life also and served his
colony in many capacities, but his aptitudes were military rather than
civil and he never became a political leader or a seeker for offices.
Governor Johnston recommended him for the council and he sat at
the board under Johnston and his successor, Dobbs, for nearly ten
years. His relations with Corbin began at least as early as 1750, when
the latter, as land agent for Lord Granville, associated him with himself as co-agent, and from that time to 1754, when he was dismissed
by Lord Granville, Innes acted with Corbin in the Granville interest,
journeying two hundred miles through the wilderness, from the Cape
Fear to Edenton, to perform his duties. None of the charges brought

against Corbin were ever seriously raised against Innes, and he emerges scatheless from an employment which, dependent as it was on fees and perquisites, created an irresistible itch for money. Innes died September 5, 1759, and two years afterward Corbin married his widow (shortly after October, 1761). Mrs. Jean Corbin was an "old woman" in 1775; what her age was when she married her second husband must be left to conjecture. People grew old early in colonial days; one was already "an old aged man" at sixty-one (*Maryland Archives*, X, 78, 165). Innes was born about 1700; she may have been a few years younger.

Francis Corbin.

The Honorable Francis Corbin, as he was frequently called, was appointed land agent for Lord Granville, September, 1744, and came to North Carolina from London in November of the same year, for the purpose of "setting off to Lord Granville one-eighth part of the colony." He was associated in succession with five co-agents, of whom Innes was one, and managed to hold on to his own position successfully till 1760. At one time or another he was a justice of the peace, an assistant judge, commissary and judge of vice-admiralty in 1754, colonel of the Chowan militia in 1757, member of the council, deputy to the assembly, and a frequent appointee on commissions and committees in the assembly and out. He was prominent in the affairs of St. Paul's Church, Edenton, and it is probable that his influence there was of material assistance in his political career. He was keen, efficient, and aggressive even to turbulence, but of a personality and character that has not endeared him to posterity. He was probably honest enough in his way, for, as far as we know, no charges of a dishonorable nature were ever made except in connection with his fees as Granville's agent, and in this particular we are not sure that he did anything strictly illegal; but at the same time it is difficult to avoid the conclusion that he was deficient in some of the qualities that make for moral uprightness and political stability. One may be prejudiced, but it seems a fitting thing that Corbin should have taken a liking for a woman whom Miss Schaw describes as not of the best character or of the most amiable manners and whose evil deeds she hopes will be forgiven. The wonder is that Jean Corbin should ever have been Innes's "loving wife."

In the performance of their duties as agents for Lord Granville,

Corbin and his first colleague, Child, were charged with acting "in concert to make the most that they could of the fees and perquisites of his Lordship's office for their own emolument, at the expense of the people, by which means they procured great sums for themselves and little for his lordship." When Bodley became co-agent, the complaints became so insistent and the abuses apparently so flagrant that the assembly appointed a committee to inquire into the matter. Though the committee reported that in the main the charges were true, the assembly took no further action and in consequence a number of Granville's grantees, exasperated because of their failure to obtain legal redress, marched to Corbin's house near Edenton, seized that gentleman, carried him off in his own chaise to Enfield, the county seat some sixty or more miles away, and there compelled him to sign a bond to disgorge. This riotous proceeding so scandalized the assembly that at its next session, in May, 1759, it sought to secure the punishment of "the authors of [the] several riots, routs, and unlawful assemblies within Lord Granville's district." But the effort came to nothing, and the chief interest in the incident lies in its reflection upon Corbin's character and the attitude of the assembly, and in its place in the history of the colony as a forerunner of the Regulators' War.

Though unmolested by the assembly, Corbin did not escape so easily in his conflict with the governor. In 1748 he had joined with others in a letter to Secretary Bedford, charging Johnston with misfeasance in office, but the secretary took no action, the Privy Council dismissed the charge, and Corbin continued to sit on Johnston's council. When, however, in 1758 he espoused the cause of the assembly against Dobbs, that excitable upholder of the prerogative suspended him from the council for prevarication and non-attendance, and removed him from his positions as assistant judge and colonel of militia. In 1760 he was dismissed by Granville from his post of agent also. Despite these humiliating experiences, perhaps because of them, Corbin was immediately elected to the assembly from Chowan county, and acting with Child, Barker, and Jones, whom Dobbs characterized as the "northern junto," resisted the efforts which Dobbs was making, during the remaining years of his administration, to maintain in unnecessarily arbitrary fashion the legal claims of the crown. Though Tryon suggested that Corbin be restored to the council in 1766, nothing came of the nomination, probably because of his death, which took place sometime in 1766 or 1767. He left no will, and his estate, except such portions as were given his wife in the marriage settlement of 1761, was disposed of at auction, at which his wife bid in some of her husband's personal property.

Corbin spent the greater part of his life in Chowan county, on a plantation two or three miles from Edenton.* In 1758 he began the erection in Edenton of the Cupola House, a famous old building which is still standing and which bears on its gable-post or ornament the initials "F. C." and the date "1758," but it is doubtful if he ever lived there.† When he went to the Cape Fear we do not certainly know, but it was before his marriage with Mrs. Innes.‡ He could have continued to represent Chowan county, even though living at "Point Pleasant," provided he retained in the county for which he stood real estate to the extent of at least one hundred acres. He was buried, as Miss Schaw says, at the bottom of the lawn on the "Point Pleasant" plantation, not far from the grave of James Innes, between whom and Corbin the old lady herself at last found rest "in a very decent snug quarter."

VIII. James Murray and John Rutherfurd.

James Murray.

THE career of James Murray is well told in the *Letters of James Murray, Loyalist*. He was connected with the Murrays of Philiphaugh, one of whom, his cousin David, the second living son of John Murray of Philiphaugh, died in Savannah, April 29, 1771. He had a brother John, who became a doctor and afterwards married Lady

---

* The exact location of this plantation seems to be unknown. In his marriage settlement Corbin describes his own property as a half acre of land and a wharf in Edenton, and Strawberry Island near Edenton, with houses, outhouses, and improvements. Dr. Dillard identifies this island with the present John Island. Perhaps the plantation referred to was there, but the identification is far from certain.

† In 1760 Corbin made a deed leaving the Cupola House to his prospective wife, Jean Innes, and after her death to his natural heirs. It went eventually to his brother, Edward Corbin (*North Carolina Booklet*, XV, 205-217).

‡ In October, 1761, he is spoken of as "late of Chowan County," so that he must have left the Albemarle region before that date (Register's Office, Conveyances, E, 88-94). His marriage was solemnized shortly afterwards.

Anne Cromartie, widow of Edmund Atkins, superintendent of Indian
Affairs in the Southern Department, who died in 1761. He was related also to the Rutherfurds, for he calls John "cousin" and had had
him in charge in London before coming to America. In fact, James
Murray, David Murray, and John Rutherfurd were all descended, in
the third generation and in different lines, from a common great-
grandfather, Sir John Murray of Philiphaugh.

James Murray came to Carolina in 1735, leaving "Johnnie" in
London. He arrived in Charles Town on November 27 of that year
and was at Brunswick at the beginning of 1736. There he rented a
house of Roger Moore and opened a store, but falling out with the
Moores he went to Wilmington, bought a house and lot there, and
entered into the business and social life of the town and province.
Later he acquired a plantation, "Point Repose," on the Northwest
at the mouth of Hood's Creek, and gradually drew out of trade in
order to devote himself to an agricultural and farming life. During
his thirty years of residence in the colony he held many important
offices in town and county and under the crown. He was at one time
or another commissioner for Wilmington, a justice of the peace,
deputy naval officer, secretary, clerk of the council and clerk of the
crown, deputy paymaster under Innes, a vestryman of St. Philip's,
and for thirty years (except for the period of his suspension, 1757-
1763) a member of the governor's council and after 1763 its president. He was on terms of intimacy with Governor Johnston, but was
unfriendly toward Governor Dobbs, who suspended him from the
council, and he was always antagonistic to the Brunswick group led
by Dry and the Moores.

He went to England in 1738, but came back the next year, bringing with him the young John Rutherfurd. Both he and Rutherfurd
were abroad from 1741 to 1743. For the third time Murray crossed
the water in 1744 to marry, as his first wife, his cousin Barbara
Bennet, who returned as far as Boston with him in 1749, but joined
him in the colony the next year. From that time, until he withdrew
permanently to Massachusetts in 1765, he continued to reside in
North Carolina. As a man of strong loyalist sympathies he was out
of touch with the revolutionary movement, whether in the South or in
New England, and toward the end of his career found himself
obliged to migrate again, and for the third time, from Massachusetts
to Halifax, where he died in 1780.

Murray was a man of strong will and of a masterful temper-
ment, though not a politician and with little liking for the responsi-

bilities of office. He preferred the quiet life of a merchant or a country gentleman, but at the express request of Governor Johnston was persuaded to accept a position under government and once in office the accumulation of posts became easier. He had energy and when in public service was inclined to want his own way. He quarrelled with Dobbs, who charged him with leading a cabal against himself, and in all his relations with Rutherfurd played the part of patron and friend somewhat more dictatorily than their relationship warranted. He suffered severely from deaths in his family, and though keeping his feelings well under control was frequently desolate and troubled in spirit. He was given to pessimistic views of life and the circumstances of the time weighed heavily upon him. He was law-abiding, conservative, and cautious, without enthusiasm or strong emotions, and he was as blind as was Miss Schaw herself to the significance of the events taking place about him. He possessed none of the qualities of a revolutionist.

John Rutherfurd.

John Rutherfurd, his protégé and the father of the children who accompanied Miss Schaw to America, was probably less than twenty years old when he came to the colony, and for a while he lived with Murray at his house in Wilmington and served as clerk in his store. In 1750, through the influence of Dinwiddie, at that time surveyor-general of customs, he was appointed receiver-general of quit-rents, the duties of which and of the deputies thereto appointed in every county outside the Granville area, were to "collect from the tenants of the king's lands the fee-farms or quit-rents reserved to the crown and to account for and disburse the same according to the instruction from the Sovereign." His profits arose from the commissions allowed upon his receipt of these rents (*N. C. R.* VII, 484). For reasons that need not be discussed here, he was removed from this position by Dobbs, at the same time that he and Murray were suspended from the council, and he was not restored until 1761, after he had made a trip to England and Scotland and had presented his case to the Treasury and the Board of Trade. After reinstatement he continued to hold the position until 1775.

Rutherfurd by all accounts was not well suited to the post, a difficult one at best and made doubly so by the unwillingness of the colonists to meet their obligations. Murray said that Rutherfurd was too good-natured and of too easy a temper to be efficient. Dobbs charged him with indolence and neglect of duty, but threw some of the blame for his earlier conduct upon Murray himself, who (he said) wrote Rutherfurd's letters and had him "entirely under his influence." It is always wise, however, to take Dobbs's charges with caution. Rutherfurd made a satisfactory defence before the Treasury and the Board of Trade and was able to impress upon them the injustice of his dismissal.

Yet when all allowances are made, the conclusion must be reached that Rutherfurd was not a satisfactory receiver of quit-rents. It is quite likely that his failure may have been due in part to the intricacies of the system and that Dobbs's action may have been prompted by a desire to break up the junto or cabal which he thought was working against him. But these reasons will hardly serve to explain Governor Martin's strictures upon Rutherfurd's conduct. Martin charged Rutherfurd with a want of "proper diligence and exertion" and recommended his dismissal a second time as one who was "in every respect utterly disqualified for the position." "Mr. Rutherfurd . . . is unhappily the receiver-general of His Majesty's revenues," he wrote Lord Dartmouth in 1774, "of excellent temper but strangely confused understanding, and actually disqualified by invincible deafness for public business" (*N. C. R.* IX, 973). Of Rutherfurd's deafness we have other evidence. In 1758, when in London, he wrote Lord Granville that he wished to resign his seat in the council, "because my hearing is so bad that I can't discharge my duty as I could wish and desire" (*ib.*, V, 959). It may be that his deafness had something to do with his failure as receiver. Yet he continued to sit on the governor's council to the end, served as a member of a court of claims in 1773, was frequently on committees, and seems to have had no trouble in carrying on ordinary conversation and doing his private business.

There are ample manifestations that Rutherfurd was energetic and efficient in many directions. In 1751-1752 he obtained a number of judgments against the estate of Colonel Robert Halton for non-payment of quit-rents, seized several parcels of Halton's lands, put them up at public vendue, and had them sold to the highest bidder (Register's Office, Conveyances, B. C., 24; Brunswick County Records, A, 12). He went to England and Scotland in 1758 and was gone three years obtaining a reversal of his suspension. He defended himself with adroitness and vigor in the letters that he sent to the Treasury and the Board of Trade. When in London in 1761 he wrote a pamphlet, *The Importance of the Colonies to Great Britain*, which was considered good enough to be printed. He and his brother Thomas,* who died in 1781, were both colonels of militia, one in New Hanover and the other in Cumberland county. Of his frequent journeyings we have ample testimony. He visited Charles Town a number of times and in 1768-1769 went as far as Georgia (*South Carolina Gazette*, March 30, 1769). He served the colony well on two important commissions, involving tedious travel and hard labor —one in 1767 to settle the boundary line with the Cherokees, and the other in 1772, an undertaking of seventy-six days, for which he was never paid, to determine the line between North and South Carolina. Henry Laurens of Charles Town, whom he visited and with whom he had business dealings, thought well of him. "A worthy man," he calls him, "a sensible worthy man, of a good fortune, and an exceedingly good planter and farmer," and again, "an agreeable worthy man, a good planter, farmer and mechanick." With him, Laurens says, he had many talks "of new methods of planting and new articles to plant" (Laurens Letter Books). Of Rutherfurd's interest in agriculture, Miss Schaw gives an interesting account, while what she says of his plantation does not suggest either indolence or inefficiency.

In 1754, sometime after May 6, Rutherfurd married Frances, the widow, first, of one Button (of whom we know nothing more), and second of Governor Johnston. She was Johnston's second wife and possibly his third, for such accounts as we have of Johnston's life before he married Penelope Galland, Governor Eden's stepdaughter, sometime between 1737 and 1741, would indicate that he had been married before.† However that may be, he married Mrs. Button in 1751 and died himself at his seat, "Eden House," in Bertie county,

---

* That Thomas Rutherfurd was John's brother appears from the latter's letter, dated March 16, 1782, from Charles Town, mentioning the death of his brother Thomas, and saying that he was now caring for his widow and children.

† In 1735 Governor Johnston traveled from Cape Fear to Edenton "with his equipage and family," and in 1737 was occupying his own plantation on Salmon Creek across the Chowan River from Edenton. It is known that the governor had two natural children, Henry, who died in 1772, and Caroline, who was probably demented or at least weak-minded. It may be that these constituted the "family" referred to. Penelope Galland had married, first, William Maule, who died in 1726; second, John Lovick, who died in 1734; third, George Phenney, who died in 1737; and some time after that date, Governor Johnston, to whom we know she was married in 1741, for Hatheway prints a deed of that year signed by both of them (*North Carolina Historical and Genealogical Register*, I, 54).

in 1752. Frances was still a "young widow" when she married Rutherfurd, and in appearance small, as we learn from Samuel Johnston's
letter to his son, 1754, in which he says, "Mrs. Rutherford has a
brother come in, one about seventeen years old, very small and like
his sister; talks and behaves like a man, makes me believe him older,
but is probably designed for Miss" (Hayes Collection).* She became
the mother of the three children of Miss Schaw's narrative and herself died early in the year 1768. Who she was or where she came from
originally we have not been able to discover.

In the settlement of Governor Johnston's will there was considerable controversy and even litigation, and Rutherfurd was engaged for
many years in closing up the estate. That he did not perform this
task to the satisfaction of the Johnston family is well known. Samuel
wrote to his son in 1757: "I don't know what to think of Mr. Rutherfurd, he has never any money. He offered me one order on you and
when it came it was after this manner, pay such and such people and
the remaining part send to your father, which I returned him"
(Hayes Collection).† The most troublesome questions were the
amount due Penelope under Henry Johnston's will and the distribution of the arrears of Governor Johnston's salary. The latter was not
effected for nearly fifty years, as will be noted elsewhere (Appendix
X). In 1752 the British government owed Johnston's estate more
than £12,000, arrears of salary. Mrs. Rutherford put in a claim for
this amount and after considerable difficulty and expense Rutherfurd
when in England obtained a royal warrant, dated February 5, 1761

---

* "Miss" was undoubtedly Penelope Johnston, daughter of the governor
by Penelope Galland. She must have been at this time about fourteen or
fifteen years old. In his will (Grimes, 269-271) the governor mentions his
daughter and earnestly requests his "dearest wife" to be a kind mother to
his "dear little girl," then (1751) perhaps ten or eleven. He left her a bequest of lands and negroes, but did not include her among those who had a
share in the residuary estate. But on the death of Henry Johnston in 1772,
she fell heir to his fifth share of that estate and was engaged for many years
in endeavoring to secure an accounting of her portion. She married John
Dawson, who died before her, and she was still living, as the widow Dawson,
in 1798.

† Among the manuscripts in the possession of the North Carolina Historical Commission is an "Account of John Rutherfurd and Frances his wife
with the Estate of Governor Gabriel Johnston," which covers the years 1752
to 1756. It was sworn to before James Murray, J. P., February 10, 1756, and
is signed by Rutherfurd and his wife. Its later pages contain accounts of
money disbursed for Eden House, Mount Galland, and Fishing Creek plantations, with items regarding Henry Johnston, Caroline or Carey, his sister, and
Penelope (education at Williamsburg = £83. 16. 6).

(Treasury 52:51, p. 437), authorizing the payment. As the North Carolina quit-rents were not sufficient for the purpose, the warrant was addressed to George Saxby, receiver-general for South Carolina, instructing him to pay over to the Johnston heirs the entire amount from the quit-rents of that province. As late as 1767 we find Rutherfurd endeavoring to obtain from Saxby, through Henry Laurens, attorney to the estate, payment of the sum authorized by the Treasury.* Before his death he had secured all but £2018 of the whole, but as we shall see in discussing the later history of the claim (Appendix X) he appropriated to his own use a larger share of what he obtained than he was entitled to receive as administrator of his wife's estate.

Rutherfurd began to accumulate property early in the fifties. In 1755, the year after his marriage, he was assessed in the Wilmington valuation of that year at £225 and his taxables were rated at ten. He had a house in Wilmington and was living there as freeholder as early as 1747. In 1749 he was elected a town commissioner, but leaving the province at the time, he was reëlected in 1751 and continued to serve for a number of years. In common with many others, among whom were his fellow Scots, Duncan, Schaw, Ancrum, Robert Hogg, and George Parker, he was frequently cited for neglecting to work on the streets, bridges, and wharves of the town—the duty of every taxable—and at one time was subject to fines running as high as £9 (Wilmington Town Records, *passim*). He was of the firm of Rutherfurd & Co., dealers in lumber and merchandise, in 1751, and from 1762 to 1766 was in partnership with Alexander Duncan. He continued to reside in Wilmington until 1758, when he went to England and Scotland, where he obtained his restoration to the council, wrote his pamphlet, secured from the Treasury the warrant authorizing the payment of Governor Johnston's salary, and in Scotland negotiated a loan of £7440 with the aid of John Murray of Philiphaugh and another Scottish friend, who guaranteed the loan

---

* On September 1, 1767, Laurens wrote to Rutherfurd: "Yesterday I called upon Mr. Saxby and received from him the sum of three thousand one hundred and fifty-seven pounds of this currency, equal to four hundred and fifty-one pounds sterling, on account of the king's warrant," and after stating that he could obtain no more at the time, adds: "I must be content to receive balances from him just when and in such quantities as he shall be pleased to pay to me. Mr. Saxby asked me what you intended to do further in this affair and hoped you would not 'start' before him in any representation on the other side of the water, adding that he would forfeit his head if you received the balance due on the warrant in ten years to come. I answered that I knew your generosity and would be surety that you would take no unfair advantages, etc." (Laurens Letter Book, 1767-1771, pp. 3-4).

with the royal warrant as security. Returning in 1761, he and his wife, with the money thus borrowed and other funds obtained from the sale of some of their Wilmington property, purchased of Maurice Moore, on December 1, a plantation of 1920 acres at Rocky Point on the north side of the Northeast beyond the bend, and removed from Wilmington to reside in the country. He named the plantation "Bowland," and with this and other landed property, some of which he acquired in 1766 (the Rockfish lands) and in 1768 (the Western Prong lands), he became, as Henry Laurens called him in 1767, a man "of a good fortune." He retained lands in Wilmington, had a tar house on Eagles Island before 1769, and in 1768 petitioned for permission to erect a public grist mill on an acre adjoining Rockfish Creek opposite the Holly Shelter "pocósin."

He was living at "Bowland" in September, 1768, but in that year his financial troubles began. His wife, the executrix under Governor Johnston's will, having died some months before, John Murray of Philiphaugh became alarmed for his security. Rutherfurd had paid £4000 of the £7440 due, but seemingly was unable to pay the remainder. Willing and desirous of giving further indemnification, for Murray was meeting the interest on the bonds, he handed over to Robert Schaw as trustee his entire property, including his £1000 legacy from Duncan and a proportion of the debts due the firm of Duncan & Rutherfurd, for the purpose of discharging the debt and avoiding a suit in chancery. But this arrangement failed to satisfy Murray, who in January, 1771, brought suit before the North Carolina court of chancery, sitting at New Bern. The matter was referred to Governor Tryon for arbitration who decided in Murray's favor and the court confirmed his decision. Rutherfurd handed over to Murray in fee simple ownership his Western Prong lands in Bladen county (4320 acres), "Bowland" (1920 acres), his Sound lands (320 acres), and his Wilmington real estate (168 acres), valued altogether at £4300 proclamation money (Register's Office, Conveyances, F. 95-102, 327-329). Of this transaction his son John said, in 1788: "Our father had nothing. John Murray of Philiphaugh stript him of everything when he went out to Carolina, except the property which my mother brought him, which was secured to her by her marriage settlement* and again secured to us by decree in chancery, when John Murray wanted to seize upon it as our father's property." In 1774 Governor Martin spoke of Rutherfurd as "bankrupt in point of for-

---

* The terms of this settlement may be found in the register's office, Wilmington, Conveyances, F, 3-4.

tune," and we know that the year before Rutherfurd had written to William Adair in London expressing his desire to leave the colony and asking that Mr. Abercrombie, the former agent, be requested to inform him "if he hears of any good office at the Boards of Treasury, Trade or Auditor's office." "At present," he adds, "Mr. McCulloh is agent, but as he probably is to be dropped soon I have no objection to being agent but do not wish to be obliged to him for any good office" (Letter to William Adair, Pall Mall, dated Newbern, March 26, 1773, Phillips Manuscripts).

But Rutherfurd did not leave the province. If Martin, writing on April 6, less than a year before Miss Schaw's arrival, is correct in his statements, then Rutherfurd must have recovered very rapidly from his financial troubles, for in the spring of 1775, when Miss Schaw visited his plantation, he was controlling "Hunthill," an estate of more than 4000 acres, lying between the Bald Sand Hills, adjoining New Exeter, on Holly Shelter Creek, ten miles from Rocky Point and thirty miles from Wilmington. "I have been at a fine plantation," she writes, "called Hunthill, belonging to Mr. Rutherfurd, [on which] he has a vast number of negroes employed in various works. He makes a great deal of tar and turpentine, but his grand work is a sawmill, the finest I ever met with." Miss Schaw's description is not exaggerated. The property had been bought for £2000 of Sampson Moseley in 1772, through D'Arcy Fowler, attorney at law of Wilmington and later a loyalist, and plats of it may be found today in the Wilmington records and among the manuscripts at Raleigh. It was a fine estate, though only in part cleared and developed. According to the testimony of John, Jr., and Samuel Graham, in charge of the forge, there were 150 slaves, many of whom were valuable tradesmen, more than 300 acres of land cleared and planted with corn and other grains, a valuable sawmill and smith's forge for the iron work, and room, timber, and water enough for two more sawmills, cutting 20,000 feet of lumber a week. There were also teams of twenty oxen, one hundred and fifty head of cattle, horses, hogs, and sheep, and a great deal of valuable furniture and many plantation implements. The whole estate furnished in 1781 enough to make several thousand barrels of pitch, tar, and turpentine for British markets and a great quantity of shingles for the West Indies. If Rutherfurd was bankrupt in April, 1774, and in possession of this property at least as early as September, 1774, when Graham says that he was first employed there, it is evident that he must have bought it with his children's money—probably the £1780 obtained from the sale of Conahoe and Possum Quarter (plantations in Tyrrell and Granville counties which had been left to his wife by Governor Johnston), and have held it in trust for them. He may have used also some of the arrears of Johnston's salary, which belonged to them as their mother's heirs; he may have been aided by Mrs. Corbin, for in her will she speaks of debts incurred and negroes loaned, of which Rutherfurd was to make no accounting; and he may have used the money left by Duncan and the debts due him as a member of the firm, for these do not appear to have been handed over to Murray in the final settlement. From a later indenture we learn that the property was bought in trust for the two boys until they should attain the age of twenty-one years (Register's Office, Conveyances, F, 14-15; H, 197-199; P, 152-155).

Rutherfurd, according to his son's statement, "having done everything in his power to suppress the distractions in North Carolina, before the arrival of his Majesty's troops, took the first opportunity of joining Lord Cornwallis. When the troops were withdrawn [from North Carolina, after the battle of Yorktown], he was under the necessity of embarking with them for Charles Town for the protection of his person from the resentment which his loyalty had stirred up against him, augmented by the discovery of his having placed both his sons in his Majesty's service. Of the negroes [150] belonging to him and his sons in their own right he could only carry off 6 for want of room in the transport." All the negroes which remained behind, the lands, mills, horses, cattle, utensils, and furniture fell into the hands of the Americans, and Rutherfurd's waiting man, Sandy, was murdered for having served as a guide in Lord Cornwallis's army. Rutherfurd remained at Charles Town until what little property he had remaining was nearly spent and his health and spirits were so much impaired that sometime after March, 1782, he had to leave America. He set forth on a vessel bound for England, but died at Cork, at the age of sixty, sometime in the same year (Son's statement, Audit Office Papers). He left no will.

The estimate of losses, as given in the son's memorial of March 23, 1784 (Audit Office, Loyalists Claims, 36, pp. 339-354), is as follows:

To attendance, etc., for running the boundary line between So Carolina and No Carolina, as mentioned in the memorial of John Rutherfurd [Sr. to the Treasury]	£ 562. 2
To balance due on the royal warrant	2018.19

Lands, slaves, plantation utensils and cattle valued by order of the prevailing persons in No Carolina in 1779 at

£36,842.18 that currency, which reduced to sterling makes £21,052.14, and which in the year 1777 £979.5 taxes were paid. [This item probably covers both the Corbin lands and "Hunthill"] 21,052.14

23,633.14

The effort of the children to obtain in part a restitution of this property is dealt with in Appendix X.

IX. The Rutherfurd Children.

ACCOMPANYING Miss Schaw to America were the three children of John Rutherfurd—Frances or Fanny, John, Jr., and William Gordon. Their father, as we know, was of the Scottish family of Rutherfurd of "Bowland," and their mother, Frances (see Appendix VIII), was the widow of Governor Gabriel Johnston of North Carolina, whom Rutherfurd had married in 1754. They were all born in North Carolina and lived there, probably at Rutherfurd's plantation, "Bowland," at Rocky Point on the Northeast branch, until after the death of their mother in 1768, when their father sent them back to Scotland to be educated.* As Rutherfurd was unable to leave the colony on account of his official duties (since except for one visit in the years from 1758 to 1761 he never saw Scotland after he left it sometime before 1735), he was obliged to entrust the children to the care of friends, and apparently placed them in charge of Alexander Duncan, a partner of his in business at Wilmington, who crossed the ocean at this time. Duncan was an intimate friend of both the Rutherfurds and the Schaws, was a Scotsman from Edinburgh, and in his will, made just before he sailed, left money to both Rutherfurd and his daughter, to the latter "in case she returns to this province and marries here." Duncan probably took the children, at that time aged ten, five, and two, respectively, with him to Edinburgh and placed them in the hands either of Rutherfurd's relatives or of Miss

---

* In the letter to William Adair of Pall Mall, March 26, 1773, Rutherfurd speaks of "my young family now on your side of the water for their education."

Schaw, wherever she may have been living. The Rutherfurds and Schaws were closely connected by marriage, for Janet's father had married Rutherfurd's aunt, and her brother, Robert, had married his eldest sister, Anne, so that it would have been natural enough for Duncan to have done either, though the probabilities are in favor of Miss Schaw. Rutherfurd's father had died in 1747, and his family was scattered: Thomas and James, his brothers, and Anne and Barbara, his sisters, were in North Carolina, and "Bowland," the Rutherfurd estate in Scotland, had passed out of the hands of the family. The children of John Rutherfurd remained in Scotland until the voyage of 1774,—Fanny at boarding school, probably in Edinburgh, —when Rutherfurd, having decided to stay in North Carolina, and with the aid of his children's money having acquired a new plantation, "Hunthill," some thirty miles from Wilmington, wished them to return to the province.

Owing to unexpected circumstances connected with the outbreak of the Revolution in North Carolina, the children, instead of remaining with their father, returned to Scotland with Miss Schaw. Soon after, the boys, at this time thirteen and ten years old, were placed in a free school in England under the protection of Lord Townshend, an arrangement having been entered into in 1768, according to which the profits from the negroes left by the father and mother were to be used during the father's lifetime to provide for their education. But in the sequel this arrangement was found to be inoperative, and the money actually used for the boys' education was £700 from the Corbin estate (originally from Mrs. Corbin's first husband, Colonel James Innes), which had been for many years in the hands of Governor Dinwiddie, an intimate friend of Innes's and lieutenant governor of Virginia from 1751 to 1758.

When the war of the Revolution came on, Rutherfurd incurred considerable ill-will in North Carolina by entering both boys in the British service, one in the army and the other in the navy. John joined the corps of engineers, became a practitioner engineer and second lieutenant in 1781, a first lieutenant in 1790, a captain in 1795, an assistant quartermaster general at Plymouth Dock in 1799, a major commandant of a corps attached to the quartermaster general's department in 1800, and in 1805 a lieutenant colonel. For a time he was stationed at Gibraltar, later at New Brunswick and Jamaica, and in 1805 was surveyor-general of the island of Trinidad. Soon after that date he was placed on the half pay list as of the Royal Staff Corps, was secretary at Gibraltar in 1810, and died sometime between February, 1816, and March, 1817. After the close of the Revolutionary War, he several times obtained leave of absence from the army, and crossed the Atlantic in an effort to obtain a restitution of the family property in North Carolina. He visited Charleston, made three trips to Wilmington, and lived for a while in New York, where he may have been entertained by his relative, Walter Rutherfurd, with whom he had financial dealings,* either at his New York house, next St. Paul's Church, or at his estate at Boiling Springs, now Rutherford, New Jersey, which he had called "Edgerston" after his old home in Scotland.† For more than twenty-five years John labored to secure, for himself and his brother and sister, the value of the land and the negroes. He was probably never married.

"Little Billie" had a more distinguished career. In 1778 he became a "Boy A B" and midshipman on H. M. S. *Suffolk*, stationed in the Channel, and there served until the end of the war. According to his brother's account, he was turned adrift in 1783, entered the merchant marine, and served as fourth mate of an Indiaman from 1783 to 1789. In 1787 he was in the East in Indian waters, but in 1789 was back in London, living at Cornhill. Soon after, he entered the royal navy again, finished his time as midshipman on various guardships, and in 1794 became acting lieutenant on the *Boyne*, in the West Indies with Sir John Jervis, afterwards Admiral Earl St. Vincent.‡ He rose rapidly in rank. In July of the same year he was commissioned commander, first of the *Nautilus*, and then of the *Adventure*, and in November was appointed post captain of the *Dictator*. In 1799 he was transferred to the *Brunswick*, then to the *Decade*, remaining with the latter in the West Indies, the Channel, and the Mediterranean as senior frigate captain under Admiral Lord Nelson, until May, 1805.‖ At that time he became acting captain of the *Swiftsure*, a new third-rate seventy-four, and at Nelson's express wish was given permanent command in July. In charge of this vessel he took part in Nelson's

---

* Walter Rutherfurd loaned John Rutherfurd, Jr., $2000, on November 9, 1790, and took as his security a mortgage on half the North Carolina lands (Register's Office, Conveyances, Y, 259-262). John was in New York at the time.

† In *Family Records and Events*, by Livingston Rutherfurd, p. 122, "Edgerston Manor" is stated to have been located in Hunterdon county.

‡ For the career of the *Boyne*, see Anson, *Life of John Jervis, Admiral St. Vincent*, pp. 88-107. Rutherfurd's appointment is dated January 9, 1794.

‖ There are many letters of this period from Captain Rutherfurd to Evan Nepean, secretary to the Admiralty Board, among the Admiralty Papers in the Public Record Office (Admiralty 1: 2398-2408), but they throw little light on his personal affairs.

famous pursuit of Villeneuve's fleet—the Toulon fleet—which had sailed for the West Indies in the summer of 1805, in order to draw the British admiral from the neighborhood of the Channel, to cross which for the invasion of England Napoleon was waiting at Boulogne. While on his return from the West Indies, Captain Rutherfurd wrote the following letter.

Swiftsure at Sea, August 4th, 1805

My dear John:

I write this at sea to go to you when an opportunity offers. When we go into harbour we are so much hurried that I have no time to write to anybody except Lilly [his wife]. Young Millikin came to me at Gibraltar last month. The boy has had a long hunt after me, as he left Dublin in December last. Fifty pounds a year will be too much for him for some time to come: he says he is to draw for money upon Mr. John Batchelor, 27 William's Street, Dublin, when he wants small sums. I will approve his drafts upon that gentleman, of which I will thank you to apprise him. I am sorry that I could do but little with Allan [not the young Millikin mentioned above]. I therefore thought it best for him to leave him in the frigate [the *Decade*] with Capt. Stewart. A stranger to him and his connections may perhaps make him do better than I could. I believe the frigate is left in the Mediterranean. We are now at sea with Lord Nelson, and from the course he steers I think we are going to England, at least I hope so; but he had not given us a hint of where we are going; all we can judge is by the course. Perhaps you and your friends may think it strange my leaving the frigate for a seventy-four, but circumstances and times must be taken into account. When the ship became vacant, I was senior frigate captain with Lord Nelson. He offered me this ship when he was in hot pursuit of the Toulon fleet [January-August, 1805]. It was impossible to refuse a fine new seventy-four when we expected to be in action with the French fleet every day. If the admiralty will allow me to keep this ship—and I see no reason why they should not—the post is certainly a more honourable one than a frigate; and I think prize-money times are almost passed, £500 a year in this ship is better than £200 in the frigate. What a chase we have had after those Toulon fellows. We have been in the West Indies; had troops embarked at Barbadoes, making certain the French were attacking Tobago or Trinidad. We went there, but no French were there. We anchored at 6 in the evening at Trinidad, and sailed at 7 next morning. I saw nothing of my brother John. We made sure they were attacking Grenada, but when we got there no French fleet was there. We then went to Antigua, where we heard the French fleet had passed that island steering to the northward five days before. We landed the troops immediately, and steered back for the Mediterranean. When we arrived at Gibraltar we heard no account of the French fleet, but we knew they had not passed that way. We got stores and water as fast as possible and the fifth day we were out of the Straits again, and I now hope steering for England. Lord Nelson, I believe, is generally thought to be merely a fighting man; but he is a man of amazing resource and abilities, more so, I think, than even Lord Vincent. I am afraid the constant anxiety he has undergone has much hurt his health. The privations this little fleet of eleven sail has gone through has been great; but it has been with cheerfulness, because Lord Nelson commanded them. All our ships have now a great many men down with the scurvy, which makes me think we must go to England. If you do not know Lord Nelson, he is the most gentlemanlike, mild, pleasant creature that was ever seen. Coming from the West Indies, I was upon salt beef and three quarts of water for a month. We had no communication from the islands to get anything either to eat or drink. Lord James is my mess-mate, and well and strong and good; his time as mid[shipman] will be out in October. Tell my sister [Fanny] George Burt [sic] is a good boy. I thought you would like to hear the history of this fleet; therefore I must put you to the expense of postage. Love to all at home.

Yours very truly,
Wм. G. Rutherfurd.

J. C. Beresford, Esq. Beresford Place, Dublin.
[Has been posted at] Brixham 208, August 30, 1805.*

From this interesting letter—interesting not only for the light it throws on "little Billie's" career but also as a commentary on Nelson and the West Indian expedition of 1805—we learn several important facts that open up a new phase of our story. John was stationed at Trinidad, Billie was married and his wife was living in Dublin, and Fanny and her husband had removed from Plymouth and had taken up their residence in the same city. We are introduced to a number of new characters—J. C. Beresford, young Millikin (William Frederick), and Lord James, of whom Beresford is the only one that calls for further mention and something will be said of him later on. The preservation of this letter, amongst the flotsam and jetsam of a genealogist's notes—a letter the author of which was entirely unknown to the writer of the volume in which it is printed—is a curious documentary accident.

From the letter we learn that Captain Rutherfurd was married.

---

* *The Rutherfurds of that Ilk and their Cadets.* Edinburgh, 1884.

This event took place, August 27, 1795, at St. Margaret's, Westminster, and the bride was Lilias or Lillias Richardson, eldest daughter of the late Sir George Richardson, Bart., of Queen Street (*Gentleman's Magazine*, 1795, p. 789). The marriage settlement is dated August 27th of that year. Lilias died sometime before 1833 without issue, but there appears to have been an adopted son, John Henry Defou, of whom Rutherfurd speaks in his will, "commonly called Henry Rutherfurd, of the age of 12 years, usually residing with me except when at school" (P. C. C. 431 Creswell). Of this child we know nothing more.

Captain Rutherfurd's later career is a noteworthy one. As captain of the *Swiftsure* he took part in the battle of Trafalgar, October 21, 1805, contributing his share to the winning of the great victory and escaping with but little loss—nine men killed and eight wounded. In the official list of the battle his name is given as "William George Rutherford" and identification would have been difficult had it not been for the discovery of his letter, his will, and the notice of his death. He remained in command of the *Swiftsure* until his discharge in November, 1807, when he was placed on half-pay; but for some reason, ten days after his discharge, he was appointed captain of the Sea Fencibles, a position that he retained until February, 1810, when he was again placed on half pay. In 1815 he was made a Companion of the Bath (on the enlargement of that order) and the next year was appointed one of the four captains of Greenwich Hospital, a position that made him an officer of the house in residence, at a salary of £200 a year with table money. Evidently the hardships which he had undergone told upon his health,* for he died at the hospital in 1817 at the age of fifty-two. Thus "little Billie," born in North Carolina, stands in history as one of the "heroes of Trafalgar." In his will he leaves his Trafalgar sword and medal to his nephew, his sister's son, and these interesting relics, the outward marks of a notable career, may still be somewhere in existence. That Captain Rutherfurd should have been promoted by Nelson himself to be a captain of a ship of the line was a rare distinction. Such an advancement must have come as a reward for services rendered, probably for good seamanship and personal bravery. North Carolina should take pride in being the birthplace of so noteworthy a man.

Fanny, who in some ways is the heroine of Miss Schaw's narrative, seems to have been an attractive girl and the frequent references to

---

* In a letter of September 2, 1802, he speaks of his own health as "much impaired" (Adm. 1:2405).

her arouse our interest and curiosity. She evidently made a strong appeal to those with whom she came into contact and at least one love affair arose during her residence on the Cape Fear (above, p. 183). But she returned to Edinburgh in February, 1776, heart free, only to find a husband within five months after her arrival. In September, 1776, she was married at Edinburgh to Archibald Menzies of Culdairs, one of the commissioners of the customs of Scotland. What romance or tragedy lies behind the bare announcement of this marriage, we do not know. Whether it was a love match or a *mariage de convenance* is equally concealed. Menzies held an important official post to which he had been appointed in 1774, and his salary of £600 a year may have been an attraction to the family. Fanny was certainly "well married," as a contemporary correspondent wrote. Whether Menzies was an elderly man or an invalid or both, we cannot say, but the fact remains that Fanny's happiness was short-lived, for her husband died at Inveresk in October, 1777, after a married life of but little more than a year. A daughter was born of this marriage, Elizabeth McKenzie Menzies, who afterwards became the wife of the John Claudius Beresford,* to whom Captain Rutherfurd wrote the letter cited above. Where Fanny, with her daughter, spent the days of her young widowhood we do not know, but she eventually found solace, for sometime in 1787—the marriage settlement is dated April 28th of that year—she was married again, and this time to her companion on the voyage to America, Janet's brother, Alexander Schaw, store-

---

* John Claudius Beresford was a banker of Dublin, doing business, in Beresford Place until 1810, and, as Beresford & Co., in Henry Street after that date. He became prominent in the municipal life of Dublin about 1815, was alderman for twenty-five years, and served his term as lord mayor. He removed from Dublin probably soon after 1841, first to Coleraine, then to Port Stewart, and finally to Glenamoyle, Londonderry county, where he died July 2, 1846. He had married Fanny's daughter sometime before 1805, but she died before 1839 and was buried in the parish church of Coleraine. The Beresfords had seven children, two sons and five daughters. The sons were John C., Jr., and Archibald. Of the daughters, Catherine married one Smyley, who died before 1847, at which date she was living with two children, John and William, at Ramsey, Isle of Man; Emily married in 1839 George Cairnes (or Henry Moore Cairnes; one name is given in the will and the other in a codicil; perhaps they were brothers) and was at first dispossessed by her father for having "wantonly and foolishly involved him in heavy debts" through "foolish extravagance"; but she was later restored to favor as having "already been sufficiently punished by the privations she suffered from a restricted income." The other daughters were Georgina, Constantia, and Kitty (*Royal Calendar, passim;* Prerogative Wills, Public Record Office, Ireland).

keeper of ordnance on the gun wharf at Plymouth, serving under the War Office at £140 a year.

Alexander Schaw was a younger brother of Janet's and at the time of the journal may have been thirty years old. We are told that he had been a writer in Edinburgh, who, having got into difficulties, the nature of which we do not know, decided to go to America and applied for a post in the customs service. By commission of March 31, 1774, he received the office of searcher of customs at St. Christopher. After leaving Antigua in January, 1775, he went to St. Kitts with his sister and the children, but did not remain, having obtained permission to go with the party to North Carolina, on the understanding that he would return as soon as possible. That he intended to do this is clear, and at one time in the summer of 1775 it looked as if he would take his sister and the children back from North Carolina to St. Kitts; but events over which he had no control brought about a complete change of plan, and in the summer of 1775 he was entrusted by Governor Martin, at that time on board the *Cruizer* in the Cape Fear River, with despatches for Lord Dartmouth. He consequently returned to England by way of Boston, and remained there during the winter, living in London. On March 6, 1776, he obtained formal leave of absence from his post in St. Christopher, and there is reason to believe that he never saw the West Indies again. As an Alexander Schaw was in Canada from 1778 to 1781, employed in surveying stores and paying corvées, it is likely that he went to Canada, remaining there until his return to England to fill the more important position of storekeeper at Plymouth.

At Plymouth Alexander married Fanny, his erstwhile companion, who had called him "uncle" on the voyage, and there they lived until in May or June, 1801, they removed to Dublin, where Alexander had secured, by appointment of the Board of Ordnance (April 28, 1801), the post of storekeeper, an office which with the additional duties of paymaster of salaries and allowances brought him in more than £500 a year with house rent and candles. From the Ordnance records we learn that in preparing for removal Alexander objected to the sloop at first provided, on the ground that it was too small, and asked for a brig, which was granted. After his arrival in Dublin (June 30), he wrote the board that his furniture and packages had amounted to sixteen tons, and as they entirely filled the vessel, he and his wife were obliged to obtain accommodation from one Canforth of the Britannia yacht tender, at a fee of ten guineas (War Office, Ordnance Book, 45 : 56 and following volumes). By the middle of the summer of 1801 he and his wife, servants, and furniture were satisfactorily established in a house in Dublin, and there they remained until sometime after 1805. On August 5, 1803, Alexander was pensioned as "superannuated" by the board, and retired on an allowance of £677 a year (Irish money), but continued to live in Dublin, until sometime before 1810, when he removed to Inveresk, Scotland. In Ireland he was one of the members of the Dublin Society, but his name does not appear in the list for 1810, and his will, which was made at Inveresk, November 22, 1810, shows that he was residing there at that time. When or where Fanny died we do not certainly know but it was probably in Scotland. From her brother's letter we learn that she was alive and living in Dublin in 1805, but in 1810, in Alexander's will, she is referred to as "my late wife." She probably died at Inveresk shortly before, aged about fifty-two or fifty-three. Alexander died in 1818.

By her marriage with Alexander Schaw, Fanny had at least one child and probably more. Alexander in his will speaks of this child, John Sauchie Schaw, as "my son and only surviving child of the said marriage." When this son was born is not quite certain, but it must have been some years after the marriage in 1787, as he was not of age in 1810 and was not married until 1828. In 1819 he was a lieutenant of artillery in Dublin, and on March 14, 1828, entered into a marriage license bond of £1000 on the occasion of his marriage with Catherine Louisa Sirr, of Dublin Castle, daughter of the Rev. Joseph Darcy Sirr. He was living at the time at Cullenswood, Dublin county. With his later career we are not concerned.

X. The Children's Inheritance.

IN the ordinary course of events, the Rutherfurd children, at their coming of age, would have fallen heirs to a very considerable property from their father and mother and Mrs. Jean Corbin, large enough to have made them in a measure financially independent. This inheritance would have been derived from three sources.

First, from their mother, who received from the estate of Governor Johnston, her second husband, (a) two plantations, Possum Quarter in Granville county and Conahoe in Tyrrell county, which with certain other lands constituted her share of the Johnston real estate; (b) a considerable number of negroes; and (c) a fifth share in the residuary estate.

Secondly, from their father, who at one time possessed (a) the extensive lands which were later seized by John Murray of Philiphaugh, (b) the legacy of Alexander Duncan of £1000, (c) his share of the debts due the firm of Duncan & Rutherfurd, and (d) the debt due him from the province for running the boundary line with South Carolina. This property had probably all been lost before 1782, for we know that Rutherfurd died insolvent.

Thirdly, from Mrs. Corbin, who at her death left the children (a) certain plantations secured to her under the terms of her marriage settlement with Francis Corbin, (b) a considerable number of negroes, and (c) a certain amount of personal property, stock, utensils, etc., in part from the "Point Pleasant" plantation. "Point Pleasant" itself was not included, as Mrs. Corbin had only a life interest in that estate and could not dispose of it by will.

Owing to various circumstances, most important of which were Rutherfurd's bankruptcy and the confiscation of Loyalists' estates during the Revolution, this inheritance had dwindled by the year 1783 to relatively slender proportions, and at that time the recovery of even a small part seemed very uncertain. The children soon found that they could count on success in three particulars only: (a) the negroes, originally numbering from 150 to 175 in all, (b) the arrears of salary, of which, in 1783, £2018 remained unpaid, and (c) the plantation "Hunthill," which had been acquired for them in trust by their father in 1772, probably from money obtained in part from the sale of Possum Quarter and Conahoe in 1768 (£1780) and in part from other sources.

It is not necessary or possible to follow in all details the early stages in the history of the recovery of these properties.* In 1784,

* At this time the children were obtaining compensation from the American Loyalist Claims Commission. On March 16, 1782, John Rutherfurd, Sr., when in Charles Town had drawn up a memorial of losses addressed to Lord George Germain, but died before he was able to deliver it. In 1784, the sons presented this memorial with another of their own and in consequence of their appeal and statement of losses were allowed compensation to the amount of £500 a year (instead of £600 asked for), a sum that was later reduced to £50, because, as the decision stated, "they had obtained a restoration of a part of their property and so had enough to live on" (Audit Office Papers). It is not clear just what property is here referred to. Even this allowance of £50 was withdrawn after January 5, 1791 (Loyalist Quarterly Pension Books).

John Rutherfurd, Jr., obtaining leave of absence from his duties at Gibraltar, went to North Carolina, "to endeavor (so his memorial states) to obtain a repeal of the sanguinary laws and resolves against himself and his family and in hopes of recovering some part of the property they have thereby lost" (Audit Office Papers, American Loyalist Claims, 36, pp. 339-354). At first the children employed as their attorneys Alexander Schaw, Fanny's husband, and Alexander Anderson, a lawyer of Princess Street, Lothbury, London, but when John, Jr., arrived in Wilmington in 1784, he put the business into the hands of Archibald Maclaine and George Mackenzie, and at a later visit, in 1786-1787, into those of John London, formerly town clerk of Wilmington and an influential merchant there. London remained the children's attorney in North Carolina for a quarter of a century. In his diary, written in 1800, he says under date June 20, "Wrote packet to Capt. John Rutherfurd and enclosed Mr. Ashe's letters and accounts to him and Capt. W. G. Rutherfurd" (North Carolina Historical Commission MSS.), and we know that he and his son, John R. London, were still acting for them in 1814.

The first attempt made was to recover the negroes. In 1786, John, Jr., given power of attorney by his sister and brother, presented a memorial to the assembly of North Carolina, asking for the restoration of the negroes bequeathed them by their mother and Mrs. Corbin (*N. C. State Records*, XVIII, 178), which had been hired out by the sheriff of New Hanover county at a money wage. The committee to which this memorial was referred recommended that the rights of the petitioners be recognized and that the negroes be returned. The Senate and House of Commons concurred in this recommendation (*ib.*, 186-187, 189, 417) and resolved, December 31, 1787, that the sheriff be required and directed "to restore to John Rutherfurd the negro slaves, the property of the said John Rutherfurd, William Gordon Rutherfurd, and Frances Menzies, widow, hired out by order of the court of said county, together with such monies and securities as he may have received for the said hire" (*ib.*, 418). As the result of this resolution, the children were enabled to sell the negroes and did so at the first opportunity. George Mackenzie acted as agent, agreeing to find purchasers for them at £40 apiece before January, 1791. On March 12, 1788, John received £960 for his share and signed a release (Register's Office, Conveyances, I, old book, 8-9) and the next year, through John London as attorney, Fanny and William Gordon received £890 (*ib.*, L, Pt. 1, 243). The number of negroes thus disposed of was fifty-seven. Though all the details of these transactions are not available, it is evident that the fifty-seven were only a part of those eventually recovered. In 1812 John London sold for John and William Gordon (Fanny being dead) a third lot (seven) for $1480 and a fourth lot (twenty-three) for $4812 (*ib.*, O, 368; P, 152). Thus as far as our record shows eighty-seven negroes were sold at an approximate return to the children of $15,500, without reckoning in anything that might have been received for negro hire.

The recovery of the arrears of Governor Johnston's salary, the most important part of his residuary estate, proved a much more difficult and litigious matter, and ended somewhat unexpectedly for the children. There were originally four beneficiaries under the residuary clause of Johnston's will: the wife, Frances, the children's mother, one-fifth; Samuel, the brother, two-fifths, for the education of his family; a sister, Elizabeth, and her heirs in Scotland, one-fifth; and a natural son, Henry, one-fifth. In the years since 1752 many changes had taken place. Frances, the wife, had married John Rutherfurd and died in 1768; the sister Elizabeth had married Robert Ferrier in Scotland, but, she dying, he became attorney for their daughters until he too died and the daughters acted for themselves; and Henry Johnston died in 1772 and left his share to Penelope, his half-sister, who later married John Dawson. More than £10,000 had already been paid under the Treasury warrant of 1761, but of its distribution we know very little. We do know that Rutherfurd, acting in his wife's name (she was sole executrix of the will), received before her death a larger portion than she was entitled to, and that consequently soon after her death in 1768, Samuel Johnston, not liking Rutherfurd's management, obtained letters of administration, and not only secured for himself some part of the arrears, but was able also to remit to others a portion of that to which they were entitled. At the close of the Revolution the amount remaining to be paid was £2018.

Soon after 1783 application was made to the Treasury by the heirs in England for the payment of this remainder, but the Treasury officials refused to comply until the heirs could agree on a plan of distribution. To meet this requirement, in March, 1791, the Rutherfurd children and the Ferriers, father and daughters, through Alexander Anderson as attorney, entered into an agreement, according to which each was to follow up the matter, bearing individually his or her part of the expense and furnishing a statement of what each had already received. Anderson procured letters of administration (P. C. C, August 31, 1791) and with these documents in hand obtained from

the Treasury the desired warrant, September 5, 1791. Having received the money, he carried out the terms of the agreement, investing
£1850 of the £2018 in three per cent consolidated bank annuities
and stock and turning over the remainder to Robert Ferrier and
W. G. Rutherfurd, representing their respective heirs. Ferrier died
at this juncture, and his daughters, dissatisfied with Anderson's conduct in the case, employed another lawyer, secured new letters of
administration, and in 1795, sued Anderson in the Court of Common
Pleas at Westminster, Easter Term. Anderson in reply charged them
with breaking the agreement and filed a bill in the Court of Exchequer. The object of these suits was to obtain control of the money
invested in consols with the accruing dividends.

The situation now became so involved and threatened to be so
expensive that the contestants agreed to submit the dispute to arbitration and selected two London merchants, Robert Barnewell and
Henry Smith as arbitrators. Under the terms of the new agreement,
each party was to pay all legal expenses hitherto incurred and to
submit without demur to the decision of the board. All living within
twenty miles of London were to be examined personally under oath
and all living farther away were to make depositions on oath before
a local justice of the peace. The examinations occupied two years.
The arbitrators questioned the parties, investigated books, papers,
vouchers, and other documents, scrutinized the accounts presented by
the different persons, and endeavored to ascertain what each heir
had already received. Captain William Gordon Rutherfurd seems
to have conducted the business for his brother and sister, as between
April, 1797, and February, 1799, he was absent from his ship on
leave, a fact demonstrated by a complete lacuna in his correspondence
with the Admiralty during that period. It was not until the latter date
that with "his private affairs settled" he announced himself ready to
join the *Brunswick* at Jamaica or to continue in any other way his
naval service (Adm. 1:2400-2402. There is not a single letter from
him in volume 2401).

The arbitrators finally rendered their award, July 10, 1798. All
lawsuits were to be stayed; the Anderson estate (Anderson himself
having died in the meantime) was to return to the heirs £57; and
the amount in dispute, £1850 in three per cent consols with £627 in
dividends, was to be distributed to the heirs. But in this distribution
the Rutherfurds were to have no share, for the arbitrators decided
that Frances Rutherfurd, as executrix (through John Rutherfurd
acting in her name), had already received £654 more than was her

due and that the Rutherfurd heirs owed the Johnston estate that amount (less one-fifth on account of Henry Johnston). Consequently they were to receive nothing until the other heirs had been paid their shares in full. As four shares of £524 each would not exhaust the principal sum, it is possible, though very unlikely, that the children eventually received some small amount from this source.*

There still remained to be recovered the real estate in North Carolina, consisting chiefly, if not entirely, of the "Hunthill" lands. These lands had been confiscated during the Revolution and a part had been regranted by patent from the state. We have not been able to discover any formal act or resolution restoring these lands to the children, as was the case with the negroes, or any court decision under the act of 1786 (*N. C. State Records*, XXIV, 795), but it is clear that in the case of the "Hunthill" property the decree of confiscation was in some way reversed. In 1811 one Israel Judge restored to John London, acting in the boys' behalf (Fanny being dead), a portion of "Hunthill," which he had obtained under a state title, for the nominal consideration of £5 (Register's Office, Conveyances, P, 154) and in 1814 London sold to one Ezekiel Lane, for the sum of $2700, which he transmitted to the boys, this tract and other tracts making up the "Hunthill" property of 4084 acres, which had been bought by John Rutherfurd of Sampson Moseley in 1772, in trust for the children (*ib.*, P, 155-156). In so doing London brought to an end a long period of service in the interest of the Rutherfurd family, during which he had been largely instrumental in recovering for the surviving members property that they were able to sell for nearly $20,000. The children's fight for their inheritance was long and costly and the per-

---

* The above account of the controversy over the arrears of Johnston's salary is based in large part upon the text of the award, contained in a document now in private hands. The controversy itself throws light on Rutherfurd's business methods and is interesting as showing that the Johnston estate was not finally settled for nearly half a century after the governor's death.

In McRee's *Life of Iredell* is printed a reference to this award in a letter from Samuel Johnston to Iredell, as follows, "By the last packet I received a letter from our cousin, James Ferrier, dated Nov., 1798. He is promoted to the rank of Major General in the army. He informs me that the dispute between my uncle's legatees and Mr. Rutherfurd's children had been left to arbitration—to two merchants of London, who had awarded that they had received considerably more than their share of our uncle's legacy and effects; and that the moneys in the hands of Anderson's executors (including what was received in England) should be divided among the other legatees." II, 545.

sistence with which they pursued the struggle to the end deserves our admiration. Fanny did not live to see the final success, and the others, including Alexander Schaw, who had some share in the business, lived but a short time after the last transaction was completed. The shadow of this great expectation, long deferred and never more than in part fulfilled, hung over them for the greater part of their lives.

XI. A Group of Provincial Leaders.

IN studying the social and political history of North Carolina one is constantly impressed with the close connection that existed between South Carolina and the Cape Fear section of North Carolina, and with the frequent intermarriages that took place among the members of a large group of intimately associated families. The widely spreading branches of one genealogical tree include names from the families of Wright, Rhett, Trott, Izard, Hasell, Smith, Moore, Quince, Dry, Eagles, Allen, Grainger, Howe, and others, many of whom came originally from the southern colony. Representative men from these families formed a strongly united provincial group, that stood at times in outspoken opposition to those in the colony who were of English or Scottish birth—Johnston, Murray, Corbin, Innes, Rutherfurd, and Schaw, newcomers and "foreigners." Though no fixed lines of cleavage can be drawn, and though the antagonisms were manifest only at certain times and in connection with certain troublesome provincial problems, nevertheless the feeling was always latent, notably between the Brunswick group led by Moore and Dry and those who were the friends and followers of Governor Johnston. The quarrels over the blank patents and the town of Wilmington are well known (*N. C. R.* IV, v-vi) and Murray facetiously referred to the situation when he spoke of "a Dryness" subsisting "between some certain gentlemen and me until the unhappy differences of the province are reconciled" (*Letters of James Murray, Loyalist*, p. 42).

Miss Schaw mentions only a few of the leaders of the provincial party, but they play a sufficiently important part in the narrative to call for brief mention here.

Richard Quince.

Richard Quince, the elder, the father of Parker and Richard, Jr., was one of the leading merchants and traders of the colony, doing business at Brunswick under the firm name of Richard Quince & Sons; which later became Parker Quince & Co., doing a considerable up-river business. He was at one time or another a commissioner of the town of Brunswick, chairman of the inferior court of pleas and quarter sessions of Brunswick county, a church warden of St. Philip's, a judge of vice-admiralty, a justice of the peace, a member of the Wilmington Committee of Public Safety, and, with his son Richard, a member of the general committee of the Sons of Liberty. He was an active participant in the Revolution, died in 1778, and was buried in the churchyard of St. Philip's, Brunswick. He was originally from Ramsgate, England, where he had a brother John (who apparently before 1768 came to Wilmington and set up as a merchant there), and where he owned a house, which he retained during his lifetime. He was also a freeman of the Cinque Ports, of which in 1741 "he produced a sufficient testimony" and was therefore excused from jury duty (Brunswick County Court Records, 1737-1741, p. 133). He lived first at "Orton" plantation and later at "Rose Hill" on the Northeast, a plantation that he left to his son Parker. The latter and his brother Richard are said to have been "gentlemen of great respectability and devoted Whigs, but quiet and unobtrusive in their characters and never mingled in public life."

William Dry.

William Dry, the collector, was fourth in descent from Robert Dry, or Drye, who settled in South Carolina about 1680, and his grandfather, father, and himself all bore the same name. William Dry, 1st, married Elizabeth, daughter of Benjamin Blake, brother of the famous English admiral, Robert Blake (*South Carolina Historical and Genealogical Magazine*, V, 109, note 6), and died about the year 1700. He was a planter of influence and property and owned a plantation, "Oak Grove," next north of the present site of the navy yard, Charleston, which he inherited from his father and which he left to his son (*ib.*, XIX, 60-61). The latter, William Dry, 2d, was one of the original grantees of lots in Beaufort Town and acquired a second plantation, two miles above Goose Creek bridge, fronting the highroad, whereon he lived and where his son William Dry, 3d, the collector, was born in 1720. This property he advertised for sale or rent in

1733 and both plantations for sale in 1734 (*South Carolina Gazette,* July 28, 1733, February 2, 1734, May 18, 1735), in anticipation of his departure for North Carolina; and he finally left the colony with his family soon after August, 1735. He had married Rebecca, sister of Roger, Maurice, and Nathaniel Moore, and it was undoubtedly through his interest in their Cape Fear project that he joined them in the enterprise. Either before his arrival or immediately after, he bought lots in Brunswick and lived there as a merchant, justice of the peace, and captain of militia until his death, which occurred in 1746 or 1747. His wife survived him about ten years.

The son, William Dry, 3d, was fifteen years old when he went with his father to the Cape Fear. He first became prominent in September, 1748, when, at the age of twenty-eight, as captain of the militia, he led the attack (aided by men from Wilmington) on an invading force from two Spanish privateers, which had landed and obtained possession of Brunswick. He became a colonel in 1754, was appointed collector in 1761, was named one of the charter aldermen of Wilmington in 1760, served in the assembly from 1760 to 1762, became a member of the council in 1764 and continued in the latter capacity under Dobbs, Tryon, and Martin, until in July, 1775, he was suspended by Governor Martin on the ground of being disloyal to the crown. He took the side of the Revolution, though he was never particularly active in its behalf; and when the new constitution was adopted, accepted a seat on the revolutionary council.

In February, 1746, Dry married Mary Jane Rhett, granddaughter, through her father, of William Rhett and, through her mother, of Nicholas Trott of South Carolina, and (as the marriage notice states) "a lady of great fortune and merit" (*South Carolina Gazette,* February 24, 1746). He had a large plantation, "Belleville," on the north side of the road leading from Wilmington across Eagles Island southward, and at his death left this plantation to his daughter, Sarah, "one of the finest characters in the country," who married Benjamin Smith, later governor of the state and the founder of Smithville (now Southport), who was of the Landgrave Thomas Smith family of South Carolina. He died in 1781, aged sixty-one, and was buried in St. Philip's churchyard. His wife survived him until 1795, when she died at the age of sixty-six. She must have been married at seventeen.

It was at Dry's residence in Brunswick that Josiah Quincy dined in 1773, and so well that he called it "the house of universal hospitality" (*Journal,* p. 459).

Joseph Eagles.

Richard Eagles, the elder, of a Bristol (England) family, lived in South Carolina until 1735, when he too joined the Cape Fear colony. In South Carolina he owned a house and store in Charles Town, which he offered for rent in 1733 (*South Carolina Gazette*, January 13, 1733), a lot in the town of Dorchester, and a plantation, "Eagles" (on Eagles Creek near Dorchester, *South Carolina Historical and Genealogical Magazine*, XX, 47-48), which he advertised for sale in 1734, with dwelling house, large store, stable, and chaise house (*South Carolina Gazette*, August 3, 10, 1734). He must have left the colony before August 30, 1735, as at that time he is spoken of as "late of Charles Town, merchant" (*ib.*, August 30, 1735). He married Elizabeth Crichton, a granddaughter of the first William Dry, and so was a cousin by marriage of William Dry, the collector. His son, Richard Eagles, 2d, married Margaret Bugnion, and was the father of Joseph Eagles, mentioned in Miss Schaw's narrative.

Joseph Eagles, who had not "come to the years of eighteen" in 1769, when his father's will was made, cannot have been much more than nineteen or twenty at the time of Miss Schaw's visit. He was "not yet major," as Miss Schaw says, and was under the guardianship of her brother Robert, who had been appointed one of the executors of Richard Eagles's estate. He had been sent to England when but a child, living probably with his father's relatives in Bristol, and had but just returned, thoroughly Anglicized. He did not go back, however, as Miss Schaw thought might be the case, but remained in the colony and married there. His wife was Sarah, surname unknown. He died in 1791, leaving two children, Richard, 3d, and Joseph, 2d, the first of whom died before 1811, and the second in 1827, each without heirs. As only an aunt remained, the wife of Alfred Moore, the disappearance of the family name from the annals of North Carolina is readily accounted for (Brunswick County Records, Conveyances, B, 84, 189, 327, 341, 368; *North Carolina Reports*, V, 267, 269).

Eagles's plantation, which Miss Schaw visited in so unexpected a way, was called "The Forks" and was inherited from his father, who was living upon it at the time of his death. It was situated a short distance above Old Town Creek, on the road from Brunswick to Schawfield, was bounded on the south by Eagles Creek, and lay a little way below Eagles Island opposite Wilmington—an island that received its name from Joseph's grandfather, who owned land there. The plantation was of considerable size, containing a house, a sawmill, and a gristmill.

Robert Howe.

Robert Howe was born in North Carolina in 1730, the third son of Job Howe, or Hows, as the name appears to have been spelt originally. His grandfather (also a Job—there were three of the name) came with the Moores from South Carolina, and Robert, through his grandmother, Mary Moore, sister of Roger, Maurice, and Nathaniel, was related to the Moores, Drys, and others among the first settlers. He was sent to England early, returning in 1748, and soon began to play his part in the history of the colony. He became a justice of the peace in 1756, was appointed captain at Fort Johnston in 1765, succeeding Dalrymple, was superseded by Collet in 1767, but resumed the post on Collet's return to England in 1769, and was finally supplanted on Collet's return in 1773. He was for a time a baron of the court of exchequer and became a member of the assembly as early as 1760. He married Sarah Grange, daughter of Thomas Grange, "a respectable planter on the Upper Cape Fear River" (*North Carolina Booklet*, VII, 169), but was separated from her in 1772 and never remarried. His political and military career after 1772 is too well known to need rehearsal here.

Howe's personality and character have been variously interpreted according to the point of view. Miss Schaw expressed the opinion common in loyalist circles. Governor Martin, while acknowledging that Howe was a "man of lively parts and good understanding," charged him with "misapplication of the public money" and with endeavoring "to establish a new reputation by patriotism." Quincy, a northerner, thought better of him, as "a most happy compound of the man of sense, the sword, the senate, and the buck. A truly surprising character." No one has ever questioned his ability, energy, or devotion to the revolutionary cause, but it may be that the "relation of his past life and adventures" (did we but have it) would be to us, as it was to Quincy, "moving and ravishing." "He was," adds the latter, "formed by nature and his education to shine in the senate and the field—in the company of the philosopher and the libertine—a favorite of the man of sense and the female world. He has faults and vices— but alas who is without them." This duality of character may explain the unpleasant impression of Howe which Miss Schaw received. Howe's opposition to Martin and his later military activity and influence stamp him as a leader of men and a determined, obstinate fighter, but certain incidents of his life and his later court-martial— though he was unanimously acquitted—seem to point to flaws in his character that have never been fully explained.

Howe's father had estates on the Sound and a plantation at Howe's Point below Brunswick. The latter, containing a large three-story frame building on a stone or brick foundation, became Robert's residence and was largely destroyed by the British on May 12, 1776. Howe died in 1786, at the age of fifty-six.

James Moore.

James Moore, colonel and major general, was grandson of James Moore, who emigrated from Ireland to Charles Town, was governor there under the proprietors, and died in 1706. His father was Maurice Moore, the pioneer and the third husband of the widow Swann, who was his mother. He was born in New Hanover precinct in 1737 and spent his early years inconspicuously, probably on his father's plantation at Rocky Point—at least until 1761 when the property was sold to John Rutherfurd. He was appointed a justice of the peace in 1759 and a colonel of militia before 1765. He took part in Tryon's campaign against the Regulators, as colonel of "all the artillery and artillery company of volunteers," with Robert Schaw as lieutenant colonel, and was present at the battle of Alamance, which ended in the defeat of the Regulators in 1771.

James Moore was one of the best types of those who conscientiously opposed the royal government in America, and from the time of the Stamp Act until his early death he was generous and high-minded in his efforts to promote the cause of the Revolution. He was appointed, September 1, 1775, colonel of the first regiment of Continental troops raised by authority of the Convention, and in February, 1776, was already in the field, prepared to oppose Brigadier General Macdonald, who, at the head of the Highlanders, serving under the royal standard, was marching on Wilmington. He was in command of the campaign which culminated in the battle of Moore's Creek bridge, and took part in the manœuvres preliminary to the battle, but through no fault of his own had no actual part in the fighting that followed. As soon as the battle was over, he directed the movement of the troops and vigorously pressed on the pursuit (Connor, *History of North Carolina*, I, 373, 385-387). As Noble says, "Moore planned the whole campaign, provided for every contingency, and drove the enemy into the hands of two brave colonels [Caswell and Lillington, each at the head of a provincial regiment] who had taken their stand at Moore's Creek. The success of the American arms is entirely due to his foresight, energy, and skill" (*North Carolina Booklet*, XI).

Moore served in the American army less than a year, dying of fever at Wilmington, January 15, 1777. His loss was deeply felt, for friends and foes alike spoke well of James Moore. Miss Schaw's comments on both Robert Howe and James Moore show the shrewdness of her judgment.

XII. A Few North Carolina Loyalists.

Robert Schaw.

OF Miss Schaw's elder brother, Robert, or "Bob" as he was known to all his friends, something has already been said. The first mention of him that we can discover in North Carolina records is as a witness to an indenture of John Rutherfurd's in 1751 (Register's Office, Conveyances, BC, 24) and the second is of date 1759, when he was cited for failure to work on the streets and wharves of Wilmington and the road from Point Peter to Mt. Misery on the east side of the Northwest (Wilmington Town Records, p. 76). He had probably begun as an apprentice in a merchant's office, for, as his sister said, he had been in trade before turning planter. Such apprenticeship might easily have been entered on at ten years of age. It would look as if he had been employed in the store of some Scotsman—probably Alexander Duncan, who was closely connected with the Rutherfurds and Schaws and with whom he was afterwards in partnership. As his name does not appear among the Wilmington taxables in 1755 or among those with houses in Wilmington in 1756, it is likely that he did not marry much before 1760, which would put his birth date at least as far back as 1740. He may have been and probably was much older. Legally to witness an indenture one would have to be twenty-one years old. That would put his birth before 1730.

He prospered in business, and sometime after 1760 became a partner, first, in the firm of Duncan, Ancrum, & Schaw, and later, after the departure of the senior member for England in 1767, in the firm of Ancrum & Schaw, doing a general merchandising business. Mrs. Burgwin once wrote, "Hoggs tea is all gone and all his handkerchiefs but one; the tea I got at Ancrums." Robert Schaw served in many important capacities, being frequently called upon to act as trustee, guardian, executor of estates, and witness of wills, and seems to have been held in high esteem as a prudent and reliable person. He became a justice of the county court in 1768, a commissioner of Wilmington in 1769, was appointed a colonel of artillery under General Waddell in Tryon's expedition against the Regulators in 1771, and on September 1, 1775, was commissioned a colonel in the revolutionary army. He was, however, always lukewarm in support of the American cause and refused to follow the lead of the radical party. In June, 1777, James Murray wrote, "Bob Schaw will be obliged to leave Carolina for not taking the oath to the states." There is reason to believe that his property was sequestrated, for in 1786, the administrators of his estate were authorized to sell lands in Bladen county, known as the Western Prong lands, and to save the personal estate for the widow and son (*N. C. State Records*, XVIII, 177, 391). As by indentures between John Rutherfurd and Robert Schaw, September 7 and 8, 1768, the latter was made a receiver of the former's property (Register's Office, Conveyances, F, 92-102), it may be that these are the lands that Rutherfurd formerly owned and that Schaw bought of Murray of Philiphaugh.

Schaw married as his first wife, Anne, the sister of John Rutherfurd, who died without issue, January 11, 1767 (*Scots Magazine*, 1767, p. 167), and as his second, Anne Vail, who is the "Mrs. Schaw" of the journal. She was the widow of Job Howe, the brother of Robert, and had one child, William Tryon Howe, by her first husband, and two children, Alexander* and Robert Schaw, by her second. Alexander was born before 1775 and died in 1802; Robert, Jr., was born before 1778 and died probably before 1788, as he is not mentioned in his mother's will. Robert, Sr., died in 1786 and his wife two years later in 1788. In the *Wilmington Centinal and General Advertiser* for June 18, 1788, is inserted a "Request" that all persons indebted to Robert Schaw, Alexander Duncan, deceased, Duncan, Ancrum, & Schaw, and Ancrum & Schaw settle and make payment or renew their obligations.

---

* This son, Alexander Schaw, who died in 1802, left one child, Catherine Schaw, as we learn from the will of her uncle, Alexander Schaw, Sr., who died at Inveresk, Scotland, leaving property to the amount of £7500. According to that will the son of Alexander, Sr., John Sauchie Schaw, was to succeed to the property. Should he die, however, before the father and there be no heirs of his body, then Catherine, the niece, was to be the heir, and should she not be living, then the estate was to be divided equally between John Rutherfurd and William Gordon Rutherfurd, Schaw's brothers-in-law (Commissary Court Books, Edinburgh). As it turned out John Sauchie Schaw inherited the property.

Dr. Thomas Cobham.

Dr. Thomas Cobham, who occupies a conspicuous place in Miss Schaw's story, was a prominent "practitioner in physics" in Wilmington, the first mention of whom in contemporary records is of date March 22, 1765, when he witnessed the will of Lieutenant Whitehurst of H. M. S. *Viper*, who, in the duel with Alexander Simpson, master of the same vessel, fought on March 18, received wounds from which he died. In his own testimony before the Loyalist Claims Commission he says that he settled on the Cape Fear in 1766 and from that time followed his profession. He had a partner, Dr. Robert Tucker, to whom he made a division of a third of the profits of his practice, but from whom he had parted before he finally left the colony. He accompanied Tryon on the campaign against the Regulators, dividing with a Dr. Haslin the inspection of the troops (*N. C. R.* VIII, 584). He was loyalist in his sympathies, and at first, on March 7, 1775, refused to subscribe to the Continental Association; but on the 13th changed his mind and in the June following sent two guineas to the Committee of Safety for the purchase of gunpowder. In August he promised, at the request of the committee, not to send medicines to Governor Martin on board the *Cruizer*, and after the battle of Moore's Creek bridge attended without pay the Loyalists who were wounded in the battle. He said afterwards that he never took any oath to the Americans but obtained a certificate from a magistrate that he had taken an oath.

Cobham planned to go to England on the opening of the war, but was prevailed upon to remain "by the executive officers of government," until the occupation of Wilmington by Craig, January 28, 1781, when he joined the British troops and was appointed surgeon to H. M. naval hospital at Charles Town and later by Admiral Digby to the same at St. Augustine. There he remained until Florida was given back to Spain in 1783, when he and the hospital were removed to New Providence in the Bahamas. He continued in the service of the hospital there until he was discharged, April 5, 1786, when in September he returned to England. There he learned from letters received soon after that his estate in North Carolina had been confiscated and sold (Audit Office Papers).

He and his wife, Catherine Mary Paine, widow of John Paine of Brunswick county, early bought land on Old Town Creek, but in 1771 they sold this property and acquired a plantation of 1300 acres, with two sawmills, in which Cobham had a half interest. In 1772 he occupied a house in Wilmington, rented of Mrs. Jane Dubois, probably on Front Street (Wilmington Town Records, pp. 154, 160), and there Josiah Quincy dined "in company with Harnett, Hooper, Burgwin, Dr. Tucker, and others" on March 29 of that year, and there too he lodged and was treated with great politeness, though, as he wrote in his journal, Dr. Cobham was "an utter stranger and one to whom I had no letters" (*Journal*, p. 460). In or about March, 1775, Cobham purchased of George Moore, for £840 proclamation money,* another house between Princess and Chestnut streets near the river, which may have been the house called "The Lodge," where Miss Schaw was entertained and from the balcony of which she saw the review. On December 5, 1778, Cobham exchanged this house for a plantation of 500 acres in the neighborhood of Wilmington, probably near Schawfield. This seems to be the plantation referred to in a deed of 1779, according to which John Rutherfurd sold to Dr. Cobham 200 acres on both sides of the main branch of Long Creek, "adjoining the mill lands of Cobham," which (according to the deed) Rutherfurd had received by the will of Jean Corbin (Register's Office, Conveyances, H, 10. There is no such bequest in Mrs. Corbin's will; the property may have been sold by Rutherfurd for his children).

Mrs. Cobham, mentioned by Miss Schaw, died sometime before 1777. There was a daughter also, Catherine Jane, whom Cobham left, together with his furniture, in the care of a lady in Wilmington when he went to Charles Town, and for whom he made provision, leaving for her, in trust, 400 acres on the west side of the Northwest, next Schawfield on Indian Creek (Register's Office, Conveyances, L, Pt. 2, 567-568).

That Dr. Cobham was highly respected in Wilmington is plainly

---

* The method of paying for this house is interesting (Audit Office, Class 13, 118), as no money actually passed from Cobham to Moore.

To amount of account due by Mr. Moore to Cobham and Tucker .	120.10.0
To Tucker's physical account paid him	39. 0.2
To cash from Estate of Thomas Jones	11.10.0
To account paid by Mr. J. Moore on account of Mr. Samuel Swan	40. 0.0
To cash paid John Ancrum (June 14, 1775)	304. 4.8
To cash paid John Ancrum on account of tar (July 24)	125. 0.0
To cash paid John Ancrum for a horse and lumber (Jan., 1776) .	78. 0.0
To cash paid John Ancrum	100. 0.0
To Cobham & Tucker's acc^t, Jan., 1775-Feb. 16, 1776	9. 3.6
To cash in part of Cobham's acc^t for medicines and attendance July, 1776-Nov., 1778	12.11.8

£840. 0.0

evident. Thomas McGuire, one of the witnesses before the Loyalist Claims Commission, said that he was a man not only of probity but of distinguished eminence in his profession. He was still living in 1797.

Robert Hogg.

Robert Hogg came to North Carolina from northern Scotland about 1756 and became a successful and prosperous merchant, living "in affluence," as the record says. He was a native of East Lothian and had two brothers, James and John, the former of whom in 1774, at the age of forty-six, came to the colony from Caithness with his wife and five children, all of the latter under eight years of age. Robert Hogg had visited Caithness in 1772, and finding his brother James tormented by local thievery and disorder, persuaded him to go to America, which he did, bringing with him a shipload of 280 persons, including his own family of sixteen, with servants, 174 passengers above the age of eight, 60 children under eight, and 30 infants. James settled first at Cross Creek, where he ran a store in close conjunction with Robert's store in Wilmington.*

We meet with traces of Robert's life in Wilmington from the Wilmington town records. In common with many other estimable citizens who preferred to pay a fine rather than work on the roads, he was occasionally cited as a defaulter. In 1769 he and John Ancrum were elected commissioners of the town, but as he wished to leave the province to go to Scotland in 1772, his place was taken by his partner, Samuel Campbell. On his return he found the revolutionary movement under way and at first coöperated with the Wilmington Committee of Safety. But in July, 1775, when the members began to advocate extreme measures, he withdrew, and in September sailed for England, with a letter of recommendation from Governor Martin to Lord Dartmouth, written on board the *Cruizer*, August 31, as follows: "A merchant of first consideration in the colony, where he has resided many years, and who is compelled by popular clamour and resentment to abandon his important concerns here, because he will not renounce his principles, which he has maintained with a manly firmness and steadiness, which do equal honour to his heart and understanding. As I know no gentleman better qualified than Mr. Hogg, both by his intelligence and candour, to represent the state of

* For his later career see Battle, in *James Sprunt Historical Monographs*, no. 3, pp. 13-16. Battle is wrong in calling James a cousin of Robert's; he was his brother.

this colony, I think it a point of duty to introduce him to your Lordship, and to give you opportunity of communication with him" (Dartmouth Papers). Mrs. DeRosset wrote soon after, "Perhaps you will be surprised to hear Mr. Hogg is in England. He was one of your *non-conformed to the times*, and so made off!" Two years later James Clarke wrote to James Hogg, at that time in Hillsboro, "I have always had a great friendship for your brother and never considered him an enemy to this country" (*N. C. State Records*, XIV, 478). Robert Hogg was one of that large class of intelligent moderates in the colonies who were unable to see the necessity of extreme measures and were literally forced into opposition against their wills. In the growth of the revolutionary movement the time had unfortunately passed when moderation was longer possible.

Robert Hogg remained in England, living in Threadneedle Street, very frugally, with an aged father to support, until the summer of 1778, when hearing of the North Carolina law, passed December 28, 1777, declaring forfeit the property of all who did not return by October of that year, he determined to sail for New York, to await the issue of the efforts of the second peace commission. He arrived before September, 1778, but died in New York the following year, leaving his brother his heir. James remained in North Carolina and endeavored to recover some of the debts due the firm of Hogg & Campbell. The debts of the firm amounted to £18,669, currency (apparently including such also as were owed to merchants in England, which they paid); the debts due them in the colony came to £34,999, currency, and among those owing the firm money may be found the names of Robert Schaw and Archibald Neilson (Audit Office Papers).

Samuel Campbell.

Samuel Campbell was a native of North Carolina and a merchant of Wilmington in partnership with Robert Hogg and for a time with Frederick Gregg. He became a captain of militia, and was compelled to take the oath of allegiance to the United States. He became captain of a company in Wilmington, which exercised privately before the battle of Moore's Creek bridge, apparently with the intention of coöperating with the Highlanders; but later was ordered by the Committee of Safety to march to Fort Johnston and dismantle it (see above, p. 205). This he refused to do and was threatened with court-martial, but in the end was neither imprisoned nor tried. He then retired into the country and paid a sum of money for a substitute.

He openly joined Craig in 1781 and was appointed a captain of militia, and when Craig marched into the country was placed in charge of the town. On the evacuation of Wilmington he went to Charles Town and was appointed by Colonel Leslie a colonel of militia, but on the failure of the southern campaign he left the city and went to Nova Scotia (*Second Report, Ontario Bureau of Archives*, pp. 54-55). There he purchased an improved farm in the neighborhood of Shelburne, settled upon it with his family, and expended upon it what property he had left. In 1786 he reported that he had not enough to live on, but in 1800 he was still there (Register's Office Conveyances, L, Pt. 2, 726). His wife, Alice, was a niece of Samuel Cornell, a man of some prominence in the political affairs of North Carolina, who became himself a Loyalist, lost his property, and otherwise suffered at the hands of the revolutionary party.

Campbell in withdrawing his allegiance to the state transferred to James Hogg all claims to the property of Hogg & Campbell, and because debarred from bringing suits in his own name, was protected by an act passed in 1787, authorizing James Hogg and two others to maintain suits in their own name as executors (*N. C. State Records*, XXIII, 187, 417; XXIV, 858-859). He said that his former income ("gains in trade") was £600 a year and that his own personal loss was £2000 sterling.

Thomas Macknight.

The case of Thomas Macknight illustrates admirably how unfortunate often was the policy of the radical revolutionaries in driving out many men in sympathy with the cause of America, but who for one reason or another were unable to adapt themselves at once to a program of revolt. Our revolution was true to type, and in the year 1775 there was no place in the revolutionary party for men who qualified in any important particular their entire submission to the will of those in control. A radical minority dominated the movement and played the autocrat without mercy, pursuing with intolerant resentment anyone who failed to see the situation eye to eye with themselves. It could not have been otherwise, for a revolution to be a revolution means the uncontrolled rule of a relatively small body of men. The hardships which the moderates suffered in the years from 1774 to 1780 are comparable, *mutatis mutandis*, with the hardships suffered by men of moderate minds and restrained opinions in the revolutions of England and France.

The documents in the Macknight case are many and voluminous, but only a few facts need to be stated here.

Thomas Macknight was a Scotsman, who came to North Carolina in 1757 and during the eighteen years that followed rapidly advanced to a position of influence and large wealth. He owned landed property in five counties in the colony, chiefly in the Albemarle region, though some of his land lay in the south near the upper Cape Fear, and he was deeply interested in shipbuilding and the export trade in conjunction with certain merchants of Norfolk, Virginia, with whom he was joined in a business partnership. His energies for many years were expended in the effort to build up the industry and trade of the northern part of the province, which in the period after the removal of the capital to New Bern and the growth of the Cape Fear section had tended to decline. When the revolutionary troubles came on, he exerted his influence to hold the Albemarle counties (notably Currituck and Pasquotank) to their allegiance, and succeeded in doing so until October, 1775. In the convention of April 4, 1775, he was present as a representative from Currituck, and when at the session of Thursday, April 6, the members were called upon to subscribe to the Continental Association, he was the only one who refused, on the ground that the doing so would involve a repudiation of a debt owed to a certain merchant in Great Britain, an act so dishonorable that he was unwilling to consider it. He asked for time in which to settle his obligations and his request was upheld by a majority of the members present, who refused at first to vote a sentence of excommunication. But the radical minority, threatening to leave if the sentence was not voted, forced the majority to pass the vote and to declare Macknight "inimical in his intentions to the liberties of America."

Macknight had already withdrawn from the convention, and, after the vote was declared, the other representative from Currituck and the two representatives from Pasquotank also withdrew. Before they did so, however, they drafted a statement of reasons and requested that it be entered in the journal of proceedings, but the convention refused their request and they were obliged to vindicate in the newspapers their attempt to rescue "the character of a gentleman we greatly esteem from undeserved obloquy and reproach." Through that medium both they and Macknight stated the facts in the case, the latter declaring "that he was greatly concerned he could not heartily concur in the vote proposed to be passed, on account of particular circumstances in his situation which obliged him to dislike some part of the Association; that he owed a debt in Britain which the operation of the non-exportation agreement would disable him to pay; and that he could not approve of a conduct in a collective capacity, which as an individual he should blush to acknowledge." He added further, "that he thought it a duty he owed to his own sincerity to mention this sentiment, but did not mean to obstruct the good purposes proposed by an union of measures; that he would cheerfully comply with the non-consumption and non-importation agreement, and should give a passive agreement to the non-exportation article; that an individual, as a member of society, ought to conform his action to the general will of it, but that opinions could not be altered without conviction or insincerely expressed without dishonesty."*

In a similar public announcement, issued by the other deputies from Currituck and Pasquotank, the latter expressed their faith in Macknight's intentions as having been "always friendly to the cause of American liberty, his actions evidently shewing to us, who are his neighbors, the uprightness of his intentions; nor did we observe any disingenuous or equivocal behaviour in Mr. Macknight to warrant the censure of the convention in the smallest degree, but some of those who were with him before, being now offended by his withdrawing from amongst them, joined the other party." Macknight in his turn publicly expressed his obligations "to the inhabitants of Newbern in general and more particularly to his friends, who by continuing their wonted civilities have discovered to the world their opinion of the proceedings of the convention relative to himself" (*North Carolina Gazette*, April 14, 1775).

From this time forward, Macknight became a marked man, "inimical" whether he wanted to be or not. He was cajoled, bribed, and threatened; finally an attempt was made to assassinate him in his own house, and his dwelling, his merchandise, his crops, and his negroes were plundered. Then he fled, first at the end of 1775 to Lord Dunmore in Virginia, and after that in February, 1776, to Governor Martin. He returned once to the Cape Fear in July or August, 1776 (*Second Report, Ontario Bureau of Archives*, p. 1231), but finally toward the end of 1776 he left permanently for England. We meet with him once or twice appearing before the Loyalist Claims Commission, in behalf of Carolina friends.

---

* "We hear that Mr. Knight is raising men in Currituck to subdue the Edenton Committee and to force open trade for the laudable purpose of paying his debts." Cogdell to Samuel Johnston, New Bern, June 18, 1775 (Hayes Collection).

During the years that followed he made long and persistent efforts to obtain compensation for his losses, in part for property confiscated in North Carolina, and in part for two vessels, one of which was commandeered by the British authorities in North Carolina, the other, cleared in September, 1775, with a valuable cargo for Lisbon, was seized by the Americans in December, and, when released, taken off Cape St. Vincent by a British man-of-war, in May, 1776, and condemned as lawful prize under the Prohibitory Act. For ten years he labored in desperation, appealing to the Treasury, Lord North, Lord George Germain, Lord Dartmouth, and the Loyalist Claims Commission, but never succeeded in securing anything that he considered an adequate compensation. Of his later career we know nothing. With the failure of his efforts he completely disappears from view. As we read through the long series of letters, petitions, and memorials to be found among the papers of Lord Dartmouth and the Loyalist Claims Commission, we are puzzled to understand the causes of his failure. Even with full allowance for the fact that the evidence is *ex parte*, Macknight's case seems a peculiarly pathetic one. (A convenient printed statement may be found in *The Royal Commission on Loyalist Claims*, Roxburghe Club, for which see the index; later letters and petitions, with one exception, are in manuscript, copies of some of which may be found at Raleigh.)

XIII. Archibald Neilson.

THE "stranger gentleman," to whom Miss Schaw refers, and with whom she was destined to become exceedingly intimate during the last few months of her travels, was Archibald Neilson. He was born in Dundee, Scotland, the home of Governor Gabriel Johnston and his brother Samuel, about the year 1745. One who, as Miss Schaw says, had seen a great deal of the world, was highly educated, and conversant with many languages, can hardly have been less than thirty at the time of Miss Schaw's visit, even though Miss Schaw does speak of him in one place as a "young fellow." We have no details of his early life, beyond the fact that he had been employed by "Mr. Grenville" in the West Indies (and if George Grenville is meant, this employment must have been before 1765) and it is possible that he there came into touch with the Martin family. He wrote to John Wilmot in 1788, "I had long been honored with the particular friendship of the deceased governor Martin on his being appointed to the government of North Carolina and, as I was at that time a young man without fixed line of employment, he in warmest and most friendly manner invited me to join him in his province. I accordingly joined him and lived with him in the most confidential manner. I was, so far as consisted, privy to the measures of his government, in forwarding many of which he did me the honour of calling on my services" (Audit Office Papers).

Neilson arrived in the province in 1771 and lived at New Bern, in the governor's "palace" with Martin for four years, acting at times as his secretary. He was serving in that capacity when the troubles broke out in March, 1775, and in May aided Martin to escape in that eventful flight from New Bern to Fort Johnston, which cost Martin his influence in the province. He aided also Mrs. Martin and the children to make their way to New York, securing the vessel and seeing them safely on board. Free then from further obligation to remain at New Bern and "after some various escapes from the popular fury," one or two of which Miss Schaw recounts, he was obliged to take refuge with the governor on board the *Cruizer*, and there he remained until he left the province in November, 1775.

Neilson was appointed to the clerkship of the courts by Martin, an appointment contested by the assembly, and he also held an agency under the governor for the Granville Grant, neither of which offices seems to have netted him anything in the way of financial return. In January, 1775, on the death of Isaac Edwards, the deputy auditor, Martin appointed Neilson in his stead, and later, in October, while both were on board the *Cruizer* and after Samuel Johnston, the naval officer, had shown his strong prediliction for the revolutionary cause by acting as moderator of the provincial congress, Martin suspended Johnston and gave Neilson his place. But the progress of the Revolution destroyed the value of both offices, the emoluments from which came from fees; and it is noteworthy that when in the summer of 1775 one Pryce arrived from England with deputations as provincial secretary and deputy auditor, he was so alarmed at the disorder of the country and disgusted with the climate that he returned to England without even calling on the governor (*N. C. R.* X, 237, 263, 269, 332).

Neilson had no property in the colony, except two houses, two negroes, some furniture and books, all of which he left behind, "being obliged to flee suddenly." It is at least worthy of remark that he should have taken no advantage of his intimacy with the governor to obtain land or accumulate wealth by any of those means which place-seekers of the time knew so well how to utilize.

Miss Schaw adds greatly to our knowledge of Neilson's activities during the summer and autumn of 1775 and of his experiences with her and Fanny in the city of Lisbon. After returning from Portugal in January or February, 1776, he went to London, where he applied to Lord Dartmouth for a commissaryship or some similar post in the British army in America, his first letter being dated May 7, from "15 Orange Street, Leicester Fields." He was evidently unsuccessful in his application, for in the same year the Treasury granted him a temporary relief, on his offering to go as a volunteer to New York. At this crisis, however, his brother died at Dundee, leaving a widow and nine children, the eldest only thirteen, and Neilson was obliged to return to Scotland in order to care for an aged mother, two sisters, a sister-in-law, and all the children. There he remained until the end of his life. All further applications to the Loyalist Claims Commission had to be made in writing, subscribed under oath before the chief magistrate of the royal borough of Dundee. In 1783 he was awarded a yearly allowance of £60, which he drew regularly until his death in 1805. In the Loyalist Quarterly Pension Books the name of his attorney appears every quarter, until in the entries for January, 1806, the word "dead" is written in pencil at the side of his name and no payment is inserted in the column (Treas. 50: 20). He never married.

During his life in the colony Neilson was on terms of friendship with Samuel Johnston and James Iredell and probably others. McRee in his life of Iredell prints a number of his letters, which show the keenness and vigor of his thought and the wide scope of his reading. In commenting upon him, McRee justly says, "He was, undoubtedly, one of the most highly cultivated men of his day and region, and though an adherent of government, highly esteemed by Iredell and Johnston" (*Life of Iredell*, I, 201-202).

XIV. Captain John Abraham Collet.

CAPTAIN John Abraham Collet may well be deemed the villain of this phase of the story, for, though possessing many natural gifts, he was domineering and unprincipled and has received little commendation from either party in the struggle. He has, however, been treated more harshly than was necessary by North Carolina historians who, following contemporary revolutionary opinion, have given him no credit for his successful handling of a difficult situation. Furthermore, North Carolina owes him something for the excellent maps that he prepared of the province—maps not generally known and never reproduced to our knowledge. One was engraved and published; the other two, now in the British Museum, with photographic copies at Raleigh and in the Library of Congress, still remain in manuscript. Of the latter, the smaller covers the lower Cape Fear; the larger, Albemarle and the back country.

Captain Collet before coming to North Carolina had served six campaigns in Germany and later for four years studied mathematics, engineering, and drawing. On May 27, 1767, he was commissioned commander of Fort Johnston, and in August embarked for North Carolina, delivering his credentials to Governor Tryon in December. He was discouraged at the miserable condition of the fort and the insufficient allowance made for its maintenance, and as an *ad interim* employment accepted Tryon's invitation to accompany him as his aide-de-camp on the expedition against the Regulators in 1768. In December of that year he returned to England, having in the meantime surveyed the province and completed a map of it, "which he afterward had the honour of presenting to His Majesty and upon the publication of which he actually lost £500." (Testimony before the Loyalist Claims Commission.) This map, engraved by Bayley, was published May 1, 1770, by S. Hooper, Ludgate Hill, London.

Though Collet carried to England recommendations from Tryon to Hillsborough, he was unsuccessful in obtaining preferment. While in England he was employed in drawing until in 1772 he was ordered by the secretary of state for the colonies to return to America and take up his post at Fort Johnston. In the meantime Governor Martin had endeavored to impress upon the assembly the necessity of making an adequate appropriation for charges and maintenance of the fort, but with slight success. Collet reached the country in 1773, and with the governor's approval "spared neither time nor pains to put [the fort] into substantial repair" and, according to his own statement, continued to maintain it at his own expense up to 1775. Martin and Collet were in fact on the horns of a dilemma: the assembly would do nothing because Collet was a British officer; and Secretary Dartmouth would do nothing because the fort "seemed calculated merely for the security and convenience of the commerce of the colony" (*N. C. R.* IX, 1008).

From the end of 1774 Collet was harassed "in every way the Americans could devise; they cut off his usual channels for provisions, and by great premiums and promises seduced his men to desert and after the first bloodshed at Lexington they declared open hostilities and more destruction to the garrison." As early as March, 1775, the rumor spread that the fort was to be attacked and Collet and his lieutenant, Richard Wilson, prepared for its defence. This activity, coupled with other rumors, true and false, convinced the Wilmington committee that it would be necessary to capture the fort and if possible to take Martin and Collet into custody. The attacking force numbered five hundred; for defence Collet had twenty-five men, reduced by desertion to less than half that number, of whom only three or four were to be depended on. The artillery was useless for want of powder. When it became evident that the fort could not hold out, Martin retired on board the man-of-war and ordered Collet and Wilson to dismantle the fort, save the guns, and embark for Boston. This they did, July 21, 1775, delivering to General Gage "a very valuable and costly set of artillery, arms, stores, and ammunition belonging to the Crown." While waiting on the transport, Collet saw his own property destroyed, losing, according to his own estimate, in house and stable, horses, cattle, carriages, hay, liquors, and furniture upward of £5900, with a total loss of "at least £10,000" (Audit Office Papers). Wilson, likewise, lost a house and stable, three saddle horses, and other property worth £400 (*Second Report, Ontario Bureau of Archives*, p. 1207). The attacking party, not content with the destruction of the fort and the houses belonging to it, shortly afterwards tarred and feathered the gunner "for expressing his loyalty," and "so grossly insulted Mr. Mulligan in particular, surgeon to the forts and garrisons in this province [South Carolina], that he was under necessity of taking refuge on board the King's ship till the packet boat sailed" (Lord William Campbell to Lord Dartmouth, South Carolina, August 19, 1775). Collet, after his arrival in Boston, continued in military service till the end of the war. He joined the Royal Fencible Americans, a loyalist regiment, served under Lieutenant Colonel Gorham at Fort Cumberland, Nova Scotia, 1777-1780, and at Fort Howe, 1781 (Loyalist Muster Rolls, MSS., 1777-1783). Of his career after his return to England we know nothing.

Collet had conspicuous faults and Governor Martin made no effort to minimize them. He charges Collet with extravagance and with conduct based upon his own gain rather than "upon any principles of justice, equity, and charity." He says that Collet was heavily in debt and contemptuous of the efforts which his creditors made to secure payment; that he was hot-headed and impetuous and so scornful of the colonials generally as to exasperate them against him. Though Martin did not believe, and probably with reason, the report that Collet was harboring and arming negroes at the fort and inciting them to insurrection, he was convinced that Collet was the wrong man for the place and hoped that he would never return to the colony.

INDEX

INDEX

Innes, Colonel James, 157 note, 171
note, 285-287, 300, 313.
Inquisition in Portugal, 221, 224,
229, 241.

Jamaica Packet, 19, 56, 132, 134, 138,
144 note.
Jews in St. Eustatius, 130-131.
Johnston, Governor Gabriel, 278,
283, 285, 286, 291, 293, 294, 307,
310, 313, 328.
Joseph I, King of Portugal, 235,
240, 245, 251.

Kames, Henry Homes, Lord, 44, 45.

Lawsons, the, emigrants, 37-38, 55,
66, 67, 72, 116.
Lindsay, Major, 238.
Lisbon, 218, 222, 226, 227, 230, 232,
242, 250, 251.
Lobscourse, 53, 58, 64.

Mackinnen, William, 89 note, 93,
107, 116.
Mackinnen, Mrs. William, 89.
Macknight, Thomas, 182, 325-328.
Maclean, General Francis, 238.
Madeira Islands, The, 58.
Magnolia, 203.
Malcolm, Dr. Patrick, 103.
Mansfield, William, Lord, 89, 110.
Manuring, 127, 160.
Maria, Senora, landlady in Setubal,
222-223, 225-226, 245.
Martin, Henry, son of Colonel Sam-
uel, 264-265.
Martin, Josiah, brother of Colonel
Samuel, 270-272.
Martin, Governor Josiah, son of
Colonel Samuel, 105, 156, 158, 173,
182, 186, 187, 188, 189 note, 193,
197, 205, 206, 207, 208, 212, 216,
265-270, 271, 281, 296, 315, 317, 321,
323, 329, 331, 332, 333.
Martin, Mrs. Josiah, wife of the
governor, 187, 265, 270, 329.
Martin, Major Samuel, father of
Colonel Samuel, 260-261.
Martin, Colonel Samuel, "Father of
Antigua," 100, 103-106; author of

Essay upon Plantership, 104 note,
129 note, 262; colonel of militia,
108, 261; biographical sketch of,
261-262.
Martin, Samuel, Jr., son of Colonel
Samuel, 105, 262-264, 268.
Martin, Samuel, M.D., son of Josiah
and nephew of Colonel Samuel,
272-273.
Martin, Young Samuel, 81, 82, 87,
95, 106, 107, 265.
Martin Family, the, 259-273.
Mediterranean pass, 62.
Memboe, colored maid, Antigua, 86,
87, 107.
Militia, Antigua, 109.
Miller, Mrs. Mary, Miss Schaw's
abigail, 22, 23, 25, 31, 45, 53, 56,
57, 86, 107, 134, 145, 180 note, 200,
210 note, 221.
Miller, Philip, author of *The Gar-
dener's Dictionary*, 168, 203.
Milliken, Miss, 116, 124, 129, 130,
132.
Miscegenation, white masters and
negro servants, 112, 154.
Mocking-bird, 168-169.
Moita, Portugal, 234.
Money, North Carolina, 214, 281.
"Monkey Hill," plantation, 131.
Monkeys, St. Christopher, 131-132.
Moore, Colonel James, 167, 178 note,
188, 205, 318-319.
Mosquitoes, 85, 86, 138, 179, 182, 200.
Moss, 151-152.
Muir, Dr. John, 109.
Murray, Mrs., of Stormont, sister of
Lord Mansfield, 247.
Murray, James, 145, 285, 289-291,
292, 313, 320.
Murray, John, of Philiphaugh, 296,
298, 300, 308, 320.

Negroes, Antigua, 78, 87, 88, 94, 103-
104, 107-109, 112; St. Christopher,
127-128; North Carolina, 163, 166,
169, 171, 171-172, 175, 176, 177, 184,
198, 199, 200, 201.
Neilson, Archibald, 181, 182, 183,
186, 188, 189, 190, 197, 200, 206,
208, 209, 214, 216, 217, 218, 220,